ALL ABOUT ROCK GARDENS AND PLANTS

ALL ABOUT ROCK GARDENS AND PLANTS · · BY WALTER A. KOLAGA

LINE SKETCHES

BY EVA MELADY

AND

SIXTY PHOTOGRAPHS

1966

DOUBLEDAY & COMPANY, INC.

GARDEN CITY, NEW YORK

PHOTOGRAPH CREDITS

Photographs by the *Author* are on pages 14, 17, 25, 27, 31, 48, and 108.
Gottscho-Schleisner, Inc. on pages 16, 18, 19, 20, 23, 27, 51, 97, and 290.
Roche on pages 24, 69, 118, 120, 134, 139, 142, 145, 156, 161, 163, 167, 172, 176, 183, 195, 199, 213, 216, 217, 227, 230, 232, 253, 265, 272, 273, 276, 278, 288, 298, 304, 316, 328, 330, 332, 335, 337, 346, 356, and 360.
Jeannette Grossman on page 125.
The New York Botanical Garden on pages 127, 136.

Library of Congress Catalog Card Number 66–10138

Printed in the United States of America

CONTENTS

To my wife
JUNE
who did all the work and the worrying.

I wish to acknowledge
my sincere appreciation to
MRS. ALICE DUSTAN KOLLAR
who first suggested I attempt
a book on rock gardening
and to
MISS CAROL WOODWARD
for her advice, encouragement,
and consistent urging to get the work done.

FOREWORD

The view that rock gardening involves the utmost in gardening skill may frighten the beginner at first, but my purpose in writing this book is just the opposite. My goal is to dispel the fear and mystery that inhibits many people who have thought longingly of the pleasures to be found in cultivating alpines and rock plants. Too often the enthusiasm of the would-be rock gardener has been dampened by the very books that were written to publicize and popularize this specialized type of gardening. Too much stress has been placed on difficult and complicated soil combinations, intricate watering systems, and innumerable gimmicks, gadgets, tricks, and professional secrets that apparently were needed to grow even the easiest plants.

It is indeed true that many of the alpines are extremely difficult to maintain, and that some of them cannot be grown in our climate no matter what is done for them. But there are countless others that are well suited to the generally adverse conditions that prevail in the United States. It is sheer folly to rule out the possibility of a lovely rock garden simply because there are some enchanting saxifrages and alpine primroses that cannot be grown.

My aim in the chapters which follow is to show, by describing the various stages of construction, how a simple, yet effective and beautiful rock garden can be built and planted in almost any part of the United States. I am most familiar with gardening in the Northeast, and the information I offer is based on my observations there. However, with a bit of improvising, this information can be applied in other parts of the country. Climatic conditions in various sections of the United States differ to such an extent that it would be impossible to cover in a general treatise all the problems that might arise. We in the Northeast are perhaps halfway between the extremes of the perfect conditions that are found in the Pacific Northwest and the trying conditions that prevail in the plains states. I consider perfect conditions to be a combination of the following: high humidity, constant moisture, warm days, and cool nights.

Rock gardens are inspired by natural scenes of poignant beauty. Few of us have ever followed a mountain path, traversed an alpine meadow, or strolled through an unspoiled woodland without wishing that we could duplicate some especially lovely view close at hand where we could enjoy it many times over. When such a thought occurs to a person, he has taken the first step toward rock gardening, whether he realizes it or not. To transplant a natural scene is to engage in natural gardening; rock gardening is its synonym. And once a rock garden is begun, any other type seems artificial.

In constructing and planting a rock garden, one strives to emulate the work of nature, whose lovely scenes seem to have been created without any planning. In a setting of sunny ridges banked with bright-colored flowers, with ferny dells and a trickling stream, a rock garden grows where plants are never tended, yet they seem to have been selected by the wisest of gardeners and put in exactly the right places. In such a spot one can commune with the infinite, shutting out all thoughts of the tense and worried civilized world.

Before attempting to define clearly just what a rock garden is —for many people have a wrong conception of it or no conception at all—I should like to rule out two ill-conceived interpretations that should be banned. One is the heap of soil that is dumped in the center of a lawn, carefully ringed with an incongruous collection of stones, and planted with *Sedum sarmentosum* or some other terrible weed. The result is a horror that would discourage almost any garden lover or homeowner from starting a rock garden.

The second atrocity is considered by most of those who see it, or resort to it, as a necessary evil. This is the bank that is left in front of a suburban house when the street has been cut in below the natural level of the land. Too often the answer to the vexing problem posed by this unsightly strip of subsoil is: make a rock garden! Not love of plants, but a hasty effort to hide an ugly scar is involved in the slipshod undertaking. Small stones are stuck all over the bank in geometric designs, and the plants are anything that can be begged or borrowed from the neighbors.

After a year or two the predominant weed is either snow-in-summer (*Cerastium tomentosum*) or the cypress spurge (*Euphorbia cyparissias*), and the over-all effect is that of an unkempt cemetery. Unfortunately, a great many people are familiar with these monstrosities and consider them rock gardens. We dismiss them with a shudder as ugly, undesirable, and in no way related to natural rock gardening.

What, then, is natural rock gardening? As we have hinted, it is man's humble effort to reproduce, usually on a small scale, a picture from nature — a natural outcropping splashed with tints of green and the bright colors of diminutive flowers.

The rocks for a garden such as this must be arranged to simulate a natural outcropping, with special stress on the symmetry of stratum lines and continuity of design. In it are established the plants that are most usually found growing wild in similar situations. There are thousands of them to choose from. Most rock-garden plants and alpines are low-growing in habit with their leaves in clusters or tiny rosettes, dense cushions, or slowly creeping mat-forming kinds. Some are herbaceous perennials, others are dwarf or diminutive shrubs and trees. Many are evergreen and produce a spectacular array of colorful blossoms.

The picture we are imagining may or may not include a bubbling stream, a tiny waterfall, and a sparkling pool to accommodate fish and some of the little bog plants. But whether there is a water feature or not, the garden should be framed by gracefully swaying evergreens, dogwood, shadblow, dark green rhododendrons, and mountain laurel. The over-all picture is a naturalistic scene that is repeated many hundreds of times all over the world but usually in remote or inaccessible places. By building your own rock garden you can enjoy and marvel at these wonders of nature every day of the year.

Many people feel that a rock garden is undertaken as a means of avoiding the maintenance work involved in ordinary gardening. This is true in only one way. In a rock garden you grow a greater variety of plants in a smaller area than you can in any other type of garden. It is erroneous to assume that once a rock garden is planted it can be left to fend for itself. Meticulous weeding is essential to successful rock gardening because the tiny alpines can be quickly overwhelmed and smothered by weeds that would not seriously disturb taller plants. Although these little plants are less troubled by diseases and insect pests, they do require the loving care you would lavish on other prized specimens. Some need be pruned and cut back, others must be trimmed to be kept within bounds, and the herbaceous perennials will of course need occasional thinning, dividing, and transplanting. Certain species like an annual feeding, a top dressing, and respond to it by blooming lavishly; others need to be mulched. And periodic watering during the hottest months is important, especially to the true alpines or mountain plants.

Many homeowners who would like to have rock gardens do not establish them because they feel that they cannot afford them. Actually, the expense of construction can be trimmed to fit almost any budget. Size is usually the dominant factor in determining the cost, but the size can be limited to a few square feet without sacrificing aesthetic principles. One of the prettiest rock gardens I have ever seen is only six feet long and about two feet wide, built as a low ledge. The owner constructed it himself in a few hours, using materials that were at hand, so that the only expenditure involved was for plants. For his little garden he selected only the rarest and smallest forms obtainable. This brought the cost of planting to a rather high figure for the area covered. By selecting good types of better-known plants he could have held the cost to an initial outlay of fifteen or twenty dollars and still have achieved an immediate effect. The cost could have been cut even more if he had had the patience to wait for some of his plants to grow and spread for a year or two.

I believe that rock gardening is the most gratifying of hobbies, offering the richest reward of all types of gardening. Those who decide to pursue it will soon be amazed at the wealth of suitable plants that are available to them. There are many thousands of known rock plants and alpines, and many thousands more still undiscovered or untried.

Novices at rock gardening will find a welcome waiting for them in the ranks of the American Rock Garden Society. As members, they are sure to enjoy the feeling of group participation that prevails and will soon find themselves exchanging ideas and swapping seeds and plants with kindred spirits.

The unlimited pleasures of rock gardening are open to everyone. Cost, we have seen, is not a detriment. It can really be considered a boon because a greater variety of plants can be grown in the space that a few costly shrubs would occupy. Here, in a small area, the gardener can express his artistic feelings in a way that is impossible in a conventional perennial border, rose garden, or other formal or semiformal garden.

In the pages that follow I hope to prove that true natural rock gardening — whether in a man-made or natural rock setting — can be easy and enchanting. It represents the peak of attainment in gardening skill.

W.A.K.

Withered limestone rock garden construction on level land with excellent design, exquisite balance, and naturalistic background. Almost the perfect garden, constructed by Zenon Schriber.

CHAPTER I

TYPES OF ROCK GARDENS

Different types of rock gardens have been developed through the years to solve specific landscaping problems or to provide appropriate settings for the successful cultivation of alpines. The most common of these is the man-made rock garden. In this type the rocks are brought to the site and arranged to resemble a natural outcropping. Such a garden can be built on a perfectly flat surface, the goal being a suitable place for the homeowner to grow tiny rock plants and alpines. Here, possibly, it reaches its peak of excellence because the site can be selected for the best possible exposure and for effective integration with the total landscape. The builder is thus able to enjoy full freedom of expression without having to contend with the problems that arise when an attempt is made to plant a naturally rocky area. Imitation rock gardens are also used on banks and slopes where lawns are difficult to maintain, or erosion is a problem.

However, a natural rock garden is the easiest to achieve because its basis is a natural outcropping, or a rocky slope or hillside. Generally, the natural rock formation is modified to blend with the surrounding landscape or to provide more suitable pockets for planting. Moving the rocks about a little, taking some away, or adding a few more will usually produce the desired effect. Fortunate, indeed, is the owner of such a situation.

The ledge is perhaps the simplest form of rock garden. It consists of a few rocks on a low level. As the name implies, it should be long, narrow, and of slight elevation. Such a planting is particularly useful for breaking the long straight lines of walks and drives, and the edges of lawns. One of the principal uses is to give character and color to great sweeps of lawn, especially where there is a natural steep incline or an abrupt curve. In planning a new lawn, keep this in mind and do not smooth out every fold

Natural ledge garden.

Small ledge garden planted with dwarf conifers.

in the elevation of the lawn. A well-planned, well-constructed ledge garden will provide an effect that will make your lawn different from your neighbor's and lend character to your landscaping plan. On a plot that is too small for a large rock garden, a small ledge along a walk or drive can provide an excellent place for the cultivation of exotic dwarf shrubs and tiny alpine perennials. A ledge only a foot or two wide and three or four feet long can accommodate as many as thirty different species of plants.

The bog garden is usually associated with a rock garden because the plants found growing in natural bogs and in alpine regions are similar in character. In fact, bogs occur naturally in mountainous regions, where water collects in shallow impervious rock basins, on the edges of mountain pools and lakes, and along the edges of rocky streams. Many of the alpine gentians, buttercups, orchids, heaths, and primroses are really bog plants, and can be grown only under similar boggy conditions in an imitation rock garden. Normally, an extensive rock garden will contain a

Granite boulder rock garden, duplicating water-eroded glacial rubble.
OPPOSITE:
Retaining wall garden — designed by Mary Deputy Lawson, L.A.

small pool or little stream which will provide a suitable place for a miniature bog garden.

The wall garden consists of a stone wall in which soil has been used as a substitute mortar. Rock plants are grown between the stones, on the sides, and on the top. It is usually constructed to serve as a retaining wall on steep banks or terraces where an ordinary brick or concrete wall would seem cold and lifeless. This is the best type of rock garden for those straight banks often seen along suburban streets, which are usually converted into the "rockeries" described in the foreword. A wall garden can also be built as a dry or double-sided wall to be used instead of a hedge or perennial border, or as a frame for a formal or semi-formal garden.

The wild or woodland garden is also associated with a rock garden. It can be part of a large rock garden or an entire rock garden in itself. Generally, it is resorted to in densely shaded areas where ordinary perennials will not thrive, and is planted with native woodland plants. Rocks are not strictly necessary in a wild garden, but they do lend a rustic charm to a rather dull setting.

Natural granite boulder outcropping.

The moraine and scree, though differing geologically, are synonymous to rock gardens. In nature, the moraine is a glacial deposit of stone chips, sand, grit, and a little organic matter, which is watered from below with ice-cold water from melting glaciers, or snow on mountain peaks. A moraine is generally a part of a rock garden, but it can be constructed as an entity. It is used by experts who wish to cultivate alpines that will not grow anywhere else. Although a very intriguing phase of rock gardening, a moraine is by no means necessary. There are few, if any, true moraine gardens, but thousands of people enjoy their successful rock gardens.

The sink garden is an English innovation which is gaining rapidly in popularity. A tiny garden is built inside an old sink, preferably a stone one, and planted with the tiniest of the alpines. The sink is excellent for growing some of the most difficult alpines — kinds that ordinarily can be grown only in a moraine. The sink idea can be modified to include window boxes, dishes, and almost any other type of container.

Cactus plants, both hardy and tender species, are often used in rock gardens, but because of their odd character, I feel they do not belong with the usual rock plants. If you wish to grow them, build a special rock garden for them, where appropriate consideration can be given to their special needs of exposure, soil, and drainage. Most northern gardeners will find that many species now considered tender will be hardy in a specially constructed cactus garden.

CHAPTER II

LOCATION AND EXPOSURE

It has been said repeatedly by other experts and nurserymen that a rock garden can be built wherever it is wanted. In effect, this is true, but on every tract of land and on every building plot there is one place that is far superior to all the others. This spot must be sought with the utmost diligence, because selecting the proper or most appropriate site is of prime importance in planning a natural rock garden.

In many instances the desirable site is indicated clearly by the topography of the land or by natural outcropping rocks. If the rocks are there, the lucky owner needs only to modify their arrangement and put in his plants. Unfortunately, many people consider these outcroppings plagues, and laboriously attempt to cover them over in order to plant the commonplace lawn, shrubbery, or perennial border. This is expensive and undesirable. By exposing the natural stone and accentuating it with appropriate plants, an outcropping can easily become the highlight of the landscape at very little cost. The only possible drawback to a natural outcropping is that of exposure. Aside from removing or planting trees to provide the desired degree of sunlight or shade, one must accept the exposure determined by nature.

The type, variety, and number of plants to be grown in a rock garden is largely determined by its exposure, the degree of sunshine that reaches it, and soil composition. Since soil composition can be modified to meet the specific requirements of all plants, it is of little importance in deciding the location of the garden. Different blends are discussed in Chapter IV. Plants can be found that will flourish in any exposure, but to assure a good natural balance and the widest range of plants a rock gardener would want to grow, the site should be planned to include sunny, shady, and semishady areas.

Natural rock outcropping with rock garden constructed at the base.

My personal choice is a site that faces southeast. This exposure makes possible the successful cultivation of the more delicate plants from the alpine arctic regions, as well as the tougher plants that can become accustomed to variable conditions. The rock garden should be in an open position, either in full sun or in partial shade from tall trees or buildings. It should not be located near large trees whose roots would quickly rob the soil of nutrients and dry up the garden in summer. The trees most important to avoid are those with wide and shallow root systems, such as the maple, ash, beechnut, elm, linden, poplar, and willow. However, a lovely tree can be used as part of the background for the garden.

Dense shade should be avoided if possible. The varieties of plants that will thrive there are sharply limited and provide color only in the early spring.

For the most naturalistic setting, the rock garden should be well apart from buildings or veiled from them with adequate

A shady nook, feathering Maidenhair ferns and Foamflower.
OPPOSITE:
Granite boulder rock garden site, selected by nature.

background planting. The exception here is the rock garden that is used as a foundation planting. A rock garden designed as a foundation planting is especially suitable for the modern, low, ranch-type house where the plants must be strictly limited in height of growth. Most of the conventional shrubs and trees used in foundation plantings soon outgrow their allotted space and become a headache to the meticulous gardener. A rock garden, on the other hand, will not vary in height, and it will grow more beautiful each succeeding year. The foundation rock garden has distinct possibilities that are overlooked completely by the general landscape artist.

Any slope or natural contour can be utilized to provide a naturalistic base for the rock garden. This will decrease appreciably the cost of excavation or filling. Drainage is by far the most important factor in the successful cultivation of alpines. Therefore, one should take advantage of the slightest incline and avoid low spots in selecting a site. The ground should slope away from the rock garden, not toward it. On nearly level ground it would be wise to observe the direction of the runoff after a rain before

making a definite choice of location. Such foresight at the beginning of the project may eliminate a few of the headaches and heartaches that are often experienced after the construction has been completed. Any natural depressions or constantly wet places can be used for pools, or for planting meadow plants, such as primroses, adjacent to the rock garden. A good deal more will be said about the all-important element of drainage in the chapter on construction.

The straight bank along a street, or the straight lines of a terrace around a house pose the problem of type of garden to be employed rather than that of choosing a location. The site of the garden is clearly defined. However, straight lines, sharp angles, and a uniform elevation are not conducive to a natural rock garden. To create an irregular contour—variations in elevation and perspective of depth—would necessitate a considerable amount of excavation at high cost. To escape the cost and labor of excavating, and to eliminate the possibility of an unsightly rockery, the best choice would be a beautiful living-wall garden which doubles as a retaining wall. In some sections, retaining walls are a necessity and they can become rather monotonous—as typified by a lovely residential area in Hillsdale, New Jersey, where most of the walls were planned by the same landscaper. In every wall garden he used the local round glacial boulders, and he planted all of them with *Ajuga, Santolina,* and *Sedum sarmentosum.* Innumerable variations of the wall-garden theme can be employed to give distinction to gardens in a retaining-wall area, with a better choice of plants, varied building materials, and individual designs.

The site of the little ledge garden is as important as the site for the large rock garden. Here are a few points to keep in mind. The ledge garden should not be placed at the highest level of the terrain, where its effectiveness would be lost in the skyline. It can be used admirably on any slope or gentle incline, but not on a perfectly level plane. The most appropriate place is any natural depression, sharp elevation, irregular contour, or fold in the ground.

If one is planning a rock garden simply for the joy of cultivating rock plants and alpines and is limited to a very small area, the desired planting can be tucked in almost anywhere and

Terraced wall garden — designed by George F. Hinricks.

Wall garden used as foundation planting.

be made to blend with the existing landscape plan. It can be located along a walk or drive, at the edge of a lawn, behind the garage, or even at the base of the barbecue pit. A rock garden for one's own pleasure need not be a spectacular affair, perched up where every passer-by can see it. A number of my friends have little rock-garden retreats that are completely screened from view in inaccessible corners. I know one man in particular who derives more pleasure from such a private outdoor den than he does from all the other plantings on his extensive grounds.

CHAPTER III

ROCK GARDEN CONSTRUCTION

Before any construction is started, I advise the rock-garden enthusiast to take several trips to the surrounding country and study natural rock outcroppings. Even casual observation will show that the most beautiful ones are those that display pronounced stratification as in the sedimentary rocks. However, a large number of natural forms and groupings would be quite unattractive. Talus slopes and deposits of glacial boulders may be natural, but they have little or no beauty and would be undesirable if imitated on the home grounds.

Expense is often a deterrent to beginning a rock-garden venture. Although the rocks themselves can usually be had for the asking or for a nominal amount, transportation is costly because of the weight involved. Since rock is the basic ingredient, it is usually the deciding factor in the over-all cost estimate. Therefore, it would be wise to choose a type of rock that is near at hand rather than one that must be hauled from a great distance.

A delightful rock garden can be built with almost any type of stone. Some types permit more freedom of plant growth than others, and some have more appealing visual characteristics. But before deciding on a type to be used, first determine its availability. If there is more than one kind of rock within easy hauling distance, it would be advisable to choose the one to which plant life adapts itself most readily. Facility of construction and attractive character should also be considered.

Although rocks may look dry, they are actually voracious hoarders of moisture, especially those that are porous and coarse grained. They absorb and store large amounts of water in wet seasons and make it available to plants in dry weather. The roots of some plants will actually penetrate an apparently solid rock in their search for moisture and nutrients. Consequently, the best rocks for rock garden construction are the comparatively soft sedimentary ones, such as sandstone, limestone, tufa, and shale.

Tufa, although extremely congenial to plant life, is difficult to use because of its predominantly rounded or lumpy shape and lack of strata. In addition, it seems devoid of the characteristics of solidity, boldness, and permanence associated with natural rock gardening. Shale is good, but usually soft or brittle. It tends to crumble and disintegrate quickly on the edges. Sandstone, especially the harder varieties, is excellent. It varies in color from dark red to light yellow, is very porous, and has a good blocky structure.

My personal preference, however, is for limestone. It has an agreeable gray color, pronounced strata, and attractively weathered fissures and crevices. It is generally available, and it is easy to assemble in naturalistic ledges and outcroppings because its blocklike structure permits it to be split readily with a crowbar. It is very porous, hence water retentive and conducive to luxuriant plant growth.

Although limestone seems to present some limitations on the choice of plants because of its lime content, this drawback can be overcome without too much difficulty. In many cases it is overlooked completely by gardeners with surprisingly good results. In most instances the incompatibility of limestone with acid-loving plants, particularly the ericaceous ones, has been grossly exaggerated. Of course, when limestone is used in a rock garden in areas of normally highly alkaline soil, the maintenance of ericaceous plants is difficult. On the other hand, in areas of normally acid soil, the use of limestone with acid-loving species is of little consequence. Although limestone is soft as rocks go, very little actual lime is dissolved by rain in the course of a year. What little lime does reach the soil is quickly neutralized by high soil acidity. It is relatively easy to maintain ericaceous plants in a rock garden made of limestone if they are planted above the stones, where whatever leaching that does occur carries the lime away from the roots of the plants rather than toward them. Lime does not permeate the soil in all directions. It moves out and downward. In nature, I have often found limestone ledges covered with wild rhododendron and mountain laurel, blueberries, wintergreen, and other acid-loving plants. I have consistently

Rock garden constructed with withered limestone.

grown heathers in display gardens constructed of limestone, and even *Gaylussacia brachycera* and *Vaccinium vitis-idaea minus* in limestone crevices. However, in all these cases, the soil used was basically acid, and its acidity was constantly being renewed from overhanging coniferous and hardwood trees.

In some localities, granite may be the only rock available. It can be used quite successfully, though with difficulty, and it should be employed only as a last resort. Granite rock usually occurs in very hard, unstratified, fine-grained masses that are not congenial to plant life. Granite formations are generally all but devoid of vegetation — which should warn the gardener against their use. If nothing is available, however, sizable fragments from talus slopes can be used to form pseudonatural outcroppings. With skillful and appropriate plantings veiling jagged edges, these granite rock gardens lose much of their harshness and inhospitality.

Gneiss, a laminated or foliated rock similar to granite, splits easily into flat slablike sections and has a pleasing dark gray color. It is readily adaptable to garden use, as is evidenced by many beautiful rock gardens in Westchester County, New York.

Glacial boulders, which abound in many areas, are often chosen for a rock garden because of their accessibility. They can be assembled to make a lovely garden, but should be judiciously selected with an eye for rocks that have been exposed to the weather for a period of years. Marks of age are more desirable than the newness of freshly uncovered surfaces. Select the largest rocks that can be found, because these will give an appearance of solidity and permanence that is totally lacking in a garden made solely of small stones. Boulders of irregular shape, but comparatively flat on top, will fit much more readily into a simulated natural setting than the common round forms.

Once you have determined the type of rock you will use, study its natural formations thoroughly. Careful examination will usually reveal a definite pattern of angles, horizontal stratum lines, and vertical joining lines. The protruding portions of the rock formation, the outcroppings, will be quite ragged, with weathered, worn, and eroded edges. Large fragments that have broken away from the ledges, leaving huge gaps in the line of rocks, appear to be strewn about in a haphazard fashion. This rough, rustic, and realistic appearance is the effect to be sought in your rock garden. It involves maintaining the pattern of natural rock formations, with close adherence to stratum lines and the angle of disposition.

All the rocks used in any single rock garden should be taken from the same source, so that they will be of uniform type and quality. Careful observation will reveal that outcroppings only a few yards apart differ noticeably in composition. If rocks for a garden are taken from two different sources, an incongruity results and the desired natural aspect is minimized. In choosing individual rocks for the garden, remember that flattish, rectangular rocks are easier to work with and lend themselves more readily to the creation of definite stratum lines. For best results, the rocks should be longer than they are high, but varying in length and thickness. Two or three very flat stones can be placed one on top of the other to create an excellent stratified subject with ideal crevices for planting some of the cespitose alpines. While choosing the rocks, be sure to mark, at least mentally, the portion that will be exposed to view in the garden. This exposed portion should be

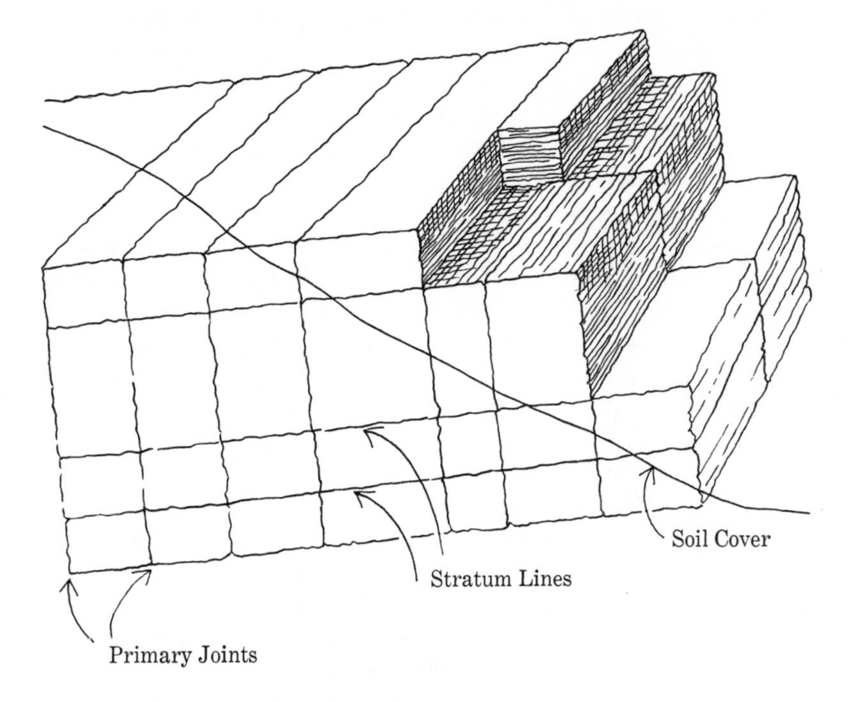

A block section of sedimentary rock showing stratum lines and joints.

Typical sedimentary rock outcropping showing effects of weathering.

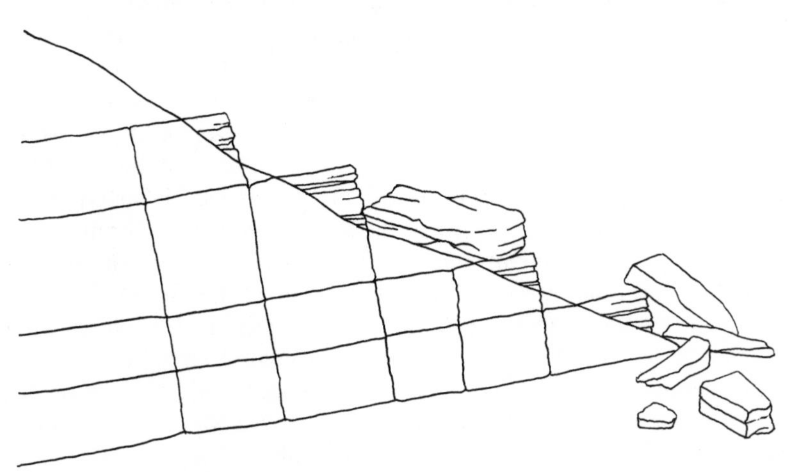

well weathered with cracks and crevices, not only to give the desired natural effect, but also to provide suitable places for planting. Some people like to use rocks that are heavily covered with mosses and lichens. These are most attractive, but unless they are given the same exposure that they had in their natural setting, the mosses will quickly die, leaving the rocks drab.

Sometimes, when rambling over fields and hills in search of stones for the garden, a natural outcropping is found that can be lifted in its entirety and taken to the garden site in well-marked sections. This has been done successfully for several famous gardens, but because of the cost, and the size of the mechanical equipment necessary to move extremely large rocks, the method is not practical for the average homeowner.

When the site has been selected, the type of rock material chosen, and the specific rocks moved to the garden area, the work of actual construction can begin. Draw a plan of the proposed garden, indicating its dimensions, high and low elevations, and any existing trees or prominent landmarks that will be included in the rock garden or the area surrounding it. The plan need not be detailed; a rough sketch will do. Its purpose is to help guide the builder in evolving the basic profile of the garden.

In making the plan, the importance of providing good drainage cannot be overemphasized because the successful cultivation of alpines and rock plants depends upon it. Most of these plants grow naturally on protuberances in wild mountain areas. The soil of their native habitat is composed mainly of rocks and fragments of rocks. Its surface consists of stone chips and dust eroded from the rocks by wind and water and enriched with decayed plant matter in the form of humus, or leaf-mold. Centuries were required to build these bits of dust, stone chips, and humus into pockets and patches of soil that could support the higher types of plant life. The roots of some of the alpines are huge in proportion to the part of the plant that is above ground. These roots sometimes travel several feet into the fissures of the rocks in their search for moisture and soluble inorganic salts and minerals that nourish the plants. A cross section of a natural alpine bed shows that it consists of a solid rock base covered with a deep layer of rock fragments, stone chips, and sand, and a top layer of stone chips, sand, humus or leaf-mold, and soil.

These are the conditions that should be duplicated or approximated in the rock garden. It is obvious that drainage of such a formation would be exceptionally good. There would be a rapid runoff of excessive water in the wet spring season, and no possible danger of excessive wetness during the winter months. In the dry period of midsummer, the rocks themselves exude sufficient moisture to prevent the thorough drying that would kill most alpines and mountain plants if they were restricted to a shallow root run.

ROCK GARDEN ON A SLOPE

The rock garden on a slope or hillside is the one most often encountered, and it is probably the easiest to build. However, most gardens are constructed with little regard for the plants they are supposed to accommodate. Often the rocks are merely placed on the top and side of the slope or bank. Sometimes they are set into the bank in a simulated naturalistic formation, but without any preliminary preparation of the subsoil. If the bank is fairly sandy, there is some hope for success; but if the subsoil is a heavy clay, most of the planting will be a total loss because the area for vigorous root action is too restricted.

In a slope or hillside garden there is a certain amount of natural drainage, but it can and should be improved upon. If the existing soil is to be used, the venture is doomed to failure from the start. Even if the soil is considered good topsoil and is fortified with fertilizers and peat moss, the number of true alpines and rock-garden plants that will flourish in it is still pitifully limited. Adequate drainage, proper placement of the rocks, and carefully prepared soil mixtures are prerequisites of a successful rock garden.

The first step in construction is to drive stout stakes into the ground to mark the limits of the garden. Use long and shorter stakes to indicate the elevations of the finished garden. The stakes should be firm enough to resist dislodgment during construction. If the base of the bank rests on poorly drained level ground, or if the slope is a gentle incline, it is wise to excavate at the lowest level to a depth of at least twelve inches. The excavation and side of the bank or slope should be filled with drainage material, consisting of broken stones or boulders varying from two to twelve inches in diameter. On top of the drainage material should be placed a layer two or three inches thick of coarse sand or fine stone chips. This layer will prevent the topsoil from washing into the space between the drainage rocks, where it would hamper the free flow of water. Next comes a layer at least twelve inches thick of prepared rock-garden soil. (Details of soil composition are given in Chapter IV.) This layer of soil should be interspersed with large rocks that will not be seen, but will support the exposed rocks and give them a solid footing. When these preliminary steps have been accomplished, the placement of the facing rocks can begin.

In placing rocks, remember the lessons learned in the study of the natural formations. You will recall that the greater portion of the rocks you saw was subterranean. Only the front face and the top level of the rocks were exposed to view. The rocks in your garden should be made to look like an integral part of the slope. They should not merely sit on top of it. The base, or approach, rocks should be as large as can possibly be moved, either by hand or with mechanical lifting equipment. With a bit of strenuous effort and the aid of a crowbar and a few planks, rocks weighing from 500 to 800 pounds can be moved without too much difficulty. When small rocks rather than large embedded ones are used on top of the soil, erosion is likely to occur. Small stones also provide an ideal harbor for destructive insects, especially the slimy slugs, most notorious enemy of the rock gardener. Avoid placing rocks on end, or at odd angles above the soil level, because this gives the garden a graveyard or signpost appearance. The stratum lines should all slant at the same angle and, for the purpose of catching rain and minimizing the possibility of erosion, all of the rocks should tilt backward into the garden. Some of the rocks should be placed close together in order to create deep and narrow crevices or pockets. Others can be spaced farther apart to provide larger beds for spreading plants and dwarf shrubs.

Strict adherence to level stratum lines and plumb joining lines should be avoided. Tilting the rocks to one side or another provides a more pleasing effect, as long as all are slanted in the

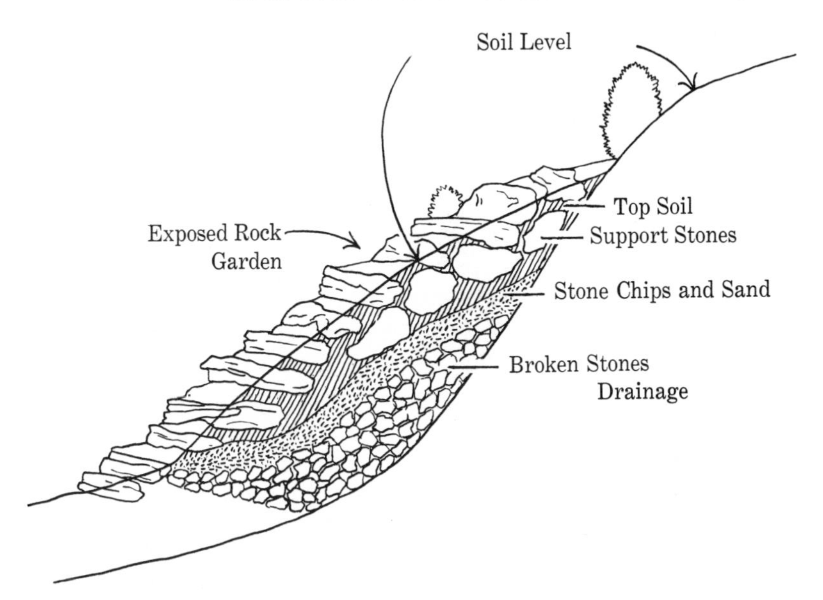

Cross section of rock garden, showing drainage material, support stones, and planting medium.

same direction. Never set the rocks in solid rows, as in a curbing, but in a natural manner with all stratum lines holding their natural alignment.

The exposed rocks of a natural outcropping are weathered and broken in an irregular line. The action of frost and erosion has undoubtedly dislodged chunks of considerable size that have rolled off the ledge and left irregular gaps in the rock formation. As these spaces eventually become filled with soil, they provide ideal footholds for plants. In a rock garden, this is the casual appearance that is desired. Avoid building a solid mass or checkerboard of rock.

The lowest rocks, at the base of the garden, should be set in place first to establish a line of demarcation. Use the largest ones for this purpose. To prevent them from slipping and turning during successive periods of freezing and thawing, embed them very firmly in the ground. It is easier to work from the base line upwards, and nearly impossible to make an attractive arrangement when you start at the top and work downward. After the

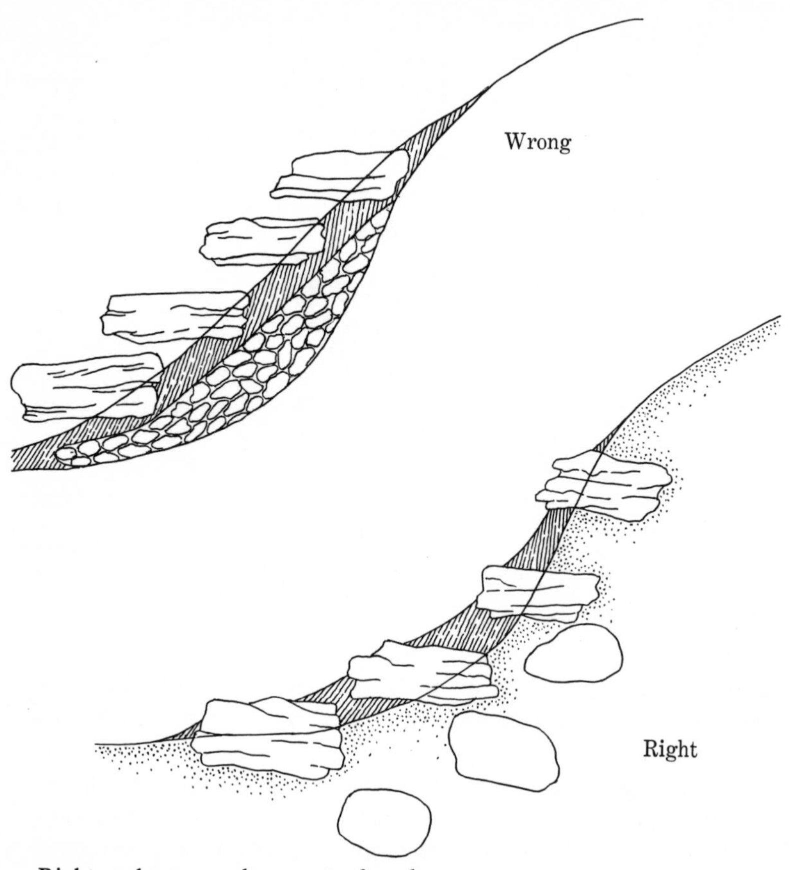

Right and wrong placement of rocks.

rocks have been properly and firmly set on their supporting stones, all spaces between them should be filled with the prepared soil mixture, as indicated in the sketch.

If the garden is to be made with glacial boulders, tufa, or granite chunks, be sure to bury most of the rock, leaving only the top surface and a small bit of the facing exposed to view. It is not possible to create the effect of strata with these rocks, but by almost covering them, you can make them look as if they are part of the terrain, not merely strewn over the surface. For best results with boulders, use the combination of three or five rocks

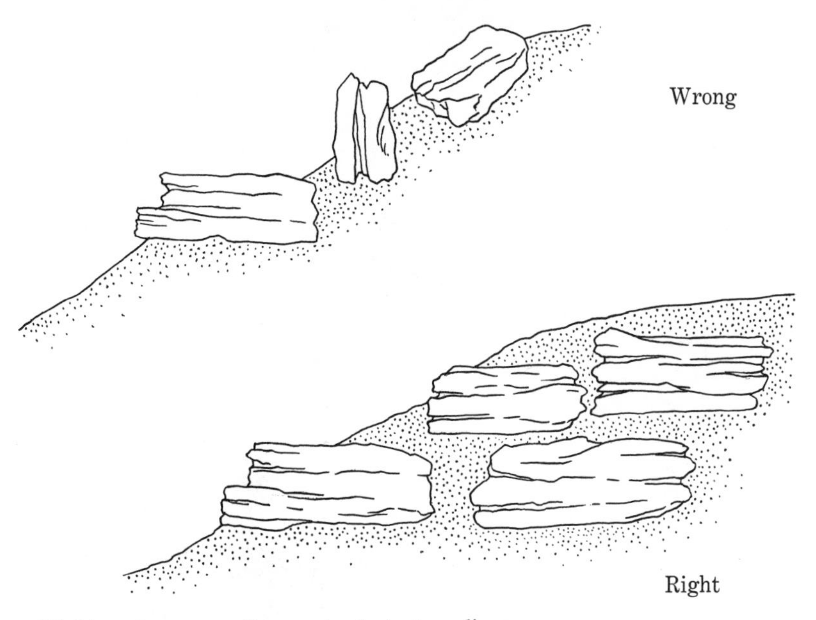

Right and wrong alignment of stratum lines.

shown in the accompanying sketch. These combinations can be expanded by using additional rocks, or repeated at various levels throughout the garden in a series of small ledges. Spaces between the ledges can be tied in with appropriate plantings of creeping species or by massing tufted plants.

If the garden is extensive, a path, or paths, and steps may be desirable. A path meandering through the garden will give the visitor a feeling of expansive rural freedom, and incidentally, facilitate planting and weeding. If steps are desired, they should be constructed of the same type of stone that is used in the rock garden. They should not be in a steep gradation of step and riser, but interspaced with level surfaces, as in a series of small terraces. The step course should be curving, and the paths winding, never perfectly straight. The paths can be partially paved with small flat pieces of the same building material, and planted with low creeping plants, such as the thymes. Other possible coverings are stone chips that blend with the building rock, or a durable organic material, such as spent tanbark or old sawdust.

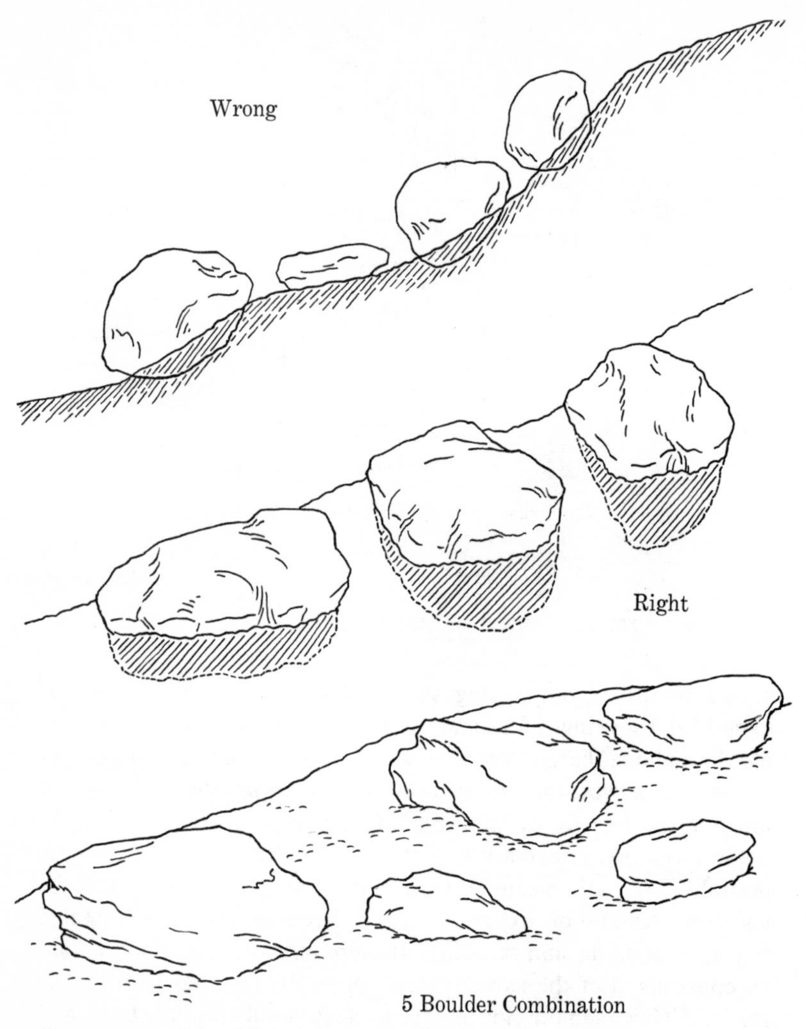

5 Boulder Combination

Proper use of boulders in constructing a rock garden.

Diagram of naturalized stone steps in a rock-garden path.

THE LEDGE GARDEN

The ledge garden is really a tiny hillside garden, and it should be constructed in the same manner. However, because of its low elevation, it may not be possible to put in the necessary drainage material without excavation. If this is necessary, make the excavation the length and breadth of the garden and from twelve to eighteen inches deep. Fill the hole to within three inches of the ground level with the drainage stone and the layer of sand or fine gravel. Then proceed with the building as for the larger hillside garden.

If the ledge is to be very low, twelve inches or less in height, use rocks that vary in thickness to create variations in elevation.

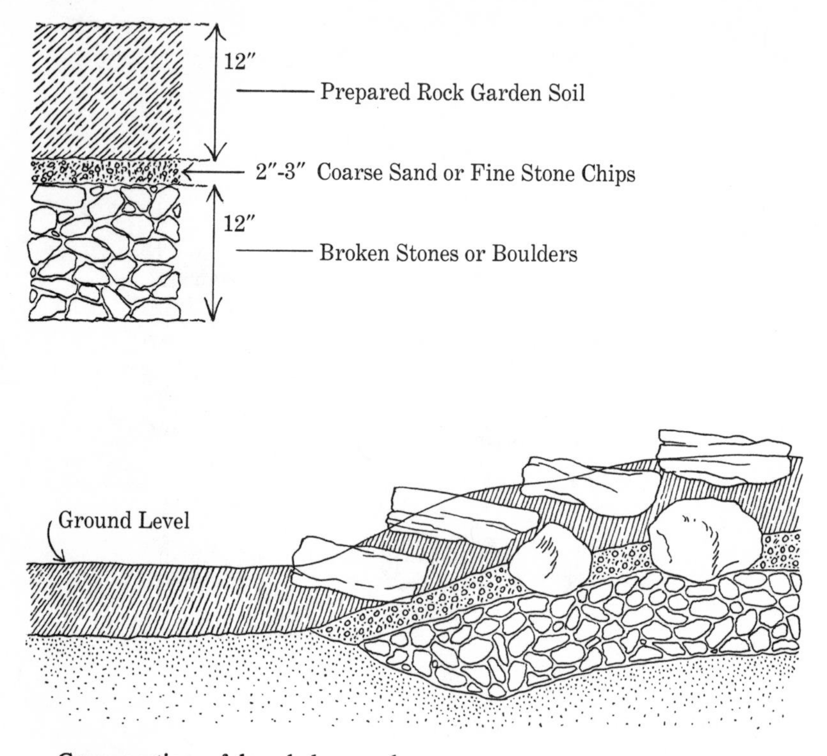

Cross section of low ledge garden.

In this type of garden, it is best to use rather flat rocks, 2 to 6 inches thick, that vary in length from 12 to 36 inches. They will give an illusion of spaciousness even to a very tiny ledge. Do not attempt to use anything but flat, rectangular, stratified rocks for the small ledge garden. Glacial boulders and granite fragments are never appropriate because it is almost impossible to make them look like a natural ledge.

NATURAL OUTCROP GARDEN

The owner of a natural outcropping will soon find that he must do more than establish plants on the rocks to build a successful rock garden. If the outcrop is of sympathetic stratified rock, the task at hand will be much easier than if it is of granite or some other eruptive fine-grained hard material. As indicated, the sympathetic stones are comparatively soft and split easily when pried with a crowbar. If the formation is almost entirely solid rock, sections can be dislodged with comparative ease to provide suitable planting areas. The pieces that are removed can be placed elsewhere in the garden to modify a contour or to build up a weak area.

Quite often only a very small portion of the rock outcropping will be exposed. Removal of some of the covering soil may reveal an extensive formation that is ideal. A rock garden in Sparkill, New York, was uncovered in this way; and without removing or adding a single rock, the owner was able to create the loveliest and most natural rock garden imaginable. If you are fortunate enough to find such a natural site, remove most of the native soil from the pockets and replace it with a prepared compost more suitable to the cultivation of the alpines and rock plants you plan to use. As for drainage, the problem can be ignored because nature has already provided it.

If the rock outcrop is a huge projection of impenetrable granite, the task of converting it into a rock garden is more involved. An outcropping of igneous or eruptive rock will support little or no life. Hence, it must be modified extensively to create a naturalistic rock garden. When the rock is on a steep incline, or in the form of a cliff, the solution is to add at the front, covering most of the natural rock with the same type of garden as outlined for the slope or hillside garden. By using rock from the same locality, the formation can be made to resemble a series of small outcroppings rather than one solid mass of rock. Precautions for adequate drainage should be undertaken here, as indicated by the accompanying sketch.

A common problem in granite areas is the huge solid-rock shelf that is almost level with the ground. Depressions in the shelf are invariably covered with two or three inches of poor soil. Any attempt to plant in these depressions is sheer folly, because nothing will grow there satisfactorily except perhaps the sempervivums and a few of the sedums. My recommendations here would be to build a rock garden on top of the shelf. However, because of the probability of thorough baking during our hot and

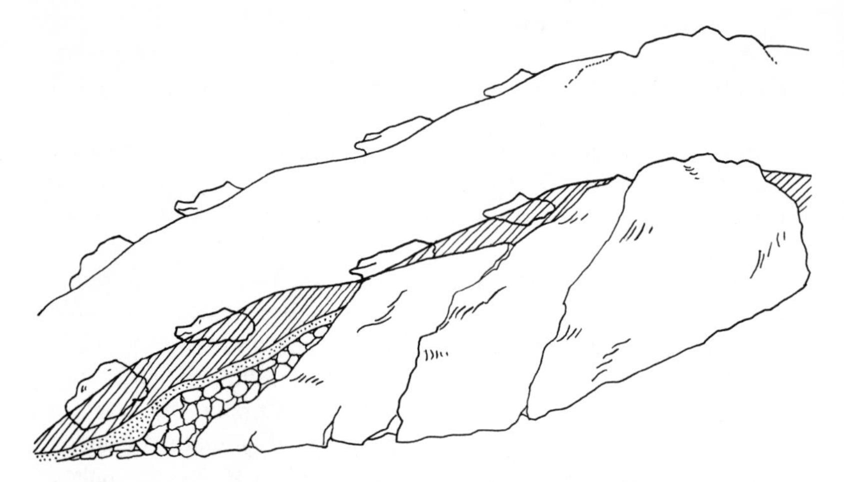

Unsympathetic granite outcropping with rock garden built in front.

dry summer months, several precautions should be taken. In order to support plant life adequately on a solid rock shelf, the soil must be at least twenty-four inches deep. A permanent foundation for this load of soil can be established by placing large rocks at the lowest extremity of the proposed garden. Use rocks of the same type as the natural outcrop, of blocky form, and as large as possible. These can be cemented in place for permanence, but avoid a solid curbing. Spaces must be left between them for planting and for the runoff of excessive rain water. Subsequent planting will screen all vestiges of the cement work from view.

After the base rocks have been placed, the bottom of the bed thus created should be filled with drainage material. Over the drainage stones goes the layer of sand or chips, and over that the 24-inch layer of prepared rock-garden soil. If there is a sharp rise, even a small one, above the rock shelf, build a garden like the one described for a hillside, using harmonious rocks. When there is no natural rise, provide a retaining wall and background planting, as described for the garden on level ground.

ROCK GARDEN ON LEVEL GROUND

For the rock garden on level ground, the site selected should be at an extremity of the property line, or where an extensive planting of large shrubs and trees, preferably evergreens, can provide a background. At the rear boundary of the proposed garden, build a retaining wall as tall as you wish your garden to be. This wall can be made of any kind of rock that is available because it will not be seen when the garden is completed. The extremities of the wall should not end abruptly, but should taper gradually until, with a backward swing, the wall blends into the natural terrain and approach planting. It can be built to curve around existing trees or shrubs that will become part of the background, or it can be made in a straight line. If it is in a straight line, the contours necessary for a lovely garden can be created with the rock work that will be seen from the front of the garden.

When the retaining wall has been completed, the preliminary drainage rocks and prepared soil mixture are laid down as outlined for the hillside garden. The finishing rock is set in place in the same manner for this garden as for all the others. A rock outcropping, however perfectly made, that rises straight up out of flat ground is as unnatural as a mound. It must be camouflaged. The rear and perhaps the sides of the garden must be appropriately planted with large evergreen shrubs and trees to conceal the wall and provide a naturalistic background. Specific species and recommendations for this purpose are given in Chapter VI.

Another exciting way to vary a rock garden on level land is to provide slopes in reverse of those just described. The result is a replica of the natural ravine or chasm often encountered in mountainous areas. Such a sunken garden can be made in the form of a shallow depression with gently sloping sides, a rather deep chasm with almost perpendicular sides, or a combination of both, graduating from one to the other. This type garden requires more labor than the others, but it is well worth the additional effort because it affords more diverse conditions and makes possible the cultivation of a larger variety of plants than any other kind of rock garden.

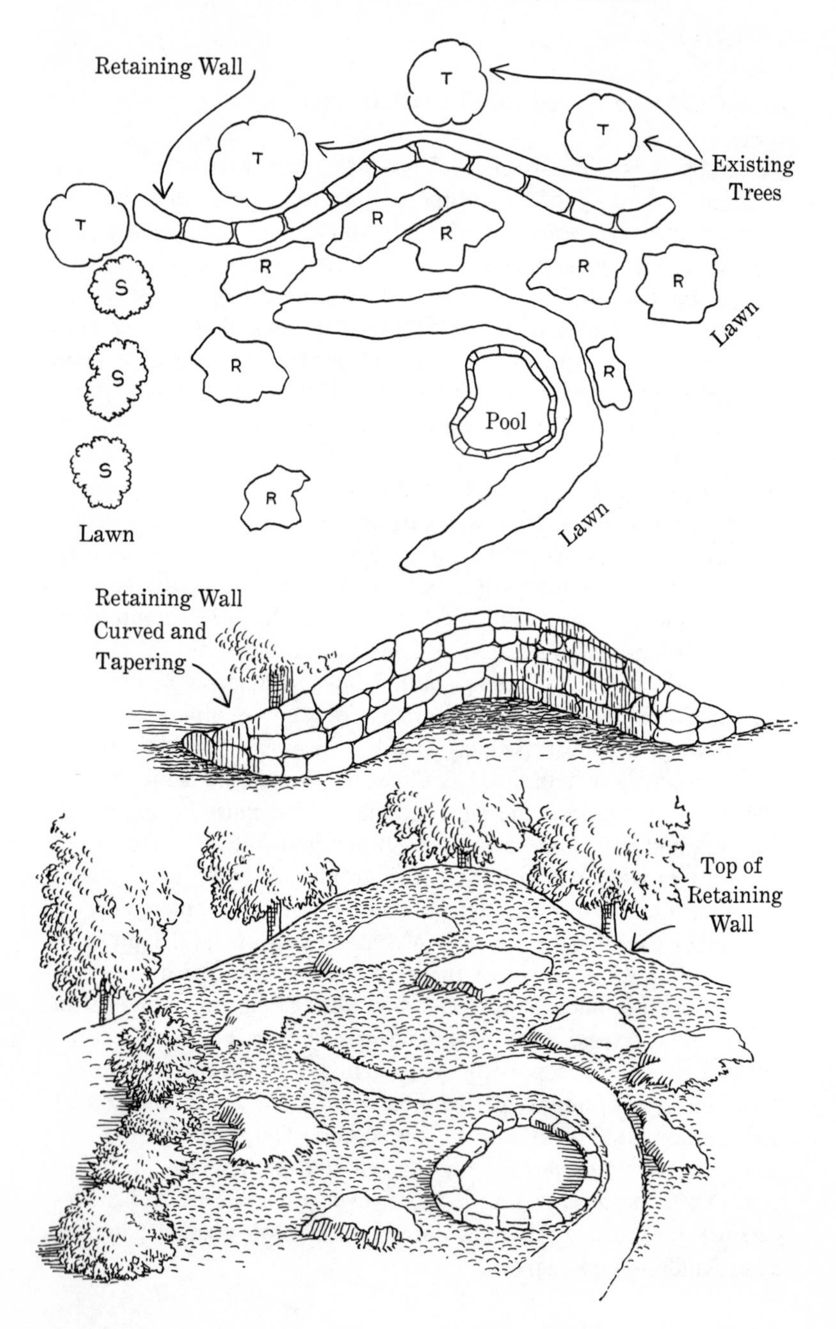
Retaining Wall
T
T
T
T
T
Existing
Trees
R
R
R
R
R
R
R
R
S
S
S
Lawn
Pool
Lawn
Lawn
Retaining Wall
Curved and
Tapering
Top of
Retaining
Wall

The first step is to dig out the soil in the center of the garden area and throw it up on both sides. The central excavated portion should be a narrow foot path that slopes gradually downward, not just a hole in the ground where water can collect. The excavation should not be on a straight line, but curving or slightly winding. The garden can, of course, be as deep as you wish to make it, unless a subterranean ledge gets in the way. The deeper it is, the greater the planting area will be. If the garden is excavated to a considerable depth, provision must be made for the drainage of excessive water that is bound to collect in the deepest part. This calls for either a dry well or a pool. And why go to the trouble of constructing a dry well when it would be just as easy to make a pool that will enhance the beauty of the garden.

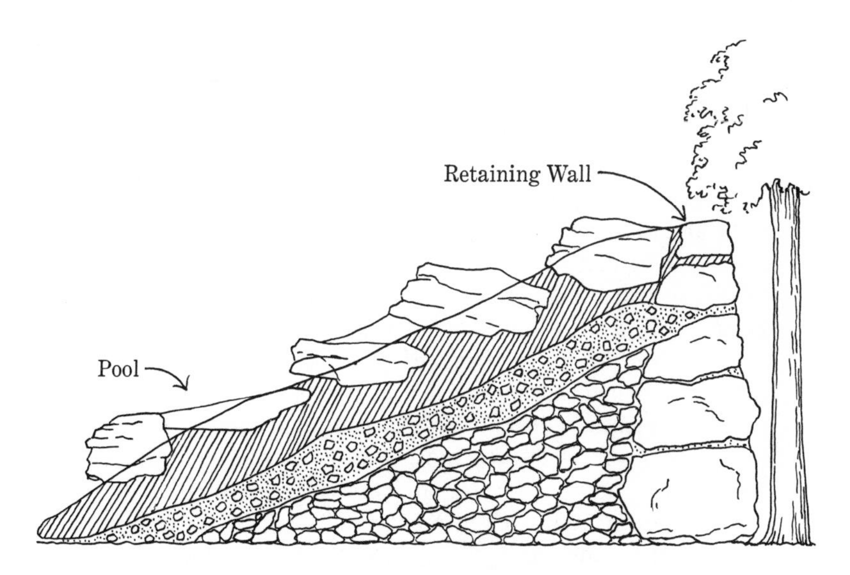

Cross section of rock garden on level ground showing retaining wall, drainage material, planting medium, and rocks.

OPPOSITE:
(Top) Plan of rock garden on level ground. (T=tree; R=rock; S=shrub.) (Center) Detail of retaining wall. (Bottom) Rock garden with soil and rocks in place.

Rock garden using well-placed slabs of gneiss.

If an extensive sunken garden is planned, with the additional labor and expense it entails, my advice is to let it start at ground level, and be quite wide with gently sloping sides. As it is deepened it should become narrower with steeper sides, and it should terminate in a very deep and narrow chasm with a glimmering pool at the bottom, perhaps with a waterfall coming over the end rocks. This deep and narrow chasm, which little or no direct sunshine reaches, will be uniformly cool and humid and will provide a setting in which the most difficult of the high alpines will flourish, whether it is located at sea level or in the hot plains of our midwestern states. Even on the hottest days the temperature maintained in this part of the garden will be several degrees lower than it is at ground level.

Throwing the soil up on both sides of the garden will create inward and outward slopes. The outward slopes should not be used as part of the garden. They can either be built up with retaining walls, as for the other garden on level ground, or they can be graded into gentle inclines that taper gradually into surrounding level ground. In either case, all sides of the garden, with the possible exception of the entrance, should be screened from view by a heavy planting of shrubs and trees. A garden of this design will never look natural without a screen planting.

Because of its central ravine, there will be exposures in the garden to all points of the compass, so that suitable conditions are provided for almost every conceivable type of plant. There will be places for the sun lovers from the hot semiarid regions, and shaded locations for those from the cold alpine and arctic climate.

GARDEN WITH ORDINARY SOIL

Some people will undoubtedly claim that all this meticulous consideration of drainage and soil composition is nonsense. I say it is all-important, if true alpines and the better rock-garden plants are to be grown. It is possible to make a rock garden by heaping up topsoil as it comes from the fields without any preparation except perhaps fertilizing. It can be made to resemble a natural outcropping with all the features of an extensive garden if the rules for placing the rocks are followed. However, the type and number of plants that will grow and flourish there are sharply limited. Many of the lowland and foothill plants, and even some alpine species, will grow well. However, these are the plants that the advanced rock gardener usually discards as being too coarse, too weedy, or too overpowering to be associated with the more delicate and desirable alpines — the gems that continually pose a challenge to the rock gardener's skill, fortitude, and perseverance. In Chapter VII, the plants described as wanting an ordinary garden soil will usually succeed in a rock garden that is made with a heavy topsoil and only moderate drainage.

POOLS AND STREAMS

Pools and streams are not essential to a rock garden, but after experiencing the initial thrills involved in his hobby, the amateur usually becomes more ambitious and wants to duplicate all the features of nature in his own little realm. Like rock gardens, pools can vary from simple to intricate and extensive projects. They can be tiny shallow basins used only to reflect the beauty of a portion of the garden, or they can be large enough to accommodate fish, water lilies, and other aquatics.

The pool can be planned for any location which, in a natural setting of hills and valleys, would collect water. Its desirability should be considered before the rock garden is started because, unless special provisions are made for it before and during construction, it will be quite difficult to create later. The pool can be placed either in the garden or adjacent to it as an approach feature. In an extensive garden there may be a succession of small pools within the garden and a larger one at the forefront. These are connected by tiny spillways resembling mountain streams or miniature waterfalls, which carry the water from one pool to the next.

If the pool is to be of simple design, as shown in the sketch, it can be kept filled easily with the garden hose. Drainage is of no particular concern here, because the flow of water will not be constant. Although the pool is simple, it will become an important part of a small rock garden, giving it an appearance of coolness and serenity.

A pool should always be irregular in shape, and any concrete used in its construction should be hidden by skillfully placed rocks. The goal is to have it blend into the garden and seem to be a natural part of it. If the pool is to be large enough to accommodate fish, water lilies, and other aquatic plants, and especially if moving water is used (a constant stream from a supply pipe), special provisions should be made to take care of the overflow. Just letting it spill over the sides is not practical. Although the wet place can be used for growing some of the bog plants and semiaquatics, it is bound to become an increasingly serious problem. If there is a natural stream nearby, it would be easy to pipe the overflow to it. However, since none is likely to be handy, the best solution is to construct a dry well. The size and depth of a dry well depends mainly on the composition of the subsoil. If it is very sandy or gravelly with good percolation, the depth need only be from eighteen to twenty-four inches. If the subsoil is heavy clay or has a thick layer of hardpan, the

Naturalistic pool, nestled in a limestone garden setting.

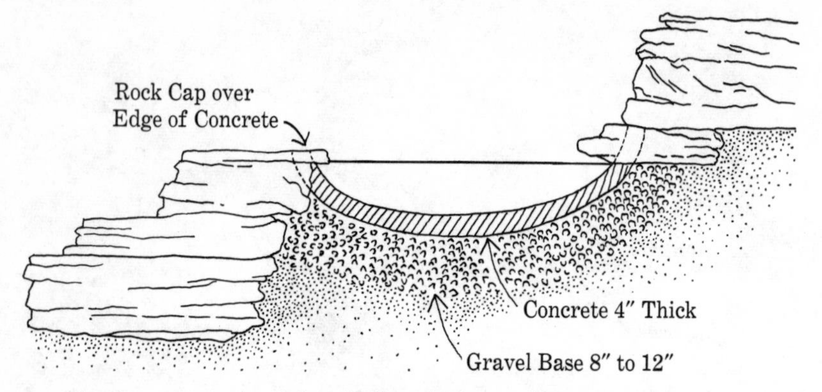

Simple construction of a shallow basin pool.

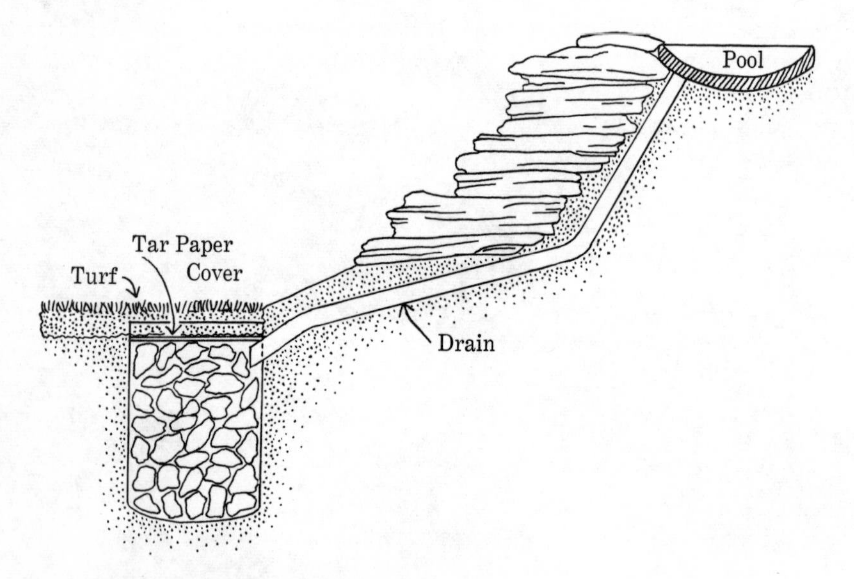

Detail of construction and proper placement of dry well in relation to garden and pool.

depth should be increased to penetrate the clay or hardpan layer to soil of a more absorbing composition. If this is impossible, the size should be increased in proportion to the estimated amount of overflow. A dry well is merely a hole in the ground that is filled with large broken stones covered over with a layer of fine gravel or sand and capped with topsoil to make it level with the surrounding ground. It should be large enough to take care of all the water in the pool when the pool is drained for cleaning.

The size of the pool is variable, according to the wishes of the owner, but its depth must be determined by the function planned for it. Eighteen inches is deep enough for most aquatic plants, which require about six inches for the roots and twelve inches of water above the crown of the plant. A pool of this depth must be drained in the winter to prevent solid freezing. If fish, plants, and water are to remain in the pool all winter, it must be deep enough to prevent solid freezing. In the New York area, thirty-six inches is sufficient, even for the most severe winters. When water is left in the pool all winter, the sides of the pool will tend to crack, even if the water does not freeze solid. This cracking can be prevented by tying a bunch of reeds together and placing them upright in one corner of the pool. The pliable reeds will take up all expansion of the freezing water and thus relieve pressure on the sides.

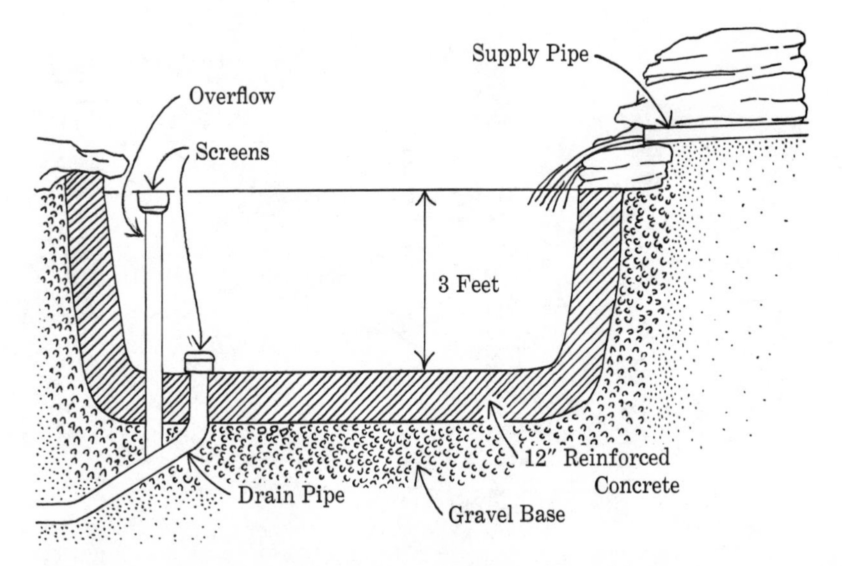

Pool construction showing supply, overflow, and drain pipes.

When a constant movement of water is desired and a continually running tap from a domestic water supply is not possible because of municipal restrictions or a seasonal shortage, the use of a small centrifugal pump may be the answer. A pipe is installed with an opening near the bottom of the pool and is connected to a pump that can be powered with a small electric or gasoline motor. The pump, in turn, is connected to the lead pipe. When the pool is filled from the garden hose and the pump is put into operation, running water is provided. This arrangement is economical because the same water is used over and over, and it eliminates the overflow problem. When evaporation reduces the water level of the pool, additional water can be supplied from the garden hose.

Streams are best not attempted unless the garden is extensive. The bed of the stream must be made of a thick shell of concrete. If it is not made of concrete or some other waterproof material, the water is absorbed by the soil, creating a soggy mess that is a constant problem. The bed of the stream should be covered with sand or pebbles to camouflage its unnatural construction.

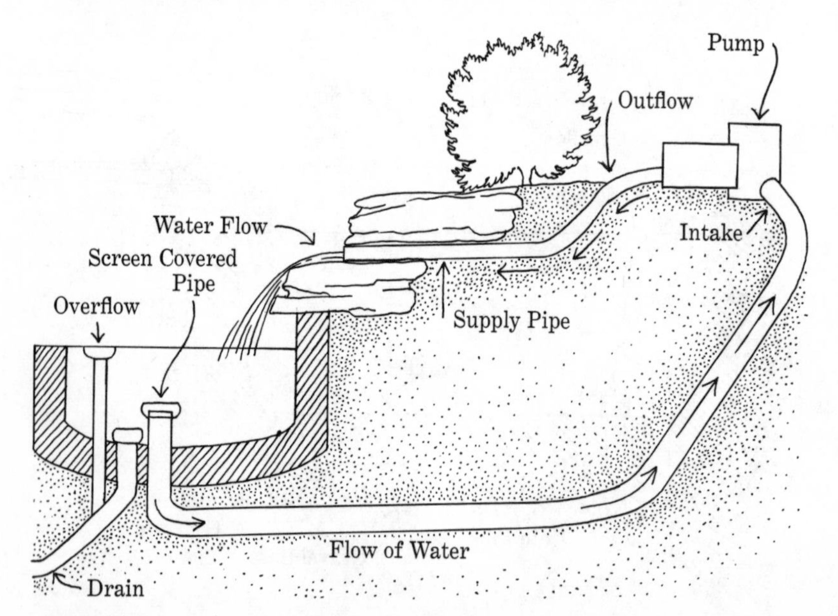

Centrifugal pump system, showing flow of water to and from pool.

THE BOG GARDEN

A bog garden is a modified water feature that can be established within the confines of the rock garden or adjacent to it. It can also be built as an entity for the cultivation of the interesting and enchanting bog plants. I have constantly stressed the importance of drainage for the successful cultivation of the alpines. In a bog garden, just the opposite is true. Bog plants should be kept wet without actually being in water. It is true that many natural bogs dry up thoroughly in summer, and the native bog plants survive from year to year. However, when the bogs dry up, the plants growing in them go dormant. We do not want this to happen in our gardens, so we plan to keep them wet. While some of the bog or semibog plants will succeed along the edges of a pool or stream where the soil is more or less damp, such locations are not suitable for the more desirable plants. The amount of moisture varies too much with the weather, and the soil in these places is not the right type for the true bog plants.

The most natural place for a bog would be at the edge of a pool, whether in the rock garden or next to it. For growing the taller bog plants and semiaquatics whose heights would be out of proportion to the plants used in the rock garden, the best place would be the edge of a pool that is adjacent to the rock garden, perhaps on the edge that is farthest removed from it. Then such plants as the cardinal flower and fringed orchids can be made to blend with the approach planting of tall perennials. Use the diminutive bog plants, such as the sundews and grass pinks, in the part of the bog that is closest to the rock garden.

The bog garden at the edge of the pool can be of any desired size. It should be a shallow concrete basin, but it can be attached to the lip of the pool so that water from the pool can seep into the bog. As pictured, the water level of the pool should be kept high enough to keep the bog constantly wet. If the water level of the pool is allowed to drop, the bog can be kept wet with the garden hose.

A suitable arrangement for a small bog garden within the rock garden can be provided by using the shallow concrete basin as illustrated for the small pool. The basin should be at least six inches deep, and it should be filled to within two inches of the top with silty sand taken from the bed or bank of a stream. If this is unobtainable, a substitute can be prepared by mixing three parts of unwashed builder's sand with one part of finely ground or screened leaf-mold or other humus material. After the soil has been placed in the basin, it is covered with a two-inch layer of living sphagnum moss. If it is impossible to obtain green living sphagnum, the dried moss, often obtainable from nurseries and flower shops, will serve. Although it looks dead, the dried material will revive quickly under favorable conditions. After the bog has been filled with the soil and moss, it should be saturated with water. When the moss is soggy wet, the bog is ready for planting. There need be no other preparation or maintenance, except to keep the bog thoroughly wet at all times. It will probably take two or more years for the sphagnum moss to resume the active growth required to make it look completely natural.

The shallow basin type of bog can be used in the rock garden without any other water feature, if it is placed in a setting of large rocks where it will look natural. It should not be placed where water is unlikely to be found in nature. The lips of the basin can be hidden easily by the judicious use of rocks and foliage.

A concrete basin is not the only kind of bog garden you can make. Any durable waterproof container can be used, whether it is an aluminum dishpan or a sawed-off hogshead. If the container is plunged into the ground so that the top is just below ground level it will serve remarkably well as a bog garden.

THE MORAINE

The moraine is an extremely desirable feature of the rock garden that enables the enthusiastic plant lover to grow some of the choicest of the alpines — plants that cannot be grown in any other location. The exquisite beauty and charm of the tiny moraine alpines do not depend upon massive arrangements. These plants are minute gems that appeal directly to the heart. Once they are seen, the beholder is consumed with an insatiable desire to have

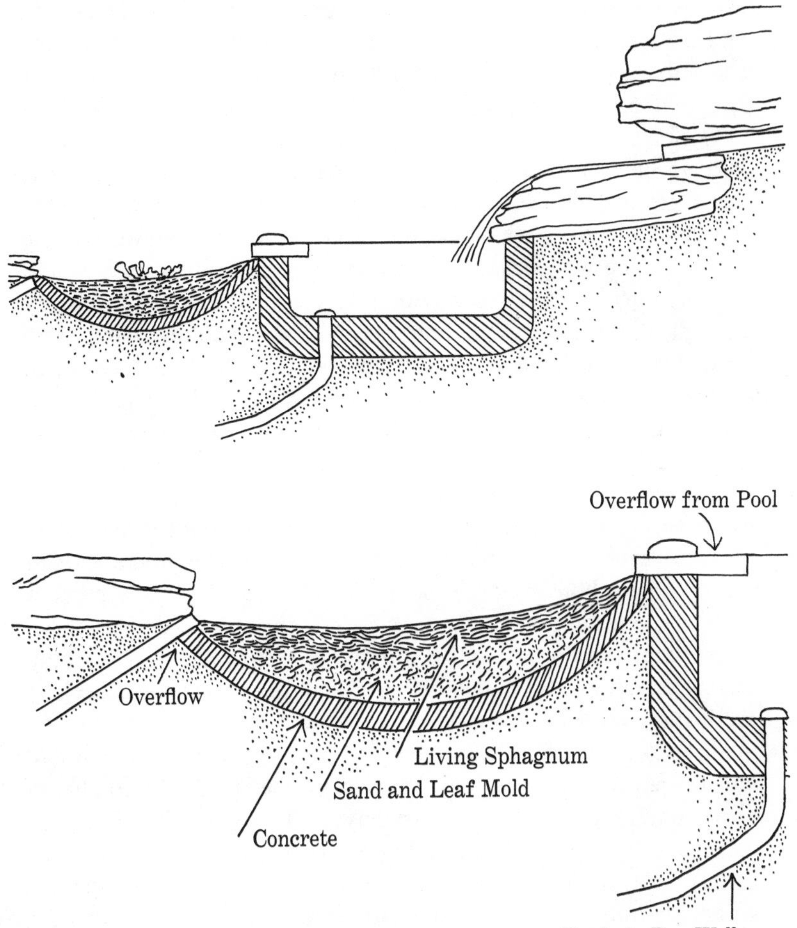

Bog garden attached to edge of pool.

them and to grow them. They are usually only an inch or two high, with foliage in tight little buds or rosettes. The flowers, though small, are usually produced lavishly, considering the size of the plant, and they are brightly tinted with the true and intense colors of the most precious stones. Such plants are grown for the gardener's own personal appreciation and edification.

Disappointments may be numerous, but when success is experienced, even with a single tiny pearl, the elation is unbounded. The larger and showier rock-garden plants are the ones that appeal to the casual viewer.

As described in Chapter I, a moraine is a bed of rock rubble built up in front of a glacier and watered from below by melting glacial ice, or snow from a mountain peak. The top surface of a moraine looks dry, but under the surface there is a constant trickle of water. The water cannot be stagnant or motionless as it would be if it collected in an impervious depression. It must flow freely through the rock rubble and be carried simultaneously away through perfect drainage. The water need not run as it would in a subterranean river bed, but the supply must be inexhaustible so that the rock rubble will be moist at all times but not soggy as in a bog.

In the alpine regions where the natural moraines are found, the base or undersurface of the moraine bed is invariably solid rock. In such a situation, the water fed into the moraine runs through the rubble the entire length of the bed and finally escapes down a slope or through fissures in the rock. In order to duplicate this process in an artificial moraine, the bed should be built up on a heavy subsoil that will prevent the water from seeping away downward immediately at the source of supply. It must be made to run the entire course of the moraine before it is diffused into the lower strata. In most cases, there need be no preliminary provision for making an impervious basin. However, in the instance of an extremely sandy hillside or subsoil, a shell of concrete or clay should be applied to keep the water from being absorbed before it has a chance to irrigate the entire area. An exceptionally fine place for a moraine garden would be the solid rock shelf described in the section on natural outcrop gardens.

The introduction of water for the moraine is an essential step that must be carefully planned before any building is started. The usual method is to use a subterranean perforated pipe, as illustrated. This is most often connected with the domestic water supply. Provision should be made for turning it off during wet weather and in the winter when it will not be needed. This is perhaps the easiest and best way to bring water to the garden, but there are other methods. One is to utilize the pool overflow if the pool is at a higher level than the moraine. The water from this source should also be piped to the moraine with a hidden overflow. It would be quite unnatural to have the moraine directly connected to the pool.

A particular aspect of the successful moraine, and one that should not be overlooked, is that of exposure. Not only do we have to duplicate the soil and water conditions of a natural

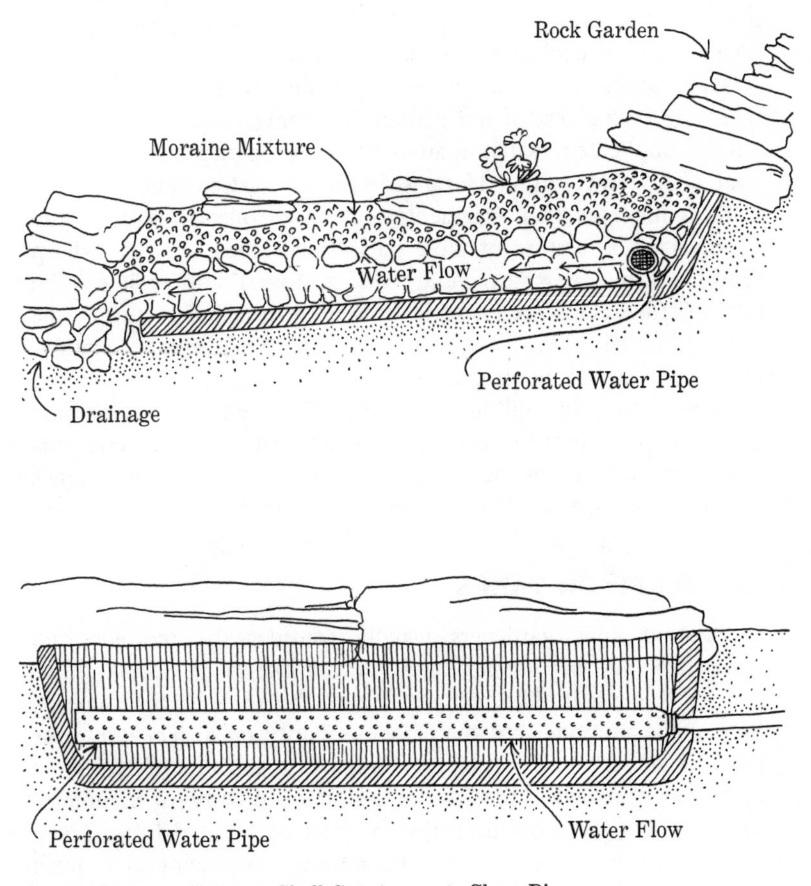

Concrete Shell Cut Across to Show Pipe

Ideal moraine construction showing shell, perforated pipe, drainage, and planting medium.

moraine, but we must also duplicate its exposures if the little moraine plants are to survive. Generally, the natural moraines are above timber line, on mountain peaks where the plants are exposed to the full blast of the hot sun, to strong winds, and to cold night temperatures. These tiny plants have become conditioned by long evolution to withstand such adversities. When they come to us they must be provided with these same conditions if they are to survive. Therefore, the moraine should be given full sun and be exposed to as much wind as possible. The combination of cool moisture below and rapid evaporation on the surface causes the temperature to remain lower in the moraine than it is in the rest of the garden. The only condition that cannot be duplicated, without an outdoor refrigeration unit, is the cold night temperature. Here we have to trust to luck.

To imitate the rock fragments that have collected at thc head of a glacier, a mixture of three parts stone chips, one part sharp sand, and one part leaf-mold will be found appropriate. The type of stone chips used is of little consequence; but to supply the needs of all the plants, it would be wise to use a mixture containing some calcareous fragments, or even better, to divide the moraine into acid and limy sections. The bed of the moraine should slope a little to insure perfect drainage. For aesthetic purposes, its surface can be varied by introducing attractive stones of the same type used in the rest of the rock garden.

THE SCREE OR TALUS

Although rock gardeners usually consider the moraine and scree identical, they are not, and I would like to define the difference at this point. The composition of the scree is the same as that of the moraine, but there the similarity ends. The scree, or talus, is an accumulation of rock fragments and bits of leaf-mold or humus collected at the base of a cliff, steep bank, or mountainside, brought there by the action of frost or by landslides. There may be subterranean water as in a moraine but, being at a much lower elevation, screes are normally very dry in summer. The plants that will succeed in a scree may resemble in many respects those that inhabit a moraine, but they must be able to withstand severe droughts during the hottest time of the year. To make a scree in the rock garden, proceed as for the moraine, but omit the concrete shell and water supply, and construct it on a steeper incline. Many of the plants from our plains states, the eastern slopes of the Rocky Mountains, northern Africa, and the Near East are habitual failures in our comparatively wet eastern states unless they are planted in a well-constructed scree.

WOODLAND GARDEN

A woodland garden can be had by acquiring a strip of woodland, removing the underbrush and other unwanted plants, and planting the more desirable kinds. Because the plants to be introduced would ordinarily be native woodlanders, no special soil preparation is required. The natural soil should suffice for most plants, but if it has been damaged by repeated burning or constant washing by rains or floods, it is advisable to enrich it with heavy applications of leaf-mold, peat moss, humus, or other organic material. Do *not* use chemical fertilizers.

This is the easiest way to start a woodland garden, but if one desires to introduce some of the little natives that normally inhabit the rocks and ledges of mountain forests, the introduction of rocks is called for. This can be accomplished by constructing within the woodland any of the rock gardens we have described, and planting them with appropriate shade-loving plants. If a rock garden cannot be built without the removal or destruction of favorite trees, the most appropriate way to introduce rocks would be to establish little ledge gardens even though the ground is fairly flat. Three rocks placed together will provide space enough to cultivate a number of the tiny woodlanders. Again, the type of rock is not important, but the same kind should be used throughout the garden.

When the land is on an incline, however slight, it is easy to make some very attractive extended ridges, without extensive preliminary work, before placing the rocks. As this is a garden mainly for the native woodland plants, natural soil and natural drainage should be sufficient for almost all the desired kinds. In making the low ledges shown in the sketch, it is only necessary to dig out enough soil to place the rocks in the incline so that they appear to be part of the natural terrain.

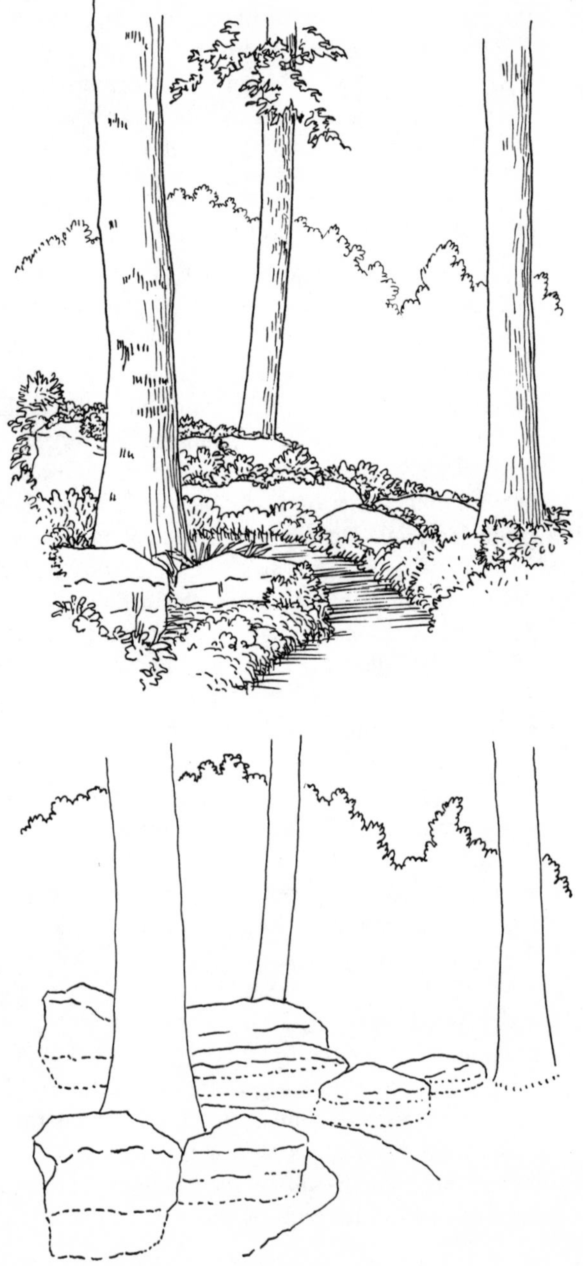

Placement of rocks in an extended woodland ledge garden.

WALL GARDEN

The wall garden is not really a naturalistic garden, but it does somewhat resemble the low cliffs that are often encountered in nature. In fact, there are many natural rock formations, mainly in sandstone or calcareous regions, that are actually a series of natural walls. These natural walls are often clothed in attractive foliage and flowers, and are sometimes copied to provide a suitable place for mural plants. However, the type of wall garden I am writing about is admittedly unnatural.

As pointed out in Chapter II, the retaining wall garden is the best substitute for the old-fashioned rockery where there is a straight bank somewhere on the home grounds. Wall gardens are also built because they are beautiful, combining rock, foliage, and flowers in a gorgeous display every month of the year. The dry-wall garden can be used instead of an ordinary hedge or as a frame for a formal or semiformal garden. There are any number of ways in which a wall garden can be used in every landscape plan, but these are often overlooked or omitted by the landscape artist. It is one of the simplest yet most effective garden features, but unfortunately it is seldom used. The maintenance of a well-constructed wall garden is negligible. Because

Diagram of trees and rocks shown in preceding drawing (T=tree).

planting areas are small, weeds are practically nonexistent, and the plants most suited for this purpose are extremely long-lived and remarkably durable. One of the finest wall gardens I have ever seen was built some forty years ago at the old home of Mayfair Nurseries in Bergenfield, New Jersey, by Mayfair's founder, Marcel LePiniec. The wall and most of the original plants are still making a fine display today. Even after years of total neglect, the wall is almost as beautiful now as it was when it was first planted. I believe it is impossible for any other type of garden, including a rock garden, to match this record of endurance.

Almost any kind of rock available, from glacial boulders to polished granite blocks, can be used for a wall garden. Even planks, railroad ties, cinder building blocks, and other handy items have been used effectively. Logs, planks, and other wood products sometimes *do* make a lovely garden, but they decompose rather quickly and become an eyesore or must be replaced after a few years. The best rocks to use are those that are most sympathetic to plant life, but their adaptability to facile and permanent construction should also be considered. Rocks for the wall garden should be in rough block form, as they come from the natural ledge. My particular favorite is sandstone. It is extremely absorbent, has good color, and breaks easily into flat or blocky pieces. Limestone is also very good; but for wall purposes, select stones of rectangular shape and avoid those that are weathered with deep crevices. The crevices would leave gaps in the face of the wall that would be almost impossible to keep filled with soil. Glacial boulders are used frequently; but because of their predominantly round shape, they are difficult to lay up into a permanent wall. If boulders must be used, choose those that are flattish and irregular in shape.

In some sections of the country, the fields are literally cut into checkerboard patterns by stone walls. These walls are a by-product of our early settlers' efforts to clear their fields for farming. Many remnants of them still exist in residential areas where the farms were subdivided into building plots. In many places the walls, or sections of them, have accumulated enough soil through the past two hundred years to support some plant life. On the whole, however, they are not suited to wall gardening without a considerable amount of rearranging. Many of my customers from

New England ask me what they can do with these ancient walls. My answer is: "Either plant them with clinging vines or pull them down and start over." Tumble-down sections can be restored easily, but the addition of soil is a tremendous and tedious task. Soil must be poked into every cranny of the wall, and the only tools that can accomplish this are a pair of hands and a stick. The person undertaking the project must show inhuman patience and perseverance. The easiest way to use the stones in these aged walls is to demolish the walls completely and rebuild them according to the following directions and sketches.

The rocks in the wall are set just as they would be for an ordinary masonry wall, but instead of using mortar to hold them together, use moist prepared soil. A layer of soil between each and every rock and a compact core of soil behind the wall are essential. The core should be free of air pockets. The backs of the stones should tilt into the wall, and the wall itself should slant backward with the top narrower than the bottom. A slant of two inches for every foot in height should be sufficient to catch all the rain and direct it back into the soil where it is most needed. The corners of the wall are the parts most vulnerable to destruction, and here the stones can be cemented together so that they will not be dislodged when bumped by garden equipment, or by the action of wind, water, and frost.

If plants are purchased before the wall construction is started, it is a good idea to plant as the building progresses. If the planting must wait until the wall has been completed, it is imperative to use small plants, preferably pot-grown ones. It would be impossible to squeeze the huge root masses of large field-grown plants into the tiny chinks of the wall. The roots of pot-grown plants are compact, and the plants will not suffer before they have a chance to develop new roots.

The retaining wall garden described above is for banks and sunken gardens. The same type of wall can be built with two sides exposed and planted; this is known as a dry-wall garden. Construction is the same, except that two sides have facings, and there is a compact core of soil between them. This core will enable the roots of the plants to penetrate into the ground below the wall, thus insuring them of a constant supply of moisture.

A semiformal wall garden, such as that at the old home of

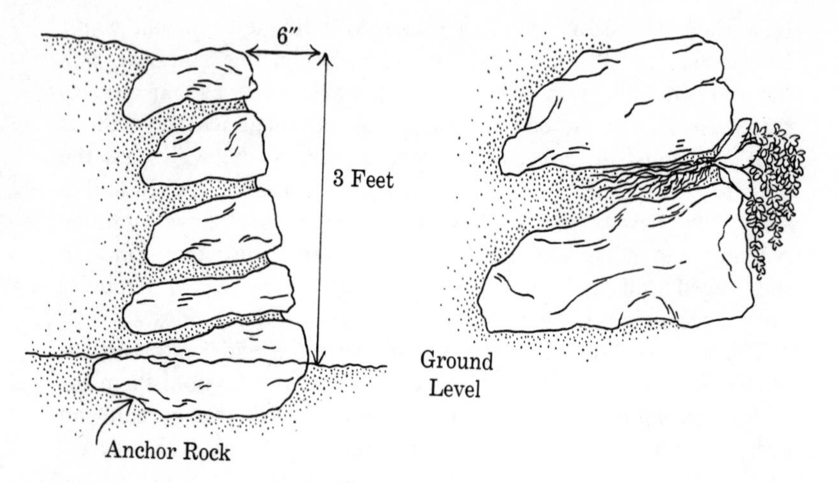

Construction of retaining wall with planting detail.

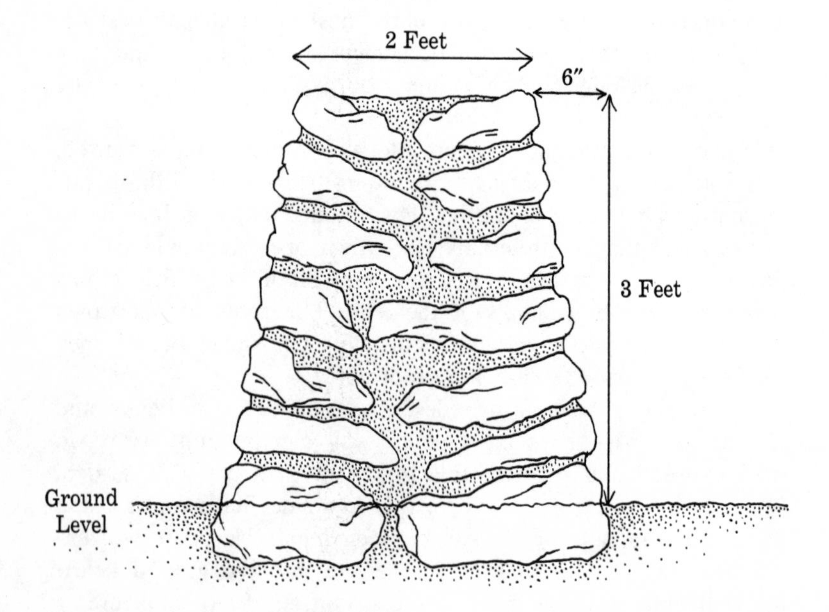

Construction of dry-wall garden.

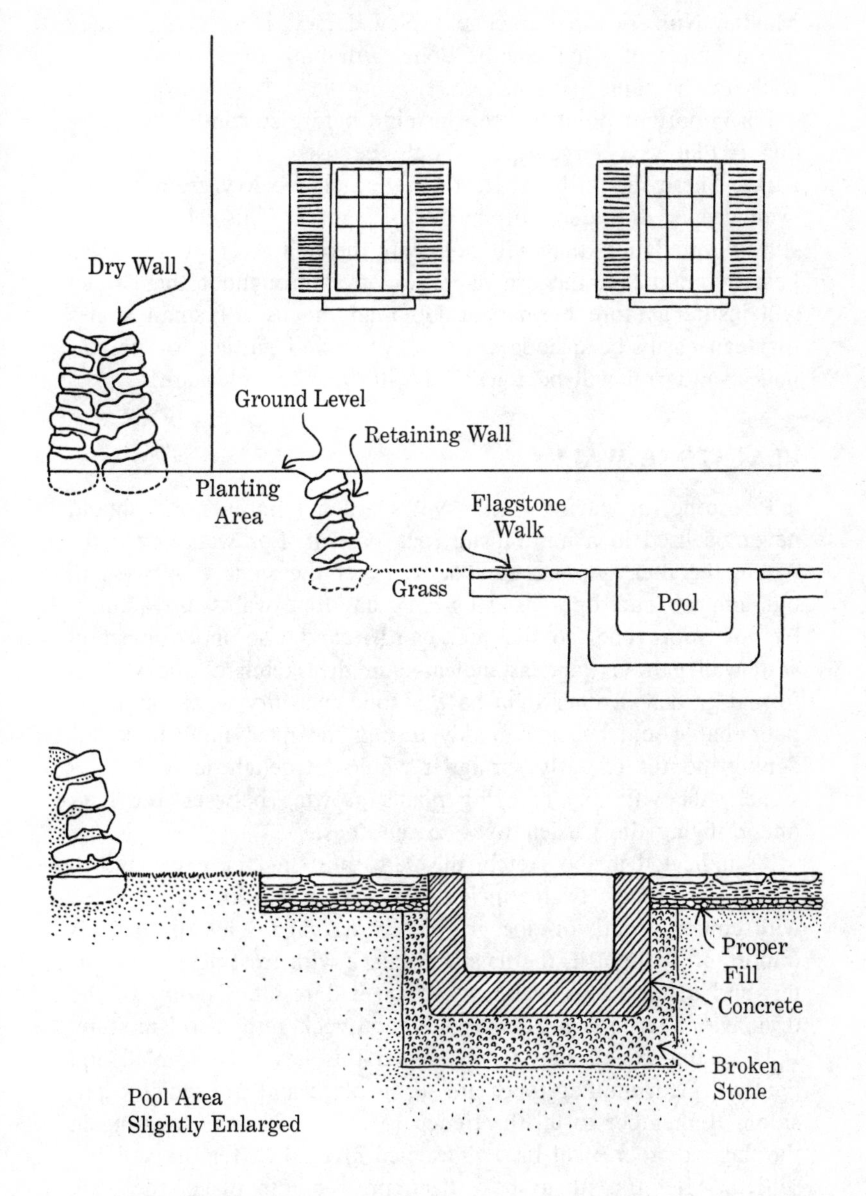

Cross section showing dry-wall garden, retaining wall, flagstone walk, and sunken pool.

Mayfair Nurseries in Bergenfield, New Jersey, is an exceptionally fine example of what can be done with both dry and retaining walls in the same garden.

An important point to keep in mind before starting a wall garden is that very large rocks should be used as base or anchor rocks. These should be at least twelve inches below ground level, even deeper if the size of the rocks permits. This will assure a sturdy foundation that will not shift through frost action. Also bear in mind that the use of large rocks throughout the garden will insure a more permanent job than the use of small stones that can easily be dislodged. Build your wall garden for permanence, and you will be rewarded with years of pleasure.

FLAGSTONE WALKS

Flagstone, or paving stone, walks are not natural and should never be used in a naturalistic rock garden. For walks or paths within the rock garden, use flat rocks of the same type used in building the outcroppings. However, flagstone walks are admirable for approaches to the rock garden and also in conjunction with wall gardens, and as indicated in the sketch of the sunken formal garden. Rather than have a solid masonry walk, or a dirt path that would become muddy during the most important gardening months of early spring, it would be delightful to have a stone walk with tiny creeping plants growing between the flags and bringing the garden right to our toes.

As indicated in the sketch, the path must first be excavated to a depth of at least twelve inches. The bottom six inches are filled with cinders, sand, or fine gravel for drainage. This drainage is important; without it, the flags will heave with frost action in winter, and a hazardous walking surface will result. On top of the drainage material is next placed a good rock-garden-soil mixture, right to the top of the trench. When this has been leveled and lightly firmed, the flagstones are set in place and pressed into position. Remember to fill the trench to capacity before pressing in the flags, or there will be a difference in grade after the soil has settled. After the stones have been pressed into place, the walk should be watered thoroughly to settle the flags and soil. When it has drained sufficiently to correct muddiness, the next step is

Flagstone walk, planted with *Thymus serphyllum album*

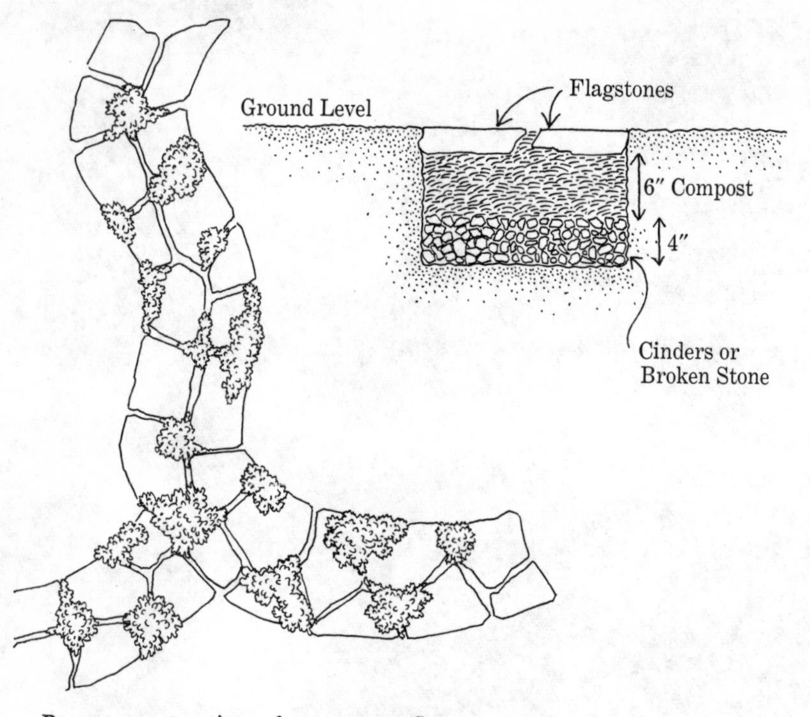

Proper construction of permanent flagstone walk.

to plant. There is a large number of low creeping plants that do not mind being stepped on and will thus thrive in a flagstone walk. Mention is made of all the walk plants in the descriptive list contained in Chapter VII.

TROUGH OR SINK GARDENS

The sink or trough garden is an innovation from England. Interest in it has been stimulated by a book written by Anne Ashberry, published in England and distributed widely in the United States. The name sink garden is derived from the fact that the old stone sinks found in rural sections of England are used for these miniature gardens. Undoubtedly, some of these old stone sinks or troughs can be found in this country on old homestead farms or at antique shops. If stone troughs are unobtainable, suitable imitations can be made of concrete. Trough gardens can be modified to window boxes, or to deep containers of crockery or earthenware. This miniature type of rock garden can become a fascinating hobby for every garden-minded person from the estate owner to the apartment dweller.

Of course, this is not natural rock gardening; but within the sink or trough, the actual tiny rock garden can be a replica of a natural rock outcropping. Here only the tiniest of plants can be used, because a single plant with even a moderately quick rate of growth will soon take over the entire garden. The best exposure for the trough is in a place where the plants will receive the slanting rays of the sun in the morning and evening, yet be sheltered from the hot midday blast that would dry up the trough and cook the plants. The garden can be set on a porch, terrace, patio, or other adjunct to the house. It can be placed anywhere in the garden — on the ground, partially submerged, or on a pedestal; never, of course, in or near a natural rock garden. If the trough is to be on the ground or partially submerged, provision should be made for drainage beneath it. This can be accomplished by digging a trench the size of the container and filling it with gravel — a kind of dry well.

Because the plants to be grown in the trough will require adequate drainage, and because the entire trough will be subjected to thorough drying, both drainage and moisture-retentive measures must be taken. The container used must have an open drain in the bottom to carry off excessive moisture, and this should be covered with a wire shield to prevent it from becoming clogged. As shown in the sketch, the bottom two or three inches should be filled with sphagnum or peat moss to hold moisture. On top of the moss is a layer of gravel for drainage. Some people recommend that these applications be reversed, with the moss on top. I believe that the plants will prefer to have their roots in moist gravel rather than in soggy moss. A layer of sand covers the gravel and then comes the prepared rock-garden soil, with or without rocks in the form of a miniature outcropping.

As stated before, only the tiniest of the alpines and the slowest-growing of the very dwarf shrubs and conifers are planted in a trough garden. Because of the restriction of the roots in their quest for nourishment and moisture, the trough garden should be treated as a potted plant. It must be fed periodically with liquid fertilizers or with a top dressing of organic plant food, such as the dehydrated animal manures. Watering the miniature garden is important and must never be neglected. Usually, one good watering will suffice for a week or more, because of the moisture-retaining moss used at the bottom of the trough. However, the garden must be checked often, especially during prolonged heat waves.

Miniature gardening in a sink or trough is a fascinating hobby that is gaining popularity rapidly, even among people with ample space for the usual types of gardening. It is particularly interesting to those unfortunates who, for one reason or another, have become cliff dwellers in the apartment houses of our big cities. For those who desire more information on this intriguing phase of rock gardening, I recommend Anne Ashberry's book, *Miniature Gardens*. She gives many specific cultural and building hints, and includes a comprehensive list of plants, dwarf trees, and shrubs suitable for the trough garden.

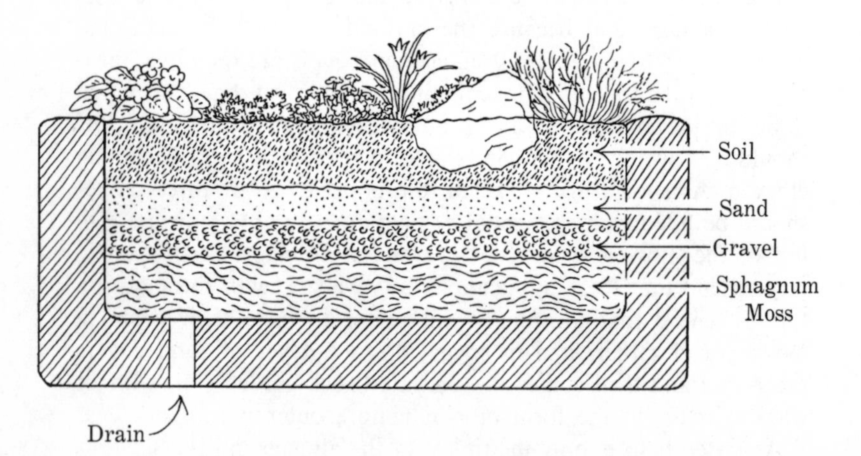

Cross section of trough or sink garden showing planting medium, drainage, and sphagnum moss moisture retainer.

THE CACTUS GARDEN

The cacti, with their curious forms, forbidding spines, and lovely flowers hold an inexpressible fascination for me and for many other people, judging by their popularity as conservatory or house plants. Despite this popularity, few gardeners understand their requirements, and hardly anyone realizes that many species and varieties are perfectly winter hardy in the North, where temperatures go as low as twenty degrees below zero, or more. Besides the kinds that are known definitely to be hardy, I believe there are many more that will prove to be so, if the conditions of their native habitats are duplicated in the garden. In the South, there is no problem in the cultivation of cacti, either in border plantings or in rock gardens. However, in the North, especially the Northeast, where we normally have wet winters and constant freezing and thawing, extra precautions must be taken to assure their survival.

The kinds that are known to be hardy and are in cultivation in the North should be given a dry scree when used in the rock garden. As we said in Chapter I, because of their odd forms, the cacti are difficult to use in a rock garden that is planted with alpines and the usual rock plants. Possible exceptions are some of the tiny mammillarias and coryphanthas with their tufty clusters of ball-shaped stems, and the little cespitose prickly pears, such as *Opuntia fragilis*. I feel that a separate garden should be built for the cacti, where special preparations can be made to duplicate the conditions that prevail in the desert and semiarid regions where they abound in nature. The cactus garden should be in full sun and exposed to as much wind as possible. It should be built well above the level of the ground for extremely rapid drainage during prolonged wet spells. The best cactus garden would be a rock garden such as those described but with soil consisting of rock fragments, stone chips, mortar rubble, or cinders and sand with only a trace of topsoil or leaf-mold. Do not give them any fertilizer, fresh organic matter, or peat moss.

For the adventurous gardener who would like to experiment with the less hardy or little-known cactus species, I advise build-

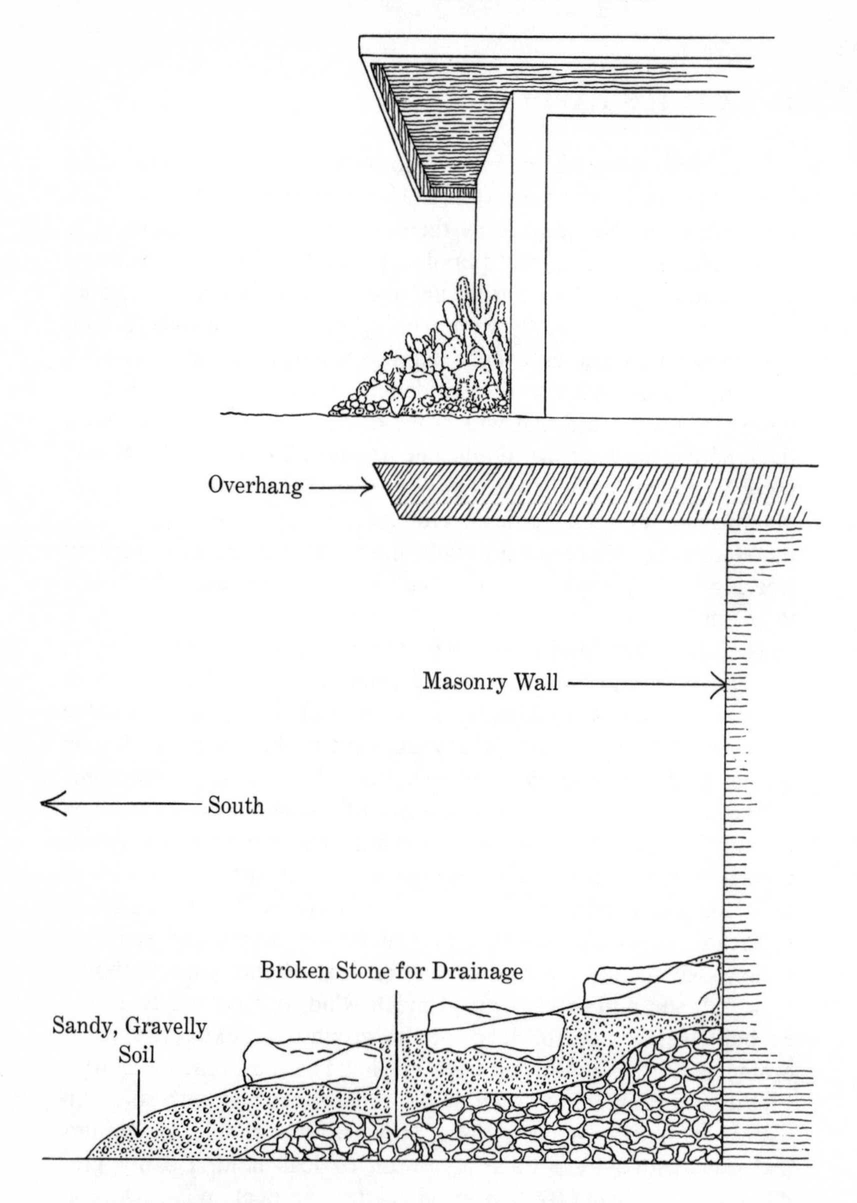

Ideal placement and cross section of cactus garden.

ing the garden against a south wall that is exposed to the full sun, especially in winter. The reflection of both heat and light from the wall will greatly increase the range of cactus species that can be tested. If the wall has a large overhang, as is now the style with our modern ranch-type houses, so much the better. The overhang will protect the cacti from most of the winter rains and snows that cause damage through breakage or excessive wetness. Cacti normally will not require watering in the Northeast, but if the garden is made under an overhang, it is advisable to supply some water during the growing season. I am sure that if a cactus garden is made in this manner, the garden enthusiast will be able to grow not only a greater variety of cacti, but also many of the interesting and beautiful echeverias and sedums that are native to our arid southwestern states and to Mexico.

ROCK GARDENING WITHOUT ROCKS

I am often asked by people who come to my nursery, and by garden club members when I show slides of rock-garden plants and alpines, if it is absolutely necessary to have a rock garden in order to grow these enchanting mountain plants. The answer is emphatically, "No!" Although many of the plants mentioned in this book need rocks to survive or to display their characteristics to advantage, a great many of them can be grown successfully in an ordinary perennial border or as edging for various types of plantings and gardens. The shrubby and semishrubby dwarfs, like candytuft, germander, and lavender cotton, are universally used for borders or edgings. Many of the dwarf evergreen trees and shrubs are used in the forefront of foundation plantings. The creeping rock-garden plants are often used as ground covers, either on slopes and banks or on level ground; and the heathers are especially attractive when they are planted in masses as ground cover in foundation plantings or in flat flower-garden beds.

There are any number of uses for the rock-garden plants; but, of course, they appear to best advantage in a rock garden that is designed to represent a bit of nature unmodified at our doorsteps.

CHAPTER IV

SOIL COMPOSITION

After the rocks for your garden have been set on a properly built base, the next step is preparation of the soil. Before you undertake this, try to determine what plants you are likely to grow, and then designate specific areas for the various soils. In this way special ground will be ready for plants of different requirements; and when a new plant is obtained, it can be planted in a place where it will live, instead of just being shoved in anywhere with a prayer for its survival.

Everyone, I believe, is agreed that soil is the basic need of plant life, just as air is basic to man and water to fish. Unlike air and water, which are essentially the same the world over, soil is divided into an infinite number of complex compositions and degrees of fertility. Therefore, in order to cultivate successfully a number of different types of plants from widely separated areas, special emphasis must be placed on the mixture of soils to be used in any garden. This is especially true in a rock garden, where the plants used will encompass a greater number of genera and species. Hence, I stress the construction of soil to simulate that found in the natural habitat of the plants that are to be grown.

Any plant endemic to a specific locality is growing there because the soil is suitable for its development. I think it is safe to say that the soil was there long before the plant arrived. Thus, it is reasonable to assume that the plant or its antecedents adapted itself to obtain sustenance from this particular soil through a centuries-long process of evolution. Man, with his impatience or ignorance, cannot upset this evolutionary development merely by his force of will or desire. When a plant is lifted from the wild and moved to a locality with an entirely contrary soil structure, it will generally die. This is particularly true of the comparatively few plants that are indigenous to areas where the soil is of marked difference in composition and fertility from that found in the generally highly fertile valleys of the world. As the rock gardener is primarily concerned with the cultivation of tiny treasures from the earth's bleak wastelands, he must pay meticulous attention to their seemingly unfathomable whims and preferences.

Plants, when discussed by amateurs, are placed in two general categories. They are acid lovers or lime lovers. In order to make simple things confusing, there is no steadfast rule to determine which plant belongs where. In fact, the line between the two classes has such latitude that most of the plants under cultivation actually fall into another group, larger than the other two combined, that can be called neutral lovers. These are the plants that are almost indifferent to soil acidity and will do equally well in soil that is slightly acid or slightly limy. Plants from the chalk cliffs and limestone ledges require lime in their diet and are recognized as definite lime lovers. Others from the deep woods, shady wastelands, and granite mountains abhor lime and so are called acid lovers. Although soil alkalinity is important, it is not significant enough to assure success with the alpines. Texture, drainage, and degrees of fertility are equally, or even more, important.

For my own edification and to facilitate the growing of many kinds of plants in my nursery, I have divided the soil types into six basic classifications. They are: ordinary garden soil, gritty lime soil, rich acid loam, acid leaf-mold soil, moraine mixture, and scree mixture.

Most of the common rock plants that are important as the backbone of the garden are easy to grow. They are easy because nature has endowed them with a versatility that enables them to become adapted to widely divergent soil and climatic conditions. Here there is no problem in cultivation. They will thrive in almost any climate and in almost any type of soil. These easy plants I have indicated as desiring an ordinary garden soil, the kind of soil that will produce good garden vegetables. This is the usual alluvial loam or fertile glacial till found on well-kept farmlands. It should have an alkalinity test from pH 6 to pH 7.5. Where a good balanced farm topsoil is unobtainable, an adequate substitute can be had by mixing the following:

3 parts friable loam	1 part leaf-mold or compost
1 part peat moss or humus	(decayed vegetable matter)
1 part sharp sand	

To this should be added a generous amount of animal manure and a sufficient amount of pulverized limestone to bring the pH value up to at least pH 6. If compost is not available, it can be replaced with an additional part of peat or humus. This is the mixture I use for most of my potting soil with extremely good results. The amount of manure to use is arbitrary. I generally use 15 pounds of dehydrated sheep manure to a mixture containing six mason wheelbarrows of the basic ingredients. The largest portion of the rock garden should be given over to this mixture, because in it you will be growing most of your plants. This soil should also be used for the wall garden, flagstone walks, and terraces. Smaller areas or pockets can be devoted to plants requiring other types of soil.

Most members of *Dianthus, Saxifraga, Androsace,* the *Cruciferae,* and other plants from limestone ledges are calcicoles and should be given the gritty lime soil made by mixing the following:

1 part loam	1 part stone chips
1 part leaf-mold	½ part limestone chips
1 part sharp sand	or crushed sea shells

This may not be exactly what the plants have in their native habitat, but I have found it to be a satisfactory medium for the easier alpines.

From the rich alpine meadows comes a wealth of rock-garden species, such as *Primula, Trollius, Anemone,* and *Ranunculus.* These require a very rich diet with an abundance of organic matter. For these plants, needing a rich acid loam, I prescribe the following mixture:

2 parts loam	½ part sharp sand
2 parts peat or humus	¼ part manure

Most of the ericaceous plants, such as heathers, rhododendrons, laurel, and an infinite number of woodlanders that find their way to the rock garden, demand a highly acid soil, made up primarily of leaf-mold. For all my ericaceous plants and woodlanders I use the following:

3 parts acid leaf-mold   1 part sharp sand

In this case the leaf-mold must be acid. The best is taken from beneath conifers, such as hemlock, pine, and spruce, and also under hardwoods, like oak and beech. If the supply of leaf-mold is limited peat moss can be substituted for a portion of it. The black domestic peats are also good. Although they usually have a mucky quality, this can be overcome to a large extent by using more sand in the mixture.

How any plant can live on a talus slope is beyond my comprehension, but live they do, and many of these hardy endemics are welcomed to the rock garden. In addition to the plants from natural screes, many others from the semiarid regions as the Middle East, Asia Minor, and the eastern slopes of the Rocky Mountains should be given scree culture if they are to be at their best in the comparatively wet eastern states and in the northwestern Pacific area. Here is my scree mixture:

1 part leaf-mold   3 parts stone chips
1 part sharp sand   a trace of manure

The most highly prized treasures of the alpine world defy cultivation except in a moraine. As pointed out in Chapter I, the scree and moraine are similar in structure, but the moraine is watered from below and the glacial debris makes it much richer in organic content and in organic salts and minerals. For the top layer of the moraine, I mix the following:

1 part loam   3 parts stone chips
1 part sharp sand   a generous application of manure
2 parts leaf-mold or compost

I honestly think that if these formulas are followed, a rock garden will be at least ninety per cent successful. Of course, any number of digressions or gradations can and should be made for plants of borderline classifications. Undoubtedly, some plants will fail repeatedly until something drastically different is tried. Most of the fun in rock gardening is found in meeting the challenge of the most obstinate subjects. If you think you will enjoy a challenge, try *Arnica montana, Eritrichium nanum, Silene hookeri, Potentilla nitida, Aquilegia jonesii, Loiseleuria procumbens,* or *Diapensia lapponica.*

CHAPTER V

PLANTING AND MAINTENANCE

As much care should be taken in placing the plants in the garden as in selecting them from the nursery or seed list. All the good work of naturalistic designing can be sacrificed by a hodgepodge planting, even when the best species and varieties are used. Maintaining a proper scale for any particular garden is imperative if the picture is to be perfectly balanced. This does not mean that the plants should all be of the same size and texture, but rather that they should be placed in relationship to each other according to their size at maturity and their habit and rate of growth.

The advocates of true alpine gardening insist that the tallest plants should be placed at the lowest levels in the garden and the diminutive alpines and prostrate growers at the highest points. This, they say, is the only natural way of planting, because in nature the lush and heavy growth is always in the valleys. As higher elevations are reached, plant growth becomes sparse and lower in stature, and trees are stunted; until finally, above timber line, all growth is reduced to tight little tufts or hummocks and prostrate creepers, only an inch or two high. This planting arrangement is commendable for rock gardens that cover large areas and have considerable elevation; but for backyard gardens of more normal size, I like just the opposite—the tallest growing plants in the background and the diminutive gems in front where they can be seen. In a small rock garden, tall plants at the lower elevation would tend to hide the smaller and perhaps more desirable kinds. In gardens of slight elevation, it is possible to use a comparatively large plant like *Astilbe* 'fanal' with a very low *Primula* 'Wanda' directly in front of it with excellent results. If the reverse procedure were followed, with the primula behind the astilbe, the primrose would bloom unseen.

Placing plants in rows, circles, or other geometric designs within the rock garden is strictly forbidden by the laws of nature. Plants in the wild never grow in formal patterns; they cannot be arranged that way in a rock garden with natural results. Using numerous plants of varying color and foliage texture in a crazy-quilt or multicolored polka-dot design is equally unnatural and quite unattractive. For the most natural and perhaps the best appearance, the plants should be placed in groups or drifts to give mass color effects. The number of plants to set in a drift or group depends mainly upon the size of the garden and the habit or rate of growth of the plant. A single plant that is a robust grower and a prolific bloomer will often create the desired effect in a small garden.

Quite a number of good rock plants are woefully insignificant when displayed singly, but in sizable groups take on a character that is unexcelled even by the flamboyant subject. Modesty and daintiness are the most appealing attributes of a desirable rock plant.

It is often said that plants should not be arranged in even-numbered groups, such as two or four or six of a kind together, because this tends to create even rows. Actually, a year or two after planting, each individual loses its identity and becomes part of a unit. Thus it does not matter how many plants are placed together or whether there is an odd or an even number to start with. In a short time they will add up to one lovely splash of color.

Each plant has a specific character that must be considered if it is to display its most striking attributes. A *Sedum sieboldii* on a flat surface is just another sedum, but when it grows in the crevice of an overhanging rock, its graceful stems arching downward and its tips upturned to display clusters of clear pink flowers, it has beauty that cannot be equaled by the most haughty plants.

Before placing a plant, know its habits. Then you can use it to its best advantage. Creeping, mat- or cushion-forming plants are used as fillers for the wide spaces between the rocks. Here they have unhampered space for spreading. The tiny tufts, or clusters of rosettes, should be planted in narrow crevices where they will not be overlooked by the viewer and where the rock itself will protect them from the encroachment of more vigorous neighbors. Hanging or decumbent plants should be set behind or above large rocks where their stems will tend to grow over the rocks, creating graceful cascades and mantles of colorful flowers. If this kind of plant were placed at the base of a rock, or on flat soil, its effectiveness would be lost. On the other hand, upright or ascending plants should be placed below the rocks where their stems will have an illusion of support and lend a softness to their hard background. Some plants, with dense clumpy foliage and tall thin stems topped by airy flower scapes, must be planted against a large rock for a proper display of their elusive beauty. A striking example of this type is *Heuchera sanguinea.* Although its flowers are colorful and pretty, they have a delicate airiness that remains undefined unless there is a solid background to emphasize their lacy loveliness.

Striking color combinations are effective in a rock garden and should be provided. Quite often the delicate beauty of one plant is accentuated when it is grown in conjunction with another. Individual taste for color affinities is the sole dictate for grouping plants in attractive arrangements. Too often plants are selected or rejected for color combinations without consideration of their blooming period. A purple flower that blooms in July obviously will not clash with the red of its nearest neighbor if the red does not appear until September.

One of the major arguments against starting a rock garden is the timeworn contention that it will look pretty when it is in full bloom early in spring but will soon become a dull and drab liability in the home landscape plan. This is true in many instances, but it is not the fault of rock gardening; it is the fault of the person who planned and planted the garden. Invariably, the person responsible visits a nursery in early spring when he is charged with his annual renewal of enthusiasm for gardening and the outdoor life. Once there, he proceeds to buy the plants that are flaunting appealing flowers, disregarding all the rest. The outcome of such a venture can only be a spring garden, sparkling with color in April and May and dull the rest of the summer. Try as he may, the nurseryman cannot convince the prospective buyer that the little plant with the tiny green leaves next to the one with showy pink flowers will offer a gorgeous display of blue trumpets in September.

Although most true alpines do flower in the spring, there are enough summer- and fall-blooming kinds to keep the garden beautiful throughout the season. If the rock gardener will look a bit farther than the end of his nose and do a bit of planning before he sets out for the nursery, he will soon learn that his rock garden does not have to be just a spring garden. By consulting garden books, visiting other gardens during different months of the summer, and above all, by seeking advice from the nurseryman and seed distributor, he will be able to plan a garden that will be his prime joy throughout the year.

Another common mistake, made especially by beginners, is to overplant. This is usually done because of a desire to cover every inch of available planting area with green growth and thus have a finished garden without waiting for nature to help. Such overplanting quickly results in overcrowding and the subsequent loss of plants, money, inspiration, and enthusiasm. Ample room must be left for natural expansion. The tiny plants that are set out first will grow and flourish only if they have room to spread without undue competition from their neighbors. Crowding never results in a well-planted garden. Only time and the healthy development of each individual can bring a garden to perfection. The new rock gardener can save money and avoid frustration by practicing the virtue of patience. His reward will be the treasures rock gardening has to offer.

I am often asked what time is best for planting. Actually, planting can be done at any time of the year when the soil can be worked, especially now when so many nursery items are being grown in pots or other containers. Winter planting is discouraging, not because it is harmful to the plants, but because the weather is not conducive to gardening and the soil is usually unworkable. Summer planting is justifiable and can be quite successful if a few precautions are taken. If container-grown stock is to be planted, there is no problem at all. The plants are tapped out of their containers carefully so as not to break the root ball, firmly set in the garden, then watered thoroughly. If drought conditions prevail, the plants should be watered twice a day for a period of a week or more. Field-grown plants that are moved in the summer should be watered more frequently and must be shaded from the hot sun for a few days or until new growth begins.

Naturally enough, spring is the most popular time for planting because most people are eager to get into their gardens after the bleak months indoors. Spring planting gives the plants a full season to become established before they must face the rigors of winter. This hardens them and minimizes the danger of heaving because their roots have taken a firm foothold in the soil. If the rock garden is ready for planting in the fall, and the gardener is undecided whether to plant immediately or wait for spring to avoid winter losses, I say plant in the fall. The few plants that may possibly be lost during the winter will be greatly offset by the increased size and production of the others. Plants set out in the fall will be far in advance of those established in the spring. Being larger, they will produce flowers the first year.

MAINTENANCE

After the initial planting has been accomplished, it is the duty of the devoted rock gardener to keep the little plants growing and happy. This can be done only by continued effort and methodic management. Although many unknowing people decide on a rock garden because they think it can be planted and forgotten, they soon learn otherwise. The rock garden, like any other garden, needs periodic weeding, feeding, watering, and grooming for satisfactory results. This may seem to imply unending hours of tedious and back-breaking work, but that is not my meaning. The rock gardener will find that each day in his garden brings its own reward. A plant in bloom for the first time, new growth on a sickling that has been carefully nursed, or a new spontaneous seedling to watch bring quiet pleasure. And not the least of his pleasures will be the looks of wonder and the exclamations of awe and envy from his friends and neighbors. Of course, there will be disappointments too, but the good will always outweigh them.

Weeding is one phase of rock gardening that cannot be neglected for any extended period. Two weeks growth of weeds will not seriously affect other plantings, but it will totally obliterate the small plants in a rock garden. Weeds can become a problem only when they are neglected. If a few are removed each day as one browses through the garden, the problem is licked before it really gets a start. Chemical weed killers should *never* be used in the rock garden. They kill more desirable plants than weeds, even though the best of them have the dubious reputation of being effective in lawns and cotton fields.

Insects, bugs, worms, snails, slugs, and fungi are always present in a rock garden as in other gardens. They can be controlled by periodic spraying, or by dusting with insecticides and fungicides. The old-fashioned spray of arsenate of lead and nicotine concentrates for insects, and flowers of sulphur and copper sulphate mixtures for fungi are still effective and are usually more reliable than a lot of the new miracle bug killers that have been ballyhooed of late. Slugs are by far the most notorious enemies of the rock gardener. Hitherto the only control was with arsenic-treated baits. Such baits are messy, not too effective, and dangerous to children and pets. Thanks to modern science, a new all-purpose insecticide has appeared on the market called Malathion. I have used it and found it effective against most garden insects. The best weapon for eliminating slugs is a new liquid killer called Sluggit. Made in England, it is still rare on the American scene, but it can be obtained from the better garden stores. For combating fungus diseases I recommend Natriphene, made primarily for mouth washes and the treatment and prevention of athlete's foot. It is about 100 per cent effective against all common fungus diseases, yet is safe for the tiniest seedling, and does not leave an unsightly residue. Usually, spraying need be resorted to only when an unusually heavy infestation occurs. Natural enemies will destroy most of the garden pests.

Changing the rock garden is a process that will continue as long as it is in existence. The changes will involve replacements for older plants that have become less desirable, and also changing plants from one location to another where they will be more appropriate or more noticeable. Many times a plant will be unhappy in one spot for no apparent reason, and a move of only a few inches will make a world of difference to it. The shadow of a building, the proximity of a large tree root, improper soil, or lack of root depth are a few of the many reasons for moving a plant. A move may not correct the trouble, but any change *might* help.

Removing obviously dead plants promptly is advisable. Their prolonged presence discourages the gardener, detracts from the appearance of the garden, and gives visitors a bad impression. But be sure such plants are really dead. In the early spring, before active growth has started, a plant may seem to be dead when, in reality, it is very much alive at the roots. If it is cut back severely and left unmolested for a time, new growth will begin and a healthy plant will emerge. Too many plants are wantonly destroyed because of the gardener's impatience in the very early spring, particularly after a severe winter.

Many rock gardens I have visited have a ragged, unkempt appearance because the gardener is too timid to trim or cut back plants. Almost all plants should be groomed after they have flowered. This means removing all vestige of dead flowers, dried seed pods, and withered stems. Such care makes a plant look presentable for the remainder of the season. Some plants should be given a general trimming of all their stems after flowering. This encourages new growth, creates an appealing shape, and generally puts the plant in a better condition to produce more flowers the following season. Annual trimming and shaping is especially recommended for the shrubby or semishrubby plants. Many plants of rambling or tumbling growth should be cut back almost to the roots after flowering. Such species as *Arabis albida, Aubrieta deltoidea, Cerastium tomentosum,* and *Saponaria ocymoides* become unattractive masses of long, tangled, half-dried stems unless they are sheared soon after flowering. If they are cut back, they soon make new growth of a neat, compact, and healthy appearance and are attractive even though they are not in bloom.

Special emphasis should be put on trimming the dwarf conifers that are so highly prized by rock gardeners. Although they are extremely dwarf and very slow growing, they sometimes do outgrow their allotted space and have to be moved to larger quarters. Annual trimming, even when the conifers are very small, will help keep them in scale with the garden for a longer period of time.

When a plant becomes old and its flowers begin to fail and applications of fertilizer do not bring a response, it undoubtedly needs rejuvenation. This can be done by thinning or dividing the old clump. Thinning is done by taking the garden trowel and relentlessly gouging out chunks of the crowded root system. After a sufficient number of chunks have been removed, the holes should be refilled with new soil. The old plant is then ready to go again. In dividing, the entire clump is dug up and the plant is pulled apart or cut apart with a large knife into numerous little divisions, each complete with roots, stems, and leaves. Again, the old soil is removed and replaced with new before the divisions are planted. Surplus plants can be set out elsewhere in the garden, potted up as donations to the garden club plant sale, or given to friends.

However, before either of these two steps is taken, determine by examining the root structure whether thinning or dividing can be accomplished without destroying the entire plant. Plants with heavy taproots, and those that become woody at the base in old age, will not take kindly to this rough treatment. Those that develop large fleshy taproots are usually comparatively short-lived and must be replaced periodically with new plants started from cuttings or seeds. Herbaceous plants that become semi-woody in old age can usually be rejuvenated by being cut back almost to the root. When new growth appears, the old rootstock should be mounded up with fresh sandy soil to encourage the new stem shoots to develop roots. Actually, one then has a new plant. Some of the plants that will respond to this treatment are: *Alyssum saxatile, Satureja montana, Santolina virens,* and *Teucrium chamaedrys.*

Water is as necessary to plants as the air that surrounds them and the soil that supports them, but overwatering and underwatering are equally detrimental. Knowing what to water and when to water it is at best always a guess, so the surest procedure is to practice moderation. Each plant set out in the garden should be watered in at the time of planting. Usually, that will carry it through the remainder of the year if the planting is done in the early spring or fall. When planting is done in the summer, at least one watering a day for several days is necessary to give the newcomer a firm foothold in its new home. In times of prolonged drought, it is advisable to water the entire rock garden to keep the soil moderately moist until relief is sent from the heavens. It is best to give the gardens a thorough soaking once every three or four days rather than a light sprinkling daily. Normally, a light sprinkling saturates the leaves and does not penetrate the dry soil at the roots. Thus, the plants are exposed to severe sun scald and dehydration through too rapid transpiration. The time of day for watering is of no consequence. High noon, or any other time available, is just as good as morning or evening. At my nursery we water continuously all day long without danger of damage to the plants. The one time not to water is in the late fall, for at least two weeks before the first frost is expected. An excessive amount of water at that time will put the plants in a state of active growth that makes them susceptible to severe frost damage.

In the spring clean-up of the garden and during weeding, most of the garden's natural plant food is removed before it has had a chance to enrich the soil. That being the case, fertilizer must be supplied from time to time to maintain normal healthy growth. The fast-acting commercial chemical fertilizers should not be used because they burn the foliage and destroy the tiny surface feeder roots. They can be responsible for the destruction of a great many valuable plants in a very short time. I speak from experience! I always advocate the broadcasting of dehydrated animal manure over the entire garden in spring and again in fall. My personal preference is for sheep manure, which is easy to use. It can be applied directly on the plants without endangering them, and can be sifted through the foliage to the roots of even the tightest growers. Because it is long lasting, its nutrients are always available to the plants at their roots.

Some plants should never be fertilized. Most important among these are the ericaceous shrubs from erica to rhododendron. These particularly abhor feeding of any kind except an annual top dressing of acid leaf-mold. It is not that they refuse to grow in fertilized soil. On the contrary, they grow like weeds; but after that, even the hardiest species will not live over the winter. Other plants that do not like feeding are those from the dry, rocky, or sandy wastelands of the world. Many of these, too, will *grow* in rich soil, but they lose all similarity to their true character.

Another method of fertilizing that has recently been growing in popularity, due to high-pressure advertising, is foliar feeding with hydroponic solutions administered by means of a sprinkling can or spray tank. In this method, water-soluble minerals, salts, and other nutrients are absorbed through the leaves, buds, bark, and stems of the plants. The nutrients are readily assimilated by the plants without photosynthesis. The plant immediately perks up, looking bright, fresh, and vigorous. This is not entirely unnatural, because essentially the same process takes place during every thunderstorm. Everyone at some time or another has noticed how fresh and green the countryside looks after a particularly violent storm. This fresh appearance is not due to the thorough washing the plants and trees have had after a dusty siege of heat and drought, but rather to the fact that they have greedily absorbed a natural application of "free" nitrogen released from the atmosphere through the chemical process of electrolysis. I think the foliar feeding should be administered only during the summer months, when the garden takes on that tired, listless look. The plants do not need it in the early spring, because at that time they have enough nutrients stored in their roots and stems to send them on their happy way. Foliar or hydroponic feeding should be avoided in the fall, because it puts the plants in very poor condition to withstand the ravages of winter. The leaves become supple, the new leaf buds swollen, and the bark soft and pliable. Plants in such a condition at the beginning of winter will most certainly suffer from blasted buds and split stems.

The hardiness of alpines and of rock-garden plants in general is constantly under discussion when enthusiasts meet. A plant will be reported to be completely hardy in one place, and in another place, not too different in climate, it will have the reputation of being tender. Much of the hardiness has to do with the condition of the plants when winter sets in, as indicated above in regard to feeding and watering. Some plants suffer more winter damage in mild climates where they are subject to alternate freezing and thawing than they do in colder areas where they have a more even temperature. Where there is constant snow cover, there is almost no damage, even to plants of doubtful hardiness. Here at the nursery we had twelve inches of snow on the ground on January 15 and 16, 1957, when the temperature fell to thirty-eight degrees below zero. There was very little frost in the ground and no winter damage resulted, even to the kurume azaleas, which are generally regarded as tender.

Winter cover for the rock garden is usually not absolutely necessary, but it is very inexpensive insurance for the safety of a large investment. A number of different materials can be used as a winter covering, among them excelsior, evergreen boughs, salt-marsh hay or slough-grass hay, and anything else that is light and airy. The cover should be put on *after* the ground has frozen hard in late fall or early winter. It is applied, not to keep the plants warm, but to keep frozen, and to protect them from scalding winter sunshine and drying winds. Mulching reduces the number of thaws, thus reducing the danger of heaving. When heaving does occur and is noticed, the plants should be pushed back as soon as the soil is soft enough to do so. A good portion of the winter damage takes place in very early spring when lovely balmy days are followed by sudden and severe cold snaps. For this reason, the winter cover should not be removed too early. Just when to uncover I cannot say, for each locality is different. The gardener must learn through the sad experience of trial and error. In northern New Jersey, I never uncovered before the first of April. Here in the hills of Pennsylvania, I cannot uncover until the middle of April.

After removing the protective material, the gardener will find that spring cleaning is in order. Fallen leaves from the surrounding trees have drifted down between the rocks; branches of shrubs may have been broken by heavy snow; clumps of dead foliage still cling to the roots of deciduous plants, and heaving and washes may have carried soil down from upper levels. These and a host of other minor casualties must be corrected. The meticulous gardener will want his garden spic and span for spring so that he can enjoy the new flowers as they appear without wading through mounds of unattractive winter debris.

When the spring cleaning has been completed, careful observation will show that the roots of many plants are partially exposed, that the crowns of others may be up above the level of the soil, and that some soil has been washed or shifted. All these areas need a top dressing of new soil. The ingredients listed in Chapter IV for all soil recipes should be kept on hand so that, when top dressing time comes around, the proper soil mixtures for the various plants will be available. The gardener will not have to use make-shift mixtures that may well be detrimental to some of the plants.

In order to keep the garden attractive at all times, and to prevent most of the washing that normally occurs on bare soils, I recommend a permanent half-inch dressing of small stone chips over the entire garden, between the plants and the rocks. This stone chip layer will discourage weeds, keep the soil cool in summer, help retain moisture, and provide surface drainage for the plants. It will help blend the rocks with the plants, and above all, it will keep the garden neat and trim. A similar mass of chips is found at every natural outcropping of rocks, so the layer will not look out of place.

Many gardeners do not care about the names of plants and even seem to be proud of their ignorance. Nevertheless, it is a good idea to learn the names of all the plants in the garden and to keep them properly labeled. Labeling will help keep track of the plants purchased and, at the same time, reduce the number of questions from visitors. The labels should be printed clearly and placed where they can be easily seen. This will discourage inquisitive visitors from pulling up the tags to read them and invariably mixing them up.

PROPAGATION

Every rock gardener at some time or another tries his hand at propagation, sometimes with success but much too often with complete failure. The reproduction of plants is not an easy task, and there are no foolproof rules to follow. Most home propagation of alpines is unsuccessful because the sole prerequisite of success, constant vigilance, is invariably impossible. Of course, there are some plants that anyone can increase without difficulty, but these are the more weedy ones that can be had by the basketful for the asking. Success in propagation is not achieved with the germination of a seed or the rooting of a cutting. The important task is to nurse the little plant to maturity.

Volumes have been filled on the subject of propagation, and it still has not been fully covered. The few notes here should be taken as general suggestions that will aid the home gardener in his endeavor to reproduce some of his own plants.

The main cause of failure, both with seeds and cuttings, is a fungus attack at the ground level, commonly called damping off. All seed flats, soils, and rooting mediums should be thoroughly drenched with a good fungicide before seeds are sown or cuttings stuck. All cuttings and seedlings should be sprayed or sprinkled with the fungicide weekly (oftener if necessary) until they are moved to permanent quarters. If this precaution is taken, almost half the battle is won. Because of the closeness of a stand of seedlings in a flat, a growth of fungus will travel quickly and kill off an entire seeding within twenty-four hours.

Fancy soil mixtures for growing seedlings, and complicated rooting mediums for cuttings, are usually prescribed. At my nursery, I use only one mixture for all seeds and cuttings with good results. That mixture is fifty per cent sharp washed sand and fifty per cent ground sphagnum moss, which in itself seems to possess some antiseptic power, thus lessening the danger of damping off. Pure sphagnum can be used, but the cuttings and seedlings are harder to separate for potting after they have rooted than when it is mixed with sand. It is very absorbent and highly moisture retentive; therefore, many waterings can be eliminated. Sphagnum is a safeguard against prolonged drying while the gardener is away from home. Such drying is ordinarily disastrous, because constant moisture is an absolute essential to successful propagation. The one digression I permit myself from my all-purpose mixture is the use of straight sand for most gray-leafed and tomentose cuttings, and for cuttings of plants from semiarid habitats. The water retained by the sphagnum is excessive for these plants and causes waterlogging or rotting even when a fungicide is used.

SOWING SEEDS

Some perennial seeds will germinate a few days after they are sown. Others will take a few weeks, and some even years. Some have a very short viability; if they are not sown immediately after ripening, they will not germinate at all. The directions on seed packets often call for stratification, or freezing, before sowing. If the seeds are sown in the sand-and-sphagnum mixture, stratification takes place automatically. We shall discuss freezing later. Whenever possible, seeds should be planted as soon as they are ripe — before they have a chance to become thoroughly dried and hardened. They will then germinate at a much better percentage, and their incubation period will be hastened by weeks and sometimes months.

Seeds should be sown in flats or shallow plastic pots. Clay pots, because of their porosity, cause the medium to dry too rapidly. The planting mixture should be firmed down tightly and then watered thoroughly before seeds are sown. Small seeds can be sown on top of the medium without covering. Large seeds should be covered lightly. The pits and humps in the sphagnum will trap them and keep them from floating away. The flats then should be watered lightly. Usually a thorough watering at the time of sowing will keep the flats moist for a period of two or three weeks unless they are exposed to direct sunshine or strong winds. For best results, the seed flats should be set outdoors but in a protected spot where strong winds and heavy rains will not hit them.

Many perennial seeds will not germinate unless they go through a lengthy period of freezing and thawing. For these, the seeds should be sown in the fall and the flats left outdoors all winter, where they will freeze solid and where snow will settle on them. Germination will then take place in the spring. Often a few seeds in a given flat will sprout in a few days, to be followed by successive germinations in the months to follow. Here once again the gardener should be patient. He should not throw out the flats if nothing happens in the first few weeks or even in the first year. If they are kept another winter, the seeds may germinate the following spring.

After the seeds germinate in sphagnum, there is very little growth and that is extremely slow. If the gardener wishes to hasten growth to facilitate transplanting, the seedlings may be sprinkled with a hydroponic solution in mild strength. When the first true leaves appear, it is time to transplant the seedlings either into flats of soil suited to their development or into small pots. I particularly like to move them to pots, because they develop new roots more quickly and there is less transplanting shock when they are finally moved to permanent positions in the rock garden.

The inhibitive properties of sphagnum have some distinct advantages. The seedlings will not grow so quickly as to crowd each other out, as they sometimes do in rich soil. If enough seedlings are moved to satisfy immediate wants, the remainder can be left in the seed flat for the next spring without detriment. When these held-over seedlings are finally moved to a proper soil mixture, they will commence to grow as normal plants without any ill effects from their year's sojourn in a semidormant state. Using this method, the gardener has on hand a supply of plants that ordinarily would be wasted or thrown out.

LAYERING

Layering is usually practiced on woody plants that do not root easily from cuttings, or when the gardener wishes to avoid the trouble of preparing cutting boxes for a relatively few new plants. It is a simple process, but slow, and only a small number of new plants can be produced at a time.

A low branch of the plant to be reproduced is selected for the layer. A notch or slit is cut into the underside of the stem, and the stem is then placed on the ground. A stone, wire staple, or hairpin can be used to hold it in place. The branch is then covered with soil at its point of contact with the ground. In some instances, rooting will take place in a few weeks; in others, it may take months. Usually, a year after the layer was prepared, it is severed from the parent plant and moved to a new location.

DIVISIONS

Most herbaceous perennials can be propagated by divisions. However, before this is undertaken, the root system should be examined to determine whether division is feasible. The entire plant should be lifted, and the soil washed from its roots. All plants with stoloniferous root systems are natural dividers. A little tug, and a piece of the plant will come off with sufficient roots to make a healthy new plant. The divisions should then be planted in small pots to encourage new root growth. As soon as they have become established, they can be removed to permanent positions. Some plants that are not natural dividers can be reproduced in this fashion with the help of a sharp knife. Before a division is made, the root structure should be studied carefully to see that the piece to be cut will come away with enough roots to sustain it, independent of the mother plant. Pieces that come off with few roots should be potted in a mixture of sand and sphagnum to encourage new root development.

CUTTINGS

Reproducing plants by means of cuttings is a much more involved process than any of the others. Each genus must be handled differently. Cuttings of some plants should be taken in the spring, others in the summer, and still others in the fall or early winter. Some will not root without special apparatus, and some must be handled under glass — that is, in a greenhouse or hotbed. In Chapter VII I have indicated when cuttings should be taken for each plant.

Cuttings should be taken early in the morning when they are still wet with dew, or on cloudy or rainy days. They should be removed from the parent plant with a sharp knife and dipped immediately into cool water. The lower leaves should be removed cleanly along the stem and the butt should be cut off neatly without any tabs of bark left hanging. The ends should not be crushed or injured in any way while being cut. The cut should be made directly below a leaf node to insure better rooting. Cuttings should be kept moist at all times during the process of making them. If they are left to wilt, or become dried out, it is best to throw them away and start over.

The cuttings should be inserted in the rooting medium deep enough to be held upright, pressed in firmly, and watered thoroughly. They should be shaded lightly for the first two weeks and sprinkled often, especially on warm sunny days in the summer. For the first few days they should be sprinkled five or six times a day. As they become progressively harder, the sprinklings can be cut to once or twice a day until rooting commences. When they have become rooted sufficiently well to permit removal from the medium without breaking off the new tender roots, they are ready to be placed in small pots containing a proper soil mixture.

Most newly rooted cuttings, seedlings, and small divisions should be carried over the first winter in pots plunged in a covered cold frame and planted out in the garden the following spring.

CHAPTER VI

BACKGROUND AND APPROACH PLANTING

The background planting of a rock garden should be planned to serve two main functions, to provide an appropriate frame for the natural picture being composed with rocks and plants, and to screen out undesirable sights, such as buildings, busy streets, and the neighbor's backyard.

An effective planting keeps the eye from straying from the main theme of the picture, the rock garden, but at the same time avoids attracting too much attention to its own composition. It should not contain brightly flowered trees or shrubs, or those with variegated or unusually colored foliage. The brilliant buddleias, quinces, laburnums, weigelas, crab apples, flowering cherries, and red hybrid rhododendrons should be used elsewhere in the home landscaping. Pyramidal, columnar, and conical forms of conifers are stiff and formal. They, too, should be avoided. The best background is graceful, subdued, and unpretentious, expressive of freedom and the informality of the wild. It should be composed of evergreen and deciduous trees and shrubs in combination. (A solid wall of evergreens lacks depth and harmony.)

All possible use should be made of any or all existing trees on the garden site, provided they are far enough removed from the planting area. Nothing could be more appropriate than a lacy canopy of not-too-distant oaks, beeches, birches, or maples. These should be tied in with the additional background planting and made a part of the entire composition. The tallest trees should be farthest from the limits of the rock garden, the shrubs gradually coming closer and becoming a part of it. The smallest of the background shrubs can be planted directly in the highest levels of the garden.

Appropriate background of Weeping Hemlock and Rhododendrons.

TREES FOR BACKGROUND

AMELANCHIER (*Rosaceae,* Rose Family). Commonly called shadbush, shadblow, or serviceberry. Mostly North American native small trees and shrubs that are distinctive for their profusion of white flowers in late March and early April before the leaves appear. They are readily adapted to various situations and soils, and are easy to transplant. Seldom offered by the nursery trade but can be moved from the wild.

A. canadensis. A small tree, to 30 feet high, with white flowers early in spring. Small silvery leaves that turn green as they mature. It has tasty edible fruit that ripens in June.

A. laevis. Very much like the preceding, except that the new leaves are purplish and the tree grows a bit taller.

BETULA (*Betulaceae,* Birch Family). The birches are well-known trees of graceful habits. The following is particularly suited to the rock-garden background.

B. populifolia. The gray, or clump, birch is well known as an invader of abandoned farms in the northeastern states. It is a small tree, from 20 to 30 feet high, with three or more trunks to a clump. The bark is an attractive silvery-gray color.

CERCIS (*Leguminosae,* Pea Family). Redbuds are large shrubs or small trees native to Europe, Asia, and North America. They are prized for their quantities of red, pink, or purplish flowers in early spring. Only one is hardy in the North.

C. canadensis. A shrub or tree, to 30 feet high, with rosy-pink flowers in little clusters all up and down the branches and twigs in late March and April.

CHAMAECYPARIS (*Pinaceae,* Pine Family). The false cypresses are represented in the horticultural world by several species and many varieties. They are evergreens, with attractive feathery, ferny, or mossy foliage, that are adapted to most sections of the United States except the Far North and the semiarid regions. Many can be used for the rock-garden background, but the following are especially commendable.

C. lawsoniana. A large tree with dark-green, ferny foliage on gracefully drooping branches. Probably the typical form cannot be found, but there are many horticultural forms from which to choose. Avoid the brightly variegated ones.

C. pisifera. The Sawara cypress is a tall tree with light-blue-green mossy foliage on drooping branches. Like the preceding, the parent has been displaced by its many attractive forms that are obtainable from most nurseries.

CORNUS (*Cornaceae,* Dogwood Family). Most of the dogwoods from Europe and Asia are useful for the rock garden, but none surpasses our native trees.

C. florida. A small tree, to about 20 feet high, with large white flower bracts in late April and May. It has clusters of scarlet fruits in September.

CRYPTOMERIA (*Pinaceae,* Pine Family). A very large tree of noble character, native to Japan.

C. japonica. An unusually fine conifer with dark-blue-green foliage. In the New York area and northward, some of the foliage may wind burn in winter, but it usually recovers the following spring.

ILEX (*Aquifoliaceae,* Holly Family). The hollies are a wonderful group of trees and shrubs. Both the evergreen and the deciduous ones have a place in the background planting.

I. aquifolium. English holly. A lovely little tree or large shrub with bright shining evergreen leaves and showy clusters of scarlet berries that remain on most of the winter.

I. opaca. American holly. This resembles the English holly but is hardier. Its leaves are larger but less lustrous. Dark-red berries in fall and winter.

I. verticillata. Black-alder or winterberry. A deciduous shrub about 10 feet tall, from the eastern states. Masses of bright-red berries in fall and winter.

MAGNOLIA (*Magnoliaceae,* Magnolia Family). Magnificent trees and shrubs, many of them too domineering or ostentatious for background planting.

M. stellata. The star magnolia is a delightful exception to the rule. It is a very slow-growing small tree or shrub, with an abundance of star-shaped white flowers in early spring before the leaves appear. The pale-green leaves make it attractive throughout the growing season. This tree is readily adaptable to training if a Japanese or oriental effect is desired in the garden.

OXYDENDRUM (*Ericaceae,* Heath Family). A deciduous tree, native from Pennsylvania to Florida, requiring an acid soil.

O. arboreum. Sourwood. A tree to 50 feet high, but of very slow growth, with bright-green shining leaves that turn scarlet in fall. Large drooping panicles of white flowers in July and August.

PINUS (*Pinaceae,* Pine Family). Most of the pines are suitable for the background. There is a free choice of many species and varieties. The ones I like best are: *P. banksiana, flexilis, monticola, parviflors, strobus, sylvestris,* and *thunbergii.*

RHUS (*Anacardiaceae,* Cashew Family). The sumacs are delightful shrubs and small trees, prized for their graceful pinnate leaves that turn brilliant colors in the fall, and for their clusters of red berries. All the species listed here are American natives and nonpoisonous.

R. aromatica. A shrub, to 8 feet high, with aromatic foliage. Spikes of yellow flowers appear before the leaves. Clusters of red berries in late summer and fall.

R. Copallina. Shining sumac. A small tree, to 20 feet high, with large ferny shining green leaves on winged branches. Pale-yellow-green flowers in July, and red berries in fall.

R. glabra. A shrub or tree, to 20 feet high, with large graceful fanlike pinnate leaves. Green flowers in June, followed by clusters of scarlet fruits in fall.

R. typhina. Staghorn sumac. A spreading stoloniferous shrub, to 15 feet high, that sometimes develops into a small tree. Luxurious pinnate leaves that turn a brilliant scarlet in fall. Green flowers and bright-crimson fruit in dense spikes in late summer and fall. If allowed to spread in its natural manner, it becomes invasive. To limit its growth, remove new stolons annually.

SCIADOPITYS (*Pinaceae,* Pine Family). A large evergreen tree.

S. verticillata, the umbrella-pine, native to Japan. A very slow-growing tree of dense pyramidal habit that is softened by airy whorls of long broad leaves at the tips of its bare twigs. A very rare and most noteworthy tree that deserves much more attention than it has been given.

TSUGA (*Pinaceae,* Pine Family). The Canadian hemlock (*T. canadensis*) is almost indispensable for the background. Its graceful pendulous branches lend the informality that we are seeking.

SHRUBS FOR BACKGROUND

Shrubs listed here are separated from the preceding list mainly because their twiggy, shrubby growth is not treelike and their stature is lower. Many of these can be planted as specimens in large rock gardens.

ACER (*Aceraceae,* Maple Family). Usually stately tall trees that are well known throughout the world. The oriental species described here are interesting subjects for the rock garden.

A. Palmatum. A low compressed shrub, usually with horizontally spreading branches, in many horticultural forms. The most desirable are those that stay dwarf and have dark-red foliage. The leaves are deeply palmately lobed in an attractive pattern.

A. palmatum dissectum. A low spreading bush with very lacy, finely pinnatifid foliage in green or dark-reddish-green. One of the most outstanding shrubs for the large rock garden or for background in smaller gardens.

AMELANCHIER (*Rosaceae,* Rose Family). The dwarf Juneberries resemble their big brothers in flower and foliage but are much lower in stature, being only 3 to 6 feet high. Normally, they are spread into broad patches by stolons.

A. alnifolia. A creeping shrub, to 6 feet high, with new leaves silvery, and white flowers in erect clusters in spring.

A. humilis. Upright shrub, to 4 feet high, with dense upright racemes of white flowers, followed by showy clusters of sweet black berries.

A. stolonifera. Similar to the others, with foliage silvery when young, and clusters of purple berries in June. Sweet and delicious.

BERBERIS (*Berberidaceae,* Barberry Family). There are many species of barberry, both deciduous and evergreen. They are most commonly known as hedging material. Most of the evergreen kinds are not hardy in the North, but the following are well adapted to the climate of the northern United States.

B. julianae. A dense, twiggy, spiny evergreen shrub, to 6 feet high, with shiny, hollylike leaves and white flowers. Showy bluish-black berries in fall and winter. Dependably hardy in the North.

B. triacanthophora. Similar to the preceding, but of lower growth and with its evergreen leaves much narrower and silvery beneath. Flowers are white, tinged with red, and the berries are blue-black. A most desirable shrub.

CLETHRA (*Clethraceae,* White-Alder Family). A group of modestly attractive, summer-blooming shrubs from warmer regions. The following is perfectly hardy and superior for our purpose.

C. alnifolia. Sweet Pepperbush. A graceful shrub from our eastern woodlands, to 10 feet high but usually lower. It has large panicles of very fragrant flowers in July and August. Var. *rosea* has flowers with a pink cast. For best results, plant in moist soil.

COTINUS (*Anacardiaceae,* Cashew Family). The smoke-tree is really a twiggy shrub 6 to 12 feet high, usually listed by nurserymen as *Rhus cotinus.*

C. coggygria. Attractive dark-purple-green leaves and massive panicles of purple, very silky-hairy pedicels that give the illusion of a smokey haze in June and July. Var. *purpureus* has dark-purple foliage.

COTONEASTER (*Rosaceae,* Rose Family). A group of wonderful ornamentals that are welcomed anywhere on the home grounds, and all those that are hardy can be used for the background of the rock garden. Several of the very dwarf forms are listed in Chapter VII. The following is particularly outstanding.

C. horizontalis. Rock spray. A graceful deciduous shrub, to 3 feet high, with very long horizontally spreading branches that are delightful to see when spread over a large rock. Small white or light-pink flowers, and showy bright-red fruit in fall and early winter. Quite often planted in large rock gardens.

ENKIANTHUS (*Ericaceae,* Heath Family). Tall upright twiggy shrubs from Japan and China, of interest to collectors of rare plants. The following is generally found in nursery catalogues.

E. Campanulatus. A tall shrub with azalealike foliage, and small bell-shaped, light-yellow flowers, with red veins, in May. In var. *palibinii,* the flowers are dark red.

ILEX (*Aquifoliaceae,* Holly Family). These are evergreen shrubby species, not usually in the form of trees.

I. crenata. Japanese holly. Dense shrubs, with small nonspiny leaves, in several varieties that are all desirable for background planting.

I. glabra. A semievergreen American native shrub, to 8 feet high, with rather loose branches and small, dull, dark-green-gray foliage. Small black berries in late summer and fall. Excellent for a wild or naturalistic setting.

I. pernyi. A most attractive little shrub of slow growth and tight habit, with the typical spiny holly leaves and large red berries.

KALMIA (*Ericaceae,* Heath Family). The kalmias are the glory of our eastern woodlands and mountains. All are welcome in the rock garden and for general home landscaping.

K. angustifolia. Lambkill or sheep laurel. A small evergreen shrub, 3 feet high, that spreads slowly by stolons. Very showy clusters of crimson or purple flowers along the tips of the stems in June. It requires an acid leaf-mold soil, in partial shade.

K. latifolia. The majestic mountain laurel. A large shrub with attractive dark evergreen leaves that somewhat resemble those of the rhododendrons, and large clusters of pink flowers in May and June. It must be planted in acid leaf-mold soil, in sun or shade.

MAHONIA (*Berberidaceae,* Barberry Family). Very ornamental evergreen shrubs with hollylike leaves. Most are not hardy in the North, but those listed here are dependable in the New York area.

M. aquifolium. Holly barberry. Very attractive shrub, 3 or 4 feet high, with spiny pinnate leaves that sometimes turn brown in winter. Large showy clusters of yellow flowers in early spring, and clusters of bloomy dark-blue berries in fall.

M. nervosa. Oregon grape. Smaller than the preceding, to only 2 feet high, but with larger shining bright-green foliage. Hardy in New England.

PIERIS (*Ericaceae,* Heath Family). Attractive and useful evergreens shrubs, usually listed as *Andromeda.* They require an acid leaf-mold soil, in sun or light shade.

P. floribunda. A dwarf, dense, dark evergreen shrub, usually not more than 3 feet high, with white flowers in upright spiky panicles in late April and May.

P. japonica. Lily-of-the-valley bush. A large shrub, 4 to 8 feet high, with bright shiny green leaves. The new growth is usually colored a most pleasing pink. Large drooping panicles of urn-shaped white flowers in early spring.

RHODODENDRON (*Ericaceae,* Heath Family). The rhododendrons are the undisputed monarchs of the heath family, and innumerable species and varieties can be used, both in the rock garden itself and in the background. For the background, I avoid those with massive flowers and flamboyant colors. Among those I usually recommend for the background are the rhododendron species *alabamensis, atlanticum, canadensis, carolinianum, catawbiense, nudiflorum, vaseyi,* and *viscosum.* This genus includes the azaleas. All species require an acid leaf-mold soil.

TAXUS (*Taxaceae,* Yew Family). The yews are familiar subjects in almost every landscape plan. The dominant species are *T. baccata* (the English yew), *T. cuspidata* (the Japanese yew), and a hybrid between the two, *T. media.* There are many, many forms and varieties of these three plants, and all are useful in the background. The smallest can be used in the garden itself.

TSUGA (*Pinaceae,* Pine Family). There are many dwarf forms of the Canadian hemlock that are perfect for the rock garden. These are listed and described in Chapter IX. The following, a semidwarf of outstanding character, should not be overlooked in planning the background.

T. canadensis pendula. Sargent's hemlock. A broad shrub with graceful pendulous or weeping branches, admired whenever it is seen. It can be planted in large rock gardens where judicious pruning will keep it within bounds.

VACCINIUM (*Ericaceae,* Heath Family). Although most blueberries and cranberries are grown for their fruit, many are ornamental and especially useful where a wild aspect is desired. They all need an acid leaf-mold soil.

V. angustifolium. An attractive deciduous shrub, to 2 feet high, with showy clusters of white flowers in late April, and large blue glaucous berries in July. Var. *leucocarpum* is a rare form with milk-white berries.

V. corymbosum. Highbush blueberry. A tall, twiggy, deciduous shrub, with nice clusters of pale-pink flowers in May, and showy, delicious, blue-black berries in July.

APPROACH PLANTING

The approach to the rock garden should not involve an abrupt change from smooth level turf to a rocky outcropping. Although such a transition can be found in nature, I think that a gradual approach is much more effective. One or two rocks (or more, if the garden is large) should extend outward from the base of the garden, and the intervening space should be planted intermittently with shrubs or dwarf conifers of a prostrate or flattish, rather open, habit. The turf can be permitted to run directly up to some of the rocks but such areas will be difficult to trim, requiring hand clipping every few days throughout the growing season. It is better, I think, to leave a narrow space between the forward rocks and the lawn, which can be planted with very low creepers that will blend the grass with the rock-garden planting and obviate hand trimming. Some excellent plants for this purpose are: *Thymus serphyllum* varieties, *Hydrocotyle peduncularis, Mazus reptans, Houstonia serphyllifolia,* and *Arenaria verna caespitosa.*

SHRUBS FOR APPROACH

JUNIPERUS (*Pinaceae,* Pine Family). The junipers are among the best subjects for the approach planting because so many varieties of different habit are available. Two species, *J. chinensis* and *J. communis,* are well represented by horticultural forms that are especially suitable for the approach to the rock garden, as well as for general home landscaping. Almost all of the usual dwarf, depressed, decumbent, and procumbent forms offered by nurserymen are variates of these two species. They are usually listed as *adpressa, andorra, plumosa, Pfitzeriana, pendula, Sargentii, compressa,* and *prostrata.* These are all good and are recommended for the foreground planting along with the following:

J. conferta. Shore juniper. A loose-growing prostrate or procumbent shrub, with sharply-pointed silvery-blue-green leaves.

J. horizontalis. Creeping juniper. A very flat prostrate creeper in several forms, usually with bluish foliage that turns purplish in fall. The most popular varieties are 'Bar Harbor' and 'Waukegan.'

J. sabina. Savin juniper. A fairly large spreading procumbent shrub, with dark-green needle-shaped leaves. Some varieties have attractive bluish foliage.

J. squamata. A low shrub, with long decumbent branches, with dense pointed gray-green foliage. Var. *meyeri* is a highly prized form of nearly upright but irregular habit, with glaucous leaves.

In addition to these junipers, the semidwarf spruces and rhododendrons, *Taxus canadensis,* the heathers, brooms (*Cytisus*), and many others of intermediate height and loose informal habit can be used for the foreground. The gardener's field here is

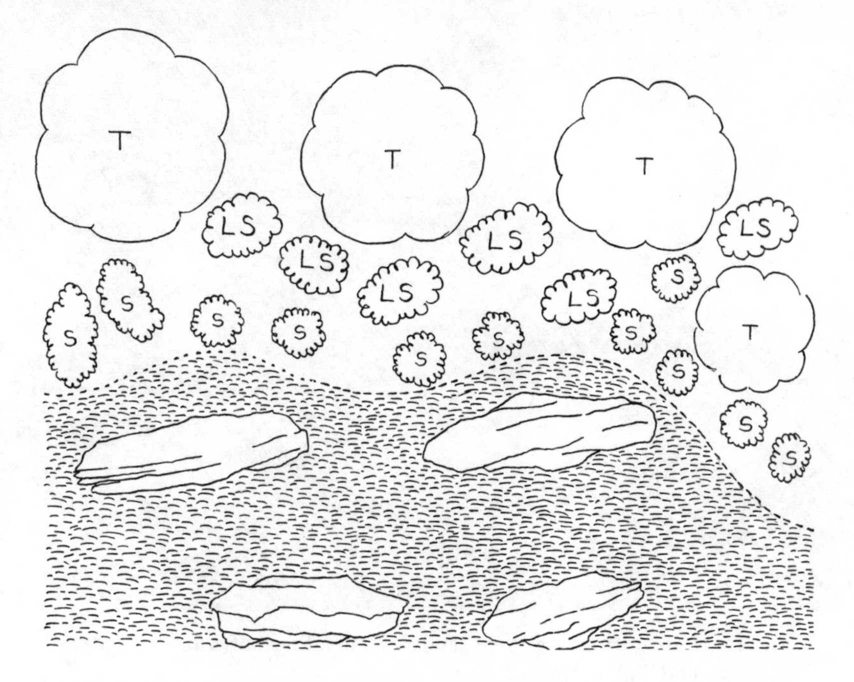

Diagram of possible placement of trees and shrubs in a background planting (T=tree; LS=large shrub; S=shrub).

Diagram of appropriate planting for the approach to the rock garden.

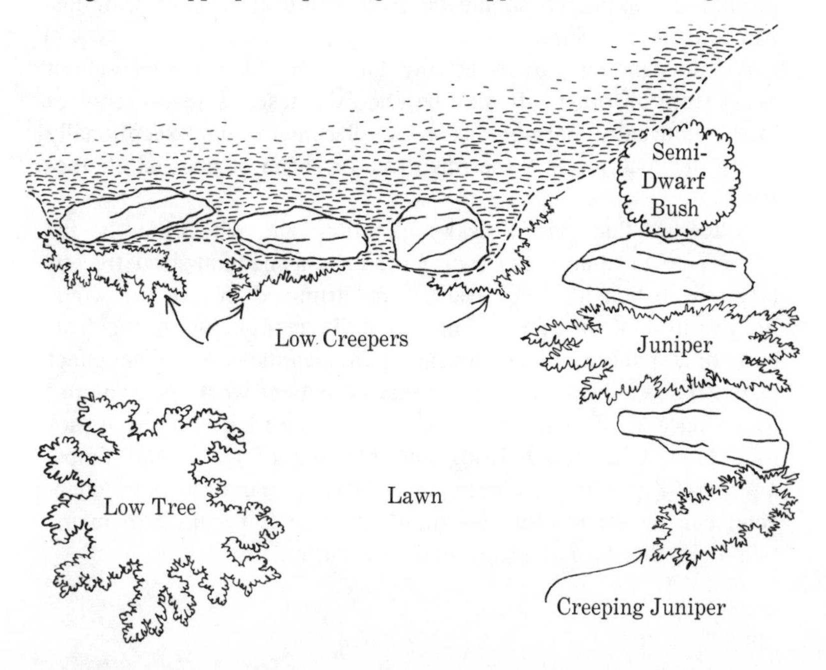

Approach featuring log steps and low plantings of *Juniperus horizontalis* and Baltic Ivy.

limited only by his resource in hunting down new plants. As the rock garden is a place for the cultivation of rare plants, the background and approach should be used to introduce choice, or unusual, trees and shrubs.

An outstanding garden usually has some feature that sets it apart from all others. It may be exquisite taste in plant arrangement, unusually harmonious rock placement, an exceptionally fine water feature, or a specimen tree or shrub of unusual character.

A feature that always draws attention, and which can be incorporated in almost any rock garden, is a medium-sized tree or large shrub that has been trained and trimmed to give the windblown effect of an oriental ming tree. In reality, this is the Chinese or Japanese art of Bonsai on a gigantic scale. The effect cannot be achieved overnight; years of patient work are required to produce it. The dwarfing process practiced in Bonsai is not used here. Only the twisting and bending of trunk and limbs, and careful pruning are necessary. After a year or two its character can be shaped, but constant attention is required to maintain it in the desired shape and inclination.

CHAPTER VII

THE BASIC PLANTS

What is a rock plant and just what is an alpine?

Obviously, for the beginner in rock gardening, these questions need clarification, and a dozen different experts will give a dozen different answers. Many people hold that any plant that can be grown in a rock garden is a rock plant, but this definition would include just about everything that grows in the world. It must necessarily be modified. Some authors in the past have limited the term rock plant to any plant that looks nice or in place in a rock garden. This is an arbitrary statement which still encompasses too wide a range. Individual preferences for plants of a certain type, geographic location, and similar factors render the definition useless. Many varieties of annual and biennial plants are used in rock gardens, but they are generally considered to be anything but rock plants.

Geographic locations must also be limited. I would be severely criticized, and rightly so, if I were to describe mesembryanthemums, peperomias, and crassulas as desirable rock plants, although they are natural saxicoles originating in tropical or subtropical regions. Definitely, comparative size is important. A plant that may look in place in one garden may be wholly unsuited to another. In a rock garden near Philadelphia I saw some twelve-foot yuccas that were perfectly lovely and in scale with the remainder of the garden, but they cannot be classified as rock plants because of their tremendous size.

My definition of a rock plant is: any herbaceous perennial, subshrub, dwarf shrub, or dwarf tree, regardless of origin, that is reasonably hardy in the area in which it is intended to grow. It must be of low stature, twenty-four inches or less, with dense compact foliage in rosettes, mats, cushions, or hummocks. It must have attractive graceful foliage, lovely flowers, or both. An evergreen plant has a decided advantage, but being evergreen is not a requisite. Twenty-four inches is rather high, but I include some of the taller perennials because of their general acceptance as rock plants. Plants like *Dicentra eximia, Ceratostigma plumbaginoides, Astilbe* 'Fanal,' and *Aquilegia canadensis,* which often reach two feet in height, are big for the average rock garden, but they are beautiful and have their usefulness. Of course, the lower, the more dense and compact, the plant is, the more acceptable it is as a rock-garden subject.

Naturally enough, most of the plants to be grown in any rock garden are native to mountains, because the prime objective of rock gardening is the cultivation of the rare, delicate, and tiny lords of the higher worlds. Some authorities contend that only alpine or mountain plants should be used in the rock garden. The argument has logic, but I see no reason to exclude all of the lowlanders when some of them are adaptable to rock culture and are in scale and harmony with the mountain plants. In fact, many plants have a range of distribution that varies from sea level to alpine altitudes. Even those who advocate the exclusion of all but the saxicolous plants often attempt to grow such things as pyxie-moss and the bird's-foot violets. The plantsman, horticulturist, and advanced amateur gardener who want nothing but alpines in their gardens are in reality advocating a specialized type of rock gardening, or alpine gardening, that is not very practical or practicable except in a few isolated places in our country.

What is an alpine? Ordinarily, the general public consider an alpine to be a plant from the European Alps because they are so familiar with the name of that range of mountains. But by comparatively recent popular usage, the name has almost come to mean any montanic plant. Specifically, an alpine is any plant from above timber line on any of the high peaks of the world. Arctic plants are usually placed in the same category as alpines because their structural characteristics and climatic conditions are similar. The name alpine plant has a forbidding or challenging ring because of the difficulty in establishing these intriguing beauties at low elevations and in seacoast areas, where the greater part of the world's population has congregated. The widespread and growing enthusiasm for rock gardening is proof enough that, with patience and vigilance, these gems of the snow-clad lands can be acclimatized at much lower elevations.

It is generally concluded that the purpose of a rock garden is the cultivation of the wild alpine, saxicole, and montane plants. This means wild species, natural hybrids, natural sports, mutations, and variants. Some eminent rock gardeners abhor the inclusion of double-flowered and variegated forms in the rock garden collection, on the grounds that they are not natural. They may not be normal, but they are as natural as life itself, and there is a definite place for them in the rock garden. Although the horticultural forms and garden variants with fancy names are too numerous to catalogue and often differ very little, they should not be entirely ruled out of the rock garden world. In the case of the heathers, where only one wild species is genuinely attractive and commands a place for itself, the garden enthusiast would be deprived of untold enjoyment if such delightful varieties as 'County Wicklow,' 'Mrs. R. H. Gray,' and 'Mrs. H. E. Beale' were excluded simply because of their horticultural origin. On the other hand, I do believe that the naming of hundreds of forms of day-lilies, irises, roses, and azaleas now borders on the ridiculous.

An interesting digression in natural rock gardening is the garden that is devoted to unusual wild forms. Albinos are especially attractive and are coveted by people who are constantly in search of new things. The odd forms and sports of ferns have long been of intense interest to plant collectors, especially the crested and wavy kinds. Variegated foliage plants, too, are always interesting. Recently, I discovered a lovely variegated form of the little merrybells (*Uvularia sessilifolia*). The typical form of this plant is pretty but not very showy as a garden subject. My find, a stand with the pale-apple-green leaves delicately tinted at the margins with sulphur-yellow, is an extremely attractive garden plant for shady areas.

Irrespective of the interest provided by sports and variants, my main object is to acquaint the beginner in rock gardening with the wondrous assortment of plants that is available from the wild without so-called improvement through cultivation, selection, and hybridization. Throughout the world, there are many thousands of plant species for the rock gardener, many of them yet untried in the garden or still undiscovered. Once the rock garden is begun, the gardener becomes involved in the endless adventure of tracking down and taming the rarest of the alpines and rock plants. The list of plants that follows is by no means a complete catalogue of the kinds that can be grown in the United States. I doubt that a complete list could be compiled in the lifetime of any one man.

I know that I will be criticized by some authorities and advance horticulturists for omitting many species, and perhaps for including others of a dubious nature. Be that as it may, I believe that I have prepared a fairly comprehensive list of the better plants and one that is complete enough to start the beginner off on the right foot.

Trying to determine what to include and what to leave out was a constant problem to me while compiling the list. To make it a worthwhile reference for the American rock gardener, I decided to list only those plants that are currently available, either through nurseries in the form of started plants or through flower-seed houses and gardening organizations that offer seed for sale or exchange. An additional condition was to include only plants with which I have had personal experience, either through actual trial at my nursery or through observation in gardens of a great many friends and acquaintances.

Another problem was to decide on the form the list should take — whether to divide it into separate lists of herbaceous perennials, shrubs and subshrubs, dwarf trees, ferns, orchids, cacti, and bulbous plants. For simplification and to avoid confusion, I decided to make a single alphabetical list embracing all the usual divisions. However, I have permitted myself three digressions. One, in Chapter VI, is a list of the semidwarf trees and shrubs that are often used in very large rock gardens and are especially good for approach and background planting in smaller gardens. Another list, in Chapter X, deals with the dwarf conifers. These are intriguing forms of trees in the pine family that are of interest to the gardening world in general and command special treatment. The third digression, in Chapter VIII, has to do with the bulbous plants. Although these are really hardy herbaceous perennials, they are usually considered a class in themselves and are offered for sale as dry bulbs for planting in the autumn. They are generally available from importers of European-grown bulbs and are not usually carried by nurseries dealing in rock plants.

I have tried to give as accurate a description as is possible with the printed word, with special emphasis on color of flower, color and texture of the foliage, period of bloom, height, and general habit of growth. The time of flowering is, of course, subject to weather and climatic conditions. The height given is the average for mature specimens and may vary according to soil conditions and exposure. Color of flower is impossible to describe to everyone's satisfaction. One pair of eyes will see a pink flower and another pair, looking at the same specimen, will see a purple one. But I have tried my best. The various color charts are almost useless unless everyone has one handy for reference. Describing *Erysimum kotschyanum* as boron-yellow, *Primula* 'Wanda' as Dodge-purple, and the helianthemum 'Apricot Queen' as brick-red according to the British Horticultural Color Council charts is comparable to calling the 'Pinocchio' rose a sky-blue-pink.

The cultural directions given are quite complete and, if they are followed, success should be assured. However, because of the great differences in climate over the country, they should be considered in many cases as a basis for experiment. I have given soil conditions and exposures as I use them successfully in my Pennsylvania nursery. Although soil acidity is important in the cultivation of many plants, the relative pH value is in most cases an arbitrary figure. It is definitely true that some species demand an acid soil and abhor lime, and that others are lime lovers and not very tolerant of an acid condition. However, the preference of most rock plants lies conveniently between these two extremes. They usually like a neutral (pH 7) soil or one that is either slightly acid or slightly alkaline. In the descriptions of these persuasive subjects, I have prescribed a neutral soil, but it can be taken to mean anything from pH 6 to pH 8. For the plants that particularly want lime, I have indicated either a limy or an alkaline soil. This would mean pH 7 to pH 8. For the remainder, or the acid-loving plants, the soil test can range from pH 4 to pH 6. Although pH 4 is a bit extreme, it will be normally possible only in a sphagnum bog. In the formula for soil requirements, a factor that should not be overlooked is that which calls for gritty, sandy, or well-drained soil. If you cannot give the plants what is prescribed, do not try to grow them. Also, plants calling for moraine or scree treatment cannot be expected to succeed in any other location. It is interesting to note that almost all woolly or gray-leaved plants require full hot sun and an extremely well-drained soil. They are particularly susceptible to fungus diseases during hot humid days in summer.

Names, of course, are important: without them we would have more confusion than exists now. Throughout the list I have used Bailey's *Hortus II,* Rehder's *Manual of Cultivated Trees and Shrubs,* and *Gray's Manual of Botany, 8th Edition,* as guides. Although trinomials are frowned upon by botanists, I have used them for the sake of convenience. I am not a botanist, merely a plant-lover and nurseryman.

The inevitable question that arises whenever a rock plant is discussed is: where can it be obtained? Unfortunately, the days are gone when rock plants were as plentiful in the United States as pansies are now. Only a few nurseries grow them in any great quantity and variety.

In addition to these nurseries that specialize in rock plants, there are any number of others that carry a limited number of them. Often small local nurseries carry a few of the better sorts for the local cash-and-carry trade.

Seeds of rock plants and alpines are available from most growers of flower seed, but usually the variety is limited. The best commercial sources for seeds are established firms in England, Switzerland, and Germany. Possibly the best source for seeds of the rarer sorts is one of the rock plant associations that make seeds available through exchange among the members. It would behoove a rock gardener, beginner or advanced, to join one or all of the following organizations:

The American Rock Garden Society
1220 Everett Place, Hendersonville, N.C.

The Scottish Rock Garden Club
Honorary Secretary, J. J. Bord-Harvey
Boonslie, Dirleton, East Lothian, Scotland

The Alpine Garden Society (England)
D. C. R. Worth, Groton, New York

PLANTS FOR THE ROCK GARDEN

ACAENA (*Rosaceae,* Rose Family). Very low-growing plants from the southern hemisphere, with inconspicuous flowers but attractive evergreen foliage. Useful as ground cover and for planting between flagstones. They must have full sun and an extremely well-drained soil (pH 6–8). They are somewhat tender and must be well protected for the winter in the North. Easily propagated by divisions at any time.

A. buchananii. Slowly creeping, with prostrate stems that root down readily. It forms dense mats of most attractive silvery-green pinnate leaves.

A. microphylla. New Zealand Bur. A faster-growing species, with leaves that are a bit larger and colored a deep rich bronze throughout the year. Both kinds are native to New Zealand.

ACHILLEA (*Compositae,* Daisy Family). Many species throughout the North Temperate Zone. Some are weedy and invasive, but many are suited to rock and wall gardens. Others are useful for cover in poor sandy soil and in hot dry spots where many plants will not survive. All can be propagated easily by divisions, preferably in late summer or early fall. Except as noted below, all the achilleas do best in a rather lean and light sandy or gravelly soil, in full sun. Good drainage is essential because the mat-forming kinds are susceptible to fungus diseases during hot, muggy, wet weather. All are hardy and can stand the severest winter without protection.

A. ageratifolia (often listed as *Anthemis aizoon*). A compact mound of long and narrow pinnatifid, silvery evergreen leaves, about 6 inches high. It has large flat clusters of white daisylike flowers on arching swaying stems 6 to 12 inches high in late May and June. This native of Greece is one of the best wall-garden plants.

A. argentea. Silvery Yarrow. Very white silvery-silky three-parted leaves in little mounds about 5 inches high, topped with clusters of white flowers in June and July. A very desirable subject from Dalmatia that requires full sun, and prefers an alkaline soil (pH 7–8). For permanence, it should be planted on the side of a wall or in a scree.

A. clavennae. A silvery-leaved species from southern Europe that is similar to *A. argentea,* but a bit larger, and with more numerous flowers in compact heads on stems to 12 inches high. For wall garden or scree.

A. lewisii. A hybrid between *A. tomentosa* and *A. argentea.* Very soft woolly gray-green leaves in dense tufts about 2 inches high. It produces masses of light-sulphur-yellow flowers on erect stems about 6 inches high in late May, June, and July.

A. nana. This native of southern Europe resembles our common wild yarrow on a miniature scale. It forms quickly spreading mats of very finely cut downy green leaves, about 1 inch high. Clusters of white flowers on 6-inch stems through most of the summer. An evergreen carpeter for hot, dry, sandy places and for flagstone walks.

A. tomentosa. Woolly Yarrow. A quickly spreading mat, with soft woolly gray-green leaves, and bright-yellow flowers in dense clusters through most of the summer. One of the basic rock garden plants, whose natural habitat embraces areas of Europe, Asia, and North America.

A. tomentosa aurea. A form with larger greener leaves and larger flower clusters in a pleasing clear yellow.

A. tomentosa 'Moonlight.' Very tiny leaves that form soft mossy evergreen mats, less than an inch high. Erect stems about 12 inches high carry very pale moonlight-yellow flowers in June and July.

A. umbellata. Dense clumps of long and narrow, soft woolly gray-green leaves, about 5 inches high. It has compact umbels of white flowers on 10-inch stems in May and June. An easy-to-grow, attractive, and permanent plant from Greece.

ACTAEA (*Ranunculaceae,* Buttercup Family). Rather tall perennials with a few coarse compound leaves, and spikes of small white flowers in spring. They are useful in a large shady rock garden. Propagated by seeds or divisions. Usually transplanted from the wild. They require shade, in a well-drained acid leaf-mold or woodsy soil (pH 5–6).

A. pachypoda (usually listed as *A. alba*). White Baneberry. Stalky stems, 18 to 24 inches high, with white flowers in spring, and remarkably handsome spikes of porcelain-white berries on thick bright-red stems in fall.

A. rubra. Red Baneberry. Similar to *A. pachypoda* but a little taller, with bright-crimson berries in summer and fall. Both are native to the woodlands of the northeastern United States.

ACTINEA (*Compositae,* Daisy Family). An interesting genus of American *Compositae*, related to the sneezeweeds but low-growing and refined. Native to the Great Plains and Rocky Mountains. They require full sun, and a well-drained lime soil (pH 7–8). To assure permanence and prolific bloom, they should be confined to the scree. Propagated by seeds or by cuttings in summer after blooming is past.

A. grandiflora (known also as *Rydbergia grandiflora*). Open tufts of slender stag-horn leaves, about 5 inches high. Large bright-yellow daisies on slender stems in May and June.

A. simplex (known also as *Actinella simplex*). Tufts, to 10 inches high, of narrow, linear, silky-silvery-gray leaves, and golden daisies on swaying stems in early summer.

ADIANTUM (*Polypodiaceae,* Fern Family). Very dainty ferns, mostly from tropics around the world. However, the following one is a Northerner and perfectly hardy everywhere. Propagated by divisions in spring or early summer.

A. pedatum. American Maidenhair Fern. Broad graceful fronds of fine lacy segments, colored a lively fresh green on purple stipes, 12 to 24 inches high. I think this is the prettiest of our native American ferns. It should be planted in shade, in an acid leaf-mold soil (pH 5–6) with good drainage but ample constant moisture. It will stand full sun in wet soil, as at the edge of a pool, but often the fronds will burn in the intense heat of August.

ADONIS (*Ranunculaceae,* Buttercup Family). Generally, a family of gaily-colored summer-blooming annuals, but a few are perennials that are well suited to the rock garden. Propagated by divisions in early spring, and by seeds sown as soon as they are ripe.

A. vernalis. An exceptionally fine plant that begins to flower early in February when the stout stems have emerged only 2 or 3 inches from the hard cold earth. With each succeeding warm spell, the flowers are more numerous and brighter.

Adonis vernalis.

It comes into full bloom in April, with multitudes of yellow anemone-like flowers, over 15-inch mounds of delicate ferny foliage. Vernalis goes completely dormant after the seeds ripen in late May and does not reappear until the following February. This interesting European plant is easy to grow and permanent in any rich, acid to neutral, soil (pH 5–7), in sun or light shade.

AEGOPODIUM (*Umbelliferae,* Carrot Family). A rather coarse weedy plant from Europe, now running wild in America. Useful in shady places, where it will help keep down other weeds. Easy to grow in any soil in shade or half-shade. Propagated by divisions at any time.

A. podagraria variegatum. Goutweed. Masses of not unattractive light green and white foliage, about 6 inches high. Umbels of small white flowers in spring.

AETHIONEMA (*Cruciferae,* Mustard Family). All the perennial stonecresses are evergreen, or nearly evergreen, dwarf subshrubs, native to the Mediterranean region, Asia Minor, and Persia. Although they come from a warm dry region, they are dependably hardy and permanent in our rigorous climate if they are treated right. They require full sun, in a well-drained, gritty or gravelly, lime soil (pH 7–8). In exposed positions in the Far North, they should be covered with straw for the winter. These are natural saxicoles and cliff dwellers that make excellent wall plants. Most gardeners consider them indispensable in a well-planted rock garden. Propagated by seeds sown in spring, or by cuttings in summer.

A. cordifolium (usually listed as *Iberis jucunda*). Lebanon Candytuft. Tiny linear leaves crowded on stiff stems that form interesting, intricate little bushlets. Upright stems, about 10 inches high, carry dense racemes of pale-pink or cream-colored flowers in May.

A. grandiflorum. Persian Candytuft. Long and narrow bluish-green leaves on upright stiff stems, about 6 inches high. The flowering stems are about 15 inches high, with large individual soft-rose flowers on slender racemes in May.

A. iberidium. A little cushion-forming shrub, about 6 inches high, with small gray-green leaves. Showy clusters of large white flowers in April and May.

A. pulchellum. Stiff, twiggy growth, with little blue-green leaves, in open mounds about 15 inches high. The upright flowering stems carry bright rose-pink flowers in May and June.

A. warleyense. An enchanting hybrid that forms compact mats, about 3 inches high. The branches trail over the ground and are crowded with fleshy, steel-blue leaves. In May and June, this evergreen plant is covered with many clusters of very pretty, deep-pink flowers on short leafy stems. One of the most popular of the stonecresses, loved by everyone who sees it. Unexcelled as a wall plant.

Aethionema warleyense.

AJUGA (*Labiatae,* Mint Family). The carpet-bugle or bugle-weed is, in a sense, a true weed, but it is charming and extremely useful. It spreads like wildfire and will grow in almost any soil, either in full sun or full shade. It is used where more desirable plants have difficulty, and in new gardens to cover freshly-worked soil quickly. Although it is a fast grower, it is easily checked when it oversteps its allotted space. It can be eradicated easily when it has outlived its usefulness. All the varieties listed here are almost deciduous in exposed positions in the North; but under favorable conditions in the mild climate, they are quite evergreen.

A. reptans. Flat mats of large dark-green leaves in May and June, with numerous 6-inch spikes of deep-blue flowers. It will cover as much as three square feet in a single season.

A. reptans alba. A form with light-green leaves and large spikes of pure-white flowers, up to 12 inches high. This seems to be a weak albino that dies out quickly and winterkills easily.

A. reptans brockbankii. A nonspreading variety that forms dense clumps of dull-green leaves, about 6 inches high. It has spikes of clear-light-blue flowers, beginning in May and continuing through most of the summer.

A. reptans metallica crispa. Larger leaves than the type, wavy and with a bronze cast. Spikes of metallic, glossy-blue flowers.

A. reptans rosea. A form with nice pink flowers almost all summer.

A. reptans rubra. Dark-purply-bronze leaves, and spikes of dark-purple-blue flowers in May.

A. reptans variegata. A nice plant with leaves variegated with pale green, white, and pale creamy yellow. It has clear-light-blue flowers in spring. This is not as strong a grower as the others and seems to prefer shade or half-shade.

ALLIUM (*Liliaceae,* Lily Family). Although these plants are related to the common garden onion and have a strong onion odor when bruised, they should not be dismissed forthwith as undesirable. Their grassy foliage has charm and elegance, and their colorful flowers appear in midsummer, when almost any color is welcome in the rock garden. Although bulbous, they are usually grown like most other perennials because many of them are evergreen, or have persistent leaves. Some have an intricate root system that binds the clusters of bulbs together as a single unit. All are easy to grow in full sun or light shade, in any ordinary garden soil (pH 6–8). Propagated by divisions at any time.

A. cernuum. Bold clumps of rather wide leaves, about 12 inches high. Large nodding clusters of light-pink flowers on stems 18 to 24 inches high, in July. Its habitat is over a wide range of North America.

A. cyaneum. A delicate little beauty that deserves a place of honor in the rock garden. Dense tufts of very thin grasslike leaves, about 6 inches high, and slender flower stems that carry loose, nodding umbels of clear-royal-blue flowers in June and July. A native of China that is easy to grow but also easy to lose if it becomes overgrown with grass. It should have a light soil with good drainage.

A. farreri. A refined species from China, for bright summer color. Eight-inch-high clumps of grassy leaves, topped with umbels of bright red-purple flowers in July.

A. flavum. Long thin leaves in loose clumps, and spectacular bursting-sky-rockets of bright-yellow bells on 18-inch stems in June and July. To display its true beauty to best advantage, this species from southern Europe and western Asia should be planted in tight groups behind shorter and leafier plants.

A. moly. A rather large plant from southern Europe, with wide flat leaves, about 18 inches high. Large upright umbels of bright-yellow starry flowers on stout stems in late spring.

A. schoenoprasum. Chives. This well-known herb-garden subject forms dense clumps of long thin leaves, about 10 inches high, with countless umbels of bright rosy-purple flowers in June and July. Besides being good to eat, it is fine for summer color in the rock garden. Many people who buy chives in the market for culinary use are amazed by its beauty when they see it in bloom.

A. senescens glaucum. This beautiful and intriguing plant from China draws attention even among the most colorful and rare alpines. It has flat, sickle-shaped, blue-gray leaves that form dense clumps. All the leaves twist in the same direction, making an attractive swirl. It has pleasing pink flowers in upturned umbels on 10-inch stems in August and September.

A. sikkimense. Short, flat, dark-green leaves in heavy clumps, and large dense flower heads of a deep-violet color on 12-inch stems, in July and August. A hardy and desirable summer-blooming plant from Sikkim, India.

ALYSSUM (*Cruciferae,* Mustard Family). The name *alyssum,* or basket-of-gold, is so popular that it is almost synonymous with "rock-garden plant." All the species are easy to grow, permanent, and reasonably hardy if given the proper conditions. They require full sun, and a rather lean, sandy or gravelly soil (pH 6–8), with extremely good drainage. Propagation is accomplished most easily by seeds sown either in fall or spring. The species listed are all from southern Europe and Asia Minor.

A. alpestrea. Tiny, oblong, soft-gray leaves on trailing stems that make a loose mat, about 3 inches high. Small clusters of yellow flowers on thin stems in April and May.

A. argenteum. Long, narrow, gray-green leaves in neat clumps, about 8 inches high, adorned with tiny yellow flowers in clusters all summer.

A. condensatum. A little trailing species, with hairy gray leaves, and lemon-yellow flowers on thin decumbent stems in April and May.

A. idaeum. Very tiny, soft-gray-green leaves on thin trailing stems, and creamy-white or very pale-yellow flowers in spring. This one does best in a scree with winter protection in the Far North.

A. moellendorfianum. Small gray leaves on semitrailing stems. Close heads of yellow flowers on nearly upright stems in spring.

A. montanum. A strong plant with grayish leaves on semitrailing stems that form an irregular mound, about 5 inches high and quite broad. Stiff, upright stems bear thick clusters of bright-yellow fragrant flowers in April and May.

A. saxatile. Basket-of-Gold. Broad spreading clumps of long, gray-green leaves, about 12 inches high. It has great masses of bright golden-yellow flowers in early spring. An exceptionally good wall-garden plant. Old plants tend to become straggly and sloppy, but they can be rejuvenated by cutting them back severely.

A. saxatile citrinum. A form with very pleasing pale lemon-yellow flowers.

A. saxatile 'Dudley Neville.' A comparatively recent introduction from England. The plant is dwarfer and more compact than the others. The leaves are smaller, and the flower stems shorter. The flowers are colored an exquisite, powdery golden-yellow.

A. saxatile flore-pleno. A more compact grower than the type. Each individual little flower is fully double. It blooms a little later and stays in flower much longer than the type.

A. spinosum. A stiff, twiggy, spiny, little gray-leaved shrub, 8 to 12 inches high. In May and June, it is entirely covered with clusters of dainty white flowers, which turn pinkish with age. It is essential that this plant have good drainage in a dry situation.

ANACYCLUS (*Compositae,* Daisy Family). Very desirable little plants from the mountains of Morocco; related to the chrysanthemums. They require a gritty, well-drained alkaline soil (pH 7–8), in full sun. Where winters are excessively wet, they should be maintained in a scree. It is advisable to protect them in the North. Propagated by seeds.

A. atlanticus. Prostrate stems with hairy, light-green ferny foliage. Large white daisies on slightly ascending stems, in May and June. The undersides of the rays are colored red.

A. depressus. Similar to *A. atlanticus,* but the flowers vary from red with white markings to white with red tips and margins.

ANDROMEDA (*Ericaceae,* Heath Family). Little evergreen shrubs, never more than 12 to 18 inches high, not to be confused with the large lily-of-the-valley bush, which is really *Pieris japonica.* Although these little shrubs are natural bog dwellers, they do not need boggy conditions for success in the garden. They require a deep acid leaf-mold soil (pH 4–6), in sun or light shade. They must be in a position where the soil does not become powder dry. Propagated by cuttings in late summer and fall. They spread slowly by short underground stolons.

A. glaucophylla. Stiff, twiggy stems, clothed with small leathery blue-gray leaves, in open mounds about 12 inches high. Very charming, light-pink, urn-shaped flowers in loose nodding umbels, in May. A very hardy native of Newfoundland.

Andromeda glaucophylla with *Gaultheria procumbens* in foreground.

A. polifolia. Long, narrow, leathery dark-green leaves on stiff branches, to 18 inches high. Shell-pink flowers in spring. Native to northern Europe, northern Asia, and northern North America.

A. polifolia grandiflora compacta. A dwarf Japanese form, with very stiff branches, 6 to 8 inches high, and attractive, blue-gray leaves. Adorable, light-pink flowers with the texture of fine porcelain.

A. polifolia montana. Dwarfer and more compact than the type, with small dark-green leaves, and brighter clear-pink flowers. The new growth varies from crimson to bronze.

A. polifolia nana. Very thin, wiry stems, and tiny, very narrow, leathery green leaves. To 12 inches. The flowers and new growth are like those of variety *montana.*

ANDROSACE (*Primulaceae,* Primrose Family). Tiny rosetted alpines, resembling miniature primroses in flower. They require sun or light shade in a gritty, well-drained alkaline soil (pH 7–8), but with constant moisture. Most species propagate naturally by offsets on short stolons. Others are propagated by cuttings and seeds. These mountain jewels are highly prized by devoted rock gardeners. While some are extremely difficult to grow, others are quite easy and permanent.

A. carnea. Tiny linear leaves in tight rosettes that form attractive close mats. The flowers vary from pink to white and are clustered in small umbels on 4-inch stems. This charmer from the Alps and the Pyrenees likes a neutral to slightly acid moraine soil.

A. chamaejasme. Rock-Jasmine. Hairy, green leaves in rosettes, and 6- to 8-inch stems, with pretty umbels of flowers that range in color from bright pink to white. This plant should have ample moisture at all times. It is widely distributed in the mountains of northern Europe, Asia, and North America.

A. foliosa. An unusual sort from the Himalayas, with large pale-green leaves on thick, almost woody stems, about 4 inches high. Rather large umbels of pink flowers with dark eyes, in May.

A. hedraeantha. Tiny mats of stiff little green leaves in tight rosettes. Bright-pink, almost red, flowers on 3-inch stems, in spring. A dainty species from the Balkans that requires moraine culture.

A. lanuginosa. One of the prettiest, easiest, and most popular of the rock-jasmines from the Himalayas. Basal rosettes send out long trailing stems that have soft, silky-silvery leaves. Large clusters of light-pink flowers are produced from late May until hard frost in the fall. At the first touch of frost, the tips of the trailing stems stop their rampant progress and develop into tight silvery rosettes for the winter. Easy to grow and permanent in a well-drained garden soil, in full sun, but will not stand a prolonged drought.

A. sarmentosa. Green leaves with silvery hairs, in neat rosettes. Six- to 8-inch flower stems spring from the center of the

Androsace sarmentosa.

rosettes in May, bearing compact umbels of lovely rose-colored flowers. New rosettes are formed all around the parent on short stolons, thus forming tight evergreen carpets. This species from the Himalayas is easy to grow in a well-drained garden soil, in sun or light shade. Moisture should be provided during dry spells. Var. *chumbyi* is similar but with woollier, grayer rosettes.

A. sempervivoides. Tiny shining green leaves in tight rosettes, about one inch across. An exquisite kind from the Himalayas, with dainty umbels of lovely rose-pink flowers, on stems 2 to 4 inches high, in May. The new rosettes are clustered around the parent, much in the fashion of a *Sempervivum.* Easy to grow in a gritty, well-drained soil, in sun or light shade.

A. villosa. Soft white woolly rosettes, to 3 inches high, and short stems, with white flowers in May. A difficult plant from Europe and western Asia that should be planted in a limestone scree, in sun or very light shade.

ANEMONE (*Ranunculaceae,* Buttercup Family). This is a large family containing many colorful and worthwhile plants for rock gardens and borders. They vary from tiny alpines to huge meadow beauties. Their natural range is in the North Temperate Zone around the world. Some inhabit dry, sunny wastelands, others moist, shady woodlands. The taprooted kinds are grown from seeds, and the others can be propagated easily by divisions.

A. alpina. A taprooted species from the high European mountains. Clumps of ferny foliage, and large white flowers on 18-inch stems, in spring. Full sun and a well-drained, gravelly garden soil (pH 6–8). Var. *sulphurea* has very showy, large sulphur-yellow flowers. This is usually listed in catalogues as a separate species.

A. baldensis. Tuberous roots produce little mounds of attractive compound leaves, and lovely white flowers, tinged with rose, in late spring. This popular plant from the Alps likes a well-drained but constantly moist soil, in light shade, and a slightly acid to neutral soil.

A. canadensis. Creeping roots from spreading colonies of large, palmately-lobed green leaves, on stems to 24 inches high, with white flowers from May to September. A North American woodlander that wants a moist or wet situation, in sun or light shade.

A. caroliniana. Little clumps of rather hairy, attractive little compound leaves from hard tuberous roots. The pretty flowers range from purple to pink and cream, on 12-inch stems, in April and May. It wants well-drained soil with ample moisture in spring, but dryness when it goes dormant in the summer. From the central plains states.

A. halleri. Little mounds of ferny leaves, covered with silky white hairs. Six-inch stems bear large lavender cups, much like miniatures of *A. pulsatilla.* This taprooted species from Switzerland needs a well-drained alkaline soil (pH 6–8), in full sun.

A. hupehensis. This is undoubtedly a dwarf form of *Anemone japonica.* Attractive clumps, about 15 inches high, of large palmate leaves. In September and October, this majestic plant is adorned with multitudes of large, wide-petaled, deep-mauve-pink flowers. It is easy to grow, and permanent in a good rich garden soil, in full sun or light shade. It will not stand prolonged drought.

A. nemorosa. European Wood Anemone. Thick creeping roots produce large carpets, about 3 inches high, of delicate five-lobed leaves. Quantities of dainty white or purple flowers, on 6-inch stems, in April and May. It is native to woodlands in Europe and Siberia, and likes an acid leaf-mold soil (pH 5–6), in shade. There are many colors and forms to choose from, such as: *Alenii* with lavender flowers, *flore-pleno* with fully-double pure-white flowers, *major* with very large white flowers, *robinsoniana* with pale blue, *rosea* with pink, and 'Royal Blue' with deep rich-blue flowers. These plants go dormant and lose their leaves after flowering in late May.

A. patens. A little taprooted species from northern Asia, Alaska, and our northern plains states. Large purple cups appear just above the ground in early spring before the little clumps of ferny foliage develop. It likes a well-drained limy soil (pH 7–8), in full sun.

A. pulsatilla. Pasque-Flower. This adorable plant is a favorite with all rock gardeners. Large, lavender, cup-shaped flowers appear with the silky, ferny foliage early in April. The exquisite flowers are followed by attractive feathery seed plumes that last for a long time. The ferny foliage stays neat and attractive all summer. Easy to grow, and permanent in any well-drained garden soil (pH 6–8), in full sun or very light shade.

A. quinquefolia. American Wood Anemone. In early spring this anemone, about 3 inches high, carpets our eastern woodlands with dainty, fragile five-lobed leaves, and delicate white flowers. Moist, acid leaf-mold and shade are essential for this plant.

A. ranunculoides. Another mat-forming species from Siberia, much like *A. nemorosa* in leaf, but the little cup-shaped flowers in early April are a rich buttercup-yellow. It requires an acid leaf-mold soil (pH 5–6), and shade.

A. sylvestris. Snowdrop Anemone. Spreading clumps of large and pure-white, very fragrant flowers, on 12-inch stems, in May and June. It likes an acid leaf-mold soil, in shade or half-shade. From Europe and southwestern Asia.

A. vernalis. Lady-of-the-Snow. Very large white flowers shaded with purple, on 6-inch stems, over little mounds of ferny foliage in early spring. This taprooted species from the Alps wants a deep, rich, well-drained soil (pH 6–8), in full sun.

ANEMONELLA (*Ranunculaceae,* Buttercup Family). Only one species in this genus, native to the woodlands of eastern North America. It likes a well-drained, acid leaf-mold soil (pH 5–6), in shade or half-shade. Propagated by divisions.

A. thalictroides. Rue-Anemone. Delicate, ruelike leaves in attractive mounds, about 6 inches high, and lovely white or pale-pink flowers for a long period in spring. If the plant is cut back after the initial flowering, it will begin to bloom all over again. It is extremely variable. Some flowers are quite large. Some are double or semidouble.

ANTENNARIA (*Compositae,* Daisy Family). Little creeping plants with white woolly leaves in rosettes, on prostrate fast-spreading stems. They have small, bristly flower heads without rays, on slender, nearly leafless stems about 12 inches high. The silvery mats are very attractive and useful for covering hot and sunny dry spots in the rock garden.

A. dioica rosea. Very quickly-spreading mats, with rather attractive, rose-colored flower heads in May. From Europe and Asia.

A. microphylla. Tiny glistening silver leaves, in very slowly-spreading mats. Nodding white flower heads on long thin stems. A native of the high Rocky Mountains that should be given scree treatment.

A. neodioica. White woolly leaves in fast-spreading mats, and white flowers on tall slender stems in May. A common plant in dry, stony pastures in the northeastern United States.

ANTHEMIS (*Compositae,* Daisy Family). Usually rather tall plants with finely cut, strong-scented foliage, and small daisy flowers. All are native to Europe. They are easy to grow in any ordinary garden soil, in sun or light shade. Propagated by seeds or divisions.

A. biebersteiniana. Undoubtedly the prettiest of the genus and a rock-garden plant of exceptional merit. Fine, lacy, silvery leaves in neat mounds, about 6 inches high, with large yellow daisies on 8-inch stems in May and June.

A. nobilis. Chamomile. Bright-green, finely-cut leaves in rounded bushlets, about 10 inches high, covered with quantities of small, yellow-centered white daisies over a long period of late spring and summer. The flowers, stems, and leaves have a very strong scent when bruised. It self-sows readily and can become a weed if not kept in check.

ANTHYLLIS (*Leguminosae,* Pea Family). Mostly vetch-like creeping plants, native to poor, stony soil in Europe. Propagated by seeds and divisions, and easy to grow in a well-drained garden soil.

A. montana rosea. Slowly-spreading mats of woolly feathery leaves, and cloverlike heads of bright-pink flowers from May to July. From the European Alps.

ANTIRRHINUM (*Scrophulariaceae,* Figwort Family). Most snapdragons are annuals, or perennials that are much too large for the rock garden, but some of the little ones are dandy. Descriptions of two of them follow.

A. asarina. Procumbent creeping stems with rather fleshy, sticky-pubescent, heart-shaped leaves that form attractive thick mats. Large creamy-white or slightly-pinkish snapdragon flowers through spring and summer. Easy to grow in well-drained garden soil, and a very effective dry-wall plant. Native to France and Spain. It should be protected in winter.

A. molle. Semishrubby, with upright stems clothed in soft, velvety gray-green leaves in nice mounds, about 12 inches high. It has loose, leafy spikes of very pale-yellow flowers in late spring and summer. A plant from the south of France that is easy to grow but rather tender in the North.

APHYLLANTHES (*Liliaceae,* Lily Family). A curious plant from the barren, dry hillsides of southern France. It must have a gravelly, well-drained dry soil, in full sun. Needs protection in the north. Propagated by divisions.

A. monspeliensis. Thin, stiff, leafless stems in little tufts, to 10 inches high, resembling a dwarf bush. Lovely clear-blue, star-shaped flowers in spring.

AQUILEGIA (*Ranunculaceae,* Buttercup Family). The columbines are elegant queens of the garden, with lacy foliage and colorful flowers. They are mostly known in the large perennial border class, with the ultimate in charm and elegance reached in the spectacular long-spurred hybrids. Some are saxicoles and alpines of exceptional merit, suitable for the rock garden. Generally, they are easy to grow and permanent in any ordinary garden soil, in sun or light shade. All are propagated by seeds, which should be sown in summer as soon as they are ripe or in early spring. Seeds sown in the summer will produce flowers the following spring.

A. akitensis. Very neat domes of deep-blue-green leaves, about 6 inches high. Large blue-purple flowers with inner petals creamy-yellow, on 12-inch stems, in May and June. From Japan.

A. alpina. Nice three-parted leaves in narrow clumps, about 10 inches high, and large dark-blue flowers in May. From the Swiss Alps.

A. bertolonii. From the high mountains of southern Europe comes this dandy for the rock garden. Small, very glaucous leaves in neat little mounds, about 4 inches high, and deep-violet-blue flowers on stems 8 to 10 inches high, in May and June.

A. canadensis. A common sight along our country roads is the bright-red and yellow display of the eastern American columbine. A rather large plant with fine lacy leaves, in open graceful clumps, 12 inches or more high. The thin, swaying stems carry multitudes of long-spurred, bright-red and yellow flowers in May and June. This is a natural cliff dweller that makes a wonderful wall-garden subject. It blooms as well in shade as it does in full sun. In height, it varies from 6 to 30 inches (*illustration page 134*).

A. clematiflora. A lovely plant of garden-hybrid origin, with delightful light-pink and blue flowers, about 3 inches across. The flowers are without spurs and thus have a flat wide-open aspect.

A. ecalcarata. A curious plant of unknown origin, with fine lacy foliage of blue-purple cast, and masses of tiny spurless dark-reddish-purple flowers on 15-inch stems, in May. It is not very showy but charming and endearing when you get to know it.

A. flabellata nana alba. Japanese Fan Columbine. Large, light-green leaves, rather fleshy and glaucous, in neat mounds to 6 inches high, and sturdy flower stems to 12 inches high, bearing large, short-spurred, pure-white flowers in May and June.

Aquilegia canadensis.

A. jonesii. A dainty little alpine from Montana that is almost impossible to grow except in its native habitat. It has been an enigma to the best of gardeners for years. Tiny tufts of rounded leaflets, about one inch high with 2-inch stems, each bearing one tiny blue flower in early spring. My observation is that it needs a very deep gravelly root run, with an acid peaty soil, in sun or part shade. It needs ample moisture in the spring but likes to be thoroughly dry in summer, when it goes partially dormant. The only way I ever succeeded in flowering it was by keeping it potted in pure sphagnum moss.

A. saximontana. Another dainty dwarf alpine, this one from Utah, that is comparatively easy to grow. A little cluster of crinkly, bluish foliage, about 2 inches high, with 4-inch flower stems carrying little blue and yellow flowers in April. It likes a very gritty, well-drained lime soil (pH 7–8), in full sun or very light shade.

A. scopulorum. Little tufts of tiny, glaucous, three-lobed leaves, and charming pale-blue flowers with long slender spurs, on stems about 6 inches high. It needs a gritty, well-drained lime soil (pH 7–8), in full sun. From the high mountains of Utah.

A. sibirica nana. Seeds sent from Japan produce dense mounds of small glaucous leaves, about 5 inches high. The 8-inch flower stems bear numerous small deep-rich-blue flowers in May and June.

ARABIS (*Cruciferae,* Mustard Family). Most of the rock cresses are alpine and montane plants. Being true saxicoles, they are rightfully very popular in the rock garden. Most are easy to grow if they are given a rather lean, well-drained, gritty or gravelly soil, in sun or light shade. They are propagated easily by divisions or seeds. Undoubtedly, many more than those listed will do well in America if seeds can be obtained.

A. albida (recently renamed *A. caucasica*). Wall Cress. Large, spreading mats of hairy, gray leaves on prostrate stems, 3 inches or more high, with large, open sprays of fragrant white flowers for a long season in early spring. Var. *flore-*

Arabis albida flore-pleno.

pleno has bold spikes of fully-double white flowers, much like the florists' stocks. Var. *rosea* or 'Rosabella' is a form that grows in tight little mounds. It spreads slowly and produces short stems of bright-pink flowers. 'Snowcap' is a dense cespitose form with multitudes of white flowers on short stems. Var. *variegata* has leaves edged with yellow. These are among the best wall-garden plants, being long-lived and permanent. The larger growing kinds, as var. *flore-pleno,* should be cut back severely after flowering to maintain a neat appearance. A worthwhile and extremely useful plant from the Caucasus.

A. androsacea. A tiny alpine from southeastern Europe that forms tight little cushions of woolly white rosettes, topped by little clusters of white flowers on 2-inch stems, in May. A rather difficult plant to grow. It should be given a limy scree soil (pH 7–8), in full sun.

A. blepharophylla. A California native, with flat rosettes of broad, dark-green leaves. Twelve-inch stems bear fragrant deep-rose-purple flowers in May. Easy to grow in a well-drained garden soil, but a place in a rock crevice will display its attractive leaves to better advantage.

A. carduchorum. Tight little mounds of shining green leaves in rosettes, about 2 inches high. It has lovely clusters of comparatively large white flowers on 3-inch stems, in April. A most adorable evergreen cushion plant from Armenia.

A. ferdinandi-coburgii. A tiny plant from Greece, with gray leaves in rosettes, and creamy-white flowers in April. The rosettes turn green in winter. It requires a gritty, well-drained lime soil (pH 7–8), in sun or light shade.

A. kellereri. A hybrid between *A. bryoides* and *A. ferdinandi-coburgii.* Tiny ash-gray leaves in tight little rosettes, and small clusters of white flowers on 2-inch stems, in April. It is a deciduous plant that looks quite dead in winter. Needs a gritty lime soil (pH 7–8), in sun or light shade.

A. lyrata. An eastern American native that clings to the side of a limestone rock in the tiniest crevice imaginable. Flat rosettes of lyrately-lobed green leaves, and airy sprays of white flowers on 10-inch stems, in May and June. If it cannot be given a tight crevice, it should have a very well-drained, gravelly lime soil.

A. procurrens. A quickly-spreading mat of bright shining green leaves. Excellent as a wall plant or ground cover in sun or light shade, in any soil available. It produces masses of white flowers on 12-inch stems, in April and May. The flowers are similar to those of the candytufts. A most prolific and dependable plant from southern Europe.

A. sturii. Apparently a dwarf form of *A. procurrens.* Little tight mounds of shining bright green leaves, about 3 inches high, and 4-inch stems bearing clusters of white flowers in May. It spreads rather slowly.

ARCTOSTAPHYLOS (*Ericaceae,* Heath Family). Most of the bearberries or manzanitas are large shrubs or small trees, native to the western and southwestern United States. They are not hardy elsewhere in the North. One, however, is exceptionally well suited for the rock garden in a rigorous climate.

A. uva-ursi. Bearberry. Dense evergreen mats of long trailing vinelike stems, with small, dark-green, leathery leaves that turn a pleasing bronze color in fall. Small white bell-shaped flowers, followed by bright-red berries in summer and fall. An evergreen ground cover for an acid sandy or gravelly soil (pH 4–5), in full sun or light shade. Propagated by seeds and cuttings taken in the fall. Its habitat is widespread in Europe, Asia, and North America.

ARENARIA (*Caryophyllaceae,* Pink Family). Usually small creeping or cespitose evergreen plants, inhabiting rather poor or gravelly soils. A rather dull group with a few bright subjects that are useful in the rock garden. Easily propagated by division.

A. laricifolia. Quickly-spreading mats of prostrate rooting stems, covered with tiny, awl-shaped, semievergreen leaves. Comparatively large and showy white flowers in airy sprays on 6-inch stems, in May and June. A Swiss alpine that is good for planting in flagstone walks, and for wall gardens.

A. montana. Long decumbent or trailing stems that make attractive mounds, about 6 inches high. It has very large, white, cup-shaped flowers in April, May, and June. An old favorite with rock gardeners that is easy to grow, and permanent in any well-drained garden soil. From southwestern Europe.

A. purpurascens. A little green mat, smothered with light-purple flowers in spring. A noteworthy species from the Pyrenees.

A. verna caespitosa. A mosslike species from Europe, no more than a half-inch high, that grows into tight little mats, which are studded with tiny white stars in early spring. One of the best plants for use between steppingstones and in sink gardens. It must have a well-drained or sandy soil, in sun or light shade. In prolonged periods of hot dry weather it may brown off, but it recovers quickly with the first rain.

Armeria juniperifolia.

ARMERIA (*Plumbaginaceae,* Plumbago Family). The sea-pinks or thrifts are admirable bright-flowered subjects for the perennial border, and the small forms are good for the rock garden. They are easy to grow and permanent in neutral to limy well-drained soil (pH 6–8), in full sun. Easily propagated by seeds, root divisions, and, in the case of *A. juniperifolia,* by cuttings.

A. juniperifolia (usually listed in catalogues as *A. caespitosa*). Dense evergreen tufts of short pointed leaves in tight rosettes, and compact clusters of white flowers on 2-inch stems, in April and May and again in the fall. This is the true form from the Guadarrama Mountains of Spain. A little gem that requires a gritty, well-drained lime soil (pH 7–8), in full sun. To prevent the crown from decaying in summer, mulch plant with a thick layer of stone chips (*illustration page 139*).

A. juniperifolia rosea. This form grows a little faster and is a more prolific bloomer. Lovely clear-rose-pink flowers, completely smothering the tiny green cushions. It carries a few flowers throughout the summer.

A. maritima. Large, fairly rapidly spreading clumps of thin, grasslike evergreen leaves, adorned with dense orbicular heads of pink flowers on 8-inch stems, in April and May. A few flowers through summer and fall. This is an old rock favorite with several forms, the most popular being var. *alba* with pure-white flowers, and var. *laucheana* with very bright-carmine flowers. The old plants should be taken up and divided every three or four years because they tend to rot out in the middle.

A. 'Six Hills Hybrid.' Probably this is more correctly called *A. caesalpina,* which is a natural hybrid. It is a nice little plant, with neat cushions of grassy foliage about 3 inches high, and a profusion of light-pink flowers on 5-inch stems, in spring and a few in the fall.

ARNEBIA (*Boraginaceae,* Borage Family). A small group of plants native to the Near East, with one perennial species adapted to the rock garden.

A. echioides. Prophet-flower. Low clumps of dark-green leaves that produce long, trailing or procumbent stems, bearing fascinating, large, bright-yellow trumpet flowers with large brown spots. The spots fade with age (to herald the coming of the prophet Mohammed), leaving the blossom pure yellow. A prolific bloomer in late April and May and a few flowers throughout the summer. Easy to grow in any well-drained garden soil, in full sun. Propagated by seeds and divisions.

ARNICA (*Compositae,* Daisy Family). Mostly small plants with yellow daisies, native to the northern Rocky Mountains, and to alpine and arctic regions. The several American species are not too difficult under cultivation if they are given a gravelly, well-drained, acid to neutral, soil (pH 6–7), in sun. Propagated by seeds or divisions.

A. montana. A difficult-to-grow subject from the European Alps. Small tufts of green leaves send up 18-inch stems, each bearing a cluster of large bright-orange-yellow flowers in May and June. It must have a moist, acid, gravelly soil, in full sun, and is most permanent in an acid moraine.

ARRHENATHERUM (*Gramineae,* Grass Family). The typical oat grass is a very large, quickly-spreading meadow plant, useful for raising fat cattle. One form, whose description follows, is well appreciated in the rock garden.

A. elatius tuberosum nanum. Dwarf Striped Oat Grass. A very attractive clump of green-and-white-striped leaves, 8 to 10 inches high. A nonspreading plant that is easy to grow in any garden soil, in sun or light shade. The subdued tones of the pale-green-and-white leaves is often a welcome change from the brilliant colors of the usual spring rock-garden flowers.

ARTEMISIA (*Compositae,* Daisy Family). Very attractive gray- or silvery-leaved shrubs and tall perennials, with loose heads of unattractive greenish or yellowish flowers. The foliage and stems are aromatic and are often used in flavoring food and beverages. Some of the dwarf or low forms are coveted rock-garden plants. All are easy to grow in a well-drained garden soil (pH 6–8), in full sun. Propagated quite easily by divisions, or by cuttings taken in early summer.

A. frigida. Neat mounds of silvery, silky, fluffy foliage, about 6 inches high, pierced by tall wands to 2 feet high, bearing small yellow flowers in nodding clusters. Even on the hottest, driest days of summer, the foliage feels very cool to the touch. From the Rocky Mountains.

A. glacialis. A tiny alpine from Switzerland. Dense two-inch-thick mats of tiny, silvery, woolly, ferny foliage on creeping stems. It needs a gritty soil with very good drainage. A wonderful plant for paved walks and wall gardens.

A. schmidtiana nana. This is the remarkable plant that is usually listed in catalogues as 'Silver Dome' or 'Silver Mound.' A perfect rounded dome of silver foam, about 10 inches

Artemisia schmidtiana nana, "Silver Dome."

high and 18 to 24 inches in diameter. An irresistible plant that is loved and wanted by everyone who sees it. The flowers are small yellow discs that should be cut off before they spoil the symmetry of the plant. It grows best in full sun, in a rather poor sandy or gravelly soil. When planted in rich soil or in shade, it flops open in the middle. If this happens, cut the plant back severely. It will then resume its fluffy round shape.

ARUM (*Araceae,* Aroid Family). Large, leafy plants with bulb-like tubers, and flowers like those of the Jack-in-the-pulpit. Native to the Mediterranean region. They require shade and a deep, rich, moist humus soil.

A. italicum. Very large, arrow-shaped leaves, on stems about 10 inches long. White flowers, followed by clubs of red berries in the fall.

A. maculatum. Lords and Ladies. Sheets of large leaves, somewhat spotted and marbled, about 10 inches high. Green spathes spotted with purple. These plants go dormant in early summer. The leaves reappear in fall and remain green all winter.

ASARUM (*Aristolochiaceae,* Birthwort Family). The wild gingers are interesting and attractive woodland plants that are very useful in shady rock gardens. They are easy to grow if they are given a moist, deep, acid, leaf-mold or humus soil (pH 5–6), in shade or half-shade. Propagated by divisions, and sometimes by seeds.

A. canadensis. A coarse deciduous plant from the woods of the northeastern United States. Large, heart-shaped leaves, about 8 inches across, on stalks 6 to 12 inches high. The leaves and stems are light green and covered with coarse hairs. Brownish flowers close to the ground early in spring.

A. europeum. Lovely evergreen mats of rounded cordate leaves of a thick, leathery texture. Greenish-brown flowers in the spring, hidden by the leaves. This species and the ones following make good evergreen ground covers in dense shade. From the mountains of Europe.

A. shuttleworthii. Leathery, heart-shaped evergreen leaves on prostrate petioles, the blades dark green and mottled with deep purple. Native in mountains of the United States from Virginia to Georgia.

A. virginianum. Similar to *A. shuttleworthii,* but with usually plain green leaves. The dark-purple flowers lie on the ground beneath the leaves early in April.

ASPERULA (*Rubiaceae,* Madder Family). Small creeping plants with square stems and tiny leaves in whorls. They are easy to grow and make an excellent ground cover for shady rock gardens and under ericaceous shrubs. They like a moist, acid, leaf-mold soil (pH 4–6). Propagated by divisions.

A. hirta. Small mats about two inches high, with hairy green leaves in whorls of six. Tiny pinkish flowers smother the plants in early spring. From the Pyrenees.

A. odorata. Sweet Woodruff. Narrow leaves in whorls 8 inches long, which form a solid thick carpet of light green. Covered with small, white, tubular, four-petaled stars in April and May. The deliciously fragrant leaves and stems are used for making May wine in Germany. Native to Europe and western Asia.

ASPLENIUM (*Polypodiaceae,* Fern Family). To me all ferns are attractive, interesting, and desirable. The species in this genus seem to be of two types: huge tropical ones as high as 8 feet, and small saxicoles native to the woods and mountains of the eastern United States, Europe, Asia, South America, and southern Africa. Those listed here are all native to our northeastern woodlands. Some are easy to grow, others very difficult. They can be propagated by divisions, but usually the plants are collected in the wild and transferred to the garden.

A. platyneuron. Ebony Spleenwort. The sterile fronds are arranged in flat whorls, 3 to 12 inches in diameter. The fertile fronds rise from the center of the plant and are about 15 inches high and to 3 inches wide. Fresh shining green pinnae on black stipes. I have always found this fern growing

Asperula odorata.

in acid soil on steep gravelly slopes, in shade or half-shade. If it is given a similar situation in the rock garden, it will thrive for years.

A. resiliens. Similar in appearance to *A. platyneuron,* except that it is much smaller, with fronds 6 to 8 inches long and 1 to 2 inches wide. This is a tough subject to grow. It must have acid leaf-mold soil in a crevice of sandstone of granitic rock, in shade. It will not grow unless it is in a crevice.

A. ruta-muraria. A tiny plant, only an inch or two high, with lacy, rounded pinnae on green stipes, that is just about impossible to grow in the garden. I have found it in the wild, only in lightly shaded, very tight cracks on the face of limestone rocks that face west or northwest. The only way I have ever had it in a garden was to take home a rock with the fern already growing in it and give it about the same exposure it had in its original setting. This is an extremely rare fern; it should not be wantonly destroyed in futile efforts to cultivate it.

A. trichomanes. Maidenhair Spleenwort. A charming little rock fern that grows in tight tufts of narrow fronds no more than 6 inches long. Shining green pinnae on black stipes. It needs full shade, and must be placed in a horizontal crevice of a limestone rock. It is easy and permanent if these directions are followed: Place a flat, square-edged limestone rock in position. Cover it with a thin layer of powdery leaf-mold. On this, spread out the roots of the fern and cover them with more leaf-mold. Place a large, flat, limestone rock on top of the roots and press it down firmly.

A. viride. Green Spleenwort. A tufted saxatile fern, with long and very narrow bright-fresh-green fronds about 8 inches long. Another difficult subject that must have full shade, and an acid leaf-mold soil in the crevice of a noncalcareous rock.

ASTER (*Compositae,* Daisy Family). A large family of bright-flowered plants. Most widely known are the tall, fall-blooming perennials. There is a good assortment of dwarf and intermediate plants that are well suited to rock gardening. Generally, they are easy to grow in an ordinary garden soil, in sun or light shade. Propagated by divisions, cuttings, and seeds. Undoubtedly, there are many more species than those listed that can be grown with ease in the rock garden. All America, from the Atlantic to the Pacific, is ablaze with bright-colored asters in the autumn, and many of them are dwarfs and saxicoles that should have a place in our gardens.

A. alpinus. Rock Aster. Neat rounded clumps of pale-green leaves, about 3 inches high. Large, solitary, light-violet-blue flowers on 10-inch stems, in June. This prolific species from the Rocky Mountains and the mountains of Europe and Asia has several forms, the most popular being: var. *albus* with pure-white flowers, var. *roseus* with bright-rose flowers, and 'Goliath' a taller more robust form with large lavender-blue flowers.

A. bellidiastrum. Broad oval leaves in little rosettes, about 2 inches high. Large white daisies on 8-inch stems, all summer long. A nice little plant from southern Europe that needs winter protection.

A. dumosus. A variable plant from the western United States, ranging in height from 6 inches to 3 feet. The plants are literally covered with small flowers in dense masses in August, September, and October. Probably the wild form is not common in gardens, but there are several named varieties that make excellent fall-blooming rock-garden plants. 'Lady Maddocks' is about 24 inches high, with pale-pink flowers; 'Lilac Time,' about 15 inches high, has light-lilac-colored flowers; and 'Little Red Boy,' about 12 inches high, has masses of bright-red flowers. 'Niobe,' about 8 inches high, has yellow-centered white flowers, very compact. 'Victor' is about 12 inches high, with thousands of lovely lavender-blue blooms.

A. farreri. A tufted plant with long, narrow, pubescent leaves, and flower stems about 18 inches high. Each stem bears a single, large, deep-blue daisy with a yellow center. From central China.

A. linariifolius. Tiny, narrow, stiff, hairy leaves on stiff, wiry stems, about 24 inches high. Large, open heads of small violet-colored flowers in September and October. If the stems are cut back once or twice during the summer before the buds begin to form, the plant will become fuller and produce more flowers on shorter stems. Native to the eastern coastal area of the United States. This plant is hardy, permanent, and easy to grow if it is given a sandy acid soil, in sun or light shade. There are several good color forms, which include var. *alba* with pure-white flowers, var. *rosinus* with charming soft-rose-pink flowers, and var. *purpureus* with very deep-purple flowers.

A. spectabilis. A pine-barren beauty, with small tufts of dark-green leaves on widely-spreading underground stolons. Large masses of bright-violet-blue flowers on stems 12 to 18 inches high, from late July to October. Very prolific and beautiful, but it is a fast creeper that must be confined in small gardens. It likes a sandy acid soil, in sun or light shade.

A. subcaeruleus. A plant from India that closely resembles *A. alpinus.* It is best known in gardens as 'Star of Wartburg.' Very large, soft-lavender-blue daisies on 18-inch stems, in midsummer.

ASTILBE (*Saxifragaceae,* Rockfoil Family). Mostly strong-growing meadow plants with attractive ferny foliage, and large, colorful plumes of fluffy flowers that bloom in midsummer. They are often listed erroneously in catalogues as *Spiraea.* All require a deep, rich, moist humus soil, in sun or light shade. They will not stand prolonged drought. However, they will stand well in dry gardens if they are planted in a humus or peaty soil, in full shade, and watered periodically during the summer. All are easily propagated by division in spring with the aid of a large strong knife. The root masses become large and woody.

A. chinensis pumila. A very dwarf plant with creeping rootstocks. It has mats of light-green, ferny foliage almost flat on the ground, and stiff, upright stems about 10 inches high, with plump spikes of colorful two-toned pink and mauve fuzzy flowers in late July and August. A choice late summer bloomer from China.

A. crispa. A tiny plant with dark-green, very stiff and crisp foliage in tight tufts, about 4 inches high. It has stiff, narrow spikes of flowers in late spring, represented in the following color forms: 'Gnome' with clear-light-pink flowers, 'Lilliput' with salmon-pink, and 'Perkeo' with deep-pink. According to Bailey's *Hortus II,* this species name is without botanical standing, but these three little plants are undoubtedly the best astilbes for the rock garden.

A. dryade. Clumps of ferny green foliage, about 8 inches high, superimposed with 12-inch feathery plumes of pure-white flowers in June and July. This is probably a hybrid of garden origin.

A. rosea. A hybrid between *A. chinensis* and *A. japonica.* A large plant with bold clumps of feathery, lacy foliage, 12 to 18 inches high, and large fluffy plumes of clear-pink flowers on stems 24 to 30 inches high. I may be wrong but I believe that most of the fancy named florists' spiraeas belong here. Among the most popular are the following: 'Avalanche' with white flowers, 'Bremen' with light pink, 'Deutschland' with white, 'Fanal' with dark-reddish-green foliage and bright-red plumes, 'Gloria' with deep-pink flowers, 'Gertrude Brix' with crimson flowers, 'Peach Blossom' with plumes colored a delicate peach-blossom-pink, 'Queen Alexandra' with carmine-pink flowers, and 'Rheinland' with white. All of these bloom from late June through July. Although they are rather tall, they are useful in large rock gardens and in open places in woodland or wild gardens.

A. simplicifolia. A plant from Japan that forms little clumps about 6 inches high. The leaves are simple and deeply lobed, not pinnate and ferny as in the other species. Tiny star-shaped white flowers in slightly nodding plumes on stems 8 to 12 inches high, in June and July.

A. simplicifolia salmonae. A taller, more robust plant, with beautiful, gracefully arching plumes of lovely salmon-pink flowers on stems about 15 inches high.

ATHYRIUM (*Polypodiaceae,* Fern Family). Large woodland ferns, most generally known in the North American species *A. filix-femina,* the lady fern. The ones listed here are Japanese woodlanders, which are among the easiest, most dependable, and elegant ferns for the rock garden. They like an acid leaf-mold soil or a humus-rich light-acid loam (pH 5–7), in shade or half-shade. Easily propagated by divisions. The rhizomes spread fairly rapidly to form large colonies.

A. goeringianum. A very lacy fern, with gracefully arching fronds about 12 inches high. The color graduates from a dark emerald-green to lighter shades toward the edges.

A. goeringianum pictum. Painted Fern. This is a most delightful fern, with graceful arching fronds tinted pink, gray, and pale-green on a dark-green background. Its effect is striking when it is set against a large rock in a shady nook of the rock garden.

AUBRIETA (*Cruciferae,* Mustard Family). A small group of choice mat-forming plants, with bright-purple flowers in early spring. Apparently, only varieties of one species are in general cultivation in the United States. Propagated by seeds, divisions, and cuttings in soil testing pH 6–8.

A. deltoidea. Purple Rock-Cress. An old favorite that is almost indispensable in the rock garden. A spreading carpet of small, evergreen, gray-green leaves that is completely covered with myriads of bright flowers from early April to June. The flowers of seedlings vary in color from mauve to deep purple. An excellent wall-garden plant, and one that is quite outstanding when allowed to tumble over the face of a large rock. Old plants may become rampant, but can be kept in check by severe clipping. A dependable long-lived plant that is easy to grow if it is given a fairly lean, gritty or gravelly, well-drained soil (pH 6–8), in sun or light shade. This versatile native of Greece and Turkey comes in several named color forms: 'Cardinal Richelieu' with brilliant royal-purple flowers, 'Dawn' with large semidouble clear-pink flowers, 'Eyerii' with dark-purple blooms, 'Graeca' with small soft-blue-purple flowers, 'Lavender' with very large wide-petaled lavender flowers, 'Whitewell Gem' with bright-pink flowers, and several others. Seed houses offer mixed Giant Hybrid or Grandiflora Hybrid seeds. These usually produce a wide variety of colors and forms.

BEGONIA (*Begoniaceae,* Begonia Family). A large family of showy tropical plants. One tuberous-rooted species from China and Japan is hardy in the North, and is used in large shady rock gardens.

B. evansiana. Large, waxy, typical begonia leaves, on 24-inch stems. Clusters of flesh-pink flowers all summer. Easy to grow in an acid leaf-mold or peaty moist soil, in shade. After the first frosts have withered the fragile stems, the tuberous roots should be covered with a 6-inch layer of leaves or straw. This should be removed in the spring.

BELLIS (*Compositae,* Daisy Family). Small tufted plants with colorful little daisies all summer. Native to western Europe and northern Africa. Although perennial, they are not reliably hardy in the North and are usually grown as biennials. Propagated by seeds, and easy to grow in any ordinary garden soil, in sun or light shade.

B. perennis. English Daisy. Small rounded leaves in little tufts, about 3 inches high. Six-inch stems carry double or single flowers in white and shades of pink all summer.

B. rotundifolia. White daisies on 6-inch stems, over little clumps of long-stalked round leaves. Var. *caerulescens* has lovely soft-blue flowers.

BELLIUM (*Compositae,* Daisy Family). One perennial species, *B. bellidioides,* a very small, mat-forming plant, no more than an inch high with tiny spatulate leaves, that spreads on very thin stolons. Tiny white daisies with pink undersides, on very thin stems about 3 inches long, all through the summer. Easy to grow in any well-drained garden soil, in full sun. A native of the Mediterranean region that needs winter protection in the North.

BERBERIS (*Berberidaceae,* Barberry Family). Generally large, thorny, deciduous or evergreen shrubs, useful for background planting and for general landscaping. A few dwarfs adapted to the rock garden are listed here. All are propagated by cuttings.

B. buxifolia nana. A very dwarf form of an evergreen Chilean species. Very tiny, dark-reddish-green, round leaves on twiggy, thorny branches in a tight ball form. Showy orange-yellow flowers in spring, and dark-purple berries in fall. Easy to grow in well-drained, acid to neutral, garden soil (pH 5–7). It needs winter protection in exposed positions in the North.

B. candidula. A very dwarf half-evergreen shrub, with bright shining green spiny leaves, in little rounded mounds about 6 inches high. Large pale-yellow flowers in May. A most interesting and useful plant from China. It needs winter protection in the North. Easy to grow in a well-drained garden soil, in sun or light shade.

B. verruculosa. A wonderful semidwarf evergreen shrub of irregular habit, growing 2 to 3 feet high. Very dark, glossy, bronzy-green, spiny leaves with glaucous undersides, on stiff, thorny branches. Large bright-golden-yellow globose flowers in May, and black berries in the fall. One of the outstanding evergreen shrubs for specimens in large rock gardens, and useful as background in small gardens. From western China. It is hardy and dependable. Likes a well-drained, acid to neutral, soil, in sun.

BERGENIA (*Saxifragaceae,* Rockfoil Family). Usually listed as *Saxifraga* or *Megasea* in catalogues. Large bold plants with huge leaves, and great heavy clusters of pink flowers on stout tall stems. They are long-lived, easy to grow, and permanent in a deep, rich, acid loam or moist peaty soil, in shade or half-shade.

B. cordifolia. Clumps of large rounded leaves, wavy and denticulate, each leaf about 6 inches across. Flower stems are 10 to 15 inches high, bearing large tight clusters of waxy-pink bells in April. Late hard frosts may damage the buds before they open. The ornamental leaves are effective in flower arrangements. A hardy plant from Siberia.

B. stacheyi. Similar to *B. cordifolia,* but the leaves are not wavy and are ciliate instead of denticulate. Pink flowers in more open panicles on 10-inch stems, in April. From India, but apparently just as hardy as its Siberian cousin.

BETULA (*Betulaceae,* Birch Family). A family of large trees, except for one dwarf from arctic regions.

B. nana. A somewhat spreading, branching procumbent or prostrate shrub, to 2 feet high. Tiny, light-green, oval leaves, and monoecius flowers, consisting of catkins and tiny cones. It is interesting and desirable for its contorted Japanese effect. Requires a gravelly, moist, acid soil, in full sun. It is best to give it moraine treatment in low altitudes.

BLECHNUM (*Polypodiaceae,* Fern Family). Very large, coarse ferns from the tropics, except for one species which is native to the Pacific coast of the United States, also Europe and Asia.

B. spicant. Deer Fern. Broad, dark-green, leathery fronds, the sterile ones in a crown flat on the ground and the fertile ones (coming from the center of the plant) stiff and upright, to 2 feet high. Propagated from spores, and with difficulty by divisions. It likes a deep, acid, peaty, or leaf-mold soil (pH 4–6), in shade.

BRUCKENTHALIA (*Ericaceae,* Heath Family). A low evergreen shrub from the Balkans, closely related to *Erica.*

B. spiculifolia. Balkan Spike Heath. A semiprostrate spreading shrub, with the upright growth about 5 inches high, clothed with very fine and dense evergreen leaves, and resembling dwarf spruce. In June and July, it is topped with innumerable short spikes of delicately colored tiny pink bells. Very hardy and easy to grow in a sandy, acid, leaf-mold soil, in sun or light shade.

BRUNNERA (*Boraginaceae,* Borage Family). A large plant from Siberia, usually listed in catalogues as *Anchusa myosotidiflora,* and commonly called Chinese forget-me-not.

B. macrophylla. Large, dull-green, hairy leaves in clumps about 12 inches high, and most attractive airy sprays of bright-blue flowers in April and May. It wants a deep, rich, moist, acid loam, in shade or half-shade. Propagation by divisions, or by seeds. If it likes the situation, it self-sows quite freely.

BUXUS (*Buxaceae,* Box Family). Very attractive evergreen shrubs, with tiny waxy leaves and inconspicuous flowers. Often used as topiary specimens, and extensively as low hedges and edgings. Easy to grow in ordinary garden soil, in sun or shade; but they sunburn very easily in the winter. Propagated by cuttings.

B. microphylla compacta. The smallest and most compact of the dwarf boxwoods, with tiny evergreen leaves. A very slow grower, it forms a tight little tuft, about the size of a golf ball, in three years from cuttings. I have seen plants from 15 to 20 years old that are less than 12 inches high.

B. microphylla koreana. A good hardy dwarf that grows into a somewhat rounded ball about 15 inches high. This is about the hardiest species, surviving the coldest winter without losing a leaf. A good plant for a bold evergreen accent, or it can be sheared to any height for low edging.

CALLIRHOE (*Malvaceae,* Mallow Family). Big, overpowering plants from the Central Plains states, with heavy taproots, digitate or palmate leaves, and large, poppylike, pink to purple flowers. They are easy to grow in a well-drained garden soil, in full sun. They like dry situations. Propagated by seeds.

C. involucrata. Poppy-Mallow. Neat little clumps of deeply-lobed leaves send out long, rambling, trailing stems, to 3 feet long or more, bearing very large, purple, cup-shaped flowers all summer. It is much too rampant for a well-ordered rock garden, but it is useful on high dry banks where little else will grow.

CALLUNA (*Ericaceae,* Heath Family). Here is the most outstanding dwarf evergreen shrub for the rock garden and for the foreground of shrub plantings — the "bonnie purple heather" of Scotland. Although closely identified with Scotland, it grows wild over most of Europe and Asia Minor, as well as in Labrador and Newfoundland. The heathers are mostly neat little rounded shrubs with tiny clasping evergreen leaves, ranging in height according to variety from 2 inches to 3 feet. They have showy spikes of colorful flowers from the first of July to the end of October and, in some varieties, to December.

Named varieties are propagated by hardwood cuttings taken in late summer or fall. They are easy to grow if given a deep, acid, leaf-mold, sandy soil (pH 4–6), in full sun. Some varieties will grow in shade, but they will not flower well. Although extremely hardy, they sometimes windburn during dry winters in exposed positions. To prevent winter damage, mulch the base of the plant heavily with peat moss or pine needles; then cover the entire plant with evergreen boughs or straw.

C. vulgaris. The one and only species in the genus. All other named sorts are natural or garden variants. The typical wild heather is a twiggy shrub about 3 feet high, with tiny evergreen leaves clasping the thin upright branches, and very small, purple or lavender flowers in long, thin spikes, in July and August. It is a plant of some economic importance in northern England and in Scotland. Grouse and other game birds live exclusively on the tender young shoots. Cattle and sheep graze on it. The long slender branches are used in making brooms and for thatching roofs. When the heather is in bloom, beekeepers move their hives to the highland moors to reap the coveted heather-flavored honey.

Many fancy named forms are available for the rock garden, the most popular being: 'Alba,' a compact rounded plant, to 12 inches high, with light-green foliage and white flowers; 'Alporti,' a tall slender plant, to 2 feet or more, with deep-crimson flowers; 'Camala,' with double soft-rose flowers; 'County Wicklow,' very dark-green foliage on arching branches, 12 inches high, and soft-pink double flowers; 'Crispa,' heavy branches of bright-green foliage, with white flowers; 'Cuprea,' masses of thin stems with golden foliage that turns coppery in the fall, and lavender flowers; 'Foxii Nana,' very tight and tiny balls of mosslike growth about 4 inches high, with short spikes of lavender flowers; 'Hammondii,' a tall slender plant, to 2 feet or more, with white flowers; 'Else Frye,' a compact plant about 10 inches high, with light-green foliage and double white flowers; 'J. H. Hamilton,' a low spreading plant with arching branches

Masses of *Calluna vulgaris* in several varieties.

about 10 inches high, and double clear-pink flowers; 'Kupholdii,' a completely prostrate plant with thin stems that grow in a swirl to make a most interesting mat or ground cover, with deep-lavender flowers; 'Mayfair,' a typical wild heather but a very prolific bloomer; 'Minima,' a most unusual form, about 6 inches high, with thick mosslike bronze foliage in tight rounded cushions, and short spikes of bright-purple flowers; 'Mrs. H. E. Beale,' a tall grower with sprays sometimes 18 inches long, and large shell-pink double flowers; 'Mrs. R. H. Gray,' a prostrate plant with thick matted growth, and long heavy sprays of lavender flowers almost flat on the ground; and 'Mrs. Pat,' little cushions of mosslike foliage about 6 inches high, with short spikes of lavender flowers. New growth of 'Mrs. Pat' is always bright pink; this is one of the most outstanding of the dwarf varieties.

Still others are 'Monstros,' a tall vigorous plant with heavy horizontally spreading branches, and dark-purple flowers; 'Nana Compacta,' small, somewhat conical, mounds of very fine, mosslike foliage about 6 inches high, with short spikes of lavender flowers, a most distinctive and refined plant; 'Plena,' a vigorous upright-grower, with dark-green foliage and double purple flowers on 18-inch stems; 'Pygmaea,' a prostrate or creeping sod-forming plant with very fine foliage, and tiny spikes of purple flowers; 'Rigida,' a 10-inch-high mound of stiff, compact, gnarled, horizontal branches of a striking fresh-green color, with short spikes of small white flowers — the only heather that does not turn bronze with frost; 'Rosea,' a strong grower with widely arching branches in mounds about 18 inches high, and heavy compound spikes of rosy-lavender flowers; 'Rubra,' an outstanding form with rich dark-red-purple flowers; 'Sister Anne,' a prostrate plant of dense matted growth, covered with fine silky down, which gives it a velvety-soft aspect, and lavender flowers in short, dense, horizontal spikes; 'Tib,' a tall form with a thin, open look that has double deep-red-purple flowers from July to the end of December; and 'Tomentosa,' a tall, stiff, sturdy plant with foliage covered by a fine gray pubescence, which gives it a dark-silvery-green sheen, particularly in fall, and vivid bright-purple flowers.

The heathers (*Calluna*) and heaths (*Erica*) (which are listed in their proper alphabetical order) are in my opinion the most versatile, the most useful, and the most rewarding small shrubs for the rock garden. The little information I have given here only begins to tell their story. For those who would like to pursue the subject further, I recommend *The Heather Garden,* a book by Fred J. Chapple.

CALTHA (*Ranunculaceae,* Buttercup Family). Showy, broad-leafed plants from marshes and swamps that are sometimes transferred to wet places on the home grounds. They can be used at the edge of a pool in the rock garden or in a bog garden. They require a wet, mucky, acid soil, in shade or half-shade.

C. leptosepala. A species from Alaska and the Rocky Mountains, with long oval leaves in little clumps about 6 inches high. Solitary blue-tinted white flowers in June and July.

C. palustris. Marsh-Marigold. A familiar early spring sight in our eastern marshes and swampy woodlands. Bright-yellow flowers over large, heart-shaped leaves in April and May.

CAMPANULA (*Campanulaceae,* Bellflower Family). An important and popular family of beautiful flowering plants, some of them tall for the perennial border, and others small and dainty enough to use in a rock or wall garden. Most are fairly easy to grow, but the tiny alpine kinds can be quite difficult. Propagation is by seeds, divisions, and sometimes by cuttings.

C. aucheri. Huge glistening deep-purple flowers, over little tufts of narrow lanceolate leaves. The entire plant is only about 4 inches high. This beauty from the Caucasus likes a gritty, well-drained soil (pH 6–8), in sun or light shade.

C. barbata. Clumps of pale-green, hairy leaves, about 3 inches high, with erect flower stems 8 to 12 inches high, bearing large soft-violet-blue bells all summer. The inside of the flower is bearded. From the mountains of Europe. Easy to grow in any well-drained garden soil, in sun or light shade.

C. carpatica. Tussock Bellflower. This old favorite from the Carpathian Mountains forms huge tussocks of large, light-green leaves, about 10 inches high, topped with large, violet-blue, cup-shaped flowers from June to September. Valuable for its long summer blooming period, and very easy to grow in any ordinary garden soil, in sun or light shade. Var. *alba* has pure-white flowers. Var. *turbinata* is a dwarfer form, with prostrate stems and wide-open flowers.

C. cochlearifolia. Often listed as *C. pusilla.* One of the best and easiest of the tiny alpine bellflowers for American rock gardens. Its creeping underground stems form dense mats of tiny shell-shaped leaves, about 1 inch high. It produces quantities of large clear-blue bells, nodding on 3-inch stems, in May and June and a few through the summer. It must have partial shade, in a moist but well-drained, gritty soil that is slightly acid to alkaline (pH 6–7). In areas where the weather is persistently hot and dry, it will be permanent only in a moraine. Var. *alba* is a dandy, with pure-white flowers. Var. *miranda,* often listed as a separate species, is a form with slightly taller stems and larger bells of silvery blue.

C. elatines. This name seems to be something of an enigma to botanists, while nurserymen almost completely ignore it. It designates a variable plant, from Italy and the Adriatic region, which has attractive, tight, slowly-spreading tufts of sharp-pointed leaves, no more than 3 inches high. The flowering stems are ascending, or trailing, to about 8 inches long, and are covered with large sprays of wide-open light-violet-blue stars in late May, June, and July. Var. *fenestrellata* is a form with smooth shiny green leaves and china-blue flowers. Var. *garganica* is the best-known form and the easiest to obtain. Its tiny, crinkly leaves are hairy but nevertheless quite shiny. A very prolific plant, with white-centered blue stars over a long period. It is admirably adapted to a wide rock crevice or to the face of a stone wall. Easy to grow in a well-drained garden soil, in sun or light shade.

C. glomerata acaulis. A small form of an extremely handsome plant from Europe and Asia. Tufts of small clumps of rather large leaves, and 5-inch stems bearing large clusters of blue bells in June and July. Easy to grow in any ordinary garden soil.

C. parryi. A particularly interesting American plant from the Rocky Mountains. Little clumps of very stiff and wavy, dark-glossy-green leaves, about 2 inches high. It has large upturned violet bells on stiff 8-inch stems, in May and June. Requires a gritty, well-drained soil (pH 5–8), in full sun.

C. pilosa. Usually listed as *C. dasyantha.* The creeping stems form low mats of broad, hairy, but shiny-green leaves, in rosettes about one inch high. Each 6-inch flower stem bears a single glistening violet-colored flower, shaped like a narrow bell, in May and June. A striking beauty from Alaska and northern Asia that is easy to grow, if it is given a very gritty, well-drained soil (pH 6–8), in sun or light shade.

C. piperi. A gem from the Olympic Mountains of Washington that is almost impossible to grow in a garden but well worthy of the challenge. Creeping stems produce little tufts of tiny serrated leaves and 3-inch stems, bearing bright glistening-blue flowers in late spring. In the wild, it grows only in very tight crevices of granitic rocks; it must be treated the same way in the garden. It can be maintained in pots if it is given a very well-drained, gritty, acid soil (pH 5–6), in light shade. Highly prized as an alpine house plant.

C. portenschlagiana. Usually listed and most generally known by the less cumbersome name of *C. muralis.* Very tight little tufts of tiny, sharp-pointed, shiny-green leaves, and masses of small upturned bell flowers of a lovely light-violet color in May and June. The flowers are on stems only 3 or 4 inches high. Easy to grow in a gritty, well-drained lime soil, in sun or light shade; but it prefers a rock crevice or the shady side of a stone wall. From Dalmatia.

C. poscharskyana. Another Dalmatian, related to the *C. elatines* group, which looks like a huge *C. garganica.* Large clumps of sharp-pointed leaves, about 6 inches high, and long, trailing stems that produce a mass of large, wide-open, light-violet-blue stars in May and June. A single plant sometimes creates a mass as much as 3 feet across. Very easy to grow in a well-drained garden soil, in sun or shade. Sometimes it becomes quite rampant in rich soil and must be checked to keep it from overrunning the garden.

Campanula portenschlagiana at home in a limestone crevice.

C. raddeana. An ornamental tuft of small, rigid, serrated leaves on slender petioles about 4 inches high, and erect 8-inch flower stems from which hang numerous glistening deep-purple bells in June and July. One of the prettiest of the bellflowers from the Caucasus. It thrives in a cool, gritty, well-drained lime soil (pH 7–8), in partial shade.

C. rotundifolia. Harebell. The famous bluebells of Scotland. Spreading clumps of small round leaves, about 4 inches high. Slender flower stems, to 18 inches high, carry open sprays of nodding brilliant-blue flowers all through the summer and fall. The leaves on the flower stems are very long and narrow. This desirable and dependable plant from around the world is easy to grow in any good garden soil, in sun or light shade. A natural rock plant, it is at home in any rock or wall garden. Valuable for its good color and long blooming period.

C. sarmatica. Little mounds, 7 inches high, of soft, hairy, gray-green leaves, and erect stems, to 8 inches high, with large, pale-violet, nodding bells in June and July. A plant from the Caucasus that is easy to grow in a well-drained garden soil, in full sun.

C. scheuchzeri. Little clumps of very narrow linear leaves, and 12-inch stems, bearing large, nodding, bright-blue bells from July to September. An easy-to-grow plant from Eurasia that is valued for its bright summer color.

C. stansfieldii. A hybrid with tiny leaves on loping creeping stems, which form broad mats, and ascending flower stems, bearing deep-purple flowers in late spring and summer. Easy to grow in a well-drained garden soil, in sun or light shade.

CAMPTOSORUS (*Polypodiaceae,* Fern Family). A one-species genus. *C. rhizophyllus* is the walking fern from the limestone mountains of the northeastern United States. Very long and narrow undivided evergreen fronds that root down at the tips, forming new little plants. It sometimes forms a solid mass on the face of moss-covered limestone rocks. To grow it in a rock garden, plant it in a shallow crevice containing limy leaf-mold, in full shade. Although it will survive for a time on a flat surface, it prefers the face of a perpendicular rock.

CARLINA (*Compositae,* Daisy Family). Thistlelike plants from southern Europe, grown as curiosity or collection items, rather than for beauty. They require well-drained, gravelly or sandy soil (pH 6–8), in full sun. Propagated by seeds or divisions.

The Walking Fern, *Camptosorus rhizophyllus,* reaching for a toe hold on moss-covered rocks

C. acaulis. Low flat clusters of prickly, pinnatifid gray-green leaves, and huge white flowers as much as 6 inches across, resembling strawflowers. The plant is stemless and flowers in May or June.

CASSIOPE (*Ericaceae,* Heath Family). Rare low-growing evergreen shrubs that are not easy to grow in the northeastern United States. They require a moist but well-drained, sandy acid leaf-mold soil (pH 4–6), in sun or light shade. In hot dry areas, they should be planted in an acid moraine. They are much easier to grow in the extreme northern parts of the United States.

C. lycopopioides. Very thin, creeping stems with tiny, dark-green, scalelike leaves in slowly-spreading mats or tufts, 2 to 6 inches high. Comparatively large snow-white bells on thin bright-red stems, in May and June. A curiously interesting and very pretty little plant from Siberia and Alaska.

C. mertensiana. A twiggy, tufted shrub about 12 inches high, with very thick, tiny leaves crowded on the stems. Solitary white bells on thin stems, in late spring. From Alaska southward to California.

CERASTIUM (*Caryophyllaceae,* Pink Family). The mouse-ears or chickweeds are familiar sights in old American gardens. They are generally long-lived and persistent, sometimes quite weedy. Easy to grow in any ordinary garden soil, in full sun or light shade. Propagated readily by divisions at almost any time. All are evergreen under ordinary conditions.

C. alpinum. A tiny plant from arctic regions that grows into a slowly spreading mat, about 1 inch high. The tiny green leaves are covered with long silky hairs. Comparatively large white flowers on short stems, in April and May. Var. *lanatum* has its leaves in tight white woolly rosettes, and white flowers in little tight clusters. This is undoubtedly the most refined and best *Cerastium* for the rock garden. It requires a very gritty, well-drained lime soil, in full sun.

C. arvense compactum. Small dense clumps of little green leaves, about 3 inches high, slowly spreading by underground stolons. Masses of white flowers on stems 4 or 5 inches high, in April and May.

C. biebersteinii. Thick spreading mats of narrow, somewhat woolly, gray-green leaves on thin creeping stems. Open sprays of small white flowers on 6-inch stems, in April and May.

C. tomentosum. Snow-in-Summer. A quickly spreading mass of silvery-gray, woolly leaves, 4 to 12 inches high, and masses of rather large white flowers in loose sprays, in May and June. A very attractive plant when young, but a very invasive, weedy, and unkempt nuisance when not kept in check. It should be cut back almost to the ground shortly after flowering to keep it in good appearance.

CERATOSTIGMA (*Plumbaginaceae,* Leadwort Family). A small family of blue-flowered plants from China and India. The following is grown in the rock garden.

C. plumbaginoides. Usually listed as *Plumbago larpentae.* This colorful plant from China can become a weed if it is not confined. It spreads by means of underground runners and forms great masses of green leaves on wiry stems 12 inches high. These are topped with clusters of vivid-deep-blue salverform flowers from August to November. Prized for its rich true-blue color and long summer blooming period. Easy to grow in almost any soil, in sun or light shade. In the extreme North, it requires a heavy mulch to keep it over winter.

CHEILANTHES (*Polypodiaceae,* Fern Family). Dainty, lacy rock ferns for dry sunny situations. They like an acid leaf-mold in the crevice of a rock. Those I have tried did not last over winter without a protective covering of salt hay. They can be propagated by divisions, but are usually collected from the wild.

C. gracillima. Lace-Fern. Dainty, lacy fronds, about 8 inches high with reflexed margins. The underside of the fronds is woolly. From British Columbia, south to California.

C. lanosa. Lacy, rusty, woolly fronds, 6 to 8 inches high on brown stipes. The easiest kind to grow and one of the hardiest. From Connecticut to Georgia.

CHIMAPHILA (*Pyrolaceae,* Shinleaf Family). Little creeping woodland plants that are quite difficult to grow away from their native habitat. I have always found them in dry woodlands, growing in a thin layer of acid leaf-mold (pH 4–5) over a gravelly subsoil. The only way I have ever succeeded with them was to take up plants from the wild early in spring, being careful not to break the runners, which should be at least 2 feet long with two or more leaf stems. The long runners are wound up in a loose ball and potted in acid leaf-mold, with stone chips in the bottom of the pot for drainage. The plants are carried over in pots plunged in a shaded cold frame for one full year, and transferred to the garden in early spring.

C. maculata. Pipsissewa. Often called spotted wintergreen or prince's pine. Usually 3 to 5 leathery, dark-green leaves marked with white along the veins, on upright stems about 5 inches high. Very fragrant, waxy-white flowers in small umbels on 3-inch stems, in July. The creeping stems make broad open patches but never dense mats. Found in the woods from Maine to Georgia.

C. umbellata cisatlantica. Decumbent stems with numerous leathery, dark-green, irregularly toothed leaves in fairly dense patches. Waxy-white flowers, 4 or 5 together, on 6-inch stems in June and July. The leaves are not variegated, and the plant somewhat resembles the Japanese pachysandra in general appearance.

CHIOGENES (*Ericaceae,* Heath Family). The only species is a creeping plant from the cold regions of North America.

C. hispidula. Creeping Snowberry. An attractive evergreen mat of small, leathery leaves on long trailing stems, studded with small white flowers in spring and snow-white berries in fall. A difficult plant for the best of gardeners. It requires a constantly moist, acid leaf-mold soil, in shade or half-shade. The only way to keep it in a garden for any length of time is to plant it in a shady bog. It invariably succumbs to summer heat at low altitudes.

The exquisite woodland beauty of *Chimaphila maculata*.

CHRYSANTHEMUM (*Compositae,* Daisy Family). A colorful family of well-known plants, usually too large and overpowering for an ordinary rock garden. However, a few from arctic and mountainous regions are suitable. They are easy to grow in a well-drained garden soil (pH 6–8), and are easily propagated by seeds, divisions, or cuttings in spring. Cushion-type chrysanthemums are often recommended for the rock garden, but I think they are all too big and floppy to fit in with the tiny alpine plants. Descriptions of some suitable kinds follow.

C. alpinum. Little tufts of ferny green leaves, about 2 inches high, and 6-inch flower stems, each with a single white daisy in May and June. A rather difficult plant from the Alps that requires a very gritty, well-drained soil, in full sun.

C. arcticum. Clumps, about 6 inches high, of segmented leaves on decumbent stems, with asterlike flowers ranging from white to lilac in summer.

C. mawii. A most interesting half-shrubbery species from the Atlas Mountains. Small pinnatifid leaves on decumbent or ascending stems, to 15 inches high. The flowers, produced in June and July, are white above and pink on the underside. This plant requires a hot sunny position in well-drained, gritty soil. As it is somewhat tender, it needs good cover for the winter.

C. morifolium gracile. A very hardy and lovely chrysanthemum of exceptional merit. It has thick, leathery, glossy-green leaves in compact mounds that are attractive all summer. Charming, 3-inch-wide, cream-colored daisies are produced in October on 18-inch stems. A wild form of the large florists' chrysanthemum that is not too big for the average rock garden.

CHRYSOGONUM (*Compositae,* Daisy Family). An American plant, native from Pennsylvania south to Florida. Propagated by divisions at any time, and easy to grow in sun or shade in almost any soil (pH 4–7) that is not too limy. It prefers shade; if grown in the sun, it must be watered periodically during dry weather.

C. virginianum. Gold Star. One of the prettiest and most useful of native American wild flowers for a shady rock garden. Low spreading clumps or mats of large hairy green leaves, and stems 4 to 6 inches high, bearing multitudes of bright-yellow stars from April to October. One of the few plants that will bloom all summer in the shade.

CHRYSOPSIS (*Compositae,* Daisy Family). Uncommon North American natives, with bright-yellow flowers in summer and fall. Propagated by seeds and divisions. Not the easiest plants to grow, but very satisfying in a naturalistic setting.

C. falcata. Loose clumps of long, narrow, woolly leaves on stiff stems, about 10 inches high, topped with clusters of small bright-yellow asters in August and September. A native of the New Jersey pine barrens that requires an acid sandy soil (pH 4–6), in full sun. It will not live in a heavy garden loam.

C. mariana. Hairy, gray-green leaves in flat mats or scattered tufts that produce immense bunches of bright-yellow asters on 2-foot stems, from July to September. Another native of the pine barrens, but this one is easy to grow in a well-drained garden soil (pH 4–7) that is not too limy.

CLAYTONIA (*Portulacaceae,* Purslane Family). Interesting and cheerful little spring-blooming plants from the woodlands of North America. They are easy to grow in a shady place in moist, acid leaf-mold. They are usually transplanted to the rock garden from the wild.

C. megarrhiza. Thick fleshy roots, and long spatulate leaves that lie on the ground. Decumbent flowering stems produce a cluster of light-pink flowers in very early spring. From the Rocky Mountains.

C. virginiana. Spring Beauty. Very long, narrow leaves that lie flat on the ground, making loose carpets. The decumbent flower stems bear comparatively large, pink-striped white flowers in March and April. The root is a hard little corm that tastes a little like potato. The leaves appear in the fall and stay green all winter. The entire plant goes completely dormant shortly after flowering.

CONVALLARIA (*Liliaceae,* Lily Family). A single species that is native to Europe, Asia, and possibly to North America. One of the best known and most beloved of springtime flowers.

C. majalis. Lily-of-the-Valley. Broad oval leaves in dense carpets from quickly creeping rootstocks. Very fragrant, bell-shaped white flowers in one-sided spikes, on stems about 6 inches high. Var. *rosea* has flowers tinged with pink. Var. *flore-pleno* has double white flowers. Easy to grow and permanent in a rich acid loam, in shade or half-shade. Propagated easily by divisions at any time.

COPROSMA (*Rubiaceae,* Madder Family). The coprosmas are mostly large shrubs from New Zealand that are used extensively in the South for hedges and general landscape work. The following is a prize for the rock garden.

C. petriei. Dwarfest of all evergreen shrubs. It forms interesting slowly-spreading mats of tiny twigs and twisted branches flat on the ground and sometimes subterranean. The tiny evergreen leaves are usually less than a quarter of an inch long. In fall, it has black berries a half-inch thick, sitting right on top of the dense little cushion. Difficult to propagate because of its minute growth. Usually, a three-year-old plant can be completely covered with a half dollar. A very slow grower that is permanent if given a well-drained, gritty lime soil, in sun or light shade, in a sheltered position. It needs winter protection in the Far North.

COPTIS (*Ranunculaceae,* Buttercup Family). Dainty little evergreen carpeters of infinite value for shady rock gardens. They all need shade and a moist, peaty or acid leaf-mold soil. Easily propagated by divisions.

C. asplenifolia. Dense feathery mats of finely dissected, five-parted leaves, about 3 inches high. Small inconsequential white flowers in spring. From Alaska southward.

C. groenlandica. Gold Thread. Dense mats of bright shiny-green, three-lobed leaves almost flat on the ground, studded with showy white flowers on erect 5-inch stems, in May and June. The underground runners are a bright golden-yellow.

They yield a dye and a medicinal drug. From our eastern woodlands.

C. laciniata. Fine, lacy, three-parted leaves in dense evergreen mats, and small greenish-white flowers in spring. From Washington and Oregon.

C. quinquefolia. The prettiest of the genus with very fine, ferny, five-parted leaves in dense little mats, about 1 inch thick. Charming waxy-white flowers on 3-inch stems, in April and May.

COREMA (*Empetraceae,* Crowberry Family). A small family of evergreen shrubs from America and Europe that are useful as ground covers where little else will grow. They require a dry, acid, sandy or rocky soil, in full sun. Propagated by cuttings in late summer.

C. conradii. A low spreading bush, about 10 inches high, with tiny sprucelike leaves, and small inconspicuous brownish flowers in early spring. It resembles a heath without flowers.

COREOPSIS (*Compositae,* Daisy Family). A family of tall annual and perennial plants, with bright-yellow or pink flowers throughout the summer. Most of them are good flower-garden subjects, but only *auriculata nana* is suited to the rock garden. Easy to grow in any garden soil in sun. Propagation is by seeds and divisions.

C. auriculata nana. Clumps, about 3 inches high, of dark-green oval leaves with little auricles at the base. Large bright-orange-yellow daisies on stems 4 to 10 inches high, from May to October. A good long-blooming plant that will give needed color through the summer, even if it is not the most pleasing.

CORNUS (*Cornaceae,* Dogwood Family). Small trees and large shrubs, extensively used for general landscape work. The following must have been created especially for rock gardens.

C. canadensis. Bunchberry. Whorls of green oval leaves on red stems, no more than 6 inches high, in thick mats from spreading creeping rootstocks. Showy white dogwood flowers

Cornus canadensis.

in May and June, and bunches of bright-red berries in late summer and fall. A cold-climate plant from northern North America that likes a cool, moist, acid leaf-mold soil (pH 4–6), in shade or half-shade. It detests the heat of summers at low altitudes. Propagated by divisions that should be kept in plots for the first year.

CORYDALIS (*Fumariaceae,* Fumitory Family). Dainty, lacy-leaved plants consisting of annuals, biennials, and perennials. Some are tuberous rooted. Usually easy to grow in ordinary garden soil. Propagated mostly by seeds, some species by divisions.

C. cheilanthifolia. A large clump of finely cut, ferny foliage, about 10 inches high, and short stems with a few small yellow flowers in late spring. A plant from China, recommended for its striking ornamental foliage.

C. lutea. A very attractive mass of delicate, glaucous, lacy foliage, 6 to 8 inches high, and loose sprays of showy yellow flowers from May to November. Much like a yellow bleeding heart. A real beauty for shaded walls and rock crevices. It is easy to grow in ordinary garden soil (pH 6–8), but will not thrive in open ground. It must be planted so that its roots can grow alongside a large rock.

CORYPHANTHA (*Cactaceae,* Cactus Family). Spiny ball-shaped cacti from the northern Rocky Mountains to Mexico. Perhaps many are hardy in the North under ideal conditions, but I have had experience only with *vivipara.* They require a dry sunny place, in very well-drained, sandy, gritty, or gravelly soil (pH 6–8). Propagated by seeds.

C. vivipara. A tiny, prickly ball cactus that slowly develops into a little mound of spiny cylinders, about 3 inches high. It has showy purple flowers in June, and bright-red berries in summer that usually stay on all winter.

COTONEASTER (*Rosaceae,* Rose Family). A large family of attractive shrubs, usually with small inconsequential flowers, but with brightly-colored berries in fall and winter. Most of them are quite large sprawling or spreading shrubs, but a few are admirably suited for rock work. They are easy to grow in any well-drained garden soil, in sun or light shade. Propagated by cuttings in summer or fall. Good kinds are the following.

C. congesta. A dwarf slow-growing evergreen shrub, 12 to 18 inches high, with sturdy, stiff, horizontally spreading branches, clothed with small, round, leathery leaves. Pale pink or white flowers in May, followed by large, showy, bright-red berries in summer and fall. A Himalayan species.

C. dammeri. Prostrate creeping rooting stems, with fairly large oval light-green leaves, that makes a superb ground cover. Small white flowers and bright-red berries. An evergreen species from China that needs some winter protection in the North.

C. horizontalis. Everyone knows "little gem," the big sprawling rockspray, but this little gem is really an outstanding variety for the rock garden. It grows into a little mound of horizontally spreading, twisting twigs, covered with tiny, shiny, green leaves that turn bright red in fall. As far as I know, it never flowers or produces berries. An extremely slow-growing form. Ten-year-old plants are only about 6 inches high and 12 to 15 inches across.

C. microphylla thymifolia. Much like *C. congesta* in habit of growth, flower, and fruit, but the evergreen leaves are very tiny and narrow.

C. pannos nana. A charming plant from China that forms a compact spreading mound, 6 to 10 inches high, with short, stiff, horizontally spreading branches and tiny, dark-green leaves. New twigs and the underside of the leaves are woolly gray. White flowers and red berries in summer and fall. It needs winter protection in the North.

CRYPTOGRAMMA (*Polypodiaceae,* Fern Family). A small family of saxicole ferns from western North America and Asia. The following is especially recommended.

C. crispa acrostichoides. Parsley Fern. This dainty rock-loving fern from the Great Lakes region and the Rocky Mountains looks like a little clump of fresh crisp parsley. Glossy-green, three-pinnate fronds on straw-colored stipes, about 5 inches high. It requires an acid leaf-mold soil (pH 4–6), in a shady moist rock crevice. It will not grow upright in open soil.

CUTHBERTIA (*Commelinaceae,* Dayflower Family). A small family consisting of two species from the Carolinas and Georgia. Closely related to *Tradescantia.* All require a moist, sandy, acid soil, in sun or light shade. Propagated by divisions.

C. graminea. One of the prettiest plants for the rock garden that I have ever seen. It consists of a little tuft of filiform leaves, 4 to 6 inches high, surmounted with bewitching bright-pink flowers, about 1 inch across, on gracefully arching stems from June to September. It resembles a miniature *Tradescantia* without the coarse untidiness and invasive characteristics of the spiderwort.

C. rosea. Similar to *C. graminea* but much larger. Tufts of flat leaf blades, 8 to 12 inches high, with rose-colored flowers in summer.

CYCLAMEN (*Primulaceae,* Primrose Family). The culmination of loveliness in foliage, flower, and fragrance. Exquisite plants from Europe and western Asia, not exclusively saxicoles, which can be used with success and satisfaction in rock gardens. They are tuberous-rooted plants that are long-lived and prolific, but they are quite particular about soil conditions and exposure. Although they can be grown in all sections of the country, they are not the easiest of plants to maintain. They like a rich, peaty or leaf-mold soil (pH 5–7) that is constantly moist but very well drained. They should be placed in a sheltered position, in shade, where strong winds will not strike them. They like a humid atmosphere, such as that found under large leafy plants and tall shrubs, but need ample air circulation and light. This may sound discouraging, without my intention. I have described ideal conditions for the best possible results. In all species, the leaves develop in the fall and stay green all winter. These plants go dormant in spring.

Cyclamen neapolitanum.

C. cilicicum. Dark-green, heart-shaped leaves almost flat on the ground, and large pale-rose flowers from August to October before the leaves appear.

C. coum. Small dark-green leaves, and odorless deep-red-purple flowers from January to April. In very cold climates, this species, and all the other winter-flowering kinds, bloom in early spring.

C. europaeum. Bright-red fragrant flowers from July to October. Large dark-green, heart-shaped leaves. One of the hardiest and easiest to grow.

C. ibericum. Green heart-shaped leaves, sometimes marbled with white. Bright red-purple flowers from February to April.

C. neapolitanum. The easiest and most prolific of all cyclamens. Great quantities of bright-rose-pink fragrant flowers in September and October. Attractive ivylike marbled leaves make a lovely solid cover for the winter.

C. rapandum. Very small, leathery, heart-shaped leaves and short stems, with bright-red-purple fragrant flowers from March to June.

CYMBALARIA (*Scrophulariaceae,* Figwort Family). Charming little creeping plants, with attractive foliage and dainty little flowers throughout the summer. They are easy to grow in an ordinary garden soil, in shade or half-shade. All, except *C. pilosa,* are somewhat tender and need good winter cover in the North. They can be propagated easily by divisions. In mild climates and good rich soil, they may become a bit weedy, spreading by underground runners to all parts of the garden. From Southern Europe.

C. aequitriloba. A very fine mat of tiny three-lobed leaves, no more than a half-inch across. The entire plant is never more than a quarter of an inch high. Dainty mauve flowers just above the leaves all summer.

C. hepaticaefolia. Rather large, 3- to 5-lobed leaves, slightly spotted and marked with white, in a mat about 2 inches thick. The leaves closely resemble those of our hepaticas. The dense mat of ornamental leaves is studded with pale-blue flowers all summer.

C. muralis. Kenilworth Ivy. A well-known plant, used for hanging baskets in homes, and often growing rampant under benches in greenhouses. It is quite tender but can be used in sheltered areas of rock gardens. Long trailing stems that root down at the nodes, with small shiny-green, sharply-pointed, three-lobed leaves, and light-lavender-blue flowers in summer.

C. pilosa. A very neat and attractive creeper with soft woolly gray-green, three-lobed leaves in dense mats, about 3 inches high. It is liberally sprinkled with charming lavender flowers from May to November. This plant proved to be perfectly hardy, without protection, at 30 degrees below zero. Unlike other species, *C. pilosa* requires full sun or very light shade. An excellent permanent ground cover over bulb patches, and a charming wall plant.

CYPRIPEDIUM (*Orchidaceae,* Orchid Family). The lady-slippers are coveted by all enthusiastic gardeners but are extremely difficult to cultivate. Usually, plants are taken from the wild and transplanted to the garden, where they promptly die. Some degree of success has been achieved by a few gardeners after painstaking preparations and many failures.

C. acaule. Moccasin Flower. Two large oval leaves about 8 inches long, and a single stem about 12 inches high, bearing an exquisite large pink orchid in late May or June. It has been grown for a number of years in a poor gravelly subsoil under a thin layer of acid leaf-mold that is annually top-dressed with pine needles. Usually, the plant produces a flower for the first year or two after transplanting, then dies.

C. calceolus pubescens. Tall leafy stems, 18 inches or more high, sometimes several from a single root. Each stem bears one or more yellow and purple-brown slippers in May and June. This is about the easiest wild orchid to grow, and it is fairly permanent if given a deep, rich, moist, humus alkaline soil (pH 7–8). In the wild, it is usually found in moist, shady places in limestone mountain areas.

C. reginae. Queen Slipper Orchid. The most coveted of the terrestrial orchids. It is listed here, not to encourage its cultivation, but to plead for its conservation. It is hardly a rock-garden plant, being almost 3 feet tall with large hairy leaves and immense white-and-rose slippers in June. Digging it up and moving it to a garden is tantamount to murder.

CYSTOPTERIS (*Polypodiaceae,* Fern Family). Natural rock-loving ferns from northeastern North America. They are easy to grow in moist, acid, leaf-mold soil (pH 5–6) in rock crevices, or on gravelly or stony banks.

C. bulbifera. Berry Fern. Long, dark-green, tapering, lacy fronds, about 12 inches high, in tufts or little clumps. Small bulblets, produced on the underside of the fronds, start new plants when they fall off.

C. fragilis. Slowly spreading clumps of lacy, gray-green fronds, about 8 inches high, from creeping rootstocks. Easy to grow in almost any acid soil, in shade or half-shade, but very susceptible to drought.

CYTISUS (*Leguminosae,* Pea Family). The brooms are odd, interesting and showy, almost leafless, green-stemmed, twiggy shrubs. Many of them are quite tall, ranging to 10 feet high, but some are well suited to rock work. Almost all are quite hardy and easy to grow if given a lean, well-drained, sandy, gritty, or gravelly soil, in full sun. They are exceptionally well adapted to use in very hot and dry situations. Soil acidity is inconsequential but they will not stand rich, heavy loam soils. Propagation is by cuttings taken in late summer and fall, and by seeds.

C. decumbens. Prostrate, somewhat leafy, grayish-green stems forming a thick tangled mat. Bright-yellow flowers along the stems in May and June. A wonderful wall plant from southern Europe.

C. kewensis. A hybrid of exquisite grace and beauty. Long, slender, nearly leafless, green stems in a decumbent bush, 12 inches or less high. Fairly large creamy-white flowers along gracefully arching stems in May. A lovely plant to drape over a large rock.

C. purgans. A dense, twiggy, upright bush, 2 to 3 feet high, quite broomy-looking. Quantities of fragrant bright-yellow flowers along the branches in May and June.

C. purpureus. A decumbent shrub, about 18 inches high, with slender gracefully arching branches, clothed in persistent cloverlike leaves. Flowers like large light-purple butterflies all along the stems in May. A rock gardener would have to look far and wide to find a plant superior to this.

DABOECIA (*Ericaceae,* Heath Family). An evergreen shrub closely related to *Erica,* called Irish heath or bell heather. *D. cantabrica* forms a dense mound, 12 to 18 inches high, with bright shining-green, glaucous-backed leaves, and bold spikes of large, nodding, purple bells from late June to November. Var. *alba* has pure-white flowers. Var. *bicolor* has purple, white, and striped flowers, all on the same plant. Like the heathers, this one prefers a sandy, acid leaf-mold or peaty soil, in sun or light shade. Being a natural bog plant, it likes ample moisture, but it will stand a dry soil that does not parch. Needs good cover for the winter. Propagated by cuttings and layers.

DALIBARDA (*Rosaceae,* Rose Family). A little tufted and creeping plant from the New England woods. *D. repens,* the star violet, makes a wonderful little evergreen ground cover in a rich, moist, acid leaf-mold soil, in shade. Small tufts of heart-shaped, violet-like leaves, about 2 inches high, produce little white starry flowers from June to September.

DAPHNE (*Thymelaeaceae,* Mezereum Family). A family of adorable fragrant flowered shrubs, some rather tall for use in shrub borders, and others dwarf or low-growing for rock gardens and edgings. They are not among the easiest shrubs to grow, mainly because their requirements are not fully understood. They are propagated by seeds, cuttings, and (easiest for the home gardener) by layering.

D. alpina. A deciduous decumbent little twiggy shrub, 6 to 12 inches high, with long, narrow, pubescent leaves. Small clusters of fragrant waxy-white flowers in early spring before the leaves develop, and showy red berries in the fall. It needs a well-drained, light fluffy lime soil (pH 6–8), in full sun. From the limestone mountains of Europe.

D. blagayana. A fascinating prostrate shrub, with thick corky branches and fairly large, rounded, glaucous, blue-green evergreen leaves. Thick clusters of fragrant creamy-white flowers in April and May. It likes a well-drained, light, acid leaf-mold soil, in half-shade. A southern European native that needs protection in the North.

D. cneorum. Garland Flower. This is the most widely known and easiest of the *Daphnes* to grow. Small evergreen leaves set closely together on decumbent or trailing branches that form rounded mounds, about 12 inches high and 3 feet or more across. Captivating clusters of deep-rose-pink, extremely sweet-scented flowers at the tips of the branches in spring and again in fall. The plants should be trimmed yearly, soon after flowering, to keep them neat and compact.

Many gardeners complain that it is very difficult to keep this plant for any length of time, but I have found the opposite true, provided it is not coddled. The best specimens I have ever seen are in old abandoned gardens where they have not been tended for years. Contrary to popular belief, they want a fluffy, light, peaty or sandy, acid soil (pH 4–6), not a limy mixture. They do best in full sun, where they are not exposed to severe drying winds in winter. They like to be crowded and detest weeding and cultivation. Weeds and grass should be allowed to grow between the branches or, if that is objectionable, another plant such as thyme or sedum should be planted with it.

Var. *alba* is an extremely rare, very dwarf form, with short prostrate branches, in a mat about 4 inches high. It has pure-white flowers. Var. *variegata* has the same kind of flowers and habit of growth as the type, but the tiny leaves are margined with white or light-yellow. The variegation is not obvious from a distance.

DELPHINIUM (*Ranunculaceae,* Buttercup Family). Majestic tall perennials, prized for their bold spikes of colorful flowers in summer. A few are not too overbearing for the average rock garden. They are easily grown from seeds (sometimes divisions) in a well-drained garden soil (pH 6–8), in full sun.

D. grandiflorum. Bouquet Larkspur. Usually listed as *D. chinense.* The type and ordinary garden forms are much too large for the rock garden, but the named variety 'Blue Mirror' is a heart-warming exception. A small plant with a few basal leaves and stems, 8 to 12 inches high, with large spurless wide-open clear glistening-blue flowers in May and June. 'White Mirror' is a similar form with pure-white flowers.

D. nudicaule. Red Larkspur. A slender plant, about 18 inches high, with long-spurred scarlet flowers in July. An outstanding plant from California that needs some winter protection in the North.

D. tricorne. Staggerweed. A tuberous-rooted plant from the eastern United States, with small finely-divided leaves and fleshy succulent stems, 12 inches or more high, bearing long-spurred flowers ranging from purple to blue and white, in April. The plant goes dormant soon after flowering.

DIANTHUS (*Caryophyllaceae,* Pink Family). It is inconceivable that a rock gardener should fail to plant several types of pinks. The *Dianthus* has long been one of the backbone families of rock-garden plants, almost as indispensable as the rocks themselves. They are generally easy to grow in a well-drained garden soil, in full sun or very light shade. A few are particular about soil compositions and exposure, as noted in the list that follows. Although they are mostly lime lovers, they will tolerate a good degree of acidity. Propagation is by seeds, divisions, and in some instances, by cuttings taken in late summer. Pinks come very readily from seeds, but they cross so easily that the form the seedlings will take is unpredictable, especially if seeds from the garden are used. A sexual reproduction is essential if the named sorts and hybrids here are to be increased. The hybrids and species listed here are evergreen. All are superb wall-garden plants.

Besides the many fancy named sorts of annual pinks (*D. chinensis*), Sweet William (*D. barbatus*), the florists' carnation (*D. caryophyllus*), and the 'Cottage' or 'Allwood Pinks' (*D. plumarius* and hybrids), there are several horticultural forms and hybrids of unknown origin that are used in rock gardening. Because I do not know their parentage and they have no botanical standing, I shall describe them here rather than in the list of species.

'Ariel' is a little cushion of deep-blue-green leaves that slowly develops into a mat about an inch thick, and produces large bright-red cup-shaped flowers in May and June. 'Bobby' or 'Little Bob' forms a little tight clump of glaucous leaves, about 4 inches high, with erect 8-inch flower stems, bearing large pink flowers. It blooms from May to October. 'Double White' has light glaucous green leaves in thick clumps about 6 inches high, and arching stems about 10 inches high, each producing two or three very large fully-double pure-white fragrant flowers in June and July. This

Dianthus "Sammy."

in my opinion is one of the most elegant of the pinks for the rock garden.

'Little Joe' is an old favorite among American rock gardeners. It has short silvery leaves in dense little mounds about 4 inches high, and 10-inch stems bearing vivid deep-crimson flowers all through the summer. 'Prince Charming' is a lovely low mat of very short silvery-blue-green leaves, about an inch thick, with stiff little stems about 3 inches high, bearing small fragrant rose-pink flowers in May and June. 'Sammy,' one of the loveliest of the hybrid pinks, was originated by Mr. N. A. Hallauer of Webster, New York. Recently, it was renamed 'Tiny Rubies' by a large nursery. It forms a dense, slowly-spreading mat of tiny blue-green leaves, about an inch high, with literally hundreds of tiny fully-double deep-pink, very fragrant flowers on 3-inch stems, in May and June. 'Wallace Red' has stiff upright dark-green, slightly glaucous leaves in clumps, about 6 inches high. Sturdy upright flower stems, about 10 inches high, carry double or half-double dark-red flowers all summer. An outstanding plant for good summer color (*illustration page 183*).

D. alpinus. Little dark-green leaves in a tuft or slowly-spreading mat, about an inch high, with very large deep-rose-to-crimson flowers in May. A temperamental plant from the Swiss Alps, it demands a moist, well-drained, gritty lime soil, in sun or light shade. It is more permanent in a moraine.

D. arenarius. A desirable species from Finland that forms large mats of short stiff light-blue-green leaves, about 3 inches high, and produces many daintily fringed, fragrant white flowers on 6-inch stems, in late May and June.

D. arvernensis. Perhaps this is a misnomer for a form of the 'Cheddar Pink.' Attractive masses of grassy glaucous foliage, about 3 inches high, and fragrant light-pink fringed flowers in May and June.

D. brevicaulis. Dainty cushions of tiny gray leaves, less than an inch thick, with 2-inch flower stems, carrying small bright-pink flowers in May. The stiff little stems with the tiny bright flowers look like beaded pins in a pincushion. Excellent for walls and rock crevices.

D. deltoides. Maiden Pink. A quick-spreading mat-forming plant with small dark-green leaves on trailing stems. Huge masses of small but very bright and showy flowers on stems 6 to 15 inches high, in May and June. There are several named forms, with flowers ranging from white to brilliant red. It makes a wonderful wall plant. A very fast grower and self-sows freely; therefore, it should be used sparingly in small rock gardens.

D. gratianopolitanus. Cheddar Pink. An old favorite from England, usually listed as *D. caesius.* Attractive mats of glaucous foliage, and 12-inch stems, displaying masses of spicy-fragrant flowers in various shades of pink and rose during May and June. There are several named forms, including *alba* with white flowers; var. *superbus* with deep-pink flowers; and var. *flore-pleno* with double or semidouble flowers. When old, the plants tend to become rather floppy and ragged. To correct this, cut them back severely after they have flowered.

D. myrtinervius. Best described as a tiny *D. deltoides.* Little evergreen mats of tiny, slightly glaucous green leaves only a half-inch high, with trailing or ascending flower stems, 3 or 4 inches long, bearing airy sprays of tiny but showy bright-pink flowers in May, June, and July. Very tolerant of acid soil and shade in dry situations. Named varieties include 'Dame Blanche,' with white flowers ringed with faint pink near the center; and 'Pastel,' with masses of delicate pastel-pink flowers.

D. neglectus. The epitome of an ideal alpine plant. A tiny cespitose plant, with sharp-pointed, prickly leaves in cushions scarcely an inch high. These are completely hidden by a tight bouquet of large deep-pink flowers on stems 2 or 3 inches high, in late May or June. Needs a very gritty, well-drained lime soil, in full sun. 'Henriette' is a minute form, with leaves about a quarter of an inch long, but with huge flowers on 2-inch stems. My parent plant is now about 15 years old and is still less than 2 inches in diameter. Each year it produces upward of 20 flowers over a period of two weeks. It is so tiny that it is extremely difficult to propagate. Once rooted, it must be carried in pots for several years before it is large enough to be moved to a crevice in the rock garden.

D. noeanus. This is usually listed as *Acanthophyllum spinosum.* It makes a neat dense cushion of short stiff spiny foliage, about 3 inches high. The cushion is prickly to the touch. Thin wiry stems, about 10 inches high, display fragrant, deeply laciniated white flowers in late June and July. This plant loves walls and rock crevices. It must have very good drainage and a stone chip collar to prevent crown rot during hot dry weather.

D. plumarius. Cottage Pink. Big spreading and sprawly mats of glaucous leaves, and flower stems, about 18 inches high, with laciniated fragrant flowers in a wide range of colors and forms. A variable plant, usually produced from seeds offered from dealers in mixed-hybrid series. This is one of the parents of the *allwoodii* pinks.

D. strictus. A small cespitose plant with light-green leaves, about an inch or two high, and thin stiff stems, each bearing a single waxy-white flower in late May or June. Var. *grandiflorus* is a large-flowered form.

D. superbus. An exquisite species from Eurasia, with soft-light-green foliage in spreading cushions. Lovely fragrant lavender flowers, laciniated and lacy, on 12-inch stems, in May and June.

D. sylvestris. Wood Pink. One of the few pinks that like shade. It forms an attractive trailing mat of soft gray-green leaves, about 2 inches thick. This is covered with a blanket of large salverform Persian-rose flowers in June and July. It takes full sun or shade in a dry situation.

Undoubtedly, there are many more species and varieties that can be grown in rock gardens. An infinite number are offered by seedsmen, especially in England and Europe.

DIAPENSIA (*Diapensiaceae,* Diapensia Family). A minute evergreen shrublet from arctic regions that is next to impossible to cultivate in areas outside its native habitat.

D. lapponica. Dense little cushions of tiny leaves, crowded on woody creeping or subterranean stems. Large white flowers nestled in the foliage in June. An extremely difficult plant that needs an acid moraine in half-shade. It will not stand hot summers at low altitudes.

DICENTRA (*Fumariaceae,* Fumitory Family). Lovely ferny-leaved plants, mainly represented in American gardens by the graceful bleeding heart (*D. spectabilis*), which is too tall for rock gardens. All other species, except *pusilla* as noted, are American natives.

D. canadensis. Squirrel Corn. Delicate, lacy, frondlike leaves in little mounds about 6 inches high, and white heart-shaped flowers nodding from slender 12-inch stems. The leaves and flowers spring from little clusters of tuberous roots in April and go completely dormant in May. It likes a well-drained, acid leaf-mold soil, in shade.

D. cucullaria. Dutchman's-Breeches. Scaly, bulblike roots produce delicate, lacy leaves, and white flowers on 10-inch stems in May. The plant is similar in growth and habit to *D. canadensis.* Each of the white flowers is shaped like a pair of Dutch colonial breeches.

D. eximia. Fringed Bleeding Heart. Large clumps of attractive ferny foliage, and loose nodding clusters of rosy-purple hearts from May to November. In rich deep soil, it sometimes grows two feet high, but is usually lower. Easy to grow in any ordinary garden soil, in shade or half-shade. It will also stand full sun if the soil is kept moist. One of the few plants that will bloom all summer in deep shade. An extremely good wall-garden plant. Var. *alba* has white flowers, usually suffused with pink, but a new find by Dr. Edgar T. Wherry in West Virginia has pure-white flowers. Its charm and grace make it one of the most outstanding white-flowered plants for the rock garden. Var. *gracilis* has long narrow deep-red-purple flowers, and the segments of the leaves are slender and elongated.

D. formosa. Clumps of glaucous, ferny foliage, and stems about 18 inches high, with light-purple flowers all summer. It forms large colonies by means of slowly creeping underground stolons. It likes a rich fluffy humus soil, in shade or half-shade. The white variety called 'Sweetheart' is a more compact plant, with light green leaves and pure-white flowers.

D. oregana. Low masses of blue-green leaves, about 8 inches high, and 12-inch stems of white flowers feathered with rose. The flowers are rather dull, but *oregana* makes a nice foliage plant for shade in an acid leaf-mold soil.

D. pusilla. "The King of the Japanese Alps." An intriguing plant from the highlands of Japan that is very difficult to grow. Little tufts of lacy, glaucous leaves, 3 or 4 inches high, and short stems bearing 2 or 3 comparatively large pink hearts in May and June. It requires a very gritty, well-drained but moist lime soil, in sun or light shade. It can be propagated by seeds if you are fortunate enough to locate some.

DIMORPHOTHECA (*Compositae,* Daisy Family). The cape-marigolds are colorful flower-garden annuals from South Africa. The one described here has proved hardy at 35 degrees below zero and makes a dandy rock-garden subject.

D. barbariae compacta. Clumps, about 5 inches high, of rather succulent thick leaves and sturdy 12-inch stems, each bearing a single large lavender daisy in May. Well-grown plants form a massive symmetrical bouquet of breath-taking beauty. Easy to grow in a well-drained garden soil, in full sun. Propagation is by seeds, which are rare, and by cuttings in summer.

DIONAEA (*Droseraceae,* Sundew Family). An intriguing little plant from North and South Carolina that is not too hardy in the North but can be carried over winter with heavy protection. *D. muscipula,* the world-famous Venus-flytrap. Small rosettes of flat petioled leaves, with two rounded lobes that snap shut when an insect alights on them. The flower stems are 6 to 10 inches high, with umbels of white flowers in May. While I was in the Marine Corps and stationed at Camp LeJeune, North Carolina, I saw thousands of these interesting plants growing in wet sand at the edges of streams and swamps. In the garden they can be grown in a bog, or at the edge of a pool where the soil is constantly wet. They take sun or light shade. This plant is now protected by the state of North Carolina, where it was formerly collected in great numbers. Propagated by seeds.

DODECATHEON (*Primulaceae,* Primrose Family). A family of little beauties, native to North America, mainly found in the Rockies from Alaska to California. They have colorful cyclamenlike flowers in the spring, ranging in color from bright red-purple to lavendar, rose, and white. The species from the Rocky Mountains are by far the prettiest and best for the rock garden. Unfortunately, they are hard to obtain and difficult to keep for any length of time. They need a peaty or acid leaf-mold soil with excellent drainage, in shade or half-shade. They require ample moisture during the growing season in early spring, and thorough and complete dryness during their dormant period, from July onward. Propagated by divisions.

D. cusickii. Tufts of soft hairy leaves, about 2 inches high, and 6-inch flower stems, nodding umbels of deep-purple flowers with reflexed petals and bright-yellow stamens in a sharp point. Much like a shooting-star. From the northern Rocky Mountains. This seems to be the only western species offered for sale by nurserymen and collectors.

D. meadia. Shooting-Star. Tufts of oval leaves about 6 inches long in flat rosettes, and flower stems, 12 to 18 inches high, bearing umbels of large shooting-stars ranging from purple to rose and white. A native of our eastern woodlands that is comparatively easy to grow. It likes a well-drained, acid leaf-mold soil, in shade. This one likes some moisture even during its dormant season.

DORONICUM (*Compositae,* Daisy Family). Most of the species of leopard's-bane are huge clumps of large leaves, with large bright-yellow daisies, very showy and useful in the perennial border. Propagated by divisions in summer and fall. The following is an excellent rock-garden subject.

D. cordifolium. Clumps of bright shiny-green, heart-shaped leaves, about 3 inches high, and flower stems, 3 to 10 inches high, each with a single large bright-yellow daisy in late April and May. A native of southeastern Europe that is easy to grow in any well-drained garden soil, in full sun.

DOUGLASIA (*Primulaceae,* Primrose Family). Charming tiny cespitose alpines that will test the skill of the best gardener. They require a very gritty, well-drained soil, in full sun. For permanence, the Rocky Mountain species should be planted in a scree composed of stone chips, sand, and a trace of leaf-mold. Propagated by seeds and divisions.

D. laevigata. Tufts of prostrate stems with rosettes of glossy-green leaves, and bright-red flowers held just above the foliage, in May and June. The entire plant is never more than 2 inches high. From the mountains of Washington and Oregon.

D. montana. Little tufts of ciliate leaves in rosettes, topped with large purple flowers in May. Found wild in Montana and Wyoming.

D. vitaliana. A comparatively easy-to-grow species from the Swiss Alps. Little cushions of prostrate stems, tipped with rosettes of tiny light-green leaves, margined and encrusted with pale yellow. Fragrant, clear-light-yellow flowers nestle in the cushion in April and May. Succeeds in a gritty, well-drained lime soil (pH 7–8), in sun or light shade.

DRABA (*Cruciferae,* Mustard Family). A misleading name for a bright and gay family of small cushiony plants, all of which are suited to the rock garden. A few are annual and biennial. Many more species than I have listed here can, and should, be grown in American gardens if seeds or plants can be obtained. Invariably, the Rocky Mountain species must be planted in a scree, in full sun. The European kinds are easier to grow; they will succeed in a well-drained garden soil, in full sun. All the species listed here make adorable evergreen cushions.

D. haynaldii. Cushions of narrow ciliate leaves in open rosettes, about 2 inches high. Thin scapes, about 3 inches high, with narrow-petaled orange-yellow flowers in early April, usually before the last snow is gone. From central Europe.

D. longirostra erioscapa. Dense cushions of tiny, dark-shiny-green leaves in tight rosettes, and little clusters of bright-yellow flowers on thin 3-inch stems, in late April and May. From the mountains of southern Europe.

D. olympica. Dense matty cushions of dark-green leaves in tight rosettes, and clusters of bright-yellow flowers on 3- or 4-inch stems, in late March and April. An easy-to-grow prolific species from Europe that makes an excellent wall and crevice plant.

D. rigida. A tiny plant with little stiff green leaves in tight rosettes, forming cushions an inch or less high. Threadlike stems, about 2 inches long, carry small clusters of yellow flowers in April. A European plant that is not too easy to grow. It should have a scree or well-drained, gritty lime soil (pH 7–8), in full sun. It loves tight rock crevices. I have had it growing in the crack of a concrete wall for years.

D. sibirica. A very quick-growing, mat-forming species from Siberia that is usually listed as *D. repens.* Creeping, trailing, prostrate stems with fairly large soft leaves in loose rosettes. A profusion of bright-yellow flowers on weak stems about 6 inches long, in early spring and again in late fall. It is virtually indifferent to soil composition and exposure, and grows well in fairly dense shade.

DROSERA (*Droseraceae,* Sundew Family). Little insectivorous plants inhabiting sphagnum bogs, mostly in eastern North America, Europe, and Asia. They are easy to grow in a bog garden or at the edge of a pool where they are constantly wet. Plants are usually collected from the wild, but they can be propagated by seeds and divisions. In all species the leaves are covered with thick hairs that are tipped with a globule of a sticky substance that traps tiny flies and other insects. These are gradually assimilated through the leaves as food.

D. filiformis. Tufts of linear threadlike leaves, about 8 inches high. Showy purple flowers in one-sided spikes on stems about 12 inches high, from June to August.

D. intermedia. Long-petioled, spoon-shaped leaves in rosettes about 2 inches high. Numerous small white flowers on 6-inch stems, in July. In this and the following species, the leaf blades curl up around the insects they catch.

D. longifolia. Similar to the preceding, but the petioles are much longer and the leaf blades are very narrow-spatulate. White flowers in July.

D. rotundifolia. I think this species is the prettiest of the lot. It has round leaves on flat petioles about an inch long, in rosettes, and white flowers on stems 6 to 10 inches high, in July. All of these interesting plants glisten when the sun strikes the sticky droplets they exude.

DRYAS (*Rosaceae,* Rose Family). Evergreen creeping shrubby plants, with small leathery leaves resembling those of a miniature oak. They are extremely hardy, permanent, and easy to grow if given a well-drained, acid leaf-mold soil, in full sun or light shade. They make a handsome half-evergreen ground cover if they like their situation. Propagated by cuttings, rooted layers, and seeds.

D. drummondii. This forms mats of bright-shining-green leaves, which are adorned with pale creamy-yellow flowers resembling tiny wild roses. It blooms profusely in May and intermittently throughout the summer. Attractive white feathery seed plumes. Native to northern North America.

D. octopetala. Grows in mats of leathery leaves similar to the preceding, with a prolific display of charming white 8-petaled flowers from May to September. Fluff seed plumes add to its charms. Native to cool regions and high mountains around the world in the northern hemisphere. Var. *minor* is an extremely dwarf form, with tiny crinkly leaves set close together to form a dense cushion, and small white flowers in summer. Var. *tenella* is another dwarf form, somewhat larger than var. *minor* but smaller than the type.

D. suendermannii. This is a hybrid between the two preceding species, with yellow buds that develop into white flowers.

DRYOPTERIS (*Polypodiaceae,* Fern Family). A family of large woodland ferns, native mostly in North America. Some are not too big for the shady rock garden. They are easy to grow in an acid leaf-mold soil (pH 4–6), in shade. Propagated by divisions.

D. hexagonoptera. Broad Beech-Fern. Large triangular fronds, about 18 inches high, in colonies from creeping rootstocks. The fronds are pinnate into pinnatifid toothed segments.

D. linnaeana. Oak-Fern. Colonies of triangular fronds, from 8 to 10 inches high. The fronds are bipinnate with smooth segments.

D. phegopteris. Narrow Beech-Fern. Spreading colonies of narrow triangular fronds, about 8 inches high and 4 or 5 inches wide. The fronds are pinnate into deeply pinnatifid segments.

ECHINOCEREUS (*Cactaceae,* Cactus Family). A large family of small cylindrical or cespitose ball-type cacti, native mostly to the southwestern United States and Mexico, with some extending to the northern Rocky Mountains. Probably more than the one species I describe here would be hardy in the North under ideal conditions.

E. viridiflorus. A very hardy plant from the Dakotas and Wyoming. A soft spiny or bristly cylinder, 2 or 3 inches across and up to 8 inches high. Small greenish-yellow flowers in a ring near the top of the plant, in July. It needs a dry, gravelly or gritty, well-drained soil (pH 6–8), in full sun.

EDRAIANTHUS (*Campanulaceae,* Bellflower Family). Lovely little montanic plants from the Balkans that are natural rock garden subjects. All species can be grown successfully in American rock gardens if seeds can be obtained, but all but two are rare. They come readily from seeds and are easy to grow in a well-drained, gritty lime soil (pH 7–8), in full sun or light shade.

E. kitaibelli. Thick tufts of thin grasslike leaves, about 3 inches high, and long trailing flower stems that radiate from the tuft, each terminating in a large dense cluster of bright violet-blue flowers in June and July.

E. pumilio. A very dwarf species, with narrow 1-inch leaves in dense tufts, and many ascending flower stems, about 3 inches high, each bearing a single large violet-colored flower in May and June.

EMPETRUM (*Empetraceae,* Crowberry Family). A small family of evergreen shrubs, with one species, *E. nigrum,* sparingly used in rock gardens. A decumbent shrub, with tiny evergreen leaves, much resembling the ericas. Small inconspicuous flowers, followed by little black berries in the fall. A native of northern North America that requires an acid, sandy or gravelly, soil with a good top dressing of acid leafmold, and full sun.

EPIGAEA (*Ericaceae,* Heath Family). A family consisting of two species, both coveted rock-garden subjects. Propagated by layers, cuttings, and seeds.

E. asiatica. Trailing or creeping woody stems and large, oval, leathery evergreen leaves, forming a very attractive mat. Clusters of fragrant waxy rosy-pink flowers in late April and May. It is hardy in the North with winter protection. A native of Japan that requires a moist, acid leaf-mold soil (pH 4–6), in shade.

E. repens. Trailing Arbutus. Broad spreading mats of leathery evergreen leaves on creeping woody stems, with numerous clusters of sweetly fragrant, waxy flowers in shades of pink and white, blooming in May. One of our beloved wild flowers, close to the hearts of all who know the eastern United States woodlands. It is permanent and easy to grow if given a well-drained, yet moist, sandy or gravelly, acid leaf-mold soil, in shade or half-shade. Often large stands of this enchanting plant are ravaged by impetuous gardeners and mercenary collectors, who tear up huge clumps and transfer them to exposures and soils that do not suit them and where they quickly die. Old plants are very deeply rooted and are virtually impossible to transplant. If small seedlings are taken, they can be moved with some degree of success. Rooted layers can be taken from old plants and carried over for a full year in pots plunged in a cold frame. When they are firmly established in pots, they can be moved to the garden, where they must be watched and watered conscientiously for the first year. If allowed to dry out, even for a short period, they are lost.

EPIMEDIUM (*Berberidaceae,* Barberry Family). These are among the most decorative and useful plants for a shady rock garden. They are easy to grow, extremely hardy, long-

Epigaea repens, the coveted "Trailing Arbutus."

lived, and dependable. They will thrive under trying conditions and solve difficult planting problems. For example, they are about the only plants I have seen in happy association with the ravenous roots of a huge maple. They will tolerate almost any soil from a light, porous, acid, leaf-mold to a heavy, clay loam, but they prefer a deep, rich, light, peaty or humus-rich soil. They prefer shade but will stand full sun almost as well. When massed, they make a most striking ground cover. They also make wonderful wall-garden plants where they get only a minimum of full sunshine. They can be increased quite rapidly by divisions in early spring.

In all species the leaves are basal, rising on stiff wiry petioles and compounded into small irregularly heart-shaped segments. They look soft, graceful, and lacy but are stiff and leathery to the touch. Although not evergreen, the leaves are persistent in sheltered positions. In the fall, they take on delightful tints of pink and red, and are liked in floral arrangements. The flowers are as elegant as the foliage, being produced in broad airy sprays just above the leaves, in April and May.

E. alpinum rubrum. Masses of lovely red-margined leaves, about 10 inches high, with short-spurred flowers, red on the outside and creamy-yellow within. From Europe.

E. grandiflorum. Dainty triternate foliage, and broad sprays of long-spurred, rosy-red flowers in April, on 10-inch stems. This species is usually sold as 'Rosy Queen.' From the woodlands of Japan.

E. pinnatum. Spreading masses of ornamental foliage about 15 inches high, from slowly creeping rootstocks. Masses of bright-yellow flowers in early spring. Var. *elegans* has larger bright-yellow flowers. Var. *sulphureum* has pale-yellow blooms. From Persia and the Caucasus.

E. youngianum. Hortus II refers the varieties listed here to *E. grandiflorum,* but they are entirely different from that species. They have finer-textured, daintier leaves in more compact clumps, from 12 to 15 inches high, and the flowers are heavier with very short spurs. The tiny individual flowers are like miniature daffodils. They bloom much longer than *grandiflorum,* from late April to the middle of June. Var.

niveum has masses of pure-white flowers, and var. *violaceum* has light-violet blooms.

ERICA (*Ericaceae,* Heath Family). A most interesting ornamental and useful family of evergreen shrubs, native to Europe and southern Africa. The tall tree heaths of southern Europe and southern Africa are not hardy with us. We can grow only the little creeping or depressed shrubs from the northern reaches of their range. However the color forms and varieties are numerous and divergent so that we do not lack ideal plants for rock garden. The tall large-flowered South African heaths are the source of the "Scotch heather" sold as cut flowers.

All the heaths require a light, acid, leaf-mold or peaty soil (pH 4–6). They grow best and flower best in full sun but will stand some light shade. Although all the kinds listed here are reasonably hardy, winter protection is essential to prevent dehydration and windburn. The pleasure derived from these remarkable plants is well worth a little effort to assure their well-being through severe winters. They should be mulched heavily with pine needles or peat moss at the base and covered over completely with evergreen boughs or salt hay.

E. carnea. A well-known European plant forming great patches on the moors of England, the sandy wastelands of Germany, and elsewhere. Creeping or trailing prostrate branches, covered with tiny leaves closely set in whorls of four, making dense carpets about 12 inches high. Individual plants will spread to many feet across. The red-purple flowers of the typical wild plant grow on one-sided terminal spikes. They begin to open in late January or February and come into full bloom in late March and April. The type is probably not much in cultivation but is represented by many named horticultural forms. 'King George' has deep-pink flowers and begins to bloom in early March. 'Ruby Glow' is a compact dwarf in the form of a low rounded bush, and has bright ruby-red flowers that begin to open in late March. 'Snow Queen' is an extremely dwarf, slow-growing plant with light green foliage. It is a prolific bloomer, with white flowers opening early in January even in very cold climates. 'Springwood' is a quickly-spreading form with long trailing stems, and long spikes of bright-clear-pink flowers from February to April. 'Springwood White' is like the preceding, but has white flowers and light green foliage. 'Vivelli' is a tight close grower, with dark-reddish-green foliage, and very dark-red flowers in March. 'Winter Beauty' has restricted growth in a rounded bush form, and bronze foliage in winter. The flowers are borne in short spikes and are rosy red.

E. cinerea. Twisted Heath. Close masses of ascending twisted branches about 18 inches high, covered with fine glossy-green leaves, make this one of the handsomest of the heaths. The little bell-shaped flowers are borne in terminals from June to September and have a glistening satiny tone. Var. *alba* has pure-white flowers. 'Atrorubens' has glowing crimson flowers. 'Domino' has white flowers with black anthers, a striking combination. 'Golden Drop' is a semiprostrate form, with lilac flowers and golden foliage. 'Violacea' has glistening deep-violet flowers. There are other named forms that I am not too familiar with.

E. darleyensis. A hybrid between *E. carnea* and *E. Mediterranea.* It grows in a compact globose form, about 2 feet high. Rosy-lavender flowers in great quantities begin to appear in November and continue to bloom all winter, reaching their peak in late March or early April.

E. mackaii plena. A hybrid between *E. tetralix* and *E. ciliaris.* This species has soft downy leaves, crowded on thin trailing stems to form a fluffy billowy carpet. It has little terminal clusters of fully-double urn-shaped waxy-pink flowers from June to August. It is not too hardy but can stand our winters with heavy cover.

E. tetralix. Cross Heath. Little mounds of prostrate branches with ascending tips, covered with soft downy dark-gray-green foliage. Large showy clusters of rosy flowers with the aspect of fine porcelain, from late June to November. Var. *mollis* is a dwarf upright grower, with light-gray-green soft fluffy foliage, and clusters of pure-white flowers throughout the summer.

Erica tetralix mollis.

E. vagans. Cornish Heath. A sturdy upright grower, with stiff stems covered with fine-textured foliage in a symmetrical globose form, 12 to 18 inches high. It displays heavy whorls of lavender-pink flowers at the tips of the branches, from early June to the end of October. Var. *alba* has white flowers with protruding brown anthers. Var. *nana* is a very dwarf form, growing in a tight little ball about 6 inches high, and bearing white flowers. 'Mrs. D. F. Maxwell' has outstanding deep-pink flowers all summer. 'St. Kevern' has lovely clear-rose-pink blooms.

E. williamsii. A hybrid between *E. tetralix* and *E. vagans.* Attractive soft light-green foliage in a billowy spreading mound, about 6 inches high. The new growth is always tinted with pink and gold. Lovely rose-pink urn-shaped flowers in close terminal spikes, from late June through summer.

ERIGERON (*Compositae,* Daisy Family). Little perennial plants, resembling small wild asters. They are mostly native to the Rocky Mountains, and many more than those I have listed here are exceptionally fine rock-garden plants. They can be grown quite easily from seeds when these are obtainable. Those listed, and all other Rocky Mountain species, require a very well-drained, sandy, gritty, or gravelly soil (pH 6–8). They like a hot, dry, sunny location.

E. compositus. Little tufts of crowded dissected woolly gray leaves, about 3 inches high, and solitary white-rayed flowers about an inch across, on swaying 6-inch stems, in May and June.

E. flagellaris. Little tufts of narrowly spatulate light-green leaves, about 2 inches high. The plant sends out long decumbent stems that root down at the tips to form new plants, thus spreading into thin mats. Tiny white daisies are borne on fragile 6-inch stems through most of the summer.

E. glaucus. Beach Aster. Little clumps or rosettes of long oval glaucous leaves, and 10-inch flower stems, bearing solitary light-violet daisies, about an inch and a half across, in May and June.

E. leiomerus. Neat rosettes of bright-green leaves almost flat on the ground, and 5-inch stems, displaying solitary deep-violet daisies in summer.

E. nanus. Dense little tufts of thin gray-green woolly grassy leaves, and thin stems, bearing tiny white daisies in May and June.

E. pinnatisectus. A lovely little plant, with light-green bipinnatifid leaves in tight little tufts, about an inch high, and charming lavender-blue yellow-centered daisies on 3-inch stems, in May and June.

E. trifidus. Little tufts of narrow woolly gray leaves, with the tips divided into three segments. White flowers on 4-inch stems, in May and June.

ERINUS (*Scrophulariaceae,* Figwort Family). A small plant from the European Alps, *E. alpinus.* Little tufts of soft-green leaves, about an inch high, and a profusion of purple flowers on thin stems, 6 to 10 inches high, from May to July. There are several named color forms, the most popular being 'Dr. Hanella' with rosy-red flowers. A temperamental little plant that needs a partially shaded position, in extremely well-drained, gritty, lime soil (pH 7–8). It does best when placed in a tight crevice on the face of a rock. Self-seeds freely when in proximity to receptive rocks.

ERIOGONUM (*Polygonaceae,* Knotweed Family). An American family of odd but interesting and decorative plants, ranging from tiny perennials to tall shrubs. Most of them have woolly gray leaves, and clusters of small yellow flowers in late spring and summer. They are native to hot, dry, sunny places in the Rocky Mountains, and will succeed in a rock garden only when planted in a sunny scree. They are propagated by divisions and cuttings, and by seeds.

E. flavum. Mats of long narrow white woolly leaves in rosettes on creeping stems. Tight umbels of bright-yellow flowers, nestled in white woolly involucres on 8-inch stems, in June and July.

E. ovalifolium. A dense mat of tiny oval leaves, covered with white tomentum like the finest velvet. Dense clusters of bright-yellow flowers on 3-inch stems, in June and July. Will grow only in a hot sunny scree.

E. subalpinum. Sulphur Plant. This is the easiest species to grow. It will do well in a sunny situation in a well-drained garden soil, where it forms neat mats of long-petioled spatulate leaves, in rosettes, on creeping stems. It has lovely pale-sulphur-yellow flowers, in compact umbels on 6-inch stems, from May to the end of July.

ERIOPHYLLUM (*Compositae,* Daisy Family). A small family of gray-leaved plants, native to the Pacific coast. The perennial species are not too tall for large rock gardens, and the following is quite popular, and deservedly so.

E. lanatum. Oregon Sunshine. Large spreading clumps of small denticulate white woolly leaves, about 6 inches high, and numerous flower stems, 12 to 18 inches high, displaying masses of small bright-orange-yellow daisy flowers in late May and June. It is easy to grow in a well-drained garden soil, in full sun. Propagated easily by divisions, cuttings in summer, and seeds.

ERITRICHIUM (*Boraginaceae,* Borage Family). Tiny cespitose plants, with bright-blue flowers, native to cold climates and high mountains in the northern hemisphere. They are difficult to impossible to grow. Cultivated to a degree for years, mainly in England and in the Pacific northwest, where growing conditions are ideal. Although perennial, the plants are most often grown as biennial. They are usually grown from seeds and carried over the first winter in pots in a cold greenhouse. They are then planted in the garden in spring, where they bloom profusely, then die.

E. nanum. A densely tufted plant, with tiny white woolly linear leaves, and 3-inch flower stems, with clusters of brilliant-blue flowers, each with a bright-yellow eye.

ERODIUM (*Geraniaceae,* Cranesbill Family). An interesting family, usually with most attractive delicate ferny foliage, and sprays of small flowers in white, pink, red, and purple. Some species are quite weedy, but a few are very good rock-garden plants. They are all easy to grow in ordinary garden soil (pH 6–8), in sun or light shade. Propagation is usually by seeds—sometimes, with difficulty, by divisions.

E. chamaedryoides. A very low dense mat of wavy large green leaves, studded with pink-veined white flowers all summer. Var. *roseum* has pink flowers, veined with red. Var. *flore-pleno* has both fully-double and single dark-pink flowers. A desirable plant but not reliably hardy in the North, where it requires heavy winter cover.

E. cheilanthifolium. Fluffy clumps of soft ferny gray-green leaves, about 8 inches high, with open sprays of white flowers, veined with rose, in May and June.

E. macradenum. Mounds of green filigree leaves, about 12 inches high, and large light-purple flowers, spotted with deeper purple. Var. *roseum* has pink flowers.

ERYSIMUM (*Cruciferae,* Mustard Family). Mostly annual and biennial species of rather tall sprawling growth, related to the wall flowers. A few cespitose kinds, one of which is an ideal rock-garden plant. All are easy to grow in a well-drained, gritty lime soil (pH 7–8), in full sun or very light shade. They are well adapted to tight rock crevices and wall gardens. Easily propagated by divisions and seeds.

E. kotschyanum. Tiny denticulate pale-gray-green leaves in tight rosettes, which form dense cushions 3 or 4 inches high. Short stems with clusters of bright-yellow, extremely fragrant flowers in early spring.

E. linifolium. Dense clumps of long linear leaves, about 6 inches high, topped with clusters of beautiful mauve flowers in April and May.

EUONYMUS (*Celastraceae,* Staff-Tree Family). Most species are large shrubs or large fast-growing vines that are widely used in general landscape work. The following two forms are useful in the rock garden. Propagated by cuttings, and easily grown in any good garden soil (pH 6–8), in sun or shade, but they prefer shade.

E. fortune minimus. (Often listed as *E. kewensis*) Very small green leaves, veined with white, on vinelike wiry stems. Somewhat tenacious, it will cling to rocks or walls. It can also be used as a limited ground cover.

E. japonicus nanus. An evergreen shrub, with close-growing stiff upright branches in a dense columnar form, usually less than 24 inches high. It is not hardy north of Philadelphia, but will stand up well farther north if planted in a sheltered position and well protected.

EUPHORBIA (*Euphorbiaceae,* Spurge Family). A large family, widely distributed throughout the world. In form, it varies from tiny creeping plants to small trees. Several species are used extensively in rock gardens, but two of the most common ones, cypress spurge (*E. cyparissias*) and flowering spurge (*E. corollata*), should be avoided at all costs. Although they are usually given away by well-wishing neighbors, they are among the most troublesome of weeds. They creep by thick underground runners and quickly take over large portions of the garden. Furthermore, once established, these plants can never be completely eradicated, because each tiny bit of root left in the soil will produce new plants. The ones whose descriptions follow behave themselves and can be used with pleasing results. They are propagated by seeds, and do well in any well-drained garden soil, in full sun.

E. epithmoides. (Usually listed as *E. polychrome*) A large plant, to 1 foot high, with woody stems, forming a broad mound of long narrow oval leaves, with huge flower bracts in early spring colored a lovely light-chrome-yellow.

E. myrsinites. A very robust plant, with long thick trailing stems and small fleshy bluish leaves. It suggests a monstrous *Seum sieboldii.* Large pale-yellow flower bracts in April and May. An outstanding plant when allowed to spread over large dry rocks.

FESTUCA (*Gramineae,* Grass Family). Common meadow and lawn grasses called fescue. The one described is sometimes used in gardens.

F. ovina glauca. (Usually listed as *F. glauca*) Clumps or tufts, to 2 feet high, of ordinary grass leaves of an attractive blue color. It is sometimes used as a filler in rock gardens and, extensively, as an edging for flower beds.

FILIPENDULA (*Rosaceae,* Rose Family). Very large attractive perennial plants, native to moist meadows in the North Temperate Zone around the world. The two described here are not too big for a rock garden and are easily grown in a rich, moist, acid loam (pH 5–7), in sun or light shade. Both are propagated by divisions, and *F. hexapetala* also by tubers.

F. hexapetala flore-pleno. Long ferny leaves that lie flat on the ground to form a thick mat that is evergreen in sheltered positions. The flower stems emerge from the center of the plant in late June and July and bear huge clusters of small double white flowers like fluffy snowballs. A plant from Europe that is extremely attractive, both in foliage and bloom.

F. palmata nana. Serrated, palmately-lobed leaflets that form an attractive low mound, and 15-inch stems that bear flat-topped clusters of clear-pink flowers from June to September. A Siberian plant that is outstanding for its long midsummer blooming period.

FORSYTHIA (*Oleaceae,* Olive Family). Everyone knows these golden-bell bushes, with their masses of bright-yellow flowers early in spring. The form described was recently introduced by the Bronx Botanical Garden, and is well adapted to rock-garden use. It is easily grown in any garden soil, in sun or light shade. Propagation is by soft cuttings in June, or by hardwood cuttings in winter.

F. viridissima bronxensis. Thin arching branches that form slowly spreading mounds about 12 inches high, and large yellow flowers in early spring when the big forsythias flower.

FRAGARIA (*Rosaceae,* Rose Family). While a rock garden is not the place to raise strawberries, two species are sometimes used. They have attractive foliage and growing habits, and they produce showy flowers and attractive delicious fruits. Both are propagated by seeds or divisions, and are easy to grow in any good garden soil (pH 5–7), in sun or light shade.

F. daltoniana. A Himalayan species, with small dark-glossy-green leaves, forming a dense mat 2 or 3 inches high. Large solitary white flowers, and bright-scarlet fruits. It spreads rapidly by long threadlike runners to form a nice ground cover.

F. vesca. An everbearing, noncreeping alpine strawberry, from the mountains of western Europe. Neat clumps of three-parted leaves, about 8 inches high. Showy white flowers in airy sprays, followed by small but delicious bright-red berries. It flowers and fruits continuously from June to November.

GALAX (*Diapensiaceae,* Diapensia Family). One species, native to the woodlands from Virginia to Georgia, *G. aphylla.* Large, leathery, glossy-green, rounded leaves on stiff petioles that emerge from creeping underground stolons. In time, it forms a wide mass of foliage that is unexcelled as a ground cover under rhododendrons and in other very shady places. It has small spikes of white flowers on wands about 18 inches high, in June. The foliage turns a beautiful bronze in fall. It requires a moist shady position, in an acid leaf-mold soil (pH 4–6).

GALIUM (*Rubiaceae,* Madder Family). A family of rather coarse weedy plants, sometimes grown in wild gardens and perennial borders. The species described here, from Europe, is not too offensive to be used in a rock garden.

G. verum. Tiny light-green leaves in whorls on square stems that trail to form a thick carpet, and airy sprays of golden-yellow flowers in June and July. It makes a good ground cover or wall plant, but is invasive and must be confined. Easy to grow in ordinary garden soil (pH 6–8), in shade or light shade.

GAULTHERIA (*Ericaceae,* Heath Family). A family of interesting and useful dwarf trailing, or creeping, shrubs for planting in mild climates. Only one is definitely hardy in the North. They are all acid-lovers, and do best in a moist, sandy, peaty, or leaf-mold soil (pH 4–6), in shade or part shade. They are propagated by divisions, sometimes by cuttings.

G. procumbens. The wintergreen or teaberry is a common sight in northeastern United States woodlands. The creeping underground runners produce mats of small leathery, dark-green evergreen leaves, about 3 inches high. Nodding white bell-shaped flowers in spring are followed by large bright-red berries. This plant was once the source of wintergreen flavoring.

GAYLUSSACIA (*Ericaceae,* Heath Family). Huckleberry bushes, native to the woodlands of eastern United States mountains. With the exception of the one listed below, all are large deciduous shrubs.

G. brachysera. The box huckleberry is a beautiful evergreen ground-cover shrub, about 6 inches high, that spreads by underground runners. It makes a solid sheet of small dark glossy-green leaves that turn a rich bronze in fall. New growth is bright crimson. A rare and coveted species, from isolated places in western Pennsylvania and West Virginia, that flowers and berries sparsely. It requires an acid leaf-mold soil (pH 4–6), in sun or shade. The leaves hold a nice red color all year when grown in full sun.

GENISTA (*Leguminosae,* Pea Family). Old and ornamental shrubs, separated from the *Cytisus* because of technical differences in the structure of the seed pod. All species like a rather dry situation in a sandy or gravelly, well-drained soil, in full sun. They grow equally well in acid and alkaline soil. Propagation is by seeds that germinate quite readily, and by cuttings.

G. delphinensis. A little mat of prostrate leafless straplike branches that are dark green and broadly winged, and short upright flower stems, bearing clusters of bright-yellow flowers in May and June. A rare and extremely slow-growing plant that looks like a miniature *G. sagittalis* and may be a form of it.

G. germanica. A compact evergreen flat-topped shrub, 10 to 15 inches high, with small persistent leaves and very spiny, dark-green branches. One of the few brooms that retains its leaves for any length of time. In May and June, it is completely covered with a mass of vivid-yellow flowers. A fast and easy grower that tolerates some shade and makes an excellent wall plant.

G. hispanica. An intricate mass of slender, spring-green branches, about 2 feet high, with yellow flowers in terminal heads in June and July. A Spanish plant that requires winter protection north of Philadelphia.

G. horrida. Similar to the above, but with stiff, gnarled, spiny branches about 12 inches high. Bright-yellow flowers in

June and July. A somewhat tender plant from France and Spain.

G. pilosa. A decumbent or semiprostrate mass of slender silky silvery-gray spineless branches, with minute leaves and clouds of clear-yellow flowers from May to July. A hardy European species that is useful for hot, dry, rock crevices and for wall gardens.

G. sagittalis. A quick-growing mat of broadly winged prostrate branches. The flower stems are about 10 inches high, upright, each with a cluster of bright-yellow flowers in May and June. A very hardy plant from the Balkans, and most striking when it is permitted to tumble over hot, dry rocks.

G. sylvestris. A rare and lovely plant from Dalmatia, with slender spiny green stems, forming dense mounds about 6 inches high. In July and August, it is covered with pure-golden-yellow flowers. Var. *pungens* is more spiny and a bit more dwarf.

G. villarsii. A tiny and extremely slow-growing plant, from central Europe. It forms a clump of spineless silky gray-green leafless stems, about 3 inches high, and produces bright-yellow flowers in May and June. Requires a very gritty or sandy, extremely well-drained soil, in full sun.

GENTIANA (*Gentianaceae,* Gentian Family). The gentians, with their rich-blue flowers, top the list of plants sought by the rock gardener. The genus contains about 300 species around the world in the North Temperate Zone. They are found growing at sea level and on high alpine peaks, in varying exposures of sunlight, and under widely divergent soil conditions. Yet, unlike other widely distributed plants, they are among the most difficult to grow and maintain in the garden. Even in prescribed soil mixtures and exposures, they often fail.

I have found that in some gardens almost all the species tried grow with luxuriant foliage and produce an abundance of flowers. In other gardens, even the easiest growers are almost impossible to maintain. I am convinced that climatic conditions are the most important factor in their cultivation. If the garden is in a favorable situation, the blue of the gentian is displayed with wanton abandon. I write this, not to discourage the rock gardener, but to warn him of the vagaries of this genus.

The species listed below are among the easiest to grow in the United States and, if the soil recommendations are followed, there should be some degree of success. There are other kinds that can, and should, be tried by the enterprising rock gardener. Propagation is usually by seeds (sown as soon as they are ripe), sometimes by divisions, and rarely by cuttings.

G. acaulis. This is the prized gentian of the Swiss Alps. It forms low evergreen mats of short broad leaves, about 1 inch high. Clear-blue flowers, as much as 3 inches long, open right on top of the mat in April and May. This plant likes a rich, acid to neutral, gravelly loam (pH 5–7), in sun or light shade. A cool root run and good drainage are essential. At low elevations, it must be shaded during the hottest part of the day. Under favorable conditions, it grows into broad dense mats, and produces as many as 50 brilliant-blue flowers to a square foot. Var. *gigantea* and var. *clusii* are often listed, but I cannot see much difference between these and the typical form.

G. andrewsi. A rather coarse plant, from the eastern part of North America. It has stout upright stems about 24 inches high, with long oval leaves, and small deep-purple-blue flowers in clusters at the top of the plant. Because the flowers never open fully, it is called the closed or bottle gentian. It grows in sun (sometimes in dense shade) in moist, gravelly, acid soil (pH 5–6).

G. autumnale. Often listed as *G. porphyrio.* Glistening deep-violet-blue flowers on thin wiry stems about 8 inches high, in September and October. When not in bloom, the plant is scarcely noticed. It consists of two or three very thin stems, with a few thin grasslike leaves. This charmer from the New Jersey pine barrens requires a moist, sandy, acid soil (pH 4–6), in sun or light shade. Var. *albescens* is a rare and singularly lovely white-flowered form.

G. calycosa. Trailing or decumbent stems, to 1 foot, emerge from a crown of small ovate leaves, each terminated with a large deep-blue flower, spotted with green, in June and July. A native of wet peat bogs in the Rocky Mountains. It requires a wet peat-moss soil (pH 4–5), in sun or light shade.

G. decumbens. Clusters of small clear-deep-blue flowers on decumbent stems, to 10 inches high, in June and July. An easy and showy summer bloomer from the Himalayas, that likes a rich, gravelly, acid loam (pH 5–6), in sun or light shade.

G. gracilipes. Rosettes of long narrow leaves, with 10-inch flower stems, terminating in loose clusters of small purple-blue flowers in July and August. An easy grower from China, that requires a well-drained, gravelly, acid loam, in sun or light shade.

G. kurroo. A tufted plant with linear leaves, and stems about 6 inches high, bearing small blue flowers, spotted with white on the inside. A summer bloomer from the Himalayas, that likes a rich, gravelly, acid loam, in sun or light shade.

G. macaulayi. An English hybrid that is a creeper, with long fragile stems and rather fleshy, very pale-green linear leaves. Very large clear-bright-blue flowers are borne toward the ends of the long trailing stems from August to October. This very desirable plant requires light shade, in a moist but very well-drained, gravelly, acid loam (pH 5–6).

G. purdomii. An erect plant, about 10 inches high, with tufts of thin leaves, and bearing tight clusters of dark-purple-blue flowers in June and July. I found this plant quite easy to grow in a rich, well-drained, garden loam (pH 5–7), in light shade.

G. scabra. A sturdy plant with large oval leaves on rather stiff stems, about 12 inches high, with large dark-blue flowers in terminal clusters in August and September. A native of China and Japan that likes a rich, acid to neutral, gravelly loam (pH 5–7), in sun or light shade. Apparently, there are several forms of this plant in cultivation. Seeds from different sources produce plants in a variety of forms.

G. septemfida. Small ovate leaves, very closely set on square stems that are somewhat erect, or decumbent, to 18 inches long. Lovely clear-dark-blue flowers in large terminal clusters in June and July. This Asian species requires a moist, well-drained, gravelly, rich, acid loam (pH 5–6), in a lightly shaded location. Var. *lagodechiana* has thin prostrate stems and large solitary flowers.

G. sikokiana. Probably the best of the gentians for novice rock gardeners. It makes a very attractive billowy low mound of small pointed leaves on long trailing stems. Very large light-blue flowers along the stems, in September and October. Two-year-old plants have as many as 75 flowers at one time. Very easy to grow in a well-drained, acid to neutral, garden soil (pH 5–7), in sun or light shade.

G. sino-ornata. A stoloniferous plant, similar in habit of growth and requirements to *G. macaulayi.* It forms a loose, quickly spreading mat of fragile pale-green leaves. The large trumpet flowers, produced from July to hard frost, are bright blue, striped with white and cream. This Chinese plant must have a constantly moist but well-drained, rich, gravelly, acid soil (pH 5–6), in light shade. It will not endure prolonged direct sunlight.

G. verna. A most difficult plant from the Swiss Alps. Tufts of small oval leaves, about 3 inches high, almost hidden by a mass of brilliant-blue starry flowers in early spring. The only success I ever had with it was under acidic moraine conditions.

GERANIUM (*Geraniaceae,* Cranesbill Family). A genus of colorful spring and summer-flowering plants, with many hardy dwarf kinds that are suitable for rock gardens. These are not to be confused with the florists' geraniums, which are pelargoniums, a close relative. Although many species of geranium are suited to rock work, only a few are generally available. I have had experience with those listed here and have found them rewarding subjects. They are easy to grow in ordinary garden soil (pH 6–8), in sun or light shade. They are generally easy to propagate by root divisions at almost any time of the year.

G. cinereum. Glaucous, five-parted leaves in mounds about 6 inches high, with large pink flowers, striped with red, produced all summer. Var. *subcaulescens* has deeper colored flowers with a very dark eye. An extremely desirable plant from the Balkans.

G. *endressii.* A charmer from the Pyrenees, with showy rose-colored flowers. Clumps more than 15 inches high of deeply-lobed leaves in June and July.

G. *grandiflorum.* Broad clumps of large maplelike leaves, about 15 inches high, with huge satiny two-toned lavender and purple flowers in May and June. Var. *alpinum* is a smaller form from China, about 10 inches high.

G. *iberidium.* A plant from China, with large deeply-lobed leaves in clumps about 18 inches high. Large glistening deep-purple flowers in May and June.

G. *macrorrhizum.* Decorative five-parted leaves in large mounds about 18 inches high, and bright-magenta flowers from June to September.

G. *maculatum.* A somewhat invasive, rather tall American native that is useful in a wild garden. Broad spreading clumps of maplelike leaves, about 24 inches high, and masses of attractive lavender flowers in May. It is a common sight at the edges of eastern United States woodlands in spring. The pure-white form, var. *album,* is rare and quite desirable.

G. *pylzowianum.* This tiny plant with the unwieldy name comes from China. Tiny five-parted leaves on thin stems that form a loose spreading mat about 3 inches high. Comparatively huge delicate rose-colored flowers on thin 5-inch stems, in May and June.

G. *renardii.* A recent discovery in the Caucasus. An attractive plant, with large velvety gray-green leaves in neat clumps about 12 inches high. Loose clusters of large very pale-pink flowers, veined with dark-red, in June and July.

G. *sanguineum.* The most common representative of the geraniums in the rock garden. Broad spreading mounds of attractive sharp-pointed, five-lobed leaves, about 12 inches high, liberally adorned with large bright-red-purple flowers from late May to October. A very low compact form that is never more than two or three inches high is var. *nanum.* Var. *prostratum* is the form usually listed as *G. lancastriensis.* It has long decumbent or trailing stems that form dense

Geranium sanguineum "lancastriensis."

mats 4 or 5 inches high, and a profusion of rose-pink flowers, veined with red.

GEUM (*Rosaceae,* Rose Family). A genus of herbaceous perennials, some attractive and quite showy. Others are dull weedy plants. The tall fancy named garden forms, mostly derived from *G. chiloensis,* are generally too overpowering for the rock garden. There are a number of species that are extremely good for rock work, but only a few are available to American gardeners. They are quite easy to grow if they are given a rather rich, moist, acid to neutral, loamy soil (pH 5–7), in full sun. Almost all the species are native to moist meadows and the edges of bogs. Propagation is by seeds and, usually quite easily, by divisions.

G. borisii. A hybrid of European origin that forms broad clumps, about 6 inches high, of large heart-shaped leaves. Masses of bright-orange-yellow flowers are produced on stems 12 to 15 inches high in May and June, and again in fall.

G. montanum. Large bright-yellow flowers on 6-inch stems, in May and June, over low mounds of large heart-shaped leaves. An easy-to-grow plant from Europe.

G. rossii. Low mats of coarsely pinnate leaves produced from creeping rootstocks. Small golden-yellow flowers on stems 8 to 10 inches high, in July. An arctic plant that likes a cool moist soil.

G. turinatum. Spreading mats of attractive feathery foliage and short flower stems, carrying small yellow flowers in June and July. A native of upland meadows in the Rocky Mountains.

G. 'X Waight Brilliant.' Tiny mounds of typical geum leaves, about 3 inches high, and 6-inch flower stems, bearing bright-orange-red flowers all summer. About the smallest and showiest geum for the rock garden.

GLOBULARIA (*Globulariaceae,* Globe Daisy Family). A small genus in a small family, but rich in rewards for the rock gardener. All species are native to southern Europe and Asia Minor. However, they are reliably hardy in the North and easy to grow in any ordinary garden soil (pH 6–8), in sun or light shade. They are readily propagated by divisions, and *G. trichosantha* also by seeds.

G. bellidifolia. Compact buns, only an inch or two high, of tiny dark-green evergreen leaves. Dainty little light-blue puffball flowers on 3-inch stems, in May.

G. cordifolia. Small heart-shaped leaves on creeping woody stems that form a lovely evergreen mat about 2 inches high. Fluffy light-blue flowers on stems 4 or 5 inches high, in May and June. A desirable and unusual ground cover for limited areas.

G. incanescens. Little mounds of orbicular light-green leaves, about 3 inches high, and light-blue globe flowers on 4-inch stems, in May. Similar to *G. bellidifolia,* but the leaves are of a lighter texture.

G. repens. Tiny compact cushions of short creeping stems, covered with leaves barely an eighth of an inch long. Bluish-white globe flowers about half an inch across, on 3-inch stems, in May. A dainty plant for rock and sink gardens.

G. trichosantha. A herbaceous species, with dull green spatulate leaves, that grows in tufts about 4 inches high; and stout flower stems, 8 to 10 inches high, with rather large, light-blue globe daisies in May and June. A very profuse bloomer.

GOODYERA (*Orchidaceae,* Orchid Family). Interesting terrestrial orchids, native to eastern woodlands of the United States. The flowers do not amount to much, but the leaves are pretty in deep shady locations. These plants are usually taken from the wild and transferred to the shade garden. They can be moved successfully if all the roots are taken up and the plants are placed in a situation similar to that of their wild home. They need a moist, acid, leaf-mold soil (pH 4–5), in constant shade.

G. pubescens. The downy rattlesnake plantain has five or six leaves, about 3 inches long, in a flat rosette. The leaves are dark green, veined and netted with white, and covered with soft down. Small white flowers are produced on 15-inch stems, in June and July.

Goodyera pubescens.

G. repens. Similar to *G. pubescens,* but the leaves are smaller and the white netting is not as pronounced. It has creeping rootstocks that form an open colony of small flat rosettes.

GYPSOPHILA (*Caryophyllaceae,* Pink Family). Generally, big sprawly plants with few leaves and masses of tiny flowers, but the small mountain kinds make excellent rock-garden subjects and are easy to grow in a well-drained garden soil (pH 6–8), in sun or light shade. Propagation is by seeds and cuttings, sometimes by divisions.

G. cerastioides. A little creeping plant from the Himalayas that makes tight inch-high mats of small downy light-green leaves. Very short flower stems, displaying clusters of red-

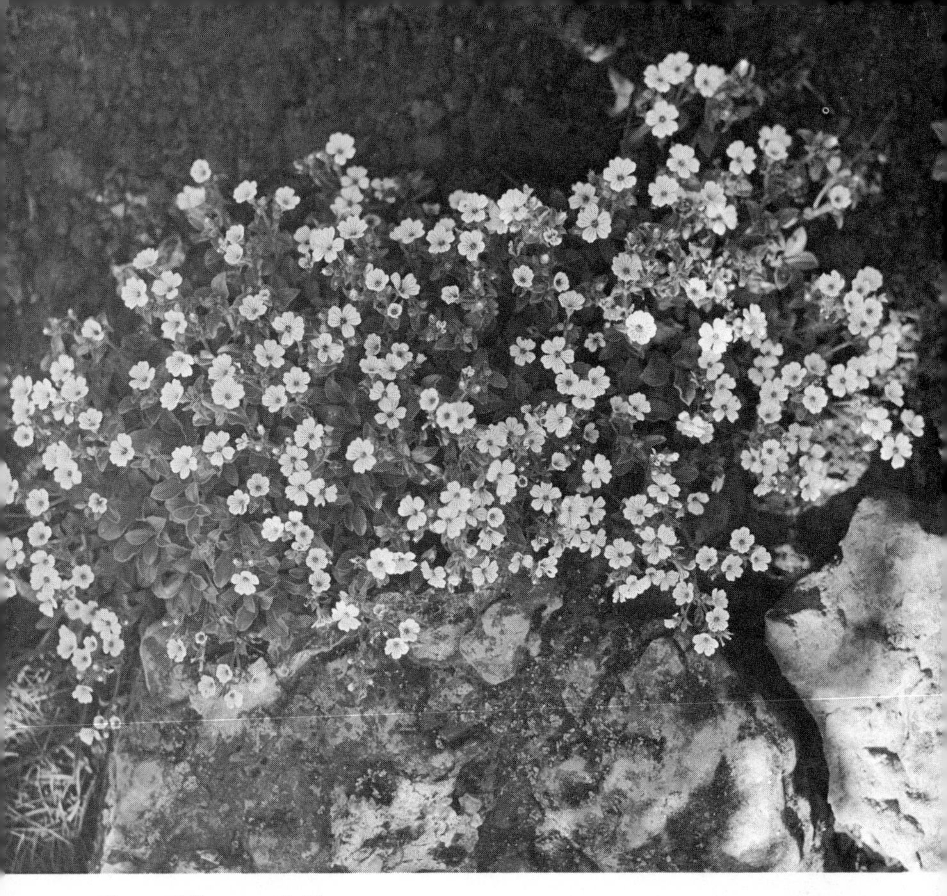

Gypsophila cerastioides.

veined white flowers in May. It needs heavy winter protection in the North.

G. fratensis. Probably a form of *G. repens.* Prostrate trailing stems with narrow, rather fleshy, glaucous leaves that form a dense semievergreen mat. Clouds of dainty shell-pink flowers just above the foliage from May to September. An excellent wall-garden plant.

G. repens. Like *G. fratensis* but a little faster in growth, with white flowers that turn pinkish with age.

HABERLEA (*Gesneriaceae,* African Violet Family). A small genus of European mountain plants that are difficult to grow but most rewarding when success is achieved.

H. rhodopensis. Neat flat rosettes of small thick oval hairy leaves that form compact colonies in shaded rock crevices. It has 4-inch stems, with rosy-lilac flowers in May and June. The flowers, as much as 1 inch across, resemble those of the African violet. It must be grown in a vertical rock crevice, in shade, in acid, leaf-mold soil (pH 5–6).

HEBE (*Scrophulariaceae,* Figwort Family). A large genus of evergreen New Zealand shrubs that are grown extensively in southern California and a few on the north Pacific coast. Most of them are not hardy in the North, but southern gardeners should find them interesting. The species described is hardy in the North, having withstood temperatures of 30 degrees below zero without apparent damage.

H. decumbens. A small evergreen shrub that forms an attractive compact mound, 12 to 15 inches high, with small gray-green leaves edged with red. It has white flowers in short dense spikes in May. Propagated from cuttings and easy to grow in a well-drained, gravelly, lime soil (pH 7–8), in full sun. An outstanding, rare, and unusual accent plant for any rock garden.

HEDERA (*Araliaceae,* Ginseng Family). Evergreen shrubs or climbing vines, typified by the well-known English Ivy. A few dwarf forms, useful in the rock garden, are listed here. These are best grown in a rich, moist, acid to neutral, loam (pH 5–7), in shade or filtered sunlight. They are propagated by cuttings taken at almost any time of the year and placed in water, sand, or directly in soil.

H. colchica. A slowly climbing vine from Persia, with thick, leathery, unlobed, heart-shaped leaves that are lightly veined with white and mottled with bronze in winter. Reliably hardy in the North if planted in a sheltered position.

H. helix. The typical English Ivy is too rapid and rampant a grower to be used, even as a ground cover in the rock garden. However, some of its dwarf forms are well adapted to this purpose. Var. *conglomorata* is a slow-growing prostrate form, with tiny crisp crinkly leaves, set close together on thick branches. Var. *meageri* has tiny deeply-cut light-green leaves on long trailing stems. Var. *minima* is an erect, non-climbing, or slightly climbing, plant with stiff branches and very small, sharp-pointed leaves, usually ranged in two rows, one on either side of the stem. When it is cut back periodically and grown in a ball form, it makes a nice accent plant.

HELIANTHEMUM (*Cistaceae,* Rock Rose Family). The sun roses are almost indispensable to a well-ordered sunny rock garden. Their attractive foliage and masses of brilliant flowers provide a pleasing contrast to other plants. Although native to the Mediterranean region, they are reliably hardy in the North. In some exposed positions, and in open winters, some damage occurs; but if the damaged parts are cut back, the plants come back quickly and make a fine show. Indeed, all of these plants should be cut back every year to keep the planting neat and compact.

All the rock roses are low-growing trailing or decumbent evergreen shrubs. The large flowers have the texture of fine crepe paper and resemble wild roses. They are propagated quite readily from seeds, or from cuttings taken in summer, and are easy to grow in a lean, gravelly or sandy, dry soil, in full sun. They do not like rich soil or fertilizers of any kind. Soil acidity or alkalinity, unless extreme, is unimportant. The plants bloom profusely during May and June, then sparsely through the remainder of the summer. If the plants are cut back about the first of July, they will again flower well in August and September.

H. apenninum. Long arching branches, with narrow silvery-gray leaves, and large white flowers in loose racemes. Var. *roseum,* usually listed as *H. rhodanthum,* is represented in the horticultural variety called 'Wendle's Rose,' an attractive plant with wide silvery silky leaves and large clear-rose-colored flowers.

H. grandiflorum. The true species is lost in the maze of fancy named garden forms of various colors listed as hybrids. Var. *multiplex* is a completely prostrate plant with small green leaves on trailing stems, and fully-double copper-colored flowers variegated with yellow which resemble dwarf pompon chrysanthemums.

H. nummularium. This is the most common species, but it probably is not available in its natural form. Seeds of this species, or its varieties, are usually offered as *H. amabile* and *H. mutabile.* Most of the fancy named garden forms are derived from this plant. The most noteworthy forms are: 'Apricot Queen,' a low spreading dense mound with large glossy-green leaves and large apricot-colored flowers; 'Ben Ledi,' a ball-shaped plant with narrow dark-green leaves and crimson flowers with bright-yellow centers; 'Ben Nevis,' yellow flower with red eye; 'Buttercup,' a compact dome of light-green leaves and masses of bright-yellow flowers; 'Fire Ball,' with fully-double bright-red flowers; 'Gold Nugget' and 'Lemon Queen' with double yellow flowers; 'Mrs. Mould,' an exquisite form, with fringed flower petals colored salmon-pink, and silvery foliage on stiff upright stems; and 'Rose Peach,' a loose-growing form with long narrow dark-green leaves and large peach-blossom-pink flowers. Many other fancy named forms are offered by nurserymen and seed houses.

HELLEBORUS (*Ranunculaceae,* Buttercup Family). A small genus of large but attractive plants that are useful for the shady rock garden. The hellebores like a deep, rich, moist, acid loam (pH 5–6), in shade or part shade. They are propagated by seeds that germinate slowly, and the young plants take years to develop. All can be easily divided for quicker results.

H. lividus. A clump of large three-parted, coarsely-toothed, thick-bodied leaves that are evergreen in mild climates. Thick, upright flower stems about 18 inches high bear clusters of green flowers in early April. In my estimation, the flowers detract from the exotic beauty of the foliage.

H. niger. The fantastic Christmas rose that is held in high esteem by all gardeners. Ornamental evergreen clumps of very thick, deeply cut and lobed dark-green leaves, 6 to 12 inches high. Large magnificent white flowers like wild roses, often 3 inches across, on stout stems, from September to

April. The flowers turn a deep pink with age, or in extremely cold weather. *H. niger* is called the Christmas rose because it blooms during the winter in mild climates. In the North, it usually produces a few flowers in the fall, which are carried over winter, and really comes into full bloom in April.

H. orentalis. Similar to *H. niger,* but somehow lacking in dignity. Large evergreen leaves in clumps about 18 inches high. The huge flowers are produced in March and April and are colored from dull-dark-green to a dark-brownish-purple.

HELONIAS (*Liliaceae,* Lily Family). One tuberous-rooted species, *H. bullata,* native to sphagnum bogs in New Jersey. The leaves are all basal, long, narrow, and 12 inches high. A stout flower stem emerges from the center of the leaves and bears a dense cluster of small pink flowers in spring. It is suitable only for a bog garden and needs a wet, acid soil (pH 4–5), in sun or light shade.

HEPATICA (*Ranunculaceae,* Buttercup Family). A small genus of woodland plants, closely related to anemones and often so listed in catalogues. The species described here are native to woodlands of the eastern United States. They require a well-drained, gravelly subsoil under a layer of acid leaf-mold, and shade. Plants are usually collected from the wild and moved to the garden, but they can be raised from seeds or propagated easily by divisions.

H. acutiloba. Clumps, about 6 inches high, of attractive sharp-pointed, three-lobed evergreen leaves, which are usually mottled in winter. Small white, blue, or pink flowers in profusion in early April.

H. americana. Very similar to *H. acutiloba,* except that the leaf lobes are rounded rather than pointed. The flower colors are predominately blue and pink, rather than white.

HERNIARIA (*Illecebraceae,* Knotwort Family). A few tiny creeping plants, native to Europe and Africa, that are sometimes used for carpeting. They generally have very tiny leaves on flat creeping stems that form a thin film of green over the soil. Flowers are small and inconspicuous. Why something better is not used, I do not know.

HEUCHERA (*Saxifragaceae,* Rockfoil Family). A group of American natives, with attractive foliage and, generally, with inconspicuous flowers. *H. sanguinea* is an outstanding exception. Propagated by seeds and divisions.

H. americana. Huge clumps of large, maplelike, evergreen leaves to dress up a dense shady situation. Small greenish flowers on thin stems about 3 feet high. Var. *begoniafolia* is a pleasing new discovery. The leaves are veined and marbled with pink, red, and bronze. It likes a moist, acid soil (pH 5–6), in shade.

H. glabra. Very neat and attractive, small, light-green, leathery, heart-shaped, evergreen leaves in tufts about 3 inches high. Eight-inch stems with comparatively large creamy-white flowers in April and May. A rare Rocky Mountain alpine that needs a gritty, acid soil (pH 5–6), in shade.

H. sanguinea. Decorative clumps of wavy, crinkly, lobed and toothed leaves, 8 to 10 inches high. It has graceful slender swaying flower stems, 18 to 24 inches high, with airy sprays of vivid-pink flowers in June, July, and August. Although native to Arizona and Mexico, it is hardy even in the Far North and easy to grow in any well-drained garden soil (pH 6–8), in full sun. Excellent in dry walls and rock crevices. This is the beloved coral-bells. The flowers are in various shades of pink and red, or white. Some named forms are 'Pluie de Feu,' 'Oakington Jewel,' 'Rosemonde,' and 'Snowflake.'

HIERACIUM (*Compositae,* Daisy Family). The hawkweeds have the reputation of being noxious weeds, and rightly so, but the two I list here make ideal rock-garden subjects. Propagated by seeds and divisions.

H. bombycinum. Flat rosettes of soft white woolly leaves, and 6-inch flower stems, displaying large heads of golden flowers in May and June. This native of the Pyrenees requires a dry, sandy or gravelly soil, in full sun.

H. venosum. Flat rosettes of small oval leaves that form loose open mats from underground stolons. The leaves are light green and most attractively veined with red and purple. Eighteen-inch stems carry open heads of deep-yellow flowers through most of the summer. This plant is native to open pine woods in the eastern United States. It likes a sandy, acid soil (pH 4–5), in sun or light shade.

HOUSTONIA (*Rubiaceae,* Madder Family). All species in this genus are little herbaceous plants, native to the eastern United States. They are good rock-garden plants, but most of them are not available at nurseries. With the exception of *H. caerulea,* they require a well-drained, acid soil (pH 5–6), rich in leaf-mold or humus, and a shady or semi-shady moist position. They are easily propagated by divisions and by seeds.

H. caerulea. The bluets, or Quaker ladies, have very tiny dark-green leaves in tight tufts about one inch high, which are completely covered with myriads of dainty, porcelain-blue, four-pointed stars in April and May, and a few through the summer. A little gem that comes readily from self-sown seed. It is easy to grow in a well-drained, acid to neutral, loam (pH 5–7), in full sun or light shade. One of the prettiest sights in the world of flowers is to see this tiny plant covering vast acres of upland pastures with a delicate blue mist.

H. longifolia. Tight little tufts of long linear leaves, 2 or 3 inches high, topped with purple buds and white flowers over a long season from May to July.

H. montana. Tufts of large broad oval leaves, with flower stems 6 to 12 inches high, displaying clusters of small deep-purple flowers in June and July.

H. serphyllifolia. Tiny rounded leaves on thin creeping stems that cover the moist ground with a dense mat of green, barely half an inch thick. The mat is covered with solitary deep-blue flowers in May and June. Unexcelled as a tiny ground cover in a moist shady portion of the rock garden.

HUDSONIA (*Cistaceae,* Rock Rose Family). Little evergreen shrubs of the eastern United States, found growing in sandy places along the seacoast and along the edges of rivers and lakes. They are seldom planted and have the reputation of being very difficult; but if given the proper conditions, they will thrive for years in a garden. They must have a moist, very sandy, acid soil (pH 4–5), in full sun or very light shade. Specimens are usually taken from the wild, and this is where the difficulty lies. Only very tiny seedlings can be moved successfully. However, the plant can be propagated by cuttings and seeds.

H. ericoides. Little mounds of slender twigs, about 6 inches high, with tiny soft downy green leaves, and a nice display of bright-yellow flowers all along the stems, in May and June.

H. tomentosa. Similar to *H. ericoides,* but the entire plant is covered with silky silvery hairs, giving it an attractive hoary luminescence.

HUTCHINSIA (*Cruciferae,* Mustard Family). A small genus of little tufted plants, very similar to the drabas.

H. alpina. A choice tiny alpine from the European Alps that forms little tufts of very finely cut, dark-green, ferny foliage about 2 inches high. Small clusters of white flowers on short stems, in April and May. It likes a well-drained, gritty, lime soil (pH 7–8), in sun or light shade. Propagated by divisions and seeds.

HYDROCOTYLE (*Umbelliferae,* Carrot Family). A group of weedy, creeping marsh plants with inconspicuous flowers, sometimes used for ground cover in wet places. One species, from Tasmania, is ideal for rock gardens.

H. peduncularis. Tiny reniform evergreen leaves on underground creeping stems that make a solid mat about half an inch high. Excellent as a ground cover over bulb beds and as edging for artificial pools and streams. Although it spreads fast, it is too small to become troublesome. Easy to grow in any ordinary garden soil, in sun or light shade.

HYPERICUM (*Hypericaceae,* St. Johnswort Family). Mostly large herbs and shrubs, characterized by large showy yellow flowers. Most species are either too large or too tender to be used in northern rock gardens. Many more than those listed here are useful for gardens in the latitude of Philadelphia. They are easy to grow in ordinary garden soil, in sun or light shade. Propagated by seeds, cuttings, and some kinds by divisions.

H. olympicum. A subshrub from Asia Minor that forms almost prostrate mats of tiny grayish leaves on long trailing stems. Large bright-yellow flowers are borne at the ends of the branches in June and July. It is hardy in a sheltered position, or with cover, in the North.

H. rhodopeum. Soft, velvety, silver-gray leaves on creeping stems, to 5 inches high, which form a most attractive silvery mat. Large yellow flowers in June and July. Excellent as a wall-garden plant or for tumbling over hot, dry rocks.

HYPOXIS (*Amaryllidaceae,* Amaryllis Family). Little-known cormus-rooted plants, mostly from the tropics. The following, native to the northeastern United States, is ideal for a shady rock garden.

H. hirsutus. Long slender grasslike leaves, and small yellow flowers on 6-inch stems in May, usually continuing through the summer. A single plant is hardly noticeable, but when it is planted in quantity, *H. hirsutus* gives late-season color to a dark shaded area. It needs a well-drained, acid, leaf-mold soil (pH 4–6), in shade.

IBERIS (*Cruciferae,* Mustard Family). The candytufts have long been garden favorites for bedding and edging purposes and for use in rock and wall gardens. All species are from southern Europe, but they are hardy in the North and easy to grow in any well-drained garden soil, in full sun. They are usually grown from seeds, and the fancy named sorts by cuttings taken in late summer.

I. gibraltarica. An evergreen mound of long narrow leaves, about 12 inches high, with large clusters of flowers, ranging in color from pale lilac to deep purple. Although perennial, it usually blooms itself to death the first year and comes back from self-sown seeds.

I. saxatilis. A very tiny plant with short twisted and gnarled branches, clothed in short, almost cylindrical, leaves, and topped with clusters of white flowers in April and May. The entire plant is seldom over 2 inches high.

I. saxavirens. A hybrid that is often listed as *I. saxatilis.* It has long prostrate trailing stems with little flat-tipped leaves, which make an attractive evergreen cushion, only 2 or 3 inches high. The entire plant is covered with small clusters of white flowers in April and May. My own origination of a form of this, which I call 'Barbara Lynch,' has the leaves and growing habit of *I. saxatilis,* but the waxy-white flowers are in large clusters that stand up well on stems 4 to 6 inches high.

I. sempervirens. This is the most popular of the perennial candytufts. It forms an evergreen mound, about 12 inches high, of small linear leaves on decumbent branches. The mound is topped with small white flowers in tight elongated clusters, in April and May. There are several fancy named forms including: 'Little Gem,' a tight ball of tiny leaves about 5 inches high, with flowers in small clusters; 'Purity,' very much like 'Little Gem' but with larger flower clusters; 'Christmas Snow,' a form that blooms almost constantly even through the winter, particularly in mild climates; and 'Snowflake,' perhaps the nicest form, with longer and broader dark-green leaves on semitrailing stems about 6 inches high, and large waxy-white flowers in large clusters.

ILEX (*Aquifoliaceae,* Holly Family). An elegant family of handsome trees and shrubs. Some dwarf forms can be used in the rock garden. Those listed here are hardy in the North but should be protected from drying winds and winter sun with a covering of evergreen boughs. They are propagated by cuttings and are easy to grow if they are given a well-drained, acid soil (pH 4–6) that is rich in leaf-mold or other organic matter.

I. crenata. A small-leaved but large-growing evergreen shrub from Japan. Only its dwarf forms can be used in rock gar-

Iberis saxavirens.

dens. Var. *hellerii* has tiny crenate leaves on short stiff horizontally spreading branches that form a most attractive flat-topped evergreen shrub, never more than 12 inches high but sometimes as much as 3 feet across in old age. It is invaluable as an accent plant, even in small rock gardens. Var. *mummularia* is a dwarf form with very stout stiff upright branches, with tiny rigid rounded leaves. A compact slow-growing shrub.

I. pernyi. Although perhaps too large to be listed among rock plants, this *Ilex* is a slow grower and, as a young plant, it can be used with justification. If it gets too big for its allotted space, it can be moved to another part of the home grounds. With annual pruning, it can be kept within scale for years. It is an evergreen with small, very spiny, bright-shining-green leaves in a pyramidal form, to 30 feet. Plants started from cuttings will begin to produce large bright-red berries in one or two years. Even unfertilized female flowers produce berries, but they are sterile.

INCARVILLEA (*Bignoniaceae,* Trumpet Flower Family). Exotic Chinese plants with huge flowers, often called hardy gloxinia. They are really too domineering for a rock garden, but they are sometimes used and make a spectacle of themselves. They are not the easiest plants to grow, but they are permanent if given the proper treatment. Most of them have very long tuberlike taproots that penetrate the soil deeply. Thus they need a very deep and well-drained, sandy soil (pH 5–6), rich in humus and a bit on the acid side. They like sunshine with ample moisture during the growing season but dry in winter. In the North, they should be given a heavy winter covering to keep them from heaving. They are usually grown from seeds, but old plants can be divided.

I. compacta. A rare plant with large thick or fleshy pinnate leaves, 6 inches or more long. The stout flower stems, about 12 inches high, bear purple flowers about 3 inches long, in May and June.

I. delavayi. Very like *I. compacta* but much larger, with the flower stems about 2 feet high and the flowers a light rosy purple.

INULA (*Compositae,* Daisy Family). Rather coarse herbaceous plants, allied to the sunflowers. A few are sufficiently small and refined for use in the rock garden. All are easily grown from seeds or divisions, and succeed in any well-drained garden soil, in full sun.

I. acaulis. Little tufts of small spoon-shaped leaves, about 2 inches high, and solitary narrow-rayed daisies on 6-inch stems, in June and July. An attractive little plant from Asia Minor.

I. ensifolia. Clumps of long narrow leaves and 2-foot flower stems, bearing heads of yellow daisies from June to September. Rather big but quite colorful during the hot summer months, when most rock gardens lack color.

IRIS (*Iridaceae,* Iris Family). No one needs an introduction to the celestial world of the iris, for we all have known this flower from childhood. A remarkable plant family, the iris is distributed over the entire northern hemisphere. Species range in height from 2 or 3 inches to several feet. In one of the marshes on my farm, I found some yellow flag iris over 6 feet tall. Rock gardeners are concerned mainly with the small, or dwarf, wild species and a few of the fancy named dwarf hybrids. There can be no general cultural recommendations, because the various species are quite individual in their preference for soil and exposures. Most irises can be grown from seeds. Usually, they are propagated by divisions.

In the list that follows, I am merely scratching the surface of the rock garden possibilities. Although these are the most commonly available to the American public from local nurseries, seeds of many more can be obtained from foreign seedsmen. I will not bother with any of the fancy named hybrids because they are too numerous, with many identical colors and forms under various names. It seems that everyone who grows a batch of seedlings names them all, regardless of their worth, and introduces them as superior strains.

I. chamaeiris. A species from France and Italy, with slightly glaucous leaves, about 6 inches high, and unbranched flower stems, about 10 inches high, with orbicular flowers

Iris cristata.

colored blue, purple, yellow, or white, in late April and May. This is often sold as *I. pumila,* but in reality most plants under both of these names prove to be hybrids between the two, with other species involved. Probably the true species is unavailable unless seeds can be found in the wild. Easy to grow in ordinary garden soil, in full sun.

I. cristata. A native of our southeastern woodlands that creeps quite quickly, forming large sheets of graceful emerald-green arching leaves about 6 inches high, with large wide-open delicate lavender-blue flowers in May and June. A lovely and rare form with pure-white flowers is var. *alba.* There are several forms with flowers of a darker tint, among them an outstanding one called 'Skylands,' with deep-violet-blue flowers. This is a very hardy and permanent plant, easy to grow in shade or light shade, in a rich, well-drained, acid, loam soil (pH 5–6).

I. douglasiana. A tall Californian native, with stiff narrow leaves about 18 inches high, and flat, narrow-petaled flowers, ranging in color from purple and lavender to creamy white. It likes part shade in a moist, rich, acid soil (pH 5–6).

I. ensata. Close clumps of long narrow leaves, and stems about 12 inches high, with small purple and white flowers in May and June. A species from China and Japan that is easy to grow in any ordinary garden soil in sun or light shade.

I. flavissima. An endearing little plant from Hungary that is a bit difficult to maintain. It has a creeping rootstock that forms small colonies of thin grasslike leaves about 5 inches high, and small but perfectly formed bright-yellow flowers in April and May. The flowers have a captivating fragrance. It wants full sun in a very well-drained, acid, sandy soil (pH 5–6). The only way I have ever been able to keep it was in a specially prepared bed, composed of three parts sand and one part acid leaf-mold.

I. gracilipes. For sheer beauty and profusion of flowers, this dainty iris takes the prize. Ruffled lavender-blue flowers veined deep lilac, held on 5-inch stems over dainty clumps of narrow arching leaves. This iris comes from Japan and blooms in May and June. Var. *alba* has pure-white flowers. Var. *flore-pleno* has curious multipetaled lavender flowers. It is easy to grow and permanent in a light acid loam, enriched with leaf-mold humus, in a shady or semishady position (*illustration page 232*).

I. graminea. Fragrant two-toned purple flowers in May, on stems 12 to 15 inches high, over thick clumps of long narrow grassy leaves. Easy to grow in ordinary garden soil, in sun or light shade. From southern Europe.

I. innominata. Thick clumps of long narrow dark-green leaves, about 2 feet long but not standing rigid. The flower stems, from 12 to 15 inches high, have dark-yellow flowers with purple veins in the typical form. There are forms with colors ranging from lilac to lavender. A native of Oregon, this iris

Iris gracilipes.

grows well in a shady location in a deep, humus-rich, acid loam (pH 5–6); but once it is established, it should not be moved or divided. New plants should be started from seeds, which germinate quickly.

I. lacustris. A dwarf and rare species from the shores of the Great Lakes that is best described as a diminutive *I. cristata.* It likes a cool, moist, acid soil, in shade or part shade. Tiny blue flowers.

I. melita. This plant is often a controversial subject among members of the American Rock Garden Society. It is usually referred to as *I. rubro-marginata,* or *I. melita* var. *rubro-marginata.* It is a tiny exotic from Asia Minor that should be included in every rock garden. *Melita* forms little colonies of 3-inch sickle-shaped leaves edged with red, which lie almost flat on the ground. The almost stemless orbicular flowers, which bloom in May and June, are about 2 inches long, subtly fragrant, and colored a dark-red-purple. This iris needs a gritty, well-drained, garden soil (pH 6–8), in full sun.

I. minuta. Another elfin queen from Japan, with little tufts of very stiff leaves about 3 inches high and a half-inch wide, and tiny brown-edged yellow flowers in April and May. A most difficult plant to keep. It demands a well-drained, rather dry, acid, leaf-mold soil (pH 4–6), in shade.

I. prismatica. A tall but extremely graceful iris from seashores and bogs along our Atlantic coast. Although it is a natural bog plant, it does well in a dry acid soil, in sun or light shade. However, it makes its best showing when placed at the edge of a pool. It grows in dense clumps of long thin leaves about 24 inches high, with slender lavender-blue flowers on thin swaying stems, in May and June. Var. *rosea* has lovely cherry-red flowers.

I. pumila. A dwarf bearded iris, from the Balkans and Asia Minor. It forms broad clumps of blue-green leaves about 6 inches high, with large flowers appearing in early April before the leaves are fully developed. The color of the wild species varies from deep purple to blue, yellow, and white. Similar to *I. chamaeiris,* except that it blooms a bit earlier, and the flowers are stemless. The true species is hard to find, but it is well represented by innumerable Latin-named garden forms and fancy named hybrids. This species and all its forms are of the simplest culture. The plants grow well in almost any soil, in sun or light shade.

I. ruthenica. A creeping plant from north China that spreads quickly into broad sheets of fine grassy foliage, 6 to 12 inches high, and sweet-scented two-toned white and purple flowers in May. It likes a deep, rich, acid loam (pH 5–6), in shade or part shade, but will stand full sun for part of the day.

I. tectorum. The beloved Japanese Roof Iris. Broad bold clumps of wide swordlike leaves, 12 to 18 inches high, with large wide flat lavender-colored flowers in May. Often called the poor man's orchid. Var. *alba* has large pure-white flowers, and the plant is considerably smaller than the type. Very easy to grow in any ordinary garden soil in full sun. A prolific bloomer, outstanding for the rock garden.

I. tenax. An Oregon native that forms clumps of tall thin leaves and flower stems about 12 inches high. Solitary flowers in May, bright violet with white centers. It needs a deep, rich, acid, leaf-mold soil (pH 5–6), in shade.

I. verna. Spreading clumps of glossy dark-green leaves, about 6 inches high, with small but very showy bright-violet-blue flowers with orange markings in May and June. A native of the Appalachian Mountains with the reputation of being difficult, but I find it permanent in a humus-rich, moist, acid soil (pH 4–6), in shade.

JASIONE (*Campanulaceae,* Bellflower Family). Nice European mountain plants, characterized by tiny blue flowers in tight globular heads. There are many species but very few are in cultivation. They are easy to grow in any well-drained garden soil, in full sun or light shade. In a rich soil, they become rank and floppy, so give them a dry, sandy soil, or plant them in dry rock crevices or in a wall garden. Best propagated by divisions.

J. humilis. Small linear hairy green leaves in tufts about 2 inches high that spread into broad evergreen mats. Leafy flower stems, 6 or 8 inches high, with small tight heads of light-steel-blue flowers in May and June.

J. perennis. Very similar to the preceding but a much larger and faster-growing plant, with clear-light-blue flowers on long stalked stems from May to July. Just outside of the town of Toms River, New Jersey, I saw a field of several acres where thousands of these blue globes were in bloom at the same time, making the field look like a reflection of the sky.

JASMINUM (*Oleaceae,* Olive Family). The jasmines are elegant shrubs and vines for planting in mild climates, but the little species from the Himalayas described here is adaptable to the rock garden. It is hardy to Philadelphia and, with protection, farther north.

J. parkerii. A compact rounded shrub about 12 inches high, with small pinnatifid pale-green leaves and bright-yellow flowers in April and May. It is propagated by cuttings, and easy to grow in a sunny location in ordinary garden soil.

JEFFERSONIA (*Berberidaceae,* Barberry Family). A genus consisting of only two species, both ideal rock plants. They are woodland plants that are easy to grow if they are given a loose, humus-rich, acid loam (pH 5–6), in shade. Both come readily from seeds, and can also be propagated by divisions.

J. diphylla. A native of our northeastern woodlands that forms broad colonies of decorative long-stalked, two-parted leaves, about 12 inches high. White flowers, about 1 inch across, in early April before the leaves.

J. dubia. A rare and coveted species from China, with large undivided leaves in lovely rounded clumps, about a foot high, and delicate light-blue flowers in early spring.

KALMIA (*Ericaceae,* Heath Family). Everyone knows the beautiful mountain laurel, but few are familiar with the small bog laurels that are suited to the rock garden. Although they are natural bog plants, they do well in a dry soil as long as it does not become thoroughly parched in summer. If given a sandy, peaty, or acid, leaf-mold soil, in sun or light shade, they will be at home with the ericaceous plants.

K. polifolia. A rather straggly, twiggy bush about 2 feet high, with a few glaucous-backed small shining-green leaves, and terminal clusters of large rosy-purple flowers in May. Var. *rosmarinifolia* has long narrow revolute leaves. Both of these have showy flowers, but the plants themselves lack charm. Therefore, I always suggest planting them behind a heather or other compact plant to hide their legginess. Var. *microphylla* is an attractive dwarf from the northern Rocky Mountains that needs no apologies for its appearance. It has small glossy leaves on short sturdy branches, 6 to 12 inches high, that form a nice compact semiprostrate bush, and clusters of large bright-lavender flowers in May.

LAMIUM (*Labiatae,* Mint Family). European weeds that sometimes make their way into a rock garden. The species described is colorful and not too offensive. It is useful as a filler or as a ground cover in an inaccessible part of the garden.

L. maculatum. A vigorous plant that forms large spreading clumps of colorful foliage, 6 to 10 inches high. The small oval leaves are crinkly and dark green, with a blotch of white in the center. In winter, the leaves are colored with purple, green, pink, and white. Showy bright-lavender flowers in spikes from May through summer. Var. *alba* has white flowers and pale-green leaves.

LAVANDULA (*Labiatae,* Mint Family). Low aromatic shrubs, mostly from the Mediterranean region, but probably only one species is cultivated in the United States. All are hardy, but it is best to give them winter cover north of the New York City area. Easy to grow and permanent in a sunny situation, in a well-drained garden soil (pH 6–8). Easily propagated by cuttings, and sometimes grown from seed.

L. officinalis. A compact rounded shrub about 3 feet high, with downy silvery small narrow leaves, more or less evergreen. Long spikes of lavender-colored flowers in June and July. Var. *nana compacta* is a dwarf, 8 to 10 inches high. Var. *munstead* is the usual rock garden form, being a compact rounded plant, 1 to 2 feet high, with lavender flowers. 'Twickle Purple' is a very dwarf plant, with silvery leaves, and short spikes of deep-purple flowers. These are nice as specimen plants in the rock garden. They are also good for the wall garden, and are used extensively for borders and edgings.

LEIOPHYLLUM (*Ericaceae,* Heath Family). A genus, according to Alfred Rehder, with only one species. Other botanists list three. They are related to ledum, the Labrador tea, but are much more handsome and better adapted to rock gardening. They go well in a planting of heathers or dwarf rhododendrons because they require the same sandy, acid, leaf-mold soil (pH 4–6), and sunny location.

L. buxifolium. A native of the New Jersey pine barrens that forms a rounded symmetrical plant, 12 to 15 inches high, with tiny glossy evergreen leaves, literally covered with tiny fuzzy white flowers in late April and May. The buds are usually deep pink, but the flowers always open white. Var. *prostratum* is an extremely dwarf, completely prostrate, form that I found near Forked River, New Jersey. This is not to be confused with *L. lyonii,* often listed as *L. prostratum,* which has an entirely different flower structure.

L. lyonii. A semiprostrate plant from the mountains of North Carolina. Those I have seen were about 10 inches high, with the main branches long and trailing and the terminal growth upright. The flowers are in looser heads, with larger petals and shorter stamens.

LEONTOPODIUM (*Compositae,* Daisy Family). Several species of gray-leaved, gray-flowered plants from the high mountains of Europe and Asia. Usually, only one species is planted in American rock gardens.

L. alpinum. This is the famous edelweiss of the Swiss Alps, associated with romantic legends. I have never been very enthusiastic about it, and after reading the accounts of Reginald Farrer and Henry Correvon, I no longer feel guilty of disrespect to this deity among alpine flora. It consists of a tuft of lanceolate gray leaves 3 or 4 inches high, with white woolly stems about 12 inches high, bearing clusters of small dull-yellow flowers, surrounded by white velvety bracts, in May. It needs a very well-drained, gravelly or gritty, lime soil (pH 7–8), in full sun. The best place to plant it is in a wall garden or rock crevice.

LEWISIA (*Portulacaceae,* Purslane Family). Beautiful little natural rock plants from the Rocky Mountains. All species are suitable for rock gardens, but only a few are ever available. I have succeeded in growing them in a deep, very well-drained, sandy, acid soil (pH 5–6), in full sun. The best soil mixture is one part fine stone chips, one part sharp sand, and one part acid leaf-mold. Best propagated by seeds.

L. columbiana. Tight evergreen tufts of thick linear fleshy leaves, about 2 inches high. Graceful airy sprays of small pink flowers on thin stems 8 to 10 inches high, in June. One of the prettiest and most persistent of the lewisias; very easy to grow.

L. cotyledon. A rather massive-looking plant with wide thick fleshy leaves, 3 to 4 inches long, arranged in rosettes and forming broad clumps. It has panicles of pink-veined white flowers on swaying stems, about a foot high, in late spring.

L. howellii. This is like a miniature *L. cotyledon,* with rosettes of small thick leaves, and sprays of comparatively large, bright-pink flowers on 6-inch stems.

L. minima. A very tiny, almost inconspicuous, plant with tiny rosettes of linear leaves about 2 inches high, and large white flowers nestled in the rosettes. The plant goes entirely dormant soon after the flowers fade in June, leaving no evidence of its existence. Hence, it is often lost or destroyed when the garden is cultivated.

L. redivia. This is the bitter-root, state flower of Montana, a spectacular and desirable plant, discovered by the Lewis and Clark expedition. It has a long carrotlike taproot, which produces a tuft of thick linear leaves, 2 to 3 inches high, in September. These remain green all winter. In June, multipetaled delicate rose-colored flowers, as much as 3 inches across, are produced on 2-inch stems. The foliage disappears completely when the plant is in full bloom, and when the flowers fade, the plant goes completely dormant for the rest of the summer. Easy to grow in the East, if given a pocket of almost pure sand with just a trace of acid leafmold for foot. If drainage is inadequate, the plant is often lost when the garden is watered excessively. Care must be taken not to uproot it during weeding and cultivation.

L. Tweedii. Large light-green, fleshy leaves in rosettes, topped with sprays of large salmon-pink flowers on 8-inch stems. One of the loveliest of the lewisias.

LIATRIS (*Compositae,* Daisy Family). Tall wandlike summer- and fall-flowering plants; generally, too large for the rock garden, but sometimes planted for the color they provide when little else is in bloom. The two species listed here are best adapted for this use. They are generally grown from seeds but are easily propagated by cuttings if the cuttings are made before the end of June. The best method is to cut the entire stem into 3- or 4-inch sections and insert them in a box of moist sand. They are easily grown in almost any ordinary garden soil, in sun or light shade. All are native to North America, mostly in the eastern states.

L. graminifolia. Slender unbranched stems, to 3 feet high, with narrow grasslike leaves, and long slender spikes of purple or white flowers from August to October. If the plant is cut back two or three times before the buds are formed, it will become rather bushy, making a gay bouquet of blooms.

L. squarrosa. A sturdier plant but only about 2 feet tall, with few but larger, flower heads.

LIMONIUM (*Plumbaginaceae,* Leadwort Family). These plants are usually listed as *Statice* and are commonly called sea-lavender. The family is large, comprised mostly of rather tall plants that have little substance. They are most usually grown in the border for use as fillers in bouquets. They are easily grown in a well-drained garden soil, in full sun. Propagation is usually by seeds, sometimes by divisions.

L. bellidifolium. Little rosettes or tufts of narrow lance-shaped leaves, about 2 inches high, with thin sprays of tiny pale-lavender flowers.

L. globulariaefolia. Similar to above but with wider leaves, in rosettes, colored a dull gray-green. The taller stems, about 18 inches high, create a haze of tiny purple flowers.

LINARIA (*Scrophulariaceae,* Figwort Family). The toadflaxes are usually tall, rather coarse, annual plants, with a few perennials that are sometimes introduced into the rock garden but are really too big for it. The following species, however, is lovely and should be encouraged.

L. alpina. Little spreading mats, about 6 inches high, of attractive blue-gray foliage, ornamented with bright blue-and-gold flowers all summer. It is a short-lived plant, but it self-sows readily, thus insuring constant renewal. It is too small to become a weed. Propagation is by seed, best sown directly in the garden. *L. alpina* thrives in a well-drained garden soil, in full sun.

LINNAEA (*Carprifoliaceae,* Honeysuckle Family). This genus has a single species, *L. borealis,* native to the northern woodlands of Europe, Asia, and North America. It is a coveted plant that is somewhat difficult to maintain because of its intolerance of summer heat and drought. The farther south it is planted, the more difficult it is to keep. Under ideal conditions, it is a quick-spreading, vinelike plant that makes an attractive ground cover, about half an inch high, of tiny round leaves. The small bell-shaped pink flowers that appear in summer are very fragrant. They are borne 2 on a stem, hence the name twinflower. This plant needs a moist, acid, woodsy soil (pH 4–5), in shade.

LINUM (*Linaceae,* Flax Family). A large family of extremely colorful summer-blooming plants that are welcome in the rock garden and in perennial borders. Those that are annual make good bedding plants. All are best propagated by seeds, and are easy to grow in a well-drained garden soil, in full sun. They are mostly native to the Mediterranean region, and should have winter protection in the North. Unfortunately, only a few species are available for planting in the United States.

L. alpinum. A mass of thin stems about 10 inches high, with tiny hairlike leaves about an inch long, topped with brilliant-blue flowers in late spring and summer.

L. flavum. The golden flax is a stout plant with sturdy stems about 18 inches high, tipped with clusters of brilliant golden flowers.

L. perenne. This is the flax usually seen, and I consider it a bit too large for the rock garden. It resembles *L. alpina* but is much larger, growing to a height of 24 inches, or more. It has thin stems, fine foliage, and bright-blue flowers.

L. salsoloides. A charming evergreen plant, with ascending stems clothed in tiny needlelike leaves, and large purple-veined white flowers. Var. *nanum* is a much smaller plant of prostrate habit that is particularly well adapted to rock gardening.

LIRIOPE (*Liliaceae,* Lily Family). The lily-tufts are a small group of Asiatic plants with much in their favor. They are reliably hardy in the North but should have some winter protection above the New York City area. They are easy to grow if given a moist, rich, garden loam, in shade or half-shade. They will stand full sun but prefer shade. Propagated by divisions.

L. muscari. Broad bold clumps of long arching grasslike leaves, which are sometimes 2 feet long but stand 12 to 15 inches high. Heavy spikes of purple, sometimes white, flowers are borne on sturdy upright stems about 18 inches high in summer. These are followed by black fruits in October. There are many fancy named varieties. Var. *variegata* is particularly handsome, with dark-green leaves striped yellow.

L. spicata. A fast-spreading plant that forms a thick ground cover of thin, grassy, almost prostrate leaves, and slender spikes of light purple to white flowers.

LITHOSPERMUM (*Boraginaceae,* Borage Family). A family of subshrubs and perennials from Europe, Asia, and North America that are particularly handsome and colorful, but few of them are available. The perennial kinds are usually propagated by seeds, the subshrubs from cuttings.

L. canescens. Puccoon. A perennial with deep woody roots, erect hairy stems, and small hairy leaves. It grows about 18 inches high, and has clusters of brilliant orange-yellow tubular flowers in late spring and summer. A native of open woodlands in the eastern United States, it needs a deep, well-drained, gravelly or sandy, acid soil, in half-shade. It is difficult to transplant because of its long woody roots.

L. diffusum. A prostrate evergreen shrub from southern Europe that requires protection in the North but is well worth the trouble involved. It forms thick mats of long trailing stems with small hairy leaves, and produces a cascade of brilliant-blue flowers from midspring to late fall. The best-known forms are 'Heavenly Blue,' and 'Grace Ward' with flowers of a lighter blue. I have found it does best in half-shade in a sandy, acid, leaf-mold soil near the top of the garden where it gets good air drainage.

LOISELEURIA (*Ericaceae,* Heath Family). A one-species genus from circumpolar regions, *L. procumbens.* This is the cherished alpine azalea. It has tiny revolute leaves on thin procumbent or creeping stems that form a mat about 3 inches high. These are studded with light-pink, sometimes white, flowers in spring. This arctic and high-alpine plant must have a moist, acid, leaf-mold soil (pH 4–5), in full sun. It is difficult to keep in the South but sometimes grows there if watered constantly in hot weather and shaded from intense sunshine.

LOTUS (*Leguminosae,* Pea Family). Low trailing plants that make attractive ground covers and are in no way related to the exotic lotus of the Orient. These plants are somewhat weedy, and are easy to grow in almost any soil, in full sun. Propagated by seeds and divisions.

L. pinnatus. A native of the north Pacific region, with stout trailing and rooting stems and attractive compound leaves, which form a thick evergreen mat. Large showy clusters of bright-yellow pea flowers are produced on stems about 3 inches high during most of the summer.

L. tenuis. An attractive carpeting plant with tiny three-parted leaves on thin stems, and small clusters of dainty yellow flowers in late spring and early summer. This is probably a variant of *L. corniculatus* and is listed in my catalogues under that name. Because it tends to be invasive, it should be planted where it will not overrun more desirable plants.

LYCHNIS (*Caryophyllaceae,* Pink Family). Colorful annual and perennial plants, mostly too large and floppy for the rock garden, but a few are welcome additions. They are all rather easy to grow, if given a well-drained garden soil and full sun. Almost without exception they should be grown from seeds. Divisions and cuttings do not come very well.

L. alpina. For my money, this tiny plant from the arctic and alpine regions is the queen of the race, although its color is not all that could be desired. Tiny tufts of narrow leaves an inch or two high, which produce remarkably sturdy 3- to 6-inch stems, each bearing a tight cluster of lavender-pink flowers in April.

L. haageana. A striking hybrid, with large light-green leaves on rather brittle trailing stems that form clumps about 6 inches high. The flowers, produced in May and June, are large and in brilliant colors, ranging from orange to scarlet and crimson.

L. viscaria. The German catchfly is the most common of the race and self-sows freely, thus becoming somewhat of a nuisance. It forms not unattractive clumps of long narrow deep-green evergreen leaves, about 6 inches high, and spikes of bright-red-purple flowers on straight 18-inch stems, in May and June. The double form var. *flore-pleno* has heavy spikes of double flowers that last much longer than the type and do not produce seeds. Thus it cannot become a pest. It is propagated by divisions, preferably in very early spring.

LYGODIUM (*Schizaeaceae,* Schizaea-Fern Family). Exotic, mostly tropical, climbing ferns. One is native to our eastern seaboard and is hardy as far north as Massachusetts.

L. palmatum. Long twining fronds that bear broad attractive palmate pinnae. It climbs as high as four feet by twining around the stems of nearby plants. It is not really a rock plant, but enthusiasts usually find a place for it in the shady background planting. This fern requires a constantly moist, acid, sandy soil (pH 4–6), in shade.

MAHONIA (*Berberidaceae,* Barberry Family). Exceedingly attractive evergreen shrubs for use in the foundation planting or background of the rock garden. The two pygmies listed are conversation pieces wherever they are found. They are usually propagated by seeds or cuttings, and are easy to grow and permanent if given an acid, leaf-mold soil (pH 4–6), in shade or half-shade. They are native to the northwest Pacific area, and are hardy in New York and lower

New England. Elsewhere, they should be protected from drying winds and winter sun.

M. nervosa. A low rounded bush about 2 feet high, with long-petioled, bright-shining-green, stiff, leathery leaves consisting of 10 to 20 ovate toothed leaflets. Large clusters of bright-yellow flowers are produced in spring, followed by bloomy dark-blue berries in fall.

M. repens. A creeping plant that forms slowly spreading clumps of small ornamental deep-blue-green compound leaves, about 12 inches high. Small clusters of bright-yellow flowers, followed by dark-blue berries.

MAIANTHEMUM (*Liliaceae,* Lily Family). A small family of unpretentious plants, sometimes used in rock gardens. They are native to acid woodlands of Europe, Asia, and North America. Our native *M. canadense* is usually transferred from the wild. It is a spreading plant that forms patches of small heart-shaped leaves about 2 inches high, and small spikes of fuzzy white flowers in May. Charming in an elfin way.

MALVASTRUM (*Malvaceae,* Mallow Family). Mostly large tropical plants, but one, which is native to the Rocky Mountains, is an ideal rock-garden subject. *M. coccineum* forms a loose spreading mat, about 12 inches high, of thin decumbent stems with finely-divided silvery foliage, and terminal clusters of bright-brick-red flowers from July to September. It does well in a rather dry, well-drained, neutral to limy, soil (pH 7–8), in full sun. It has long, deep, woody roots, and spreads by means of underground shoots, which emerge as far as three feet from the original planting. It is best grown from seeds and is difficult to transplant.

MAZUS (*Scrophulariaceae,* Figwort Family). Small mat-forming trailing plants from Asia and Australia that look very much alike. *M. reptans* from the Himalayas is the species usually planted. It forms very quickly spreading mats of fresh-green tiny leaves, about an inch high, studded with comparatively large lavender flowers in May and June. It does well in almost any soil but prefers shade or filtered sunlight.

MENTHA (*Labiatae,* Mint Family). A genus of strongly aromatic and flavored plants that are too big for the rock garden but are cherished in the herb garden. One tiny species *M. requienii,* from Corsica, is a favorite where it is hardy. It will grow as far north as the New York City area with winter protection. This plant produces a creeping green film of minute round leaves, and tiny whorls of lavender flowers in late spring. It will grow in sun or light shade, but is so tiny that it is usually lost. The entire plant is extremely aromatic when bruised.

MERTENSIA (*Boraginaceae,* Borage Family). Pretty, fragile little plants from thickets and open woodlands of Asia and North America. Almost all of them are suited to rock gardens, but only a few are ever available. Most of them are tuberous-rooted and most easily grown from seeds.

M. longiflora. Little tufts of delicate blue-green leaves, about 3 inches high. The flower stems are about 10 inches high, with clusters of long tubular blue flowers in April and May. The plant goes dormant soon after flowering. It likes an acid, peaty soil, in sun or light shade, with ample moisture during the growing period, but perfect drainage and complete dryness during its dormant season.

M. longifolia. Little tufts of blue-green leaves, and flower stems, 6 to 8 inches high, with nodding clusters of lovely deep-blue flowers in April and early May. This is another Rocky Mountain native that goes dormant early. It should be treated like the preceding. It self-sows freely, producing numerous spontaneous plants throughout the garden.

M. virginica. A large plant with monstrous tuberous roots, as much as 6 inches in diameter and about 15 inches long. It makes clumps of large light-blue-green leaves, about 15 inches high. Stout stems bear large clusters of purple-tubed blue flowers in early spring. Like others of this species, it goes dormant shortly after flowering. It likes a deep, rich, acid to neutral, loam (pH 5–7), in shade and part shade. There are also desirable white and pink forms.

MICROMERIA (*Labiatae,* Mint Family). A family of aromatic trailing plants, closely resembling thyme. They are easily propagated by cuttings and divisions, and will grow in any ordinary garden soil, in full sun. There are several useful species, but I have had experience only with the following.

M. juliana. A trailing billowy mat of soft silky gray-green evergreen foliage, 4 or 5 inches high. Showy spikes of light-purple flowers in summer and early fall.

MITCHELLA (*Rubiaceae,* Madder Family). A monotypic genus from North American woodlands.

M. repens. This is the well-known partridge-berry or checker-berry. Trailing rooting stems with small orbicular white-veined light-green leaves make a delightful ground cover. Tiny, very fragrant, pale-pink twin flowers in late spring are followed by large bright-red, edible but not very tasty, berries in fall. It requires shade or half-shade in an acid, leaf-mold soil (pH 4–6). Can be increased by divisions and cuttings. Generally, it is collected from the wild.

MITELLA (*Saxifragaceae,* Rockfoil Family). Attractice evergreen or semievergreen foliage plants, with small inconsequential flowers. They are native to northern woodlands of the United States, and require shade in an acid, leaf-mold soil (pH 4–6) for best results. Easily increased by divisions, but the plants are usually brought home from the woods.

M. diphylla. Little clumps or mats of attractive heart-shaped leaves, about 3 inches high. The flower heads are clasped between two small directly opposite leaves, hence its name. It has short spikes of small white flowers in April. The petals of the individual flowers are finely laciniated and resemble a miter, or Bishop's cap.

MONESES (*Pyroplaceae,* Shinleaf Family). One species, *M. uniflora,* native to North America, Europe, and Asia, and found in deep shade in acid woodlands. It forms open mats of shiny-green and bronzy round leaves that lie almost flat on the ground. Only one or two leaves show from each underground stem and a single waxy-white or light-pink nodding fragrant flower appears in May. This plant is difficult to move and establish. The best and usual method is to find a small isolated patch in the woods and move it as a sod, with lots of soil and all its roots.

MONTIA (*Portulacaceae,* Purslane Family). Small, almost insignificant, plants from our western states, often called miner's lettuce. I have had experience only with the following.

M. parviflora. Although *Hortus II* lists this as an annual, I have found it to be perennial. Attractive little mounds of fleshy, bright shining-green leaves, about 3 inches high, and long arching flower stems, bearing a few, but quite large, deep-pink flowers in late spring. It spreads radically by long slender runners, much like a strawberry. Although fairly hardy, it should have winter protection in the North. It likes a moist, acid soil, in shade or filtered sunlight.

MUEHLENBECKIA (*Polygonaceae,* Knotweed Family). A small genus of wiry-stemmed vinelike plants from New Zealand and Chile. The following is hardy in the North, and a good rock plant.

M. axillaris (Usually listed as *M. nana*). Low mats of very thin, wiry stems, covered with small orbicular dark-green leaves. The flowers are tiny and inconspicuous. This is an excellent plant to use as a cover over bulb beds in the rock garden. It will grow in almost any soil, in sun or light shade.

MYOSOTIS (*Boraginaceae,* Borage Family). These are the ever-popular forget-me-nots. There are several species from around the world, but only two are usually planted. Propagated by seeds and sometimes by divisions.

M. scorpioides (Usually listed as *M. palustris*). Mounds of soft gray-green foliage on procumbent stems, 10 or more inches high. Masses of showy bright-blue flowers with pink, white, or yellow centers. Var. *semperflorens* is a more compact dwarf form that blooms all summer. It likes a rich, moist soil, in light shade.

M. sylvatica (Usually listed as *M. alpestris*). Mounds of soft gray-green leaves to 2 feet, topped with open clusters of blue flowers. This species is a biennial or, at most, a short-lived perennial that must be renewed annually. Blue yellow-eyed flowers, varying to white and pink. Listed under several fancy names.

NARTHECIUM (*Liliaceae,* Lily Family). These are strictly bog plants. Our eastern native *N. americanum,* the bog-asphodel, is found in the bogs of the New Jersey pine barrens. To succeed at all, it must be kept constantly wet in a mucky, acid soil (pH 4–5), in sun or light shade. It is not a very showy plant but an interesting one. It forms slowly spreading clumps of long, narrow, grasslike leaves a foot or more high, and has light-yellow flowers in small terminal clusters on 18-inch stems, in May and June.

NEOBESSEYA (*Cactaceae,* Cactus Family). Little cespitose globe cacti from the Great Plains. Those from the northern regions are hardy and make fine rock garden subjects. They require a sandy, well-drained soil (pH 6–8), in full sun. About the only means of propagation is by seeds.

N. missouriensis. Interesting cylindrical or globose cacti, very spiny, that eventually reach a height of 12 to 18 inches. The small yellowish flowers are borne in a circlet near the top of the plant.

NEPETA (*Labiatae,* Mint Family). These are mostly rather tall and floppy, strongly aromatic herbs from Europe and Asia. A few are suitable for use in the rock garden. They are easily propagated by divisions, and will grow in any ordinary garden soil.

N. hederacea. This is the common ground ivy that has become widely naturalized in America. It forms thick fast-spreading mats of large rounded leaves, 4 or 5 inches high, with quantities of light-blue flowers in small clusters in late spring. It does equally well in full sun or deep shade, and makes an effective ground cover. Somewhat invasive but easily controlled by uprooting.

N. mussinii. A strikingly handsome plant that forms large billowy mounds of small silvery-white leaves, about 15 inches high, topped with short spikes of light-lavender-blue flowers in late spring and summer. An excellent wall-garden subject that requires full hot sun.

NIEREMBERGIA (*Solanaceae,* Nightshade Family). Attractive colorful plants from Argentina. Only one is hardy in the northeastern United States, but it is exceptionally fine. Others are grown as annual bedding plants.

N. rivularis. The lovely white-cup. Little mats, about 2 inches high, of small oval leaves that rise from creeping underground stems and stand almost erect. Large creamy-white, cup-shaped flowers are nestled in the leaves from late May to September. *Rivularis* is hardy in the New York City area, and can be kept farther north with a heavy winter cover. It likes a rich, moist, acid to neutral, loam (pH 5–7), in light shade or filtered sunlight. Easily increased by divisions.

OENOTHERA (*Onagraceae,* Evening-Primrose Family). A large genus of annual and perennial species, with some spectacularly handsome rock garden subjects. They are of wide distribution, mostly in North America, and in some cases of wide cultural difference. Almost all are easy to grow. They come best from seeds, but some kinds can be reproduced by divisions and cuttings. Many more species than those I list here are good rock plants if they can be found.

Oe. caespitosa. Little tufts or clusters of long narrow-toothed leaves, about 3 inches long, that lie almost flat on the ground. Pure-white or light-pink flowers, 3 inches or more across, are produced in May and June. This exotic from the badlands requires full sun in a gravelly or sandy, well-drained, neutral to limy, soil (pH 7–8).

Oe. fruticosa. Attractive evergreen mats of small dark-green oval leaves in rosettes that send up woody flower stems, 18 to 24 inches high, each bearing a showy cluster of 2-inch bright-yellow flowers in July and August. It is a rather rapid spreader that is easy to grow and permanent in any well-drained garden soil, in sun or light shade. Var. *youngii* is shorter and more floriferous than the type.

Oe. lavendulaefolia. Neat little mounds of thin wiry stems, about 6 inches high, with silvery-gray leaves like those of the lavenders. It has bright-yellow broad-petaled flowers that are almost square when fully open. It blooms over a long period from May to August. A native of the Great Plains that requires a dry, well-drained soil (pH 6–8), and full sun.

Oe. missouriensis. A spectacular plant from the Missouri valley, with stout trailing or ascending stems with long narrow dull-gray-green leaves that form an attractive low broad mound about 6 inches high. The very large clear-yellow flowers, often 4 inches across, are displayed in the afternoon or early evening during June and July. It likes a dry, well-drained, sandy lime soil (pH 7–8) in full sun.

Oe. perennis. A small, charming, and extremely floriferous sundrop, from sandy places in the eastern United States. The plant starts as a tiny rosette of oval leaves and begins to bloom when it is only about 2 inches high. As the season advances, it increases in size and height, eventually ascending to about 18 inches. There is a continuous display of bright yellow flowers from spring to late fall. Although its native habitat is sandy wasteland, it makes itself happy in almost any soil in sun or light shade.

Oe. serrulata. Dense clumps of tiny, bright-green, serrated leaves on wiry 6-inch stems; and lovely, quite large, bright yellow flowers, with wavy petals, in June and July. A desirable little plant for the wall garden, or for a sunny, dry location (pH 6–8) in the rock garden.

Oe. triloba. Large clumps of long shining-green leaves that look like those of the dandelion, with large bright-yellow flowers nestled in them. You have to get up early to enjoy the attractive flowers. They open in the evening after dark and close at about 9 in the morning. Easy to grow in any well-drained garden soil, in sun or light shade.

OMPHALODES (*Boraginaceae,* Borage Family). A small genus from Europe and Asia, related to the forget-me-nots. The plants are easy to grow, showy, and permanent, if they are given a rich, moist, acid loam (pH 5–6), in shade or half-shade. They are usually propagated by divisions.

O. verna. Creeping stems from attractive mats of long, pointed, heart-shaped leaves, 4 or 5 inches high. Lovely open sprays of small bright-blue flowers in spring. The white form, var. *alba* is a lovely companion.

OPHIOPOGON (*Liliaceae,* Lily Family). Little sod-forming plants from Japan, often called mondo grass. They are easy to grow in a deep, rich, acid to neutral, moist loam (pH 5–7), in sun or shade. Propagated by divisions. Reasonably hardy as far north as New York, but do better with a generous winter cover.

O. jaburan. This species forms dense mats of thick cordlike roots and grassy leaves, to 2 feet long and a half-inch wide, that lie on the ground and form an attractive cover. Short spikes of white flowers are followed by deep-violet-blue berries. There are forms that have leaves striped with white or yellow.

O. japonicus. This plant forms a low dense mat that spreads quickly by means of underground stolons. It has very narrow, grasslike leaves, 10 to 12 inches long, and small lilac flowers, followed by blue fruits.

OPUNTIA (*Cactaceae,* Cactus Family). These are the well-known prickly-pears from desert regions of the West. Most species are not hardy and are too large for rock gardens, but some grow as far north as the arctic area and are small enough to use. Many more than those I list here can be used if care is taken to give them a hot, sunny location and extremely well-drained soil (pH 6–8). They are best planted high up in a rock garden, or in a wall garden. They can be grown from seeds, but it is a slow process. Almost all of them root easily if a joint is carefully cut off and inserted in a bed of barely moist sand.

O. compressa. A spreading mat of oval joints, which are sometimes 6 inches long. It produces quantities of large silky frilly yellow flowers in June, followed by small red "pears" in late summer. Native to open, sandy and rocky wastelands of the eastern United States.

O. fragilis. Little mounds of tiny orbicular spiny joints, an inch or two long, with small but showy pale-yellow flowers in early summer. This hardy little plant extends from Texas to northern Canada.

O. polyacantha. Wide flat joints, thickly covered with hoary spines, which form slowly spreading prostrate or ascending mounds, about 6 inches high. The large silky flowers are produced in early summer and range in color from lemon-yellow to brilliant orange and scarlet.

O. rhodantha. Dark-green, long, narrow joints, with long, sharp spines and lovely red or pink flowers.

O. rutilla. Clumps of long, cylindrical joints, with small spines and large deep-red flowers make this one of the best.

ORCHIS (*Orchidaceae,* Orchid Family). Terrestrial orchids from woodlands and marshes that are difficult to grow. Our eastern native *O. spectabilis* is sometimes collected from the wild and moved to gardens. It requires a deep, rich, moist, acid soil, in shade or half-shade. The best advice concerning this vanishing American is to enjoy it when you find it in the woods and *leave* it there.

PACHISTIMA (*Celastraceae,* Staff-Tree Family). Two small evergreen American shrubs.

P. canbyi. This species, a native of the mountains of Virginia, is the only member of the genus that I have worked with. It forms spreading semiprostrate mounds or mats, to 1 foot high, of thin woody stems and tiny shining-green leaves. The flowers are all but invisible when they appear in early spring. This shrub does well in sun or shade, in an acid leaf-mold soil. It spreads by underground stolons and, if left alone, will make an effective ground cover. If trimmed, it develops into an attractive little bush. Perfectly hardy to 25 degrees below zero, and easily increased by means of hard wood cuttings taken in fall.

Opuntia compressa.

PACHYSANDRA (*Buxaceae,* Boxwood Family). Woodland plants from North America and Japan that are attractive, useful, and easy to grow in a rich, acid to neutral, loam (pH 5–7), in shade or filtered sunlight. They are propagated by cuttings taken in early summer and sometimes by divisions.

P. procumbens. This native of the Alleghenies is scarcely known to American gardeners, but it is a handsome ornamental. Broad noncreeping clumps of pale-green denticulate leaves, about 10 inches high. In the fall and winter, the leaves remain green but lie flat on the ground. In early spring, large broad spikes of white flowers are produced from the base of the stems before the new foliage unfurls.

P. terminalis. This is the well-known evergreen creeper that is so extensively used as a ground cover. To 12 inches high. I have never seen it used in a rock garden, but it is often employed in conjunction with it. It has small insignificant white flowers in short terminal spikes. Var. *variegata* is an interesting form, with the leaves edged and marked with yellow.

PAPAVER (*Papaveraceae,* Poppy Family). The poppies are well-known flamboyant flower-garden subjects. Most of them are annuals or very large perennials. A few select species make excellent rock- and wall-garden subjects. They are invariably grown from seeds. The best method is to sow them where you want the plants to stand. They thrive in any well-drained garden soil, in full sun. The three species listed here are, I believe, the best for our purpose.

P. alpinum. A charmer from the European Alps. Small clumps of delicate pinnate glaucous foliage, and delicate fragrant flowers, colored white, yellow, or pink, on thin 10-inch stems, throughout the summer. It is short-lived but free-flowering, and self-sows readily in a situation that is particularly to its liking.

P. nudicaule. This is the favorite Iceland poppy from the Arctic that forms handsome mounds of lobed and cut hairy leaves, and stems about a foot high, bearing large silky flowers that range in color from white to yellow, orange, and red. There are numerous fancy named color forms.

P. rupifragum. This Spanish poppy makes broad flat tufts or rosettes of neatly divided hairy pale-green leaves, with 18-inch flower stems, bearing large orange to light-red flowers throughout the hottest part of the summer.

PARNASSIA (*Saxifragaceae,* Rockfoil Family). A few not too showy marsh plants from Europe, Asia, and North America. They are called grass-of-Parnassus, but why, I do not know, because they do not in the least resemble grass. I am familiar with only one, *P. caroliniana,* native to the marshes and swamps of northeastern mountains of the United States. Clumps of orbicular leaves, 3 or 4 inches high, with erect 18-inch flower stems, each bearing a single small, yellow-veined white flower in late spring. This plant requires a wet, mucky, alkaline soil (pH 7–8), in sun or light shade. Propagated by seeds or divisions, but usually collected from the wild.

PARONYCHIA (*Illecebraceae,* Knotwort Family). Small tufted plants from the Mediterranean region and the United States, with not much to recommend them except their silvery sheen. They like a hot, dry, well-drained soil (pH 6–8), in full sun. Propagated by seeds and divisions.

P. argentea. A tiny prostrate plant, with minute lanceolate ciliate leaves, and small flowers without petals, surrounded by glistening silvery bracts.

P. argyrocoma. Tiny silvery silky leaves on procumbent stems, forming billowy mats about 8 inches high. The tiny flowers are hidden by the large glistening silver bracts.

PEDICULARIS (*Scrophulariaceae,* Figwort Family). Attractive American woodland plants, with terminal spikes of showy flowers incased in bracts, and nice fernlike foliage. They are believed to be partially parasitic on the roots of oak trees and perhaps some other plants, and if they do not make the right connections they soon perish. They like an acid, woodsy soil (pH 5–6), in shade or filtered sunlight.

P. canadensis. Large, finely-divided fernlike leaves that lie almost flat on the ground, forming mats. The flower stems, about 15 inches high, bear short spikes of curly-looking yellow flowers, marked with red, in May and June.

PELLAEA (*Polypodiaceae,* Fern Family). Lime-loving rock ferns, mostly from the tropics, with a few northern ones that are ideal for rock gardens. The one most often attempted is *P. atropurpurea,* the purple cliff-brake, native to North America. It has lovely gray-green, simple-pinnate fronds with purple stipes, about 12 inches long, in neat noncreeping tufts. This fern is rather difficult to establish. It needs a tight, well-drained, limestone rock crevice with rich, black, pulverized leaf-mold (pH 7–8), in sun or light shade.

PENSTEMON (*Scrophulariaceae,* Figwort Family). A gloriously rich family of perennials and evergreen shrublets from North America. Almost all of its members are natural rock plants, a seemingly endless number of species and varieties. A few lowlanders from the northeastern United States are acceptable, but the best ones are found in the northern high Rocky Mountains. The taller weedy species have flowers somewhat like the foxglove, with colors ranging from dirty-white to muddy-purple. The best kinds have striking flowers, in colors ranging from deep rich purple to bright cherry-red and an intense clear blue. I have listed only 10 species here, to illustrate their versatility. Many more kinds are obtainable, mainly from collectors of seeds and plants in the Rocky Mountain states.

The perennial kinds are propagated by seeds and divisions, and the shrubby ones by cuttings taken in summer. Almost categorically, they require a very well-drained, sandy or gritty, gravelly, acid soil (pH 5–7), in full sun. Overwatering, the tendency of the modern gardener, usually means death to these prized plants.

P. alpinus. A herbaceous perennial, making tufts of long lanceolate leaves, about 4 inches high, with flowering stems, about 10 inches high, bearing spikes of large purple flowers in May and June.

P. angustifolius. Like *P. alpinus,* but with narrower leaves and flowers of a charming metallic blue.

P. caespitosus. A tiny evergreen shrublet, with thin creeping or decumbent stems and tiny spatulate leaves, studded with little racemes of lilac flowers from May to July. The entire plant is never more than 2 inches high, but it spreads into a fine mat, about 12 inches across.

P. crandallii. A somewhat loping, billowy mass of entwined stems, clothed in tiny linear leaves to form an attractive broad mound or mat, to 8 inches high. Short spikes of clear-light-blue flowers in summer.

P. davidsonii. This species is one of my favorite mat formers. Long, stout trailing stems with thick dark-green rounded leaves make a dense mat, about 1 inch thick. The comparatively large bright-purple flowers are produced on ascending stems, about 4 inches high, in May and June and a few through the summer. An exceptional fast-creeping ground-cover plant.

P. hirsutus. A fine example of eastern United States species. Large leafy clumps of dark-reddish-green sticky-hairy leaves, about 8 inches high. Bold spikes of light-purple flowers on upright stems, as high as 3 feet. There are several color forms, listed under the names *purpureus, rosinus, albus,* etc. Var. *pygmaeus* is a good rock-garden form that makes dense little mounds, about 3 inches high, with wide wavy-edged leaves. Heavy heads of light-purple-blue flowers rise just above the foliage on 5- or 6-inch stems.

P. menziesii. A noble and noteworthy little shrub about 6 inches high, which makes an attractive spreading mound of thick, decumbent or creeping branches, clothed in thick dark-green leathery evergreen leaves. It has huge purple trumpets on 6-inch stems, in May and June. An excellent wall-garden plant, and one of the easiest of the westerners to grow.

P. nitidus. Charming little tufts of long, narrow, glaucous leaves, about 6 inches high, with bright clear-blue flowers in loose spikes in June and July.

P. rupicola. This is one of the handsomest of the alpine penstemons and perhaps the most difficult to grow. It forms a dense compact bun of thick leathery leaves on decumbent stems, about 4 inches high, with large cherry-red flowers in July and August. *Rupicola* is one of the most desirable of the dwarf evergreen shrubs for rock and wall gardens. It must have a very well-drained, gravelly, acid leaf-mold soil, in sun or light shade. A rock ledge, where its roots will be kept cool and moist against the rock, is ideal.

P. tolmiei. A beautiful herbaceous species that forms low leafy clumps of broad, oval, dark-glossy-green leaves, about 3 inches high, and erect stems, about 8 inches high, bearing showy spikes of fragrant lavender flowers in May and June.

PERNETTYA (*Ericaceae,* Heath Family). Showy and interesting evergreen shrubs for mild climates and for sheltered and protected spots in northern rock gardens. They require a cool, moist, acid, leaf-mold soil (pH 4–6), in sun or light shade. They are increased by cuttings, divisions, or suckers from underground shoots.

P. mucronata. A dense, twiggy bush about 24 inches high, with small, oval, shining-green leaves, and small urn-shaped white to light-pink flowers. The main attraction of the plant is its conspicuous crop of brightly colored berries that hang on all through the winter. In the typical form, the berry is red. There are several named forms with variously colored berries, as *rosea* with pink, *alba* with white, *purpurea* with deep-purple, and *lilacinea* with light-purple berries. *Mucronata* is native to the southern reaches of South America.

P. tasmanica. As the name indicates, this tiny creeping plant comes to us from Tasmania. However, it will survive our severe winters with a little winter protection, particularly from drying winds. It forms a mat, about 3 inches high, of thin wiry stems with very tiny, pointed, shining bright-green leaves, and has tiny solitary white flowers with a liberal sprinkling of showy bright-red berries.

PETALOSTEMUM (*Leguminosae,* Pea Family). Interesting hardy subshrubs from the North American plains. Some are a little tall for the rock garden, but all make interesting conversation pieces. Several species grow wild, but I have grown only one.

P. villosum. Loose, open mounds of finely-divided silvery-silky foliage, about 12 inches high, with short dense spikes of silky purple flowers in June and July. It has deep, woody roots, which make it rather difficult to move after it has become established. *P. villosum* requires a rather dry, well-drained, gravelly or sandy, lime soil (pH 7–8), in full hot sun.

PETROPHYTUM (*Rosaceae,* Rose Family). Miniature prostrate or cespitose evergreen *Spiraeas* from the Rocky Mountains. They require a gritty limestone soil (pH 7–8), in sun or light shade. They can be propagated by tiny cuttings and, with care, by divisions.

P. caespitosum. Dense mats, only an inch or two high, but under ideal conditions spreading in several years to 2 feet or more wide. The woody stems are prostrate or subterranean, and the leaves are barely half an inch long. Dense little spikes of white flowers are about 3 inches long.

PHLOX (*Polemoniaceae,* Phlox Family). Colorful old-favorite garden plants. Some are tall and best planted in the perennial border, but many are natural rock plants of numerous varieties and different color forms. The phloxes are all endemic to North America, and we are justly proud of the flamboyant touch they add to our gardens. A mass of mountain-pinks, bursting into brilliant purples, pinks, and whites on a south bank in April is difficult to match. Other flowers may be the harbingers of spring, but when the mountain-pinks flower, we know spring has come to stay.

Except for the few annual species, and the very tall ones, like *P. carolina* and *P. paniculata,* all species are acceptable rock plants. Their cultural requirements are as varied as the kinds and are therefore indicated under the species listing. Phloxes can be propagated by seeds and cuttings, but the usual and easiest method is by divisions.

P. adsurgens. A most beautiful species from Oregon. Eastern members of the American Rock Garden Society disagree on the subject of its ability to flower and its cultural requirements. It is a trailing evergreen plant with broad, oval, dark-green leaves, and ascending stems with clusters of large salmon-pink flowers in spring. I have been able to grow it in an acid leaf-mold soil over a well-drained gravelly subsoil, in shade or half-shade. The flowering shoots are produced on the old stems, never on new shoots coming from the roots. It is not thoroughly hardy away from its natural range, and if it dies back to the roots it will never flower. With ample winter cover, it will retain its old stems and flower profusely.

P. bifida. Large tumbling mounds about 10 inches high, with stiff almost woody stems bearing long and narrow, quite stiff awl-shaped leaves, colored a dull gray-green. Large, loose panicles of light-purple to white flowers in May, with the petals of the individual florets divided almost in two. It requires a well-drained, sandy soil (pH 6–8), in full sun.

P. divaricata. The wild sweet William is native to eastern United States woodlands. It is easy to grow in a rich, acid, loam soil (pH 5–6), in either shade or sun. In full hot sun and dry soil, it goes partially dormant, losing most of its leaves and presenting a poor appearance. It is best in shade or half-shade, where it forms a spreading mass of large oval, more or less evergreen leaves, and flowering stems about 18 inches high. Delightful masses of light-violet-blue fragrant flowers appear in May. Var. *alba* is a good form, with pure-white flowers. Var. *laphamii* has deep-blue-violet flowers.

P. nivalis. Broad mats of long trailing stems with evergreen sharp-pointed, awl-shaped leaves. This species resembles the mountain pink *P. subulata* in growth habit and is often confused with it. It has large pale-pink flowers, displayed well above the leaves on stems about 5 inches long. There are several named forms, with flowers in white, blue, and various shades of pink. The most popular, 'Camla,' has large salmon-pink flowers. This species blooms two or three weeks later than the mountain pinks, and usually again in the fall when warm weather comes after the first hard frost. It is easy to grow in any well-drained garden soil, in full sun.

P. ovata. Large mats of big oval leaves, about 3 inches high, that spread by underground shoots. The flower stems in late

May and June are about 15 inches high and bear large flat clusters of deep-purple flowers. An extraordinarily fine form discovered by Dr. Edgar T. Wherry in the mountains of Alabama is var. *pulchra.* It has dark-veined pastel-pink flowers with a delicate fragrance. *P. ovata* is easy to grow in sun or light shade, in a fairly rich garden loam that is slightly on the acid side (pH 5–7).

P. pilosa. Mounds of stiff wiry stems, about 10 inches high, with long, narrow hairy 3-inch leaves. The flowers are borne in late spring in small clusters and vary from white to pink and purple in the type. It likes a sandy or gravelly, well-drained, acid soil (pH 5–6), in full sun.

P. procumbens. A hybrid that is often listed as *P. amoena.* Dense little decumbent mats of small dark-green spatulate leaves, about 3 inches high. Huge clusters of bright rosy-purple flowers on 6-inch stems, in April and May. Var. *variegata* is an interesting plant with yellow-striped foliage. Easy to grow in any ordinary garden soil, in sun or light shade.

P. stononifera. Attractive quick- and wide-spreading evergreen mats of broad, oval leaves that lie flat on the ground. It makes a most desirable ground cover even without its colorful flowers. Nodding clusters of large light-purple flowers are carried on 6-inch stems, in April and May. There are several good named color forms, the best being 'Blue Ridge' with large clear light-blue flowers, and 'Lavender Lady' with narrower smaller leaves and flowers the deepest mauve imaginable. A woodland plant that requires an acid leaf-mold soil (pH 5–6), in shade or filtered sunlight.

P. subulata. This is the versatile, colorful and ever-popular mountain pink, or moss pink, of roadside banks. A native on rocky hillsides and mountains from New York to North Carolina, it is easy to grow in full sun on almost any well-drained soil. It forms broad spreading evergreen mats of tiny sharp-pointed leaves that are prickly to the touch, and masses of small flowers tight on the foliage. It comes in various color forms, often listed under fancy names, from white to all shades of pink and purple and even ranging into blue. Var. *brittonii* is an unusual sort, making a very tight mat of tiny leaves, with small bright-pink flowers conspicuously notched at the apex. One of the most desirable of the fancy named sorts is 'Schneewitchen.' It forms an extremely compact little mat of silky gray-green leaves, with tiny white flowers in profusion.

PHYLLODOCE (*Ericaceae,* Heath Family). Little evergreen shrubs, resembling the ericas in foliage and habit of growth. They are arctic or high alpine plants that are difficult to maintain in hot dry climates. Phyllodoces require a constantly moist, acid leaf-mold soil (pH 4–6), with sun or light shade in their native habitat, but do best in shady situations at low altitudes. They can be propagated by cuttings and by the removal of self-layered branches. There are six or seven species, but only one or two are available.

P. caerulea. Stout, stiff, ascending branches that make spreading bushlets about 6 inches high, with terminal clusters of urn-shaped flowers in spring. This is called blue heather, but the flowers are not blue. They range in color from pink to purple. From the Arctic, but ranging as far south as the White Mountains of New Hampshire.

P. empetriformis. A rounded little bush about 8 inches high with stiff, upright branches, thickly garbed in very fine needlelike dark-green leaves. The bell-shaped flowers are a glistening rosy-purple color. A native of mountain bogs from British Columbia south to northern California.

PHYSARIA (*Cruciferae,* Mustard Family). A few odd tufted plants from the Rocky Mountains that are sometimes furnished by collectors and planted in the rock garden. They require a sandy, well-drained lime soil (pH 7–8), in full hot sun.

P. didymocarpa. Broad, oval soft-silvery leaves on decumbent stems about 6 inches long, and clusters of small yellow flowers in spring, followed by odd large inflated seed pods.

PHYSOSTEGIA (*Labiatae,* Mint Family). A couple of very tall, rather weedy plants, found in moist soil in the eastern United States, that are sometimes planted in rock gardens.

P. virginiana is a resplendent summer-blooming border perennial that grows about 4 feet tall and spreads rapidly by long underground runners. Some of its forms, however, are adaptable to rock gardens. Var. *alba* is a noncreeper that forms little mounds of long narrow denticulate leaves, about 6 inches high, from which emerge erect 12-inch stems, bearing spikes of pure-white flowers in July and August. A fancy named form called 'Vivid' has bright-red flowers on stems about 24 inches high. It is a good color form but must be planted with care because it spreads rapidly and can become a nuisance. Both of these forms are easy to grow in any ordinary garden soil in full sun.

PHYTEUMA (*Campanulaceae,* Bellflower Family). A large group of rather tall and floppy perennials from Europe and Asia. Some are interesting, showy, and desirable for the rock garden. They can be propagated by seeds or by divisions without difficulty, and are easy to grow in any well-drained garden soil, in sun or light shade. Phyteumas are excellent wall-garden plants, too, and, like the campanulas, do best when their roots can run along an underground rock. They are seldom offered in the United States, but most of them can be obtained from Europe in the form of seeds. In all species, the flowers are borne in orbicular clusters. The buds are hornlike, never open fully, and thus have a bristly look.

P. scheucheri. Soft-looking clumps of long, narrow leaves, about 6 inches high, with flower stems about 18 inches long, bearing light-lavender flowers in May and June.

P. sieberi. Attractive little mounds of lance-shaped toothed leaves, and flower stems about 6 inches high, with tight globose heads of deep-blue flowers in spring and early summer.

PIERIS (*Ericaceae,* Heath Family). Handsome evergreen shrubs from North America and Asia, known chiefly in the species *P. japonica,* the lily-of-the-valley bush. They are large shrubs, used extensively in home landscaping. One tiny arctic species and two or three dwarf forms of *P. japonica* can be used in the rock garden. They are increased by seeds or cuttings, and succeed in an acid leaf-mold soil (pH 4–6), in sun or half-shade.

P. japonica var. *variegata*. An exquisite dwarf plant that eventually reaches a height of about 3 feet. The attractive shiny-green leaves are edged and feathered with yellow. New growth in early spring is pink and crimson and, along with the green and yellow of the mature leaves, makes a striking display. This plant has showy nodding, or drooping, panicles of white flowers. Var. *compacta* is a dwarf green form that originated through a regression of the variegated one to green but retained its dwarf characteristics.

P. nana. A miniature arctic plant, usually listed as *Arcterica nana*. It consists of a tiny mound of decumbent branches, about 3 inches high, with tiny leaves about a half-inch long in whorls of three. Tiny white urn-shaped flowers in groups of three appear in early spring. Although *P. nana* is an arctic plant, it is difficult to keep over winter without a constant snow cover.

POLEMONIUM (*Polemoniaceae,* Phlox Family). Gorgeous little perennials, mainly from the high Rocky Mountains. Besides the common Jacob's-ladder, very few are ever available. If you are lucky enough to find someone who collects seeds of these plants, you will be the envy of fellow rock gardeners. The plants are rather easy to grow in a fairly rich garden loam, in sun or light shade.

P. pulcherrimum. Lovely little tufts of ferny foliage, 3 or 4 inches high. Nodding little clusters of flowers in subdued tones, from violet to rose.

P. reptans. Masses of light-blue flowers over large clumps of attractive ferny foliage, about 12 inches high. This native of the eastern United States prefers light shade, in a fairly moist soil.

P. viscosum. Attractive tufts, about 3 inches high, of sticky-pubescent, round-lobed leaflets, and clusters of large blue flowers held scarcely above the foliage in early spring.

Pieris japonica variegata.

POLYGALA (*Polygalaceae,* Milkwort Family). An interesting family of annual and perennial shrubby plants. Most of them are either too large or too tender for northern rock gardens, but there are some fine exceptions.

P. calcarea. Small, slowly-spreading mats of oval evergreen leaves, barely an inch high, which are almost smothered with countless bright-clear-blue flowers in early spring. A Swiss alpine that requires a gritty, very well-drained, limestone soil, in full sun or very light shade. To insure its permanence, it should have moraine culture.

P. chamaebuxus. A little creeping evergreen shrub from the woodlands of southern Europe. It has green stems about 12 inches high, with little leathery boxwoodlike leaves, and fairly large yellow flowers in spring. It is not thoroughly hardy, but can be brought through the winter with ample protection in a sheltered position. It likes a deep, acid, leaf-mold soil, in shade or half-shade.

P. paucifolia. The colorful little gaywings of our eastern woodlands. It has creeping underground stems that form loose open mats, 6 to 7 inches high, of small oval, more-or-less-evergreen leaves. The bright wide-winged rosy-purple flowers are an enchanting find when you visit the woods in early April. Gaywings requires a moist, cool, leaf-mold soil (pH 4–5), in rather dense shade. It is rather difficult to establish in the garden, apparently because it is partially parasitic. Unless its roots join the proper host plant, it will not remain for very long. In the wild, it is most often associated with *Maianthemum canadensis.* Therefore, I believe that if these two are planted together the gaywings will succeed.

P. vayrediae. A little evergreen shrub about 6 inches high with long, narrow, leathery leaves that droop down close to the stem. Bright purple and yellow flowers in early spring. This is a tender species from southern Europe that requires winter protection in the North. It requires an acid leaf-mold soil (pH 4–6), in shade or filtered sunlight.

POLYGONUM (*Polygonaceae,* Knotweed Family). A large group of rather coarse and invasive perennials or viny shrubs. One or two of the Himalayan species are suitable for rock work.

P. vaccinifolium. A trailing perennial with woody stems and tiny, oval, pointed leaves, somewhat resembling the cranberry. It forms a wide-spreading, billowy mat, 6 inches or less high, which is almost covered with short spikes of rose-pink flowers in August and September. A tender species that does well in the Philadelphia area, but requires heavy winter protection farther north. It likes any well-drained garden soil, in full sun.

POLYPODIUM (*Polypodiaceae,* Fern Family). A large collection of huge tropical ferns, with a few dwarf northerners that are adaptable to rock gardening. They are generally typified by the common wall-fern of our rock ledges in shady woodlands.

P. vulgare. Broad spreading mats of small leathery fronds, about 6 inches high, sometimes taller. It is usually found growing on top of flat rock ledges in a two- or three-inch accumulation of leaf-mold, or on the face of rock cliffs in a layer of damp sheet moss.

POLYSTICHUM (*Polypodiaceae,* Fern Family). Mostly evergreen ferns of northern woodlands, some not too tall for rock garden work. All of those listed here require an acid leaf-mold soil (pH 4–6), in shade or filtered sunlight. Most of them can be propagated by divisions, but usually they are collected from the wild.

P. acrostichoides. Handsome and boldly decorative Christmas ferns, often used for table decoration and in flower arrangements. This fern is about 24 inches high, with fronds 4 or 5 inches wide and long lance-shaped, leathery pinnae colored a bright shining green.

P. braunii. A large plant with fronds about 2 feet high and 12 inches wide, in handsome clumps. The 2-pinnate fronds have a lacier aspect than the preceding.

P. lonchitis. This is the mountain holly fern, much like the Christmas fern but shorter in stature, to 2 feet, and much narrower.

POTENTILLA (*Rosaceae,* Rose Family). A long list of useful and colorful perennials and a few little shrubs, many of them natural rock plants. Many more than the 10 species listed here can, and should, be used in rock work. With few exceptions, they are easy to grow in ordinary garden soil, in full sun or light shade. Some of the alpine forms need special attention. Almost all of them are easy to increase by divisions. Shrubby ones can be propagated by cuttings taken in early summer.

P. alba. Elegant, slowly spreading mounds, about 5 inches high, with green palmate leaves that are silky white on the underside, with enough showing to create a glistening effect. Sprays of large white flowers are carried on stems about 10 inches high, in May and June. A rare beauty from central Europe.

P. atrosanguinea. Mounds, about 12 inches high, of strawberrylike leaves that are covered with silvery-silky down. The brilliant-scarlet flowers are borne in large sprays on 18-inch stems, in May and June and sometimes in July. A handsome, nonspreading plant from the Himalayas.

P. flabellifolia. Little mounds of dark-green 3-parted leaves, about 3 inches high. Sprays of bright-yellow flowers on 10-inch stems, in May and June. From the Rocky Mountains.

P. fruticosa. A large shrub that reaches a height of 4 feet. It is much too large for the rock garden, but there are several dwarf forms from around the world that are admirably suited to it. Var. *vietchii* grows into a nice rounded shrub, about 2 feet high, with large pure-white flowers from May to October. Var. *pumila* is a very tiny plant with stiff little twigs that grow into a ball, 4 or 5 inches high. The leaves are silky-gray-green and the flowers bright yellow. Var. *tenuiloba* grows about 18 inches high, with thin stems, and the leaves are divided into fine, long, and narrow segments. The flowers are bright yellow, and it blooms all summer. Var. *rigida* is a sturdy plant, about 12 inches high, with stiff, upright branches and bright-yellow flowers. Var. *mandshurica* is a creeping, or prostrate, shrub with gray-green silky leaves and large white flowers. Besides the botanically recognized varieties, there are several fancy named garden forms, such as 'Catherine Dykes,' 'Gold Drop,' 'Lemon Drop,' and 'E. P. Bowles.'

P. nevadensis. A little prostrate or tufted plant from Spain, 3 inches or less high, with tiny palmately-lobed, 5-parted leaves. Both leaves and stems are covered with fine silvery-silky hairs, which give it a hoary look. Sprays of yellow flowers on 3 or 4 inch stems, in May. This one demands a very well-drained, gritty lime soil (pH 7–8), in full sun.

P. nitida. A rare and coveted plant from the Swiss Alps that is difficult to grow. It consists of a little tuft of silvery-silky 3-parted leaves, about an inch high, with large lovely rose-colored flowers on 1-inch stems in spring. It must have a tight rock crevice, with lime soil and full sun. The one and only plant that I have been able to keep for any length of time was in the west side of a dry-wall garden.

P. tormentillo-formosa. A hybrid that is often listed as *P. tonguei.* Little mounds of dark green 3- to 5-parted leaves, about 4 inches high. It sends out long trailing stems, sometimes 2 feet long, which form a lovely mat covered with a continuous display of showy pale-yellow flowers with red centers, from July to September. This plant is not a creeper; the trailing flower stems die off in winter, leaving only the central clump of leaves. An unexcelled wall flower, with the trailing stems hanging down like a waterfall.

P. tridentata. This native of eastern North America is a delightful evergreen ground-cover plant. Its creeping underground stems form quickly-spreading broad mats of dark-green shining 3-parted leaves, about 2 inches high, when it is grown in full sun, in a poor sandy soil. When it is given a rich garden loam it grows about 6 inches high. Airy sprays of small white flowers in May, June, and July. Easy to grow and permanent in an ordinary garden soil that is a bit on the acid side (pH 5–7).

P. verna. Close-growing evergreen mats of tiny palmate leaves, only about 2 inches high, almost completely hidden by quantities of bright-yellow flowers in very early spring. The usual form is called var. *nana*. Whether this is different from the natural species, I do not know. After the flowers fade, the plant remains an interesting ornament because of its dark evergreen leaves. Easy to grow in any ordinary garden soil.

P. villosa. This fast-creeping plant from Alaska forms neat evergreen mats, to 1 foot high, of small three-parted silky gray-green leaves that are liberally sprinkled with large clear-yellow flowers from April to June. A good wall plant and ground cover that is easy to grow in any ordinary garden soil, but it must have full hot sun.

PRIMULA (*Primulaceae,* Primrose Family). There is no need to extol the beauty of the primroses, for they are well known to all gardeners. This is a huge genus made up almost exclusively of colorful and desirable plants, most of them hardy in the North. Some are rather tall marsh plants, but the majority are ideal rock-garden subjects. They are native to Europe, Asia, and North America. The most desirable ones are the saxicoles from high mountains and the Arctic. These are also the most difficult to cultivate, mainly because they are intolerant of summer heat and need cold at their roots.

The thorough study of primroses would require a lifetime of work and fill volumes. This small space will be devoted to the species and varieties that are usually encountered in rock gardens. These are of simple requirements, and are permanent under adverse conditions. To those who would like to experiment with primroses, the door to adventure is wide open. There are literally hundreds to choose from. *Hortus II* lists about 140 species, and Henry Correvon almost 200. Add to these the countless varieties, hybrids, and as yet undiscovered and unnamed kinds, and your horizon recedes into the far distance. Periodically, seeds of these rare and lovely alpines are obtainable from botanists and collectors, who have gathered them during field trips.

The basic requirements for the simple, yet lovely and desirable, primroses treated here is a good, rich, acid loam (pH 5–6), rich in organic material, ample moisture, and shade or filtered sunlight. They are propagated by seeds, which germinate best from fresh seeds, or by divisions in late summer.

P. auricula. Tufts or low clumps, to 8 inches high, of thick, rather leathery, large light-green leaves about 4 inches long. Flower stems, about 8 inches high, with large clusters of yellow flowers in the wild species. There are numerous garden and color forms with fancy names. Flowers range from brown to almost black, with every shade of yellow and red imaginable.

P. denticulata. Large clumps of long crinkly denticulate light-green leaves about 10 inches high. Sturdy stems, 10 to 20 inches high, carry dense orbicular clusters of purple flowers in early spring before the leaves appear Var. *cashmeriana* is a color form that is often listed as a separate species.

P. japonica. The queen of the candelabras. Somewhat tall for the rock garden, but often planted at the edge of adjacent pools. Broad clumps of large ovate leaves, about 6 inches high. The flower stems, which appear in late May and June, have successive whorls of flowers, beginning when they are about 6 inches high and eventually reaching a height of about 2 feet. The color varies from white to all shades of pink and red. For best results, it should have full sun and wet mucky soil (*illustration page 272*).

P. juliae. A tiny plant from the Caucasus, which forms little spreading mats about 2 inches high. Dark-red or purple-red flowers are borne singly, scarcely above the foliage, in early spring.

P. polyantha. Probably the easiest, and by far the most popular, of the primroses in United States gardens. It is a hybrid of mixed parentage that forms rather large clumps of long light-green leaves, about 10 inches high. The huge flowers are borne in large flat clusters on stems 8 to 15 inches high. The colors include all shades of yellow, red, pink, purple, buff, bronze, and blue. There are several strains and numerous fancy named color forms.

P. sieboldii. Spreading mats of soft, light-green, crinkly leaves, about 3 inches high, that go dormant soon after flowering.

Primula japonica.

Primula sieboldii.

Very large flowers in umbels appear in early spring. The flowers, of crepe-paper texture, are white or tinted in delicate tones of rose and mauve.

P. veris. The famous cowslip from the meadows of England. Low spreading mounds of soft-green leaves, about 4 inches high, and numerous stems, about 8 inches high, bearing large nodding umbels of fragrant yellow flowers in spring. There are numerous hybrids and garden forms, with flowers of every color of the spectrum. One of the nicest is var. *duplex,* with hose-in-hose flowers of delicate moonlight-yellow.

P. vulgaris. Low clumps of wrinkled leaves, about 3 inches high, with large yellow, blue, pink, or purple flowers nestled in the leaves, one flower to a single thin stem. Here again, there are several named garden forms, many of them hybrids.

P. 'X Juliana.' These are hybrids of *P. juliae* and other low-growing species and some of the best plants for rock work. They are all mat-formers, with leaves 2 to 4 inches high. The flowers of some are borne singly, of others in clusters like the polyanthus primroses. Some of the fancy named forms are 'Dorothy' with pale yellow flowers, 'Primose Lodge' bright purple-crimson, 'Kimlaugh Beauty' delicate salmon, 'Lady Greer' creamy-white, 'Mrs. McGillivary' mauve-pink, 'Nettie Gale' pure-white, and the best of all 'Wanda,' a persistent permanent, and floriferous variety with deep wine-red flowers in early April.

PRUNELLA (*Labiatae,* Mint Family). Weedy herbaceous perennials that are hardly worth the space they occupy. One species, *P. grandiflora,* is often used when nothing better is on hand. It makes broad creeping clumps of not unattractive large oval evergreen leaves, about 6 inches high. It has spikes of purple typical labiate flowers on stems about 12 inches high, in June and July. There are several color forms as indicated by the names, *alba, rubra, rosea,* and *carminea.* Easy to grow in any ordinary garden soil, in sun or light shade. Propagated by divisions or seeds.

PTEROCEPHALUS (*Dipsaceae,* Teasel Family). A small group of herbs from the Mediterranean region, related to the scabiosas. I know only one species, *P. parnassi.* It forms a low wide-spreading mat of gray pubescent pinnatifid lyre-shaped leaves, about 3 inches high. Tight heads of mauve-pink flowers are produced on 3-inch stems in late spring and summer. It requires a deep root run of fairly dry, well-drained, gravelly, lime soil (pH 7–8), in full sun. An excellent wall-garden plant. Propagated by divisions and sometimes by cuttings.

PULMONARIA (*Boraginaceae,* Borage Family). Large, rather coarse, but still showy and desirable plants with blue flowers resembling those of the mertensias. They are easy to grow, and permanent in a good rich garden soil, in half-shade. They will stand full sun if the soil does not become parched, but the leaves tend to brown at the edges. Propagated by divisions in late spring.

P. angustifolia. Low spreading clumps of long, narrow, hairy green leaves, about 12 inches long but standing only about 4 inches high. Terminal nodding clusters of long-tubed clear-blue flowers in early spring. Var. *azurea,* often listed as *P. azurea,* is said to have lighter-blue flowers, but I have never been able to see the difference.

P. officinalis. Bold clumps of very large light-green leaves, mottled and spotted with silvery white, standing about 12 inches high. In early spring, the flowers open red and gradually turn to a deep blue-violet, giving them a two-toned effect. The foliage is an attraction throughout the summer, even without the flowers.

P. saccharata. Much like *P. officinalis,* but the leaves are spotted, rather than mottled, with white, and the flowers remain reddish-violet. There are several named forms, the best being 'Mrs. Moon' with salmon-pink flowers.

PYROLA (*Pyrolaceae,* Shinleaf Family). Little mat-forming woodland plants, related to *Moneses* and *Chimaphila,* that are almost impossible to maintain in a garden. They make low mats of roundish shiny-green leaves and have large waxy white, rose, or light-purple flowers in June, on stems 4 to 10 inches high in later summer. They require an acid leaf-mold soil (pH 4–5), in dense shade. There are several species native to Europe, North America, and Asia. The best method of handling these enchanting plants is to enjoy them where you find them in the woods and leave them there.

PYXIDANTHERA (*Diapensiaceae,* Diapensia Family). Two creeping evergreen shrublets, native to sandy pine barrens in the eastern United States. They require a constantly moist, sandy soil with acid leaf-mold (pH 4–5), in shade or filtered sunlight. They can be grown from seeds, but it is a slow painstaking operation. The usual method is to dig them

Pyxidanthera barbulata.

in the wild, plant them in the garden, and watch them die. If small isolated seedlings are selected, they can be moved successfully, but they require constant care for at least the first year.

P. barbulata. This is the famous pyxie moss of the New Jersey pine barrens. Tiny shining bright-green leaves on creeping woody stems that make a dense mat about half an inch high, but spreading to 3 feet or more. This fine mosslike growth is liberally studded with white stars that open from pink buds in early spring. *P. brevifolia* from North Carolina is distinguished only by technical differences.

RAMONDA (*Gesneriaceae,* Gesneria Family). Since the growth in popularity of the saintpaulias, these are best described as hardy African violets. They are natives of the high mountains of Europe, and are, to say the least, difficult to grow. They require perfect drainage, an acid leaf-mold soil (pH 4–6), shade, and a tight vertical rock crevice, preferably under an overhanging rock. They will not stand being wet in winter.

R. nathaliae. Rosettes of thick, hairy, large, ovate, wavy-toothed evergreen leaves. Sprays of large lavender-blue flowers with golden centers on 6-inch stems, in May (*illustration page 278*).

R. pyrenaica. Much like *R. nathaliae* with thick, hairy, deeply-toothed leaves, and the flowers a deep purple. Var. *alba* has white flowers, and var. *rosea* pink.

RANUNCULUS (*Ranunculaceae,* Buttercup Family). These are the true buttercups of florist shops and gardens. They are showy, but also tall and rangy. A few of the dwarf mountain species make ideal rock plants. They generally require a moist acid loam (pH 5–6), in sun or light shade, and are easily propagated by divisions. Besides the two Europeans I list here, there are several choice kinds from the Rocky Mountains that should be introduced to our gardens. I offered two or three of them several years ago, but, like too many plants from our native American flora, they were spurned in favor of the better-known plants.

Ramonda nathaliae in a vertical crevice under an overhanging rock.

R. crenatus. Little tufts of rounded, wavy, denticulate leaves about 3 inches high, and large white flowers on 4-inch stems in early spring.

R. montanus. A tiny, slowly creeping plant that forms little mats of attractive leaves divided into linear segments. Solitary bright yellow flowers are carried on 6-inch stems in spring.

RAOULIA (*Compositae,* Daisy Family). Little creeping plants from New Zealand. The flowers are insignificant, but the silvery leaves are attractive. They are not hardy, but I have had some success with *R. australis* in a sheltered place and with heavy winter cover. It forms little mats, about an inch high, of tiny leaves covered with a silvery-yellow tomentum. Needs a sandy or gritty, well-drained, lime soil (pH 7–8), in full sun.

RHEXIA (*Melastomaceae,* Melastoma Family). Interesting plants, native to bogs and marshes of the eastern United States. I am familiar only with the meadow beauty, *R. virginica.* It forms neat clumps of small oval leaves on square stems about 10 inches high, and has vivid rosy-purple flowers with prominent yellow anthers from July to September. Although native to wet ground, it will succeed in a dry soil that does not become parched. It likes sun or light shade, in an acid loam or leaf-mold soil (pH 5–6). Self-propagated by means of numerous little tubers.

RHODODENDRON (*Ericaceae,* Heath Family). These are the aristocrats of the woody plants that are well known to every homeowner. They are mostly large shrubs, used extensively in general home landscaping, but there are numerous tiny arctic and alpine species, as well as dwarfs of the better-known larger forms, that are adaptable to rock garden work. All require an acid leaf-mold soil (pH 4–6), in full sun or light shade. Some of the arctics prefer shade when grown at low elevations in warm climates. There are many more species and hybrids than those listed that can, and should, be introduced into our rock gardens. The botanists have grouped all the azaleas with the rhododendrons, and so I list them here together.

Hardiness, or the lack of it, is a dominant factor in the cultivation of rhododendrons. Some are hardy in stem and leaf but lose their buds every year, and thus are almost worthless to northern gardeners. Many species that can be grown along the seacoast are tender a few miles inland. It is up to the individual gardener to select ones that will do well in his particular locality. I have found that some of the kinds that have the reputation of being tender can be grown in my cold climate where temperatures of 20 or 30 degrees below zero are not uncommon. They come through the coldest of winters, if they are planted on the north side of a building where they get absolutely no sun in winter and the soil never thaws. Another precaution is to protect them from severe drying winds. Many of the arctic and alpine species require heavy winter protection in areas where a continuous snow cover is lacking.

R. atlanticum. A deciduous azalea from the Carolinas that forms an attractive rounded bush about 24 inches high, with glaucous-green foliage. The large clusters of long-tubed creamy-white flowers, suffused with bluish-pink, appear in early spring before the leaves. Although a southerner, *atlanticum* is perfectly hardy in the North.

R. canadense (*Rhodora canadensis*). A bog plant from eastern Canada that spreads slowly by means of short stolons. The stiff sturdy branches stand upright, 2 feet or more, and are clothed with very small blue-green leaves. The lavender flowers, with corolla divided into narrow petals and prominent stamens, are produced in March and early April. Var. *alba* is a dwarfer, more compact plant, with pure-white flowers. Contrary to the belief that this plant is difficult, I have found it easy to grow and permanent, even in a very dry soil.

R. carolinianum. A shrub, to 6 feet high, that should be relegated to the background of the rock garden. However, there is a dwarf form, recently discovered by Mrs. Mary G. Henry in the mountains of South Carolina, that grows only 3 feet high, with more or less spreading or decumbent branches. The flowers are deep pink to dark red, and the leaves have a dark reddish-green color. An excellent rock-garden subject.

R. ferrugineum. The famous "Alpen rosen" of the Swiss Alps. Small, narrow, shining green leaves on compact bushes, about 3 feet high after many years of growing. Clusters of bright-carmine, funnelform flowers in July.

R. flavidum. A low twiggy shrub about 2 feet high, with small pale-green scaly leaves, and little clusters of light-yellow flowers in spring. This one needs protection in the North.

R. hirsutum. A dense, bushy plant with bright-green ovate leaves, ciliate with long hairs. Flowers similar to *R. ferrugineum,* varying from pink to carmine. It is said to like limestone soil, but I grew it in acid leaf-mold.

R. impeditum. This dwarf flowering shrub from the mountains of China is one of the best for rock work. It is very slow-growing, tight, and twiggy, with leaves scarcely half an inch long. I have seen plants 30 years old that were only 18 inches high and about 30 inches across. In late April or early May, it produces small but showy clusters of deep-violet-blue flowers. A closely related species *R. fastagiatum* is sometimes confused with it, but it is taller than *R. impeditum,* more open in its habit of growth, and its leaves, instead of being dark green, have a bluish cast.

R. indicum. A tender evergreen azalea from Japan, which florists often force to produce holiday plants. The typical form is worthless to us, but var. *Balsaminaeflorum* is the most lovely azalea imaginable. It is not thoroughly hardy but is reasonably dependable in the New York City area and can be carried over farther north and inland with ample winter protection. It is a dwarf semiprostrate plant that makes a little mound about 12 inches high, with small dark-green hairy leaves. The fully-double large roselike salmon-colored flowers are displayed in late May and June. There are several other good garden forms, among them 'Hakatishiro,' 'Flame Creeper,' and 'Angustifolia.'

R. keiskei. A magnificent yellow-flowered rhododendron from Japan that is a little on the tender side but can be maintained with protection. It is really too big for the rock garden, but it is useful as a young plant and can be kept in proportion for a number of years by annual shearing. It grows into a broad procumbent shrub, about 4 feet high, with small dark-green ciliate leaves. In May, it is covered with lovely lemon-yellow flowers.

R. keleticum. A twiggy prostrate shrub, about 6 inches high, with tiny sharp-pointed ciliate leaves, and small bright-crimson flowers marked with deep purple.

R. laetevirens. Usually listed as *R. wilsonii.* A hybrid between *R. carolinianum* and *R. ferrugineum,* this is a dense, twiggy shrub with long and narrow, petioled dark-green leaves. It eventually reaches a height of about 3 feet. Clusters of small bright-rose-colored flowers appear in May. Perfectly hardy, even in the most severe winters under adverse conditions.

R. lapponicum. A tiny prostrate plant from the Arctic and from high mountains of Europe, Asia, and North America. Tiny oval dark-green leaves on prostrate stems that make dense little mats, 3 or 4 inches high, but spreading to about 3 feet wide. Comparatively large bell-shaped purple flowers in June.

R. myrtifolium. A dense globe-shaped hybrid between *R. hirsutum* and *R. minus* that is said to grow about 5 feet high, but I have never seen one more than 2 feet tall. A dense ball-shaped plant, with leathery dark-green leaves, and loose clusters of long-tubed pale-pink flowers in May. An extremely handsome and perfectly hardy plant. It has withstood a temperature of 35 degrees below zero in an exposed position without the loss of a single leaf or bud.

R. obtusum. A rather large evergreen azalea from Japan, with many well-known varieties and garden forms, among them *amoenum, kaempferi,* and the *kurumes.* Most of these are either too tall or too tender for northern gardens. Some kurumes, such as *Hinodegeri,* the flame azalea, are reasonably hardy and of slow and compact growth. They are literally covered with red flowers in May. The one I am particularly concerned with is var. *japonicum,* a perfect doll among rock-garden plants. It is a dense, twiggy semi-prostrate plant, which is never more than 12 inches high but spreads about 3 feet wide. Its tiny dark-green shining leaves are almost evergreen, but they are barely visible through the dense bouquet of lavender-pink flowers that appears in late April and May. Hardy under the most adverse conditions.

R. racemosum. A large tender shrub from China that, in its typical form, is useless to rock gardeners. Through careful selection (mainly by Mr. Guy G. Nearing) over many years, a dwarf hardy strain has been developed that is ideal for the rock garden. A very slow grower, 20-year-old plants have a height of about 18 inches and a spread of two feet. It has small persistent evergreen leaves and is extremely floriferous, with flowers produced both in the axils of the leaves and from terminal buds. Most of these shrubs are grown from seeds, and the plants vary in leaf structure and in the color of their flowers. The flowers that are produced in late April or early May range in color from rose to deep pink.

R. *radicans*. A tiny prostrate plant, about 6 inches high, with very small shining green leaves. The dark-purple flowers are borne singly from terminal buds. A difficult plant from the Himalayas that requires heavy winter protection in areas where a continuous snow cover cannot be counted on.

R. *williamsianum*. A magnificent low spreading shrub, usually about 2 feet high, with small long-petioled heart-shaped leaves. Large bell-shaped pale-pink flowers in May. Unfortunately, this handsome plant is not very bud hardy. It fails to flower, even though its leaves and stems come through rigorous winters. Fortunate, indeed, are those who garden in a climate mild enough for this plant. Several hybrids and named forms are available, all with the characteristic cordate leaves.

Besides these species and botanically recognized hybrids, there is a large number of garden forms and fancy named hybrids that should not be overlooked by the enthusiastic rock gardener. In fact, some of the best of the rhododendrons are in this category. Many new named kinds are introduced each year, which makes it impossible to know and list them all. Among the best, and one of my favorites, is 'Ramapo' a dwarf introduced by G. G. Nearing. It is a small, dense, twiggy plant in the form of a perfect globe, about 15 inches in diameter. The leaves are small and leathery, and light-blue-purple flowers cover it in May. Hardy in almost any climate, it has withstood a temperature of 35 degrees below zero in an exposed position without losing a leaf or bud. Another excellent form is an old hybrid, which is little known outside of its native state, Massachusetts. This one is called simply 'P.J.M.' after its originator P. J. Mezet. It grows into a compact, rounded bush that eventually reaches a height of 3 feet. The leaves are small and a dark-reddish-green color. Myriads of bright-pink flowers cover the bush in late April and May.

ROSA (*Rosaceae,* Rose Family). The enchanting beauty of 99 per cent of the roses is not for the rock garden. However, two or three native North American wild roses are small enough and are sometimes used, particularly in wild sections. *R. arkansana* from the plains states and *R. nitida* from New England grow about 18 inches high, and have delicate single-petaled pink flowers. *R. carolina* is planted occasionally, although it grows about 3 feet high in a loose fashion and spreads radically by underground suckers. The memorial rose *R. wichuriana* is sometimes used as a ground cover in large rock gardens or in conjunction with a rock garden. This is an attractive and useful plant that forms immense blankets of long prostrate branches with shining evergreen leaves and clusters of fairly large fragrant white flowers.

Our main concern here is with the delightful dwarf fairy roses. These are derivatives of *R. chinensis* var. *nana,* a rose originally imported to England. Apparently lost to cultivation for a while, it was rediscovered in a window garden in Switzerland and reintroduced by Henry Correvon as *Rosa rouletti.* This is a perfect rock-garden subject. It grows about 15 inches high, has typical rose foliage, and quantities of double pink flowers bloom from June to October, or ever later in mild climates. *R. rouletti* is reasonably hardy but should have winter protection in exposed positions in the North. In recent years it has grown in popularity and has been complemented with several new varieties under such names as 'Pixie,' 'Bo Peep,' 'Tom Thumb,' 'Jackie,' 'Baby Gold Star,' 'Oakington Ruby,' and 'Sweet Fairy.' Flower colors are predominantly pink and red, but there are also good yellows and whites. Apparently, the new varieties were originated through seedlings of the parent *rouletti* and by crosses with other garden roses.

Recently, a new race of dwarfs has been introduced, characterized by slightly taller growth, with single or semidouble flowers in clusters. These are sometimes called dwarf polyanthas and were probably originated through work with *R. multiflora nana.*

SALIX (*Salicaceae,* Willow Family). Most willows are tall trees, but the arctic region and the high mountains of Europe, Asia, and North America harbor some exquisite dwarf matted or creeping forms that make ideal rock plants. I am familiar only with the two listed here, but several others with similar habits are found in the wild. The following are both arctic plants. They dislike summer heat but can be grown in hot climates if a few precautions are taken. They should be planted close to rocks, where their roots will remain cool, and shaded from the hot noonday sun. They need a moist, acid, leaf-mold soil (pH 4–6). Propagated by cuttings in late summer.

S. reticulata. A depressed shrub, almost ubiquitous in the tundra of Alaska and northern Canada. It grows only 5 or 6 inches high but spreads to considerable size. The tiny dark-green leaves are about a half-inch long, roughly and conspicuously netted. Some reddish-purple catkins are produced with the first leaves in early spring.

S. uva-ursi. This is the tiny creeping bearberry willow, which forms a dense twiggy mat, never more than 2 inches high. The leaves are a bright-green, glossy above and glaucous on the underside. Small rosy-red catkins are produced tight on the branches in early spring.

SANGUINARIA (*Papaveraceae,* Poppy Family). An interesting and attractive one-species plant from eastern United States woodlands. This is the bloodroot *S. canadensis,* with thick red-fleshed tuberous roots. In the first warm days of early spring, striking 8-petaled white flowers appear on stems about 6 inches high, each clasped in the tight folds of an unfurled leaf. The flowers do not last very long, but they are abundant and delightful. The leaves are large and palmately lobed, about 12 inches wide and just as high. The plant goes entirely dormant by the end of May. It is easy to grow in shade in a woodsy soil (pH 5–8), either limy or slightly acid. Var. *multiplex* is the coveted double form with exquisite fully-double flowers, like tiny water lilies. They are easily increased by root division.

SANTOLINA (*Compositae,* Daisy Family). Strongly aromatic subshrubs from the Mediterranean region, used extensively for low borders. They are also good as accent plants in the rock garden and make nice wall-garden subjects. Relatively hardy, they are easy to grow in any well-drained garden soil, in full sun. They come readily from cuttings taken in summer. For best effect, they should be cut back annually almost to the base. If this is not done, they tend to become straggly and unattractive.

S. chamaecyparissus. Commonly called lavender cotton, this plant is usually listed under the less cumbersome name of *S. incana.* Neat mounds, about 12 inches high, of silvery-gray, minutely pinnatifid leaves, evergreen in mild climates and sheltered positions. Globular yellow flowers on tall stems about 18 inches high in summer. The flowers resemble the yellow centers of daisies.

S. virens. Similar to the preceding, but the foliage is a bright-fresh-green color. It is a little hardier and not as floppy.

SAPONARIA (*Caryophyllaceae,* Pink Family). Annual and perennial herbs from Europe and Asia. They are rather coarse, but a few are ideal rock plants. Easily propagated by seeds, and sometimes by cuttings and divisions.

S. caespitosa. A tiny cushion plant from the Pyrenees, with thick, fleshy, pointed evergreen leaves, usually about an inch high. It has very large rose-pink flowers with inflated calyxes in May. A neat little plant that should have a place in a sunny scree, or in a tight rock crevice with lime soil (pH 7–8).

S. ocymoides. One of the old reliable rock plants. It forms broad, tumbling evergreen mounds, about 6 inches high and as much as 2 feet across. Masses of bright-pink flowers from May to August. An excellent wall-garden plant that is easy to grow in any ordinary garden soil, in full sun. It should be cut back severely after flowering to keep it compact.

SARCOCOCCA (*Buxaceae,* Boxwood Family). Highly ornamental evergreen shrubs from China and Tibet that, unfortunately for northern gardeners, are not too hardy. They are really too tender and too big for rock work, but one variety *S. hookeriana* var. *humilis* is useful as a young plant or when cut back annually to maintain scale. It spreads slowly by stolons into more or less rounded bushes with shining, leathery, bright-green leaves. Small clusters of fragrant white flowers in the early spring are followed by fleshy black fruits. It likes an acid leaf-mold soil (pH 4–6), in shade. Propagated readily by cuttings.

SARRACENIA (*Sarraceniaceae,* Sarracenia Family). These are the world-famous pitcher plants, insectivores native to swamps and sphagnum bogs of the eastern United States. Strictly bog plants, they will not live unless their roots are wet. They can be planted at the edge of a pool or in a bog garden. Sometimes they are planted in pots of mucky acid soil that are set in pans of water. Pitcher plants can be propagated by seeds, but are usually obtained from the wild. They are found mostly in the southern states, but *S. purpurea,* native from Labrador to Florida, is hardy. It forms a large rosette of tall tubular hooded leaves, which are the pitchers that trap the insects. The leaves are usually striped with green and purple. The curious, nodding, dark-purple flowers are produced in May and June on stems about 24 inches high (*illustration page 288*).

SATUREJA (*Labiatae,* Mint Family). These are the savories, so useful in culinary practice. They are attractive little aromatic plants that make nice rock-garden subjects. All are easy to grow in any ordinary garden soil, in sun or light shade. Those listed here are hardy in the North. The shrubby kinds are propagated by cuttings, the herbs by divisions.

S. calamintha. Often listed as *Clinopodium calamintha.* Broad evergreen mats of small oval leaves on creeping stems, about 3 inches high. Quantities of attractive lavender flowers, in whorls between the leaves, in May and June.

Sarracenia purpurea.

S. glabella. A curious little plant from Kentucky westward, with thin creeping stems and tiny dark-green leaves flat on the ground, a mat with absolutely no height. It has open sprays of showy purple flowers on 3-inch upright stems. The leaves have a very strong scent when bruised.

S. montana. Winter Savory. A little rounded or decumbent shrub with small light-green leaves, and spikes of lavender flowers in July and August. A good summer-blooming plant that grows about 12 inches high. Var. *pygmaea* is a smaller form with white flowers. The nicest one is var. *subspicata* that forms a tight little ball of upright stems, to 6 inches high, topped with tiny spikes of lavender flowers in August and September.

SAXIFRAGA (*Saxifragaceae,* Rockfoil Family). Rockfoils are the *sine qua non* of rock-garden plants and their successful cultivation is the rock gardener's crowning achievement. These are rock plants and alpines in the truest sense. With the exception of a few tall unattractive weedy swamp plants and lowlanders, all are ideal for our purpose. In fact, most of them cannot be successfully cultivated anywhere else. They are from the arctic and high alpine regions of the northern hemisphere, with a few woodlanders from Asia. These woodlanders are the easiest to grow at low elevations when they are given the proper soil. Special note is made of their requirements in the list that follows.

The arctics and alpines are easy to grow in the Far North, but are progressively more difficult as they are moved southward and to lower altitudes. They invariably need a very gritty, limestone soil (pH 7–8), well drained but with ample moisture at their roots. In their native habitats, they are exposed to full sun and blasting winds. However, it must be remembered that cold water from melting snows trickles continuously over them, and that they are constantly bathed in alpine mists. The only situation in which these conditions can be duplicated, even approximately, is in a limestone moraine. In fact, most of them will not endure for any length of time unless they *are* in a moraine. Many fanciers, who are fortunate enough to have greenhouses, can grow these

Sempervivum arachnoideum and *Saxifraga aizoon*.

enchanting miniatures with ease because temperatures and humidity can be controlled to suit their needs.

There still remain many kinds that can be grown in an ordinary rock garden, if care is taken in their placement and in their basic soil requirements. They will not live for even a short time if they are planted on a sunny clay bank, like some of the easier rock plants. At low altitudes and in warm climates, they must have shade, or at most filtered sunlight, gritty, well-drained, limestone soil and, in the absence of continuous subterranean watering, periodic sprinkling, particularly on hot days. Often they suffer considerably in summer, with browning leaves and a generally depressed look. However, they perk up in the fall and recover any ground they have lost. These are essentially cold-weather plants that look their best from October to December and from March to May. I do not want to discourage anyone from trying them, but neither do I want to imply that they are easily grown.

The genus *Saxifraga* comprises hundreds of species and natural hybrids, as well as numerous horticultural crosses and forms with fancy names. The botanists have divided the genus into several sections, according to their technical differences. Since I am not a botanist and this is not a technical work, I will not burden my readers with descriptions of these divisions. However, growers of saxifragas all over the world do divide the genus into three general groups. These groups are used in almost all of the catalogues that offer saxifragas for sale. They are 'encrusted,' 'kabshia,' and 'mossy.' All other species and cross-sectional hybrids are listed under a fourth division arbitrarily called 'miscellaneous.'

Plants in the encrusted section have leaves in rosettes and somewhat resemble the hens-and-chicks, but the leaves are hard and very stiff, encrusted with lime on the edges. They form attractive little mounds or mats, with the rosettes close together. The flowers are usually white, creamy, or pink, often with darker dots, and are displayed in May and early June. Some are the easiest of the alpine sorts to grow.

The kabshias are usually very small plants with pointed

leaves in tight rosettes, which form dense little mats or pincushions about an inch high. Some of them have more or less trailing stems that form little creeping mats. The flowers are comparatively large and cup-shaped, one or two on a stem 1 to 3 inches high, usually in very early spring. They are most colorful, with flowers ranging from white to all shades of yellow, pink, and purple. Most of them are quite difficult to grow, requiring moraine culture.

The mossy saxifragas are characterized by soft dark-green mossy foliage, usually finely divided, on long trailing stems that form broad evergreen mats. The large flowers, in good shades of red, are produced on fragile stems, 3 to 6 inches high, in early April and continue into May. The high-alpine species require moraine culture. Lime not being essential, they can be grown in a slightly acid soil (pH 5–8).

All other species are listed in the miscellaneous group because most growers have only a few of each of the other technical sections and it would be awkward to list them separately. Some of these are quite easy to grow under ordinary garden conditions, while others demand an acid leaf-mold soil as noted in the descriptions that follow.

The list which follows describes only a fraction of the desirable rockfoils. Many more can be grown and are available in the form of seeds, mostly from European sources. Propagation by seeds will result in variable plants because they cross quite readily. Propagation of specific species and color forms is best done by divisions.

S. aizoon. (Encrusted) This is the prototype of the encrusted section, occurring in Europe, Asia, and North America. The rosettes are usually about 2 inches across, and flowers white, spotted with pink or purple, on stems about 12 inches high. There are several geographical variants and innumerable named forms differing in the color of the leaves. Leaf colors range from pale green to silver and silver-blue. They also differ in the size of the rosettes. The smallest var. *baldensis* has rosettes only a quarter of an inch across; var. *major* has rosettes 3 inches or more in diameter. The color of the flowers varies from pure white in var. *alba,* to yellow in var. *lutea,* and bright pink in var. *rosea.*

S. andrewsii. A hybrid between *S. aizoon* and *S. geum,* to 6 inches, with beautiful large rosettes of long, narrow, pale-green leaves. The leaves are sharp-pointed, with saw-tooth edges and some encrustation. Airy sprays of white flowers with crimson dots, on stems about 18 inches high, in May. This seems to grow equally as well in a gritty lime soil and a sandy, acid leaf-mold soil.

S. spiculata. (Kabshia hybrid) Little spreading mats of tiny linear leaves, about 3 inches high, with rich yellow flowers in April. Var. *alba* has light-green leaves and white flowers.

S. arco-valleyi. (Kabshia hybrid) A tiny pincushion about 1 inch high, with large bright-red flowers in April.

S. boeckeleri. (Kabshia hybrid) Tiny silvery-green rosettes in dense little tufts about an inch high, and charming vivid yellow flowers marked with red in early spring.

S. burseriana. (Kabshia) Tiny silvery-gray pinpoint leaves, in tight tufts 4 inches high, and solitary white flowers in April. Var. *major* has large white flowers on thin red stems. Var. *crenata* has frilled white flowers. Var. *sulphurea* has delicate pale-yellow flowers.

S. cartilaginea. (Encrusted) Little globular rosettes, to 9 inches high, with wide leaves of a fresh green color, with cartilaginous edges rather than lime encrustation. A profuse bloomer with white flowers on 8-inch stems, in May.

S. cochlearis. (Encrusted) Small, narrow, spoon-shaped leaves of silvery-gray rosettes, about 1 inch or slightly more. Large white flowers on 10-inch stems, in May.

S. cortusaefolia. A Japanese woodlander with long-petioled rounded and lobed leaves in rosettes 3 or 4 inches across. The leaves are shiny green and fleshy. Delicate sprays of white flowers on swaying wands about 15 inches high. The flowers are irregular, the two lower petals being much longer than the upper ones. This plant forms broad mats by producing new rosettes on long runners like the strawberries. It is tender, requiring winter protection. Easy to grow in shade, in an acid leaf-mold soil (pH 4–6).

S. cotyledon. (Encrusted) A very large plant with long, wide, spoon-shaped leaves in stiff, gray rosettes about 4 inches across, and airy plumes of pink-veined white flowers on stems 2 feet or more high.

S. crustata. (Encrusted) Small linear leaves heavily encrusted with lime, in tight silver and white rosettes. Twelve-inch stems with white flowers, marked with purple at the base.

S. cunefolia. A European woodland plant with small rounded and toothed leaves, in tight little mounds about 3 inches high. The thick leathery leaves are smooth and dark green. It has tiny white flowers, in airy sprays on 10-inch stems, in May. Easy to grow in a slightly acid garden loam or acid leaf-mold soil (pH 4–6), in shade or filtered sunlight.

S. decipiens. (Mossy) Finely divided soft-green leaves, in mossy mats about 3 inches high but spreading quite broad. White flowers in May, on stems 6 or 8 inches high. This is the prototype of the mossy section. There are innumerable hybrids and fancy named garden forms, with flowers ranging from white to all shades of pink and red. All are extremely desirable rock-garden subjects.

S. geum. Fairly large orbicular leaves of thick leathery texture, colored a shiny dark green. The broad rosettes form lovely tight mounds, 3 or 4 inches high, topped with sprays of tiny white flowers in May. Easy to grow in acid loam or leaf-mold soil, in shade or filtered sunlight. Found in Europe and eastern Canada.

S. grisebachii. (Kabshia) Short wide sharp-pointed leaves, in gray rosettes about a quarter of an inch across, forming tight little tufts. It has small deep-crimson flowers on fuzzy red stems, about 3 inches high, in late March or early April.

S. haagii. (Kabshia hybrid) Mats of trailing stems about 2 inches high, with light-green needlelike leaves, and bright golden-yellow flowers in April.

S. irvingii. (Kabshia hybrid) One of the prettiest and most floriferous of the group. Very tight cushions of tiny pinpoint gray leaves, adorned with large clear-pink flowers dangling on red stems, in March and April. One of the easiest of the kabshias to grow.

S. lingulata. (Encrusted) A large species with silvery rosettes, 4 or more inches in diameter. Long, narrow, spoon-shaped leaves with the margins recurved and heavily encrusted.

Stems 12 to 18 inches high, with broad open sprays of white flowers in May. There are several varieties with rosettes of varying size. Var. *leichtlinii* and Var. *rosea* have pink flowers.

S. longifolia. (Encrusted) Very like the preceding, except that the leaves are not thickened at the ends. The white flowers are produced on stems 2 to 3 feet high.

S. macnabiana. (Encrusted hybrid) A magnificent plant with rosettes about 4 inches across of thick long leaves, heavily and attractively encrusted with lime. The handsome white flowers, produced in spiky panicles, are set close together on stout stems, 12 to 18 inches high, in May. Quite easy to grow under ordinary garden conditions.

S. Marginata. (Kabshia) Tiny silvery rosettes, compressed into a compact little cushion about an inch high. The leaves are ciliate and cartilaginous. Tight clusters of white flowers on black stems, about 3 inches high, in late May and June, sometimes in July.

S. moschata. (Mossy) Mossy little mounds of tiny linear leaves on trailing stems, to 3 inches high. In the typical form, the flowers are creamy white or pale yellow, but the wild form is seldom seen. There are numerous fancy named forms and hybrids, with flowers in all shades of pink, red, and purple. Growers specializing in saxifragas usually have long lists of the mossy kinds which are comprised of variants of this species and *S. decipiens,* and hybrids of the two. Most growers do not know or care about their parentage and list them only with their fancy names, such as 'Sir Douglas Haig,' 'Rosy Dawn,' 'Guildford Seedling,' and 'Mme Pompadour.'

S. paulinae. (Kabshia hybrid) A prickly silvery cushion less than an inch high, with delicate pale-yellow flowers almost an inch across, on 2-inch stems, in late March and April.

S. sancta. (Kabshia) A bright emerald-green mat of prickly leaves on long trailing stems, and a profusion of bright orange-yellow flowers in early April. A kabshia that is easy to grow.

S. sarmentosa. This is the well-known house plant called strawberry-begonia or mother-of-thousands that few people realize is quite hardy. It is easy to grow in an acid loam or leaf-mold soil, in shade or filtered sunlight. As everyone knows, it forms numerous new plants on long runners. When planted in a garden, these make broad mats, to 2 feet high, of hairy, fleshy, rounded leaves on long petioles. The attractive flowers are produced in loose sprays, on stems about 18 inches high, in June and July. The two lower petals are very long, making the flowers look like tiny butterflies. Var. *variegata* is not quite as hardy but it is an attractive plant with leaves marked with green, yellow, pink, and red. An excellent plant for a shady wall garden.

S. tennesseensis. A plant from the limestone ledges and shale cliffs of the southeastern United States. While not as pretty as its alpine cousins, it is still a desirable little plant. It has light-green leathery leaves, oval in shape and roughly toothed, in flat rosettes that form low mats on the sheer face of the rocks with only a precarious root hold in little crevices. The tiny white or creamy-white flowers are produced in broad open clusters on sturdy stems, 6 or 8 inches high, in April and early May. It likes finely pulverized limy leaf-mold in tight rock crevices, in either sun or shade. When grown in full sun, the leaves are small, very thick, and colored deep-red beneath; in shade, the leaves grow much larger and have a fresh bright-green appearance.

S. trifurcata. (Mossy) The attractive staghorn saxifrage. The bright-green shiny leaves are rather stiff and stand upright, 3 or 4 inches high, from trailing stems that form lovely broad evergreen mats. Each leaf is divided into three sharp-pronged divisions and resembles a stag's horn. The large flowers are a clear milk-white on stems about 5 inches high, in April and May. This is definitely the easiest mossy to maintain.

S. umbrosa. A European woodland plant that is extensively planted as a dooryard plant in England and affectionately known as 'London Pride.' It has large oval leaves on long petioles formed into funnelform rosettes that are abundantly reproduced to make broad mounds, about 6 inches high. The tiny white or pink flowers give a misty effect about 6 inches above the foliage. Var. *primuloides* is smaller in all its parts except its flowers, which are deep pink.

S. virginiensis. An American native from Canada down to Georgia on shale cliffs and limestone ledges (*illustration page 298*). It is just like *S. tennesseensis,* except that it is smaller and the numerous small white flowers are carried in dense flat-topped heads, in April and early May.

SCABIOSA (*Dipsaceae,* Teasel Family). Popular, rather large, and sometimes weedy garden flowers from Europe and northern Africa, called mourning bride or pin-cushion-flower. They are annual and perennial plants, easy to grow in any ordinary garden soil in a sunny location. Three or four kinds make nice rock-garden subjects. Propagated by cuttings and divisions.

S. graminifolia. An attractive plant with long, linear, silvery-silky leaves on stiff, almost woody stems about 10 inches high. It has large dense heads of pale-blue flowers in May and June. A fine wall-garden subject.

S. scabra. A pretty dwarf scabiosa with a name that I cannot verify in any of my reference books. Probably a form of *S. caucasica.* It has small, broad, oval evergreen leaves that form mats or little mounds, about 3 inches high. The branching flower stems, about 10 inches high, display lavender pin-cushion flowers all summer.

SCHIVERECKIA (*Cruciferae,* Mustard Family). Little alyssumlike perennials from Asia Minor. *S. bornmuelleri* is the only one I know. It has soft light-gray-green leaves in dense evergreen buns, about 3 inches high. A profusion of showy sprays of small white flowers on 6-inch stems, from late March to the end of May. Easy to grow in a well-drained garden soil, in full sun. A fine wall-garden plant.

SCUTELLARIA (*Labiatae,* Mint Family). Colorful annuals and perennials, often weedy, and too tall for the rock garden. Some, however, are ideal. They are easy to grow in any ordinary garden soil, in sun or light shade. Propagated by divisions. Only one, *S. alpina,* is seen in American rock gar-

Saxifraga virginiensis growing on the face of a moss-covered rock.

dens. It is a creeping plant that forms mounds of small oval leaves about 10 inches high, topped with spikes of hooded purple or white flowers all summer. Var. *lupulina* has yellow flowers.

SEDUM (*Crassulaceae,* Orpine Family). Without sedums you wouldn't have much of a rock garden. They are almost as necessary as the rocks. The family, extremely large and somewhat confused, is rich in natural hardy rock plants. Some are too weedy or too tall to associate with our choice plant selections, and a few from Africa and southern Asia are not hardy; but generally speaking, all sedums are good rock plants. With a few exceptions, they are easy to grow in any ordinary garden soil, in full sun or light shade. Many like the hottest, driest situations possible and can be used admirably to fill the cracks of hot, dry rocks and in dry-wall gardens. Propagated by divisions. Usually, every tiny piece broken from a plant will take root wherever it touches ground.

S. acre. The ordinary and ubiquitous stonecrop. A fast-spreading evergreen plant that forms broad mats of tiny, almost cylindrical, pale-greenish-yellow leaves. It is covered with clusters of yellow star flowers on 3-inch stems, in April and May. Var. *minus* is a small form, with very tiny leaves compacted in tight buns that are always neat.

S. album. A fast-creeping evergreen, forming billowy mats about 6 inches high, with cylindrical leaves about a half-inch long. Airy sprays of white stars in July and August. Var. *murale* is an interesting form, with deep-purple foliage and pink flowers.

S. brevifolium. A tiny plant, forming dense little evergreen mats about 2 inches high, with minute ovoid mealy leaves in four rows crowded on the fragile stems. Small white flowers on 1-inch stems in midsummer. This is an extremely small and delicate plant, easily overrun by the smallest weed growth. It must have a very dry and gritty lime soil (pH 7–8), in full sun. A treasure for the fancier.

S. cauticolum. An exquisite Japanese sedum with thick orbicular blue leaves, on 5-inch stems, in noncreeping tufts. Tight showy clusters of deep-red flowers in September and October. This is one of the good sedums that stays where you plant it. It is completely deciduous, with both leaves and stems dying back to the ground in winter.

S. *chrysanthum*. Hairy, light-green, soft fleshy leaves in globular rosettes that form little rounded mounds. Fiddleheads 6 inches high rise from the centers of the rosettes, producing tight heads of chartreuse flowers in early summer. This one looks more like one of the hens-and-chicks and is usually listed as *Umbilicus chrysanthus*.

S. *dasyphyllum*. A dainty plant, forming a slowly-spreading mat of tiny ovoid silver-blue leaves on thin fragile stems, up to 2 inches high. The neat evergreen foliage is completely hidden by multitudes of pink buds that open to perfect little white stars in May.

S. *ewersii*. A deciduous-leaved species from Mongolia, with large, broadly oval, blue leaves on twisted persistent, almost woody, stems. It forms a broad mat or mound about 5 inches high, with masses of pink flowers in August and September. Var. *homophyllum* is only an inch or so high, with blue leaves about a quarter of an inch long. This species prefers partial shade during the hottest part of the summer.

S. *gracile*. A dense mat-forming evergreen plant about 3 inches high, with very fine linear leaves about half an inch long, closely arranged on the stems. Masses of red-dotted white flowers on 1-inch stems, in May. In winter, the foliage has a dark bronzy color.

S. *gypsicolum*. An intriguing plant that forms loose mats of long, loping, thick, fleshy stems and large cylindrical leaves, spaced rather far apart. The leaves are light green, marked with red. The white flowers are born in small clusters in July. A rare and interesting species from Spain that needs some winter protection.

S. *kamtschaticum*. A clump-forming plant from Siberia, with large wide leaves on trailing stems, about 4 inches high. Large clusters of bright-yellow stars in July and August. The old stems die back in the fall, but new ones appear from the center of the clump and remain green all winter. Var. *floriferum* has more decumbent stems with narrow light-green leaves; it begins to flower early in May. A very attractive form is var. *variegata,* with light-green leaves marked with yellow, pink, and red. After the flowers fade, on all varieties, the seed pods turn dark red and remain attractive all summer.

S. lineare. A delicate and attractive Japanese species that needs winter protection. It forms a mound of upright stems about 6 inches high, with long and narrow cylindrical, pale-green, soft, fleshy leaves. Clusters of yellow stars in summer. In var. *variegatum* the fragile leaves are margined with white.

S. middendorffianum. A most interesting plant from Manchuria. Everyone that sees it for the first time asks, "What kind of candytuft is that?" It forms a very compact mound of trailing or decumbent stems, about 5 inches high, with very dark-green leaves much like the candytuft. A shy bloomer, but when it does flower, it is quite handsome with bright-yellow blossoms. It is a good wall plant, and the only one I have seen in flower was growing on an extremely hot dry wall. The old stem dies back in fall, and new ones come from the center that remain green with a rich bronze cast all winter.

S. nevii. Lovely little silvery-gray leaves with a pinkish cast, in tight rosettes compressed into small buns or slowly spreading mats, about 2 inches high. It has white flowers with purple anthers that give a pleasing rosy effect in June. A native of the mountains of Virginia that prefers partial shade, in an acid soil (pH 5–7).

S. populifolium. A handsome deciduous shrub from Siberia. The stiff woody stems form an open rounded bush about 18 inches high, with dark-green, thick, fleshy leaves resembling those of the tulip tree. Loose clusters of white star-flowers in June. It likes an acid leaf-mold soil (pH 4–6), in shade or partial shade.

S. pruinatum. Fast-spreading evergreen mats of creeping stems, about 4 inches high, with thin linear very blue leaves. In fall and winter, the foliage turns deep purple. Large dense clusters of pale-yellow flowers on stems about 15 inches high, in May and June.

S. *purdyi.* A rare and lovely plant from the mountains of California. Thick, fleshy, spatulate green leaves in flat rosettes. It forms lovely little mats by producing new rosettes on the ends of short red stolons. Dense little clusters of white flowers in late spring. It prefers partial shade, in a neutral or slightly acid soil (pH 6–7).

S. *sieboldii.* An old favorite rock-garden plant and still one of the best. Beautiful clumps, about 6 inches high, with gracefully arching stems. Thick, leathery, silvery-blue round leaves in successive whorls of three all along the stems, terminating in a cluster of bright pink flowers in September and October. The leaves have conspicuous red edges, and in var. *foliis medio-variegatus* (var. *variegatum*), the center of each leaf has a spot of yellow. It is most pleasing when the stem can arch out from a high rock crevice or from the side of a wall.

S. *spathulifolium.* A beautiful species from the Rocky Mountains, with long, spoon-shaped, mealy gray leaves in tight rosettes that form slowly-spreading evergreen mats, about 2 inches high. Showy bright yellow flowers on 3-inch stems, in June. It is a native of the woodlands; but if it is planted in the sun, it stays more compact and takes on a pleasing red hue. Var. *Capo-Blanco* is a dwarf form, like a gnarled little shrub, about 2 inches high, with thick stems crowded with small powdery-white rosettes.

S. *spectabile.* The common big live-forever, popular as a cemetery plant, and sometimes planted in rock gardens. It makes bold 18-inch clumps with large glaucous leaves, and is topped with pale-pink flowers in large clusters in September. Var. *brilliantissimum* has bright-pink flowers. Var. *variegatum* is an interesting form, with the leaves marked with yellow.

S. *spinosum.* A rare and beautiful species from China that looks more like a sempervivum and is usually listed as *Cotyledon spinosa* or *Umbilicus spinosus.* Very tight globular rosettes, and the tip of each leaf armed with a long white spine. Spikes of yellow flowers that spoil the effect of the plant. Quite slow-growing, with new rosettes forming little rounded mats about an inch high.

S. spureum. A good fast-growing evergreen ground-cover plant, with long creeping stems and wide, light-green, fleshy leaves. Clusters of pale-pink or white flowers all summer. Var. *splendens,* usually listed under the name 'Dragon's Blood,' has red-green foliage that turns dark red in winter, and large clusters of blood-red flowers in summer.

S. subulatum. A handsome plant, forming evergreen mounds about 6 inches high, with thick decumbent stems and terete linear, sharply acute, little blue-gray leaves. Clusters of white flowers, on stems about 12 inches high. A good foliage plant that is spoiled by the appearance of the flowers; I always cut them off.

S. tatarinowii. A rare species from China, with the habit of *S. sieboldii* but much smaller, growing only about 4 inches high. The leaves are narrow and deeply lobed at the apex, and the flowers are pale pink.

S. ternatum. A ground-cover plant from southern mountains of the United States, not too choice. It has thin creeping stems and light-green leaves, widely spaced in whorls of three. White flowers in May and June. It likes an acid leaf-mold soil (pH 4–6), in shade.

SEMPERVIVUM (*Crassulaceae,* Orpine Family). The rosette is the symbol of a true rock plant, and here we have rosettes by the thousand. This genus is really comprised of only a few species from the mountains of Europe and north Africa, but botanically it is one of the most confused. There are hundreds of hybrids and thousands of variants, or so the story goes. Quite often a single type will have a hundred different names. Not a botanist in the world can make heads or tails out of this muddle, so I shall not try.

Without reservation, I can say that all the sempervivums, or hens-and-chicks as they are commonly called, are excellent rock- and wall-garden plants. All are rosetted plants that multiply quickly by producing new rosettes at the ends of short stolons, thus forming little mounds or mats and, in some kinds, widespread carpets. I once had a garden in New Jersey where a single plant spread to cover the face of a dry wall 3 feet high and six feet wide. These little

Sempervivum globiferum.

plants are almost indestructible. They require only sunshine and good drainage. They will grow in deep soil and will subsist on bare rocks with only a trace of nourishment. Once they gain a foothold in the tiniest crevice, they will spread over the face of the rock, nourished by their own dead leaves and whatever dust blows into them.

The size of the rosettes in mature plants varies from tiny dots an eighth of an inch in diameter to monstrous ones 12 inches across. The texture of the leaves varies from smooth sheen to every degree of hairiness. Some are soft and downy, others are covered completely with long, cobwebby, silver hairs. The color of the leaves is equally diverse, running from various greens to all shades of blue, brown, pink, red, purple, and every imaginable shade between. Often the degree of moisture in the soil, the richness of the soil, and the amount of exposure to sun and wind will cause a single kind to have a hundred different aspects. Mr. Frederick V. Guinzberg of Chappaqua, New York, has a small rock garden planted exclusively with sempervivums. The various textures and colors of the plants make it look like an exquisite Persian carpet.

The color of the flowers varies from greenish-yellow to all shades of yellow, pink, red, and purple. The individual flowers are star-shaped, in large flat clusters, usually on stems from 6 to 24 inches high, depending on the variety. Although the flowers in themselves are attractive, they are usually out of proportion to the plants that produce them.

I am not listing or describing any of the species or varieties, because I feel that to do so would further disturb already troubled waters. Usually, the growers of rock plants have dozens of different kinds. It is better to buy by sight rather than through descriptions. Another word of precaution: do not depend on listed catalogue names, because they are usually meaningless.

SERRATULA (*Compositae,* Daisy). A small group of European plants, related to the centaureas. I am not even sure the one I want to discuss even belongs here. It came to me labeled *S. shawii,* a name I cannot verify; but whatever it is called, it is a good fall-blooming rock plant. Low clumps of deeply cut, almost fernlike foliage of a pleasing dark-bronzy-green color, about 4 inches high. It has branched flower stems about 10 inches high, with a multitude of deep-purple flower heads in September and October. In general appearance it resembles a dwarf spineless thistle. Easy to grow in any ordinary garden soil, in full sun. Propagated by divisions.

SHORTIA (*Diapensiaceae,* Diapensia Family). A small family of exquisite dwarf woodland plants, ideal for the cool shady rock garden. They require a deep, moist, yet well-drained, sandy, acid leaf-mold soil (pH 4–5), in shade. They will stand some filtered sunlight but prefer dense shade where it will be cool all summer. Propagated by seeds (which are slow to mature) and by divisions.

S. galacifolia. The glorious oconee-bells from the mountains of North Carolina. Slowly-spreading clumps of bright-shiny-green evergreen leaves, about 4 inches high. In fall and winter, the foliage turns to rich bronze and red. The new growth is also brightly tinted in spring. Quantities of large white bells in early spring. I consider this one of the best plants in the American flora; it is revered the world over.

S. soldanelloides. Best known as *Schizocodon soldanelloides.* A wonder from the Japanese Alps. Little evergreen tufts of small, round, coarsely-toothed, leathery leaves, about 3 inches high. Finely-fringed white or bluish-pink bells, four or five on a stem about 4 inches high. Almost impossible to grow unless it is given shade in an acid moraine.

S. uniflora. The Japanese counterpart of our delightful oconee-bells. The leaves are heart-shaped with wavy margins, and the large bells are a delicate shade of pink.

SILENE (*Caryophyllaceae,* Pink Family). Annuals and perennials of wide distribution. Many of the perennial kinds are natural rock plants, but very few of them are ever available to American gardeners. Even our very worthwhile natives are, for some reason, overlooked. Most are easy to grow in ordinary garden soil, in sun or light shade. A few need preferential treatment, as noted in the list. They are all best propagated by seeds, although a few of the tufted ones can be divided.

S. acaulis. Little mosslike tufts or mats with tiny pointed leaves in rosettes, very close together. Large bright-pink flowers are nestled in the foliage from May to August. The entire plant is never more than an inch or two high. An alpine from Europe and North America that should have moraine treatment at low altitudes.

S. alpestris. An endearing alpine from the European Alps that forms little mats of linear leaves, produced from slowly creeping rootstocks. Airy bouquets of small white flowers, about 6 inches high, all summer. Var. *flore-pleno* has fully-double white flowers like tiny carnations.

S. caroliniana. Usually listed as *S. pennsylvanica.* Clumps of lanceolate sticky-hairy leaves, 6 inches high. Great masses of large pink flowers, just above the foliage, in May and June. Exceptionally fine in a wall garden. The flowers vary from white to deep carmine. *S. wherryi* is the same, except that it is not sticky.

S. Keiskei. An attractive tuft of stiff little dark-reddish-green leaves, about 3 inches high, and short 4-inch stems, producing quantities of brilliant carmine flowers in August and September. It likes a well-drained, gritty or sandy, acid to neutral, soil (pH 5–7), in full sun.

S. maritima. Large clumps of trailing stems, with soft glaucous foliage, about 10 inches high. White flowers with the petals deeply notched and the calyx greatly inflated. Blooms all summer. Var. *flore-pleno* is a prostrate plant with the blue leaves quite fleshy, and the great double flowers as much as 3 inches across.

S. pumilio. A tiny tufted plant from the European Alps, with bright-fresh-green fleshy leaves, barely a half-inch high. It has pink flowers, about an inch across, sitting right on top of the little close cushion. A difficult plant that requires moraine treatment.

S. Schafta. An old favorite and always dependable rock plant. It has soft light-green leaves in very dense tufts, 3 or 4 inches high, and masses of bright-pink flowers in August and September. An alpine from Europe that is about the easiest to grow.

S. virginica. The brilliant fire-pink from our eastern mountains. It is a bit tall for the average rock garden, growing about 2 feet high, but its fiery scarlet color in summer makes it important in many gardens. It forms evergreen clumps of long narrow leaves, about 6 inches high, and produces masses of brilliant-red flowers from June to September.

SISYRINCHIUM (*Iridaceae,* Iris Family). Blue-eyed grass. Graceful little grassy plants from North and South America. Those from the United States are hardy and easy to grow but are seldom offered to the public, probably because they are not spectacular like so many of our garden monstrosities. These have an unobtrusive fairy grace that appeals to the connoisseur. They are easy to grow in a sandy, well-drained acid soil (pH 5–6), in full sun. Propagated very simply by divisions. All are tufted plants with long grasslike leaves, usually winged, and with small star-shaped flowers in late spring and summer.

S. birameum. About 15 inches high, with yellow-eyed dark-blue flowers.

S. boreale. Eight or ten inches high, with clear-yellow flowers.

S. douglasii. Fairly large bright-red-purple flowers.

S. idahoense. Glaucous foliage, and deep-violet-blue flowers.

S. mucronatum. Dense tufts of narrow winged leaves, and an abundance of pale-blue flowers. Var. *alba* is a charmer, with pure-white flowers.

SOLDANELLA (*Primulaceae,* Primrose Family). Exquisite, but almost endemic plants, from the alpine regions of Europe. About the only way it can be grown is to provide it with a perfectly duplicated acid moraine.

S. alpina. Little tufts of orbicular leaves, about 2 inches high, from which rise thick fleshy 4-inch stems, with large fringed light-purple bells in March or early April before the ground has thawed completely.

S. minima. Like *alpina,* with tiny round leaves, shorter stems, and pale-blue or white bells.

SOLIDAGO (*Compositae,* Daisy Family). These are the goldenrods, so bright and lovely in our autumn countryside. Most of them are tall and have no place in the rock garden; but two tiny ones, from isolated mountain tops in New York State, are ideal for this purpose. They are propagated by divisions and are easy to grow in any well-drained garden soil, in full sun.

S. brachystachys. Tiny mats of little dull-green oval leaves, about 1 inch high, and short spikes of bright-yellow flowers on 4-inch stems, in September and October.

S. cutleri. Attractive evergreen leafy clumps of fairly large leaves, about 4 inches high. Masses of fuzzy yellow flowers, on 6-inch stems, in June and July.

SPIRAEA (*Rosaceae,* Rose Family). A group of large shrubs, used extensively in landscaping the home grounds, typified in the ubiquitous bridal wreath. A few dwarf forms make exceptionally fine rock-work specimens. They are propagated by cuttings, and are easy to grow in any ordinary garden soil in full sun.

S. bullata. (Usually listed as *S. crispifolia*) A dense, twiggy little shrub about 15 inches high, with small crispy-crinkly leaves, topped with small flat clusters of bright-pink flowers all summer. A neat, dense, and compact grower.

S. decumbens. Rounded mounds, to 10 inches high, of thin procumbent stems clothed in small smooth pale-blue-green leaves, and small clusters of white flowers in June. A rare European species.

S. normandii. This is really a dwarf form of *S. bumalda.* It forms little mounds of very thin twiggy stems, 6 inches high, or less. The tiny leaves have a rich reddish-green color and turn a brilliant scarlet at the first touch of frost. I have never seen it flower.

STACHYS (*Labiatae,* Mint Family). Rather coarse and tall, more or less weedy plants. One species from Europe, *S. lanata,* is extensively grown as a bedding plant. It also makes an attractive rock-garden subject. It is called lamb's-ears because its leaves, exactly the size of a lamb's ear, are covered with soft white woolly down. It grows in a dense evergreen mat about 3 inches high, and has spikes of purple flowers on straight 15-inch stems, in May. When the leaves or flowers are bruised, they smell like fresh blueberries. Easy to grow in a well-drained garden soil, in full hot sun. Propagated by divisions.

STYLOPHORUM (*Papaveraceae,* Poppy Family). A perennial, native to open woodlands of Pennsylvania and westward, *S. diphyllum.* About 18 inches high, with large pinnately-cut light-green-blue leaves, and loose clusters of bright-yellow floppy flowers, about 2 inches across, in May and June. It likes a rich woodsy loam, in partial shade. Not a spectacular plant but an interesting filler in a wild woodland setting.

SYMPHYANDRA (*Campanulaceae,* Bellflower Family). A few species much like the campanulas from Europe. I am familiar with only one, *S. wanneri.* Low clumps of soft, hairy, long, lanceolate, sharp-toothed leaves, about 6 inches high, and nodding bell-shaped deep-violet-blue flowers in late spring. It likes a well-drained garden soil, in sun or light shade. Propagated by seeds and divisions.

SYNTHYRIS (*Scrophulariaceae,* Figwort Family). Curious, rather than beautiful, plants from the Rocky Mountains. They are reminiscent of the heucheras, having the same general appearance. *Synthyris* forms little mounds of long-stalked leathery leaves, 4 to 10 inches high, spiked with small purple or reddish flowers in late spring. The leaves are dark green and of a tough leathery shiny texture, round or reniform, and wavy-toothed. They like a rich, mucky, acid soil (pH 4–6), in shade or filtered sunlight.

TALINUM (*Portulacaceae,* Purslane Family). Small plants with soft fleshy foliage, and an abundance of small but bright pink, red, and yellowish flowers over a long season in late spring and summer. There are some rather big ones from tropical America, but the tiny ones for the rock garden are mostly from our plains states and are hardy if treated right.

Talinums require a sandy soil with perfect drainage, and a hot sunny situation. They will not stand water around their roots in winter. They are easily propagated from seed and, once established in a garden, will produce a never-ending supply of new plants from self-sown seeds. There are several species in addition to those listed, but they are seldom offered for sale because of their delicate nature.

T. calycinum. Long green terete leaves, on 4-inch stems, with a halo of fire-red flowers from June to October. The flowers are displayed only in the afternoon on bright sunshiny days.

T. teretifolium. Similar to the preceding, except that the plant is taller, and the flowers are smaller.

TANAKAEA (*Saxifragaceae,* Rockfoil Family). Only one species, *T. radicans,* from the mountain woodlands of Japan. Thick leathery dark-green leaves in tufts, about 2 inches high, and inconspicuous greenish-white flowers. It makes an attractive evergreen mat by producing new plants on long runners. Likes an acid leaf-mold soil (pH 4–6), in cool dense shade.

TEUCRIUM (*Labiatae,* Mint Family). Several ornamental evergreen shrubs and perennials from Europe, Asia, and North America. Some are outstanding rock- and wall-garden subjects. They are easy to grow in any ordinary garden soil, in full sun. Propagated usually by cuttings, the perennials sometimes by divisions. Only one or two are ever available to American gardeners.

T. Chamaedryas. Germander. A shrublet, about 12 inches high, with small bright-green shiny leaves on brittle stems, and spikes of lavender flowers in July and August. It is extensively used as an edging plant or low hedge, and can be sheared to any height desired. For years I grew a plant called var. *prostrata.* I am sure that this is a misnomer, but I do not know where else to put it, so I will describe it here. Its leaf resembles that of *T. chamaedrys* but is thinner. It forms a wide evergreen mat, about 3 inches high, by means of underground stolons, and is very floriferous, with long decumbent spikes of lavender flowers.

T. montanum. A prostrate evergreen mat with soft light-gray-green foliage, and large clusters of pale-yellow flowers in June and July. Exceptionally well suited to the wall garden.

THALICTRUM (*Ranunculaceae,* Buttercup Family). Elegant and delicate ferny plants, but few of them are small enough for the rock garden. They are easy to grow in a moist acid loam (pH 5–6), in partial shade. Propagated by divisions. The flowers are small, in hazy masses, and consist mainly of large dangling anthers.

T. alpinum. An arctic plant, forming mounds of ferny compound leaves with oval segments, about 12 inches high. Misty green and yellow flowers.

T. kiusianum. A delicate little plant from Japan that forms small colonies of purple-blue ferny leaves, about 3 inches high. Comparatively large and showy purple flowers in May and June.

T. minus. Mounds 15 inches high, with delicate, lacy, blue-green foliage. The dainty, fine-textured leaflets are about a quarter of an inch across.

T. venulosum. Mounds of stiff stems with lacy blue-green foliage, about 18 inches high, and a misty bouquet of pale-green flowers. This one is from the northern Rocky Mountains and will stand a dry soil, in full sun.

THLASPI (*Cruciferae,* Mustard Family). Little alpine plants with leaves in low dense mats or rosettes, and flowers like the candytufts. They require a gritty, well-drained lime soil (pH 7–8), in full sun. Propagated by seeds, sometimes by divisions.

T. alpestre. Little mats, to 12 inches high, of small glossy-green leaves in rosettes, and clusters of white flowers tinged with red, on 10-inch stems, in April and May.

T. rotundifolium. A small cespitose plant, to 8 inches high, that spreads slowly by stolons. Little cushions of thick rounded leaves, and spires of pale-lilac flowers.

THYMUS (*Labiatae,* Mint Family). Little evergreen shrubby plants from southern Europe that are almost indispensable in rock and wall gardens. They are extremely hardy and will grow almost anywhere in a sunny position, in any kind of soil. They are particularly suited to dry walls, dry sunny slopes, and rock crevices. In fact, they perform much better in poor, gravelly or sandy soil than in good, rich soil. Some are grown commercially for food flavoring, others for medicinal purposes. Propagated by divisions.

T. herba-barona. Long trailing stems with tiny dark-green leaves that form dense mats, an inch or two high. The mat is literally covered with small clusters of purple flowers in June and July. The leaves have a strong caraway scent when bruised.

T. nitidus. An elegant little rounded mound, about 8 inches high, with rather stiff stems and tiny silvery-gray leaves. Short spikes of pale-lavender flowers in late spring. This is called French thyme and is highly prized in poultry seasoning.

T. serphyllum. Broad spreading mats of small shining evergreen leaves, about 3 inches high. Flowers in the typical form, which is seldom if ever available. This is the ubiquitous mother-of-thyme, used extensively for planting between flagstones and in ground-cover work. There are several named forms with variously colored flowers, and foliage of different textures and colors. Var. *albus* is a tiny creeper with minute fresh-green leaves, and sheets of tiny white flowers in late spring. Var. *aureus* has leaves variegated with yellow; and var. *variegatus,* leaves variegated with white. Var. *coccineus* has dark-reddish-green foliage and bright red-purple flowers. Var. *vulgaris* is strongly lemon-scented and is usually listed as *T. citriodorous.* Var. *lanuginosus* is the woolly thyme, with its green leaves covered with woolly gray down. Var. *rosea* has pink flowers.

T. vulgaris. Broad decumbent mounds of dark-green leaves, about 10 inches high, and spikes of lavender flowers in summer. Var. *argenteus* is a smaller, more compact plant, with attractive silver and white variegated foliage.

TIARELLA (*Saxifragaceae,* Rockfoil Family). Lovely North American woodlanders, with decorative foliage and attractive flowers. They are hardy, easy to grow, and permanent in a good rich acid loam (pH 5–6), in shade or filtered sunlight. Propagated by divisions.

T. cordifolia. The lovely, delicate-looking foam flower of our eastern woodlands. It spreads by long runners, forming broad mats of large heart-shaped leaves, about 4 inches high. The flower stems are about 12 inches high, with spikes of foamy fuzzy white flowers in April and May. An important recent discovery is var. *collina,* a noncreeping form, with bold spikes of pink buds that open to foamy bluish flowers.

T. wherryi. A lovely clump-forming noncreeping species, with white flowers and variable foliage. The heart-shaped leaves are deeply indented, divided, or lobed in a very decorative pattern.

TOWNSENDIA (*Compositae,* Daisy Family). Exquisite miniature daisies from the Rocky Mountains and plains states. There are several species in the wild, but I know only *T. exscapa.* It consists of a tiny tuft of pale-gray-green linear leaves, about 1 inch high, and in late spring, large thin-rayed pink daisies, about 2 inches across, nestled in the foliage. Needs a very well-drained, gritty or sandy, lime soil (pH 7–8), in full sun. It grows best in a dry rock crevice or in a scree.

TRILLIUM (*Liliaceae,* Lily Family). The glorious trinity lilies of the deep North American woodlands. There are about 25 species, but only half of them are suitable for the garden. The others have small inconspicuous greenish or brownish flowers. They all like dense shade in a deep, moist, acid loam (pH 4–6), in a cool situation. Although they are usually collected from the wild, they can be propagated by divisions or by cutting the tubers into sections. They are more or less clump-formers, with thick tuberous roots, rather thick succulent stems, 6 to 18 inches high, with three leaves to a stem, and the flowers with three petals. All bloom in April and May.

T. erectum. Dark-red flowers held erect, well above the leaves. About 12 inches high.

T. grandiflorum. The best and most common of the trilliums and the easiest to grow. It forms wide clumps, to 18 inches high, of long ovate leaves, and has very large white flowers that turn pink with age. It will grow in an ordinary garden soil that is slightly on the acid side, and will take full sun if the soil does not parch. Var. *flore-pleno* is a rare and coveted form, with large fully-double white flowers (*illustration page 316*).

T. nivale. Like *T. grandiflorum,* a miniature, but about 6 inches high. A rare species found from Pennsylvania to Kentucky.

T. stylosum. To 18 inches high, with very large-petaled flowers, colored a delicate rose.

T. undulatum. The renowned painted trillium. About 18 inches high, with white flowers exquisitely marked with red and purple.

T. vaseyi. A rare plant from Tennessee, with dark-red-purple fragrant flowers, as much as 6 inches across, on stems to 18 inches high.

TUNICA (*Caryophyllaceae,* Pink Family). A few small plants, related to the *Dianthus,* from the Mediterranean region. One species, *T. saxifraga,* the tunic-flower, is a well-known bedding and rock-garden plant. Also, a very fine wall-garden plant. It forms mounds of thin wiry stems, about 10 inches high, covered with small, very narrow leaves, and produces masses of small pink or white flowers, suggestive of the baby's-breath, all summer. Var. *flore-pleno* has fully-double flowers, like tiny carnations. Easy to grow in a well-drained garden soil, in full sun. The double form is sterile and must be propagated by cuttings, but the single one is a prolific seeder, and tends to become weedy in an unobtrusive way.

UVULARIA (*Liliaceae,* Lily Family). Interesting woodland plants from the northeastern United States. They are not showy, but modestly attractive, and useful for dressing up a shady nook. Can be propagated by divisions, but are usually transplanted from the wild. They like a rich, acid

Trillium grandiflorum.

leaf-mold soil (pH 4–6), in shade or filtered sunlight. All kinds form broad colonies by means of thick creeping rootstocks.

U. grandiflora. Large, glossy-green, perfoliate leaves on stiffish stems, about 15 inches high, with a prolific show of huge pendulous yellow bells with curly petals, in April and May.

U. perfoliata. Clumps of zigzag stems, about 15 inches high, with roundish perfoliate leaves, and straight-petaled pale-yellow bells in early spring.

U. sessilifolia. Spreading masses of straight or arching stems, to 1 foot high, with small, oval, very light-green leaves sessile on the stems, and small pale-yellow flowers almost hidden by the foliage.

VACCINIUM (*Ericaceae,* Heath Family). Creeping viny plants or upright shrubs, producing the edible berries called cranberries, blueberries, and huckleberries. They are too tall or lack the necessary character, for rock-garden use, with a few remarkable exceptions. All the vacciniums require an acid leaf-mold soil (pH 4–6), and grow equally well in sun or shade. They are propagated by cuttings and divisions. Native kinds are collected from the wild. Three types of lowbush blueberries are sometimes used as fillers in large rock gardens, usually in areas where they are common in the wild. They are *V. angustifolium, V. caespitosum,* and *V. canadense,* all with the same general characteristics. They are deciduous twiggy shrubs, 6 to 12 inches high, with small ovate gray or blue-green leaves, and clusters of small white or pale-pink urn-shaped flowers in spring, followed by delicious bloomy berries in midsummer. They prefer a rather dry situation, in full sun or light shade.

V. crassifolium. Long trailing stems with tiny shining evergreen leaves, forming a solid carpet, about 3 inches high and several feet in diameter. Pale-pink flowers, in April, followed by small black berries in summer. An exceptionally fine evergreen ground cover for shade or sun.

V. vitis-idaea. An elegant little shrub, about 12 inches high, with upright stems densely covered with dark-glossy-green leathery leaves, forming a compact bush. In early spring, it has tight clusters of white bell-shaped flowers. These are followed in the fall by large, very bright-red berries that hang on most of the winter. It creeps by underground stolons, thus forming rather broad patches. Should be cut back periodically to keep it dense and compact. In fall, the leaves turn a rich bronzy color. Early spring growth is pink and red. Var. *minus* is an exciting dwarf carpeting form, found on top of Mt. Washington in New Hampshire. It grows only about 3 inches high, forming dense mats with bright-green shining leaves. Big bunches of showy pink flowers in spring, and huge bright-red berries in fall and winter. Of inestimable value because of its fine evergreen foliage, colorful flowers, and bright berries.

VALERIANA (*Valerianaceae,* Valerian Family). Perennial plants with strongly scented roots, grown from antiquity for perfume manufacture. Most of them are big plants, but a few dwarfs are ideal rock plants. These dwarfs are seldom offered in America, and I have grown only *V. arizonica,* an attractive little plant that forms slowly-spreading mats of ovate leaves, about 3 inches high, topped with dense clusters of pink flowers in June. The creeping roots are very sweetly scented. A hardy native of Arizona that likes a dry, gravelly lime soil (pH 7–8), in full hot sun. Propagated by divisions, if you are lucky enough to obtain the plant.

VANCOUVERIA (*Berberidaceae,* Barberry Family). Attractive, delicate-looking woodland creepers from the Pacific northwest, closely resembling the epimediums in habit. There are three species with the same general characteristics: *V. chrysantha* with golden-yellow flowers, *V. hexandra* with white, and *V. parviflora* with white or lavender blooms. They are called inside-out flowers, because the small petals are reflexed and the long stamens protrude to a point. The flowers are borne in loose airy sprays, about 15 inches high, over delicate clumps of lacy, ternately compound leaves. They require an acid leaf-mold soil (pH 4–6), in shade or filtered sunlight. Easy to increase by divisions. Blooms in late spring.

VERBENA (*Verbenaceae,* Vervain Family). A gay assortment of creeping or tall colorful plants, native to North and South America. Mostly, they are either too tall for the rock garden, or are not hardy and must be grown as annuals in the North. Fortunately, there are two fine exceptions that are reasonably hardy and easy to grow in any well-drained garden soil, in full sun. Increased easily by seeds or divisions.

V. bipinnatifida. A hardy and prolific plant from the northern plains states that forms a wide mat, about 3 inches high, of creeping stems with finely divided deep-green leaves. It has clusters of lilac-purple flowers from May to hard frost.

V. canadensis. A misnomer for a plant from Virginia. In the South it is considered a weed, but in the North it is valued as an ideal rock-garden subject. A quickly spreading clump of trailing, creeping, or decumbent stems, about 8 inches high, with deeply-toothed, crinkly green leaves. It produces masses of large-clustered heads of bright-red-purple flowers from May to November. One of the most spectacular and persistent bloomers in the garden. It is reasonably hardy, but in severe open winters it may succumb, and that is of little consequence because it always produces an abundance of self-sown seedlings.

VERONICA (*Scrophulariaceae,* Figwort Family). A large genus, rich in garden subjects both tall and dwarf. Almost all of them are easy to grow and dependable in an ordinary garden soil, in sun or light shade. Propagated by divisions. There is much confusion in the names, particularly the varietal names, and many more than I list here are desirable rock- and wall-garden plants.

V. armena. A very pretty ground-cover plant with long trailing stems, clothed with deeply-divided, mossy, light-green, evergreen leaves, about 2 inches high. Vivid-blue flowers in loose racemes from May to July.

V. chamaedrys. Large spreading clumps of crisp green leaves, about 10 inches high, and loose sprays of lovely vivid-blue flowers in May and June. Var. *alba* has delicate pure-white flowers.

V. fruticans. A compact little shrubby plant, forming rounded mounds, about 6 inches high. Tiny, closely set, dark-green shining leaves, topped with short spikes of vivid-royal-blue flowers in May and June.

V. gentianoides. Neat attractive clumps, about 4 inches high, with leaves remarkably like those of *Gentiana acaulis.* In May and June, stems 12 to 18 inches high bear long spikes of lovely clear-pale-blue flowers, like a dwarf delphinium.

V. incana. Gorgeous clumps of soft silvery-white leaves, about 4 inches high, topped with bold spikes of brilliant blue flowers in June and July. Undoubtedly, one of the nicest summer-blooming plants for rock and wall gardens. Like all plants with silvery leaves, it needs full hot sun. Var. *rosea* has spikes of deep-pink flowers.

V. pectinata. A fast-growing evergreen ground cover that forms 2-inch-thick carpets of pretty woolly green leaves, adorned with short dense spikes of deep-blue flowers in April and May. It is especially delightful when draped over a large rock or down the side of a dry wall. The foliage of var. *rosea* is more silvery and the flowers are pink.

V. repens. A tiny plant from Corsica, indispensable for trailing in rock crevices or filling in between steppingstones. It has creeping stems that form a solid little mat, about a quarter of an inch high, of very small shining-green leaves, studded with comparatively large, very pale-blue flowers from May to July. Prefers light shade, especially when planted in flagstone walks and terraces.

V. rupestris. A confused name for a charming little evergreen mat-former. It forms thick carpets by spreading both above and below the ground. Tiny, dark-green, toothed leaves, and showy spikes of clear-bright-blue flowers, 3 inches high, in May and June. Var. *rosea* has lilac-rose flowers; and var. *alba,* a fast grower, has very pale-green leaves and white flowers.

V. spicata. An old-favorite garden plant that is too big and overpowering for a well-ordered rock garden, except for var. *nana,* a fine dwarf form. It makes little spreading mounds of soft green leaves, about 3 inches high, and produces a superabundance of short heavy 6-inch spikes of bright-blue flowers in June, July, and August. An exceptionally fine summer-blooming plant. Var. *nana alba* is a bit taller, with 10-inch spikes of fuzzy white flowers.

VIOLA (*Violaceae,* Violet Family). All perennial violets are acceptable rock plants. Their size is right, their growth habit suitable, and they have pretty flowers of various colors. Often, though, they are overlooked because they are so common. Some species are weedy and invasive and should be avoided, but there are dozens of others that are perfect for rock gardens.

Of the hundreds of species, both native and foreign, I have selected only a few that I know well. Throughout the United States, there are many others that can be planted with loving pride.

Almost all the violets, including the large pansy-flowered violas of Europe, like a cool, fairly rich, moist soil that is acid to neutral (pH 5–7), and a shady or partially shady location. Special note is made of the dry-land and sun-worshiping violets in the following list. Almost all can be propagated by divisions or by seeds. If using seeds, remember that they have a very short viability.

V. arenaria. Dense mounds of small ovate leaves, about 3 inches high, and quantities of pale-violet flowers all summer. Var. *rosea* has vivid bright-pink flowers.

V. blanda. Small white sweet-scented violets with reflexed petals, over little carpets of small fresh-green leaves in early spring.

V. canadensis. A big sprawly plant with stems about 12 inches high, and large heart-shaped leaves. Violet-tinted white flowers all summer. Likes deep shade.

V. conspersa. Mounds, about 3 inches high, of small cordate leaves, and many pale-violet flowers striped with deep purple in early spring.

V. cornuta. The parent of our large-flowered bedding violets that is probably unavailable unless seed is collected from wild plants in the Pyrenees. Many fine fancy named kinds are available from nurserymen and seed houses, with white, yellow, and purple flowers.

V. fimbriatule. Flat rosettes of small ovate pubescent leaves, and hairy purple flowers in May. The entire plant is never more than 3 inches high. It likes a dry situation in filtered sunlight.

V. jooi. A cushion of little pink flowers in April, before the leaves appear. It makes a pretty tuft of sharp-pointed, heart-shaped leaves, about 3 inches high.

V. lanceolata. A wet-soil plant that forms patches of long, narrow, upright leaves, and tiny white violets on stems about 4 inches high.

V. nana. A tiny plant that forms mats no more than a half-inch high, with bright shining leaves about one-quarter of an inch long, and tiny pale-lavender flowers from May to July.

V. nuttallii. Clumps of long, narrow leaves, and bright golden-yellow flowers in spring. It likes a fairly dry situation, in partial shade.

V. odorata. This is the sweet violet of the florists. It forms broad clumps of heart-shaped leaves, 6 or 8 inches high, on running stems. The deep-purple flowers are very fragrant. There are many named forms with white, pink, violet, and yellow flowers, and a particularly good form with fully-double flowers called 'Double Russian.'

V. palmata. Low tufts of palmately-divided leaves, about 4 inches high, and fairly large, deep-purple flowers in May.

V. papilionacea. Our most common violet and the one that should be most avoided. It is attractive, with very large crisp green leaves and purple flowers on long stems, but it is very invasive and persistent. Seedlings come by the thousands from underground cleistogamous flowers.

V. pedata. This is the lovely bicolor bird's-foot violet, gem of our native species. It makes little tufts of finely-divided leaves suggesting the foot of a bird, and has adorable pansy-like flowers on stems about 4 inches high. The two upper petals are a bright velvety purple and the three lower ones are pale blue or lavender. Var. *alba* is a rare form with pure white flowers. In var. *lineariloba,* all the flower petals are a lovely pale violet. Why it is called *lineariloba,* I will never know; its lobes are no more linear than the bicolor form. This is a dry-land plant that requires a very sandy, acid soil (pH 4–5), in full sun.

V. pedatifida. Six-inch high clumps of large leaves, palmately parted and the lobes again divided into linear segments. Long-stemmed violet flowers in May.

V. priceana. The famous Confederate-violet with masses of white flowers, each with a blotch of blue in the center, over broad-spreading clumps of fresh-green heart-shaped leaves, about 4 to 6 inches high. It blooms for several weeks in spring. Quite invasive, so be careful where you plant it.

V. primulifolia. Clumps of long oval leaves, about 10 inches high, with purple-veined white flowers in spring. It likes a very moist situation.

V. rotundifolia. Flat rosettes, to 4 inches high, of thick rounded leaves, and showy bright-yellow flowers in May. A mountain plant that likes a dry situation in partial shade.

V. sagittata. Long, tapering, arrowhead-shaped leaves, and bright violet-purple flowers in spring.

V. stricta. Attractive rounded mounds of small orbicular leaves on ascending stems, to 18 inches high. Masses of delicate pale-yellow flowers with lavender stripes, from May to July. This is a particularly good violet.

V. walteri. Evergreen mats of light-green, hairy leaves, mottled with purple and dark green, and dark-purple flowers on 2-inch stems, in early spring. Requires dense shade.

WALDSTEINIA (*Rosaceae,* Rose Family). Two evergreen ground covers, from the woods of Siberia and the eastern United States. *W. fragarioides,* the barren-strawberry, is our useful and attractive native. It forms a spreading mat, about 3 inches high, of shiny three-parted leaves, and has open corymbs of bright-yellow flowers in May. A good ground cover for sun or shade in an acid to neutral loam (pH 4–7).

WOODSIA (*Polypodiaceae,* Fern Family). Small tufted ferns from Europe, Asia, and North America. They like rock crevices and moist, acid, leaf-mold soil (pH 4–6), in shady locations.

W. alpina. Narrow lacy fronds, about 5 inches high, with the ovate segments pinnately lobed. A high-alpine and arctic fern that needs pampering during hot summer weather.

W. ilvensia. Fronds about 10 inches high, with rust-colored hairs and scales along the stipes and on the underside of the leaves.

W. obtusa. A fairly common woodland fern that grows about 15 inches high. The wide fronds are bipinnate, and the segments are roughly toothed. Easy to grow in any woodsy setting.

XYRIS (*Xyridaceae,* Yellow-Eyed Grass Family). Humble sphagnum-bog plants with a sylphidine grace that compensates for their lack of brilliance. *X. flexuosa,* the nicest one, forms slender tufts of long twisted leaves, about 6 inches high, with a tall wand bearing a leathery globose head with a few tiny yellow flowers from July to September. It requires a wet, acid, mucky soil (pH 4–6), in full sun.

ZINNIA (*Compositae,* Daisy Family). Well-known annual bedding plants. One hardy perennial, *Z. grandiflora* from the Rocky Mountains, is a happy note on which to end this long list. It forms loose, open mounds of stiff stems, about 8 inches high, with narrow hairy linear leaves, and yellow flowers about 2 inches across in summer. With age, the rays turn white and the center disks a bright red. It requires a very well-drained, gravelly, lime soil (pH 7–8), in full hot sun.

CHAPTER VIII

ROCK GARDEN BULBS

Nothing elates the rock gardener more than the first flower of the year to appear in his garden. Usually, it is one of the tiny bulbous plants, a wild crocus or a delicate lavender-blue chionodoxa that has broken through the cold bare ground. Long before the first of the alpines begin to stir, the tiny winter-blooming bulbs turn the pockets and slopes of the rock garden into a multicolored galaxy of blossoms that promises new hope and joy, just as the rainbow does after a storm.

These brave little harbingers of spring have a short time to display their colors, but they make a show that is not soon forgotten. The tiny spring-flowering bulb plants are not to be confused with the large hybrids and horticultural varieties that are offered to the public in brightly-colored advertisements in the fall. They are the neglected and almost forgotten wild species from the far corners of the world. Their natural daintiness and modesty have not been violated by man in his effort to make everything bigger and better.

The little plants from these wild bulbs are insignificant when planted singly. They should be set in large drifts or groups where masses of their small flowers can make a vivid splash of color. Where to plant them is dictated by their soil and exposure requirements and by the personal taste of the gardener. While most of these wildings are tiny, some are vigorous and invasive, with comparatively heavy foliage. The grape-hyacinths, star-of-Bethlehem, and snowdrops should be confined or checked so that they will not overrun some of the rare and choice alpines. Most are early spring bloomers that display their flowers before the herbaceous perennials begin their spring activity. Others bloom in late spring, summer, or autumn.

Most bulbous plants go dormant early in the season. Therefore, to avoid bare spots in the garden, they should be over-planted with a ground cover. The ground cover selected should be as low as possible and without heavy matted woody stems that would prevent the fragile stems of the bulbs from emerging. Some of the best covers for this purpose are: *Veronica repens, V. pectinata, Mazus reptans, Hydrocotyle peduncularis, Arenaria laricifolia, A. verna caespitosa, Muehlenbeckia axillaris, Phlox stononifera, Houstonia serphyllifolia, Gypsophila repens, Dianthus myrtinervius,* and *Bellium bellidioides.* Many others are listed in Chapter VII.

Although these bulbous plants differ greatly in appearance and habit of growth from the usual herbaceous perennials associated with a rock garden, they have a definite place in it. Many are natural saxicoles, and others are true alpines. Because of the different culture required for the production of bulbs on a commercial scale, they are not usually grown by American nurserymen, and do not generally appear in their lists and catalogues. Most often the bulbs are offered for sale in special catalogues issued in the summer and fall by importers of European-grown bulbs. Holland, Belgium, and parts of France, where soil and climate are ideal for their development, are the main sources, and the bulb growers there have developed techniques in handling and marketing flower bulbs that makes competition by American growers practically impossible.

I have separated the species listed below from the general list of rock plants contained in Chapter VII because there is such a marked difference in their character and in the method of handling them. Many of the Alliums have persistent or evergreen foliage; they must, therefore, be treated like the usual herbaceous perennials and are thus included in the general list. Most of the native North American tuberous plants, like the trilliums, are listed in Chapter VII because they are usually grown in American nurseries or listed by collectors of wild flowers along with other perennial species.

BULBS FOR THE ROCK GARDEN

ANEMONE BLANDA (*Ranunculaceae,* Buttercup Family). Delicate clumps of finely-cut dark-green leaves, about 4 inches high, with lovely sky-blue flowers in April and May. Var. *artrocoerulea* has deep-dark-blue flowers, var. *rosea* pink, and one called 'Fairy' by the trade has white flowers. Likes an acid leaf-mold soil, well drained, in open shade. It will tolerate full sun but will not grow there to best advantage (*illustration page 328*).

BLETILLA STRIATA (*Orchidaceae,* Orchid Family). Usually listed as *B. hyacinthina.* A hardy terrestrial orchid with little tufts of long thin leaves, and racemes of adorable little purple orchids on 2-foot stems in June. It thrives in ordinary garden soil, in full sun.

BRODIAEA (*Liliaceae,* Lily Family). Most of these plants are native to the Pacific coast states. They have a few grass-like leaves and umbels of lovely delicate flowers in shades of blue, pink, purple, and white. They are of doubtful hardiness in the North and East, but can be grown successfully on the Pacific coast and in the South. One species, *B. uniflora,* usually listed as *Triteleia uniflora,* has proven to be reliable in northern New Jersey. It has solitary star-shaped light-blue flowers on 6-inch stems in April and May. A native of Argentina that grows in sun or light shade, in ordinary soil.

BULBOCODIUM VERNUM (*Liliaceae,* Lily Family). A pretty crocuslike flower of bright violet-red in very early spring or winter in warm regions. Easy to grow in ordinary soil, with good drainage and full sun. The leaves appear after the flowers have faded.

Anemone blanda.

CALOCHORTUS (*Liliaceae,* Lily Family). The wonderful mariposa lilies or globe-tulips are native to the Pacific Northwest and Rocky Mountains. Most of them are hardy but need protection from alternate freezing and thawing. There are many species, ranging in height from 6 inches to 3 feet. Flowers are white, or in shades of pink, yellow, blue, and purple, appearing in spring and summer. Many of them are striped or spotted with contrasting colors. These bulbs are hard to find in the trade. When acquired, they should be planted in a very gritty, well-drained, acid soil, in sun or very light shade.

CALOPOGON PULCHELLUS (*Orchidaceae,* Orchid Family). The lovely and dainty grass pink. It has a single grasslike leaf and a thin stem, 12 to 15 inches high, with numerous little deep-rose orchids in June and July. It should be planted in a bog garden or a wet place in the rock garden, in full sun.

CAMASSIA (*Liliaceae,* Lily Family). Slender plants suggesting fairy wands that are a bit tall for the ordinary rock garden but excellent in a wild-flower collection.

C. esculenta. Lovely pale-blue star-shaped flowers on stems, to 2 feet high, in May. This and the following like neutral to acid loam, in partial shade.

C. quamash. A taller species from the Pacific Northwest, with dark-blue stars.

CHIONODOXA (*Liliaceae,* Lily Family). Glory-of-the-snow. Early in March, these dainty plants begin to show their lovely blue color, often breaking through late snows. Once planted, they increase rapidly by offsets and seeds to form dense carpets of blue. They thrive either in sun or light shade, in any ordinary garden soil.

C. luciliae. Arching stems, to 6 inches high, with bright-blue white-centered flowers, an inch or more across. Some kinds have white or pink flowers. Var. *gigantea* is taller, with larger flowers of lavender-blue (*illustration page 330*).

C. sardensis. A very dark-blue-flowered species, without the white center.

Chionodoxa luciliae gigantea.

COLCHICUM (*Liliaceae,* Lily Family). Often called autumn-crocus because the huge flowers that appear without leaves in September resemble those of the crocus. Most species are native to southern Europe and the Near East, and are easy to grow in full sun, in ordinary garden soil. *C. autumnale* is the species most usually grown. It has purple flowers, 4 inches high and 4 or more inches across. It also comes in pink, white, and deep purple. *C. speciosum* is about 12 inches high, with violet flowers, 6 inches in diameter. *C. parkinsonii* and *C. variegatum* have rose or white flowers checkered with purple.

CORYDALIS (*Fumariaceae,* Fumitory Family). Most species are annual or perennial herbs with fibrous roots. A few species have hard tubers that are treated like bulbs. They are easy to grow and permanent in good well-drained garden soil, in full sun or light shade.

C. hallari (Usually listed as *C. solida*). Dense tufts of delicate, ferny foliage about 4 inches high, topped by large clusters of rosy-purple flowers in April and May.

C. nobilis. Ferny foliage, to 8 inches high, with creamy-yellow flowers tipped with deep purple in May.

CROCUS (*Iridaceae,* Iris Family). These crocuses are not the large-flowered hybrids and sports usually found in gardens but dainty small-flowered wild species. They all have little tufts of grasslike leaves, and produce flowers of many colors in late winter or very early spring. A few, as noted, bloom in the autumn. Easy to grow in an ordinary garden soil that is well drained, in full sun or very light shade. These wild species usually seed themselves freely, forming broad patches a few years after the initial planting. A few of the best and most easily obtained are listed here.

C. biflorus. The parent of most of the garden sorts. White flowers shaded with purple. Varieties of this species have flowers ranging from pure white to deep purple.

C. chrysanthus. Flowers bright orange-yellow in late winter. There are several garden forms, with flower colors of different intensities.

Crocus Imperati.

C. etruscus. Delicate mauve flowers in later winter.

C. Imperati. Lilac flowers with deep-purple stipes.

C. laevigatus. White flowers feathered with lilac in the fall before the leaves.

C. sativus. (Saffron) Very large and lovely lilac flowers in autumn. The commercial flavoring saffron is derived from the stamens of this species.

C. sieberi. One of the prettiest of crocuses. Soft-lavender-blue flowers with golden throats in spring.

C. speciosus. Large, purple, lavender, or white flowers in September and October.

C. susianus. Cloth-of-Gold. The outer petals of the bright-yellow flowers are feathered with a glossy brown. Blooms in March and April. One of the finest for naturalizing.

C. tomasinianus. Tiny flowers of soft, silvery lavender-blue in great masses just an inch above the ground in April. This and 'Whitewell Purple,' with deep glistening purple flowers, are my favorites for the rock garden.

C. zonatus. Large rosy-lilac flowers, veined with purple and spotted lightly with soft orange on the inside. It flowers in September and October.

ERANTHIS (*Ranunculaceae,* Buttercup Family). Winter Aconite. The little tubers of *E. hyemalis* should be planted close together to form dense mats of lacy, bright-green foliage, sparkling with bright-yellow buttercups on 6-inch stems, in early March. Needs a rather moist situation in an acid leaf-mold soil, in shade. Var. *cilicia* has larger flowers and bronzy foliage. *E. tuberginii* is a hybrid or sport, with large sterile flowers that last much longer.

ERYTHRONIUM (*Liliaceae,* Lily Family). Adder's-Tongue. Trout-Lily or Dog's-Tooth Violet. Excellent for the shady rocky or wall garden. The long thin bulbs should be planted deep in a well-drained, acid, leaf-mold soil. *E. americanum* likes a moist or wet situation. Each bulb produces two leaves, often attractively mottled, and a flower stem, from 6 inches to two feet high, depending on the species. One lilylike flower in shades of white, yellow, purple, and red.

E. albidum. Leaves light green, sometimes mottled. White or pink flowers on 12-inch stems, in April.

E. americanum. Leaves attractively mottled with brown and white. Flower stems, usually 6 inches high, with a nodding light-yellow lily.

E. californicum. Leaves distinctly mottled, and creamy-white flowers on 12-inch stems.

E. dens-canis. The only European species. Bronze mottled leaves and 6-inch stems, with flowers ranging from rose to bright red and deep purple. Var. *album* has white flowers. Several fancy named horticultural forms are available.

E. hendersoni. Leaves mottled, and deep-purple flowers with recurved petals. To 12 inches high.

E. revolutum. Twelve-inch stems, with wide-open starlike flowers of a delicate shade of lavender.

E. tuolumnense. Light shining green leaves, and bright-yellow flowers on 12-inch stems.

FRITILLARIA MELEAGRIS (*Liliaceae,* Lily Family). Checkered Lily, Snake Head, or Guinea-Hen Flower. A species native to Europe, with thin grassy foliage and 12 to 15 inch stems, each bearing two or three nodding, tuliplike flowers in May. The curious flowers are checkered with pink, purple, or maroon. There are many forms, with a color range from pure white to darkest purple. Excellent for the rock garden and for naturalizing in partial shade. Easy to grow in an ordinary garden soil.

F. pudica. A species from the northern Rocky Mountains with few leaves and 8-inch stems, with small clear-yellow flowers. It needs a very gritty, well-drained soil, in full sun. There are several other species native to Asia and the Pacific Northwest that are desirable but hard to find.

GALANTHUS NIVALIS (*Amaryllidaceae,* Amaryllis Family). The lovely snowdrops are among the first to bloom, often appearing early in February. Self-sown seedlings come up freely, forming dense mats of shining green leaves, topped with myriads of green-tipped white flowers on 10-inch stems. Easy in almost any soil, in sun or light shade. Var. *flore-*

Erythronium americanum.

pleno has double flowers, and var. *maximus* is a tall form with very large flowers. Native to Europe. There are other species that are almost never seen in the United States.

HYACINTHUS AMETHYSTINUS (*Liliaceae,* Lily Family). A dainty plant from the mountains of Spain, with clear-light-blue nodding flowers on 6-inch stems, in May. Easy to grow in an ordinary garden soil, in sun or light shade. At its best when massed in clumps.

IRIS (*Iridaceae,* Iris Family). Everyone knows the tall bearded irises, and most rock gardeners are familiar with the dwarf species and hybrids, but few know the dwarf bulbous kinds whose bright colors and delicious fragrance lend enchantment to the garden in early March and April. Most of them are native to the semiarid regions of the Near East, where summer conditions are extremely dry. Therefore, they need a very hot, sunny location, with perfect drainage. Otherwise, they are easy to grow in ordinary garden soil.

I. danfordiae. Bright yellow flowers, on stems 2 to 4 inches high, in March. Each bulb has two very stiff four-sided leaves, to 12 inches high.

I. histrioides. Bright blue-purple flowers, scarcely above the ground in early spring.

I. orchidoides. Leafy stems, about 10 inches high, with three or more deep-yellow flowers in April.

I. reticulate. The most popular of the dwarf bulbous irises, with elegant flowers in various shades of blue, very close to the ground, in early March. There are several fancy named horticultural varieties, ranging in color from a pleasing sky-blue to deep violet.

I. sindjarensis. Three or four large light-lilac flowers, on 9-inch stems, in late March and April.

LEUCOJUM (*Amaryllidaceae,* Amaryllis Family). The snowflakes somewhat resemble the snowdrops but bloom later, and the flowers open wide. Left undisturbed, they form thick colonies in any ordinary soil, in sun or light shade.

Galanthus nivalis.

L. aestivum. Nodding clusters of white flowers, on 12-inch stems, in late May and June.

L. autumnale. White flowers tinged with red, on 8-inch stems, in September. Very thin grassy leaves after the flowers appear.

I. vernum. Nodding wide-open solitary white flowers, on 12-inch stems, in April.

LILIUM PUMILUM (*Liliaceae,* Lily Family). The dainty little coral lily is usually listed as *L. tenuifolium.* Lilies are rarely adaptable to the rock garden because of their rather formal and stiff upright habit; but *L. pumilum,* with its thin wiry stems that seldom go above 24 inches, is an exception. It has a few thin leaves, and a crown of nodding bright-scarlet flowers in June and July. Easy to grow in a well-drained garden soil, in full sun.

L. philadelphicum is another low species, 24 to 30 inches high, that is sometimes planted in shady rock gardens and in woodland gardens. It requires shade, and an acid leaf-mold soil. It usually has one bright orange-red flower to a stem, in May.

LYCORIS SQUAMIGERA (*Amaryllidaceae,* Amaryllis Family). This charming native of Japan is often listed as *Amaryllis hallii.* Some call it the 'Mystery Lily.' In the spring, it produces narrow basal leaves, which soon disappear. In June or July, the bulb sends up a stout stem, to 12 inches high, with a large umbel of fragrant pink flowers. This plant is easy to grow in ordinary soil, in full sun. There are other species with yellow, white, and bright-red flowers that are rarely seen in America.

MUSCARI (*Liliaceae,* Lily Family). The grape-hyacinths are well known around the home grounds and are particularly well suited to rock gardening. They thrive in an ordinary soil, in sun or light shade, and increase rapidly by natural offsets and seeds to form dense colonies of blue, pink, or white grapelike flowers in heavy spikes in April and May.

M. armeniacum. Long, thin prostrate leaves that begin to grow in August and stay green all winter. The bulbs produce 6-inch spikes of deep-violet flowers in late April and May.

M. botryoides. This is the species most usually grown. Stems to 12 inches high, with blue flowers in the spring. Var. *album* has white flowers; var. *carmeum,* pale pink; and var. *coerulem,* brilliant blue flowers.

M. comosum monstrosum. (*M. plumosum*) A curiosity in which all the flowers are sterile and transmuted into fine hairlike shreds with the airiness of a violet-blue ostrich feather.

M. conicum. Represented in the trade by the form called 'Heavenly Blue.' Very clear-light-blue flowers.

M. neglectum. Nine-inch spikes of extremely dark-blue fragrant flowers.

M. paradoxum. The starch-hyacinth is a very distinctive species, with large deep-blue-black flowers of good size and form.

NARCISSUS (*Amaryllidaceae,* Amaryllis Family). The daffodils are represented in the garden mainly by the large-flowered and gaily-colored hybrids and horticultural forms. These are not too large for the rock garden but are seldom planted there because of their association with garden borders and edgings. Most of the wild species have a dainty and refined character that is best displayed in the rock garden. They thrive in a well-drained, slightly acid garden soil, in sun or half-shade.

N. bulbocodium. The petticoat daffodil has very fine grassy leaves, and thin 8-inch flower stems with bright-yellow flowers that have a blown-out hoop-skirt appearance. Var. *citrinus* has lemon-yellow flowers, and var. *conspicuous,* the usual form, has large yellow flowers in May.

N. cyclamineus. Extremely slender and dainty, with small lemon-yellow flowers with reflexed segments that resemble those of the cyclamen.

N. jonquilla. The true jonquil, with rushlike foliage, and clusters of very fragrant yellow flowers, on 12-inch stems, in May.

N. minimus. (*N. nanus*) *Hortus II* says this is a dwarf garden form of the large trumpet daffodil, *N. pseudo-narcissus.* It is one of the prettiest for the rock garden, with perfectly formed tiny trumpets, on 3-inch stems, in late March and April.

N. odorus. The campernelle has fine grasslike foliage, and clusters of bright-yellow fragrant flowers, on 10-inch stems.

N. tazetta. (Usually listed as *N. canaliculatus*) This is the well-known paper-white narcissus of florists, with clusters of fragrant white flowers.

N. triandrus. Angel's-Tears. Usually three slender white flowers together on a 12-inch stem in May, over thin rushlike leaves.

OXALIS ADENOPHLIA (*Oxalidaceae,* Wood-Sorrel Family). A little gem from Chile that is hardy in a sheltered spot in a sunny rock garden. It must have well-drained soil. Little tufts of glaucous cloverlike leaves, topped with charming pink flowers in May. Another species, *O. violacea,* a native of the United States, is sometimes planted in the rock garden. It is an attractive plant with trifoliate leaves, and violet or rose-purple flowers in June and July.

PUSCHKINIA SCILLOIDES LIBANOTICA (*Liliaceae,* Lily Family). Lovely squill-like, soft-blue flowers in dense racemes on 12-inch stems, in April. Another form has white flowers, faintly veined with blue. Easy to grow in ordinary soil and sun.

SCILLA (*Liliaceae,* Lily Family). The early-flowering squills are almost a necessity in the well-planted rock garden. These tiny plants should be massed among the deciduous plants, where they will make a carpet of blue in the early spring sunshine. They like a well-drained garden soil, in full sun or very little shade. The taller and later-blooming Spanish and English bluebells prefer partial shade.

S. bifola. Two thin leaves to a plant, and intensely deep-blue star-shaped flowers on 6-inch stems, appearing with the winter-aconite in early March.

S. chinensis. The Chinese squill forms its leaves in the fall and loses them before the flowers appear in August. It has 12-inch stems, with dense spikes of rose-pink flowers tipped with green.

S. hispanica. (Usually listed as *S. campanulata*) The Spanish bluebells are rather tall for the rock garden, with stems to 20 inches, bearing campanulate nodding blue flowers in mid-May. There are pink, white, and deep-blue varieties.

S. nonscripta. (Usually listed as *S. nutans*) The English bluebell goes to 12 inches high, with spikes of tubular blue flowers in May. There are pale rose, white, and red forms.

S. sibirica. This is the plant almost everyone means when speaking of squills. Usually, three nodding, deep-blue star-shaped flowers, on 4-inch stems, in March and April. The horticultural form, 'Spring Beauty,' has very large flowers of an intense delphinium-blue, on 8-inch stems. Var. *alba* is a rarity with white flowers.

TULIPA (*Liliaceae,* Lily Family). Tulips, with all their gay colors in the springtime, are wondrous things, but the giant hybrids most people are familiar with must be relegated to the perennial border or to formal beds. The rock gardener is primarily concerned with the dwarf botanical tulips or wild species. Exquisite in form and brilliant in color, these tulips have a carefree, informal habit that makes them very desirable additions to the garden. Most of them are native to southern Europe, northern Africa, and southwestern Asia. They require full sun, in a very well-drained garden soil. *T. saxatilis* must be planted in a scree to succeed in the northeastern states.

T. acuminata. Thin wavy leaves and 12-inch stems, with wide-open light-yellow flowers in May. The petals are long and pointed.

T. australis. Dainty little yellow flowers, flushed with red on the outside, on 10-inch stems, in May.

T. batalinii. Five-inch stems, with wide-petaled, soft-chrome-yellow flowers in early April. Very rare and most desirable.

T. biflora. A tiny plant with two or three very narrow leaves, and 6-inch stems, bearing 2 small pale-yellow flowers tinged with purple in early April. Var. *turkestanica* (listed as *T. turkestanica*) is larger, with as many as 10 flowers to a single, somewhat decumbent stem.

T. chrysantha. One of the smallest, with bright-yellow flowers tinted red on the outside, on 6-inch stems, in April.

T. clusiana. The lady-tulip, or candy-stick tulip, is a charming species with the outer petals cherry-red and inner ones white. Slender stems, to 15 inches high, with fragrant flowers in May.

T. dasystemon. Five-inch stems carry 3 to 5 small canary-yellow flowers in early May. The petals are narrow and edged with white.

T. eichleri. The leaves are broad and long-pointed. Six-inch stems bear large scarlet flowers, with golden markings and a deep-blue-black center.

T. fosteriana. A robust tulip that is too cumbersome for the rock garden, parent of the famous 'Red Emporer,' but it has a smaller form called 'Princeps' that is admissible in large rock gardens.

T. greigii. Broad dark-green wavy leaves and 10-inch stems, with large flame-colored flowers in April.

T. hageri. Globular flowers of a dark-scarlet color, shaded with copper on the outside, and a black base. Usually 3 or 4 on a 6-inch stem, in April.

T. kaufmanniana. This dandy is called the water-lily-tulip. Very large wide-open creamy-yellow flowers shaded with red, nestled in broad glaucous leaves, in April. There are several named sorts, with colors of different intensities and combinations. All are highly recommended.

T. kolpakowskiana. A rare species. Yellow flowers feathered with red, on 8-inch stems, in April.

T. linifolia. Glowing scarlet cup-shaped flowers with conspicuous black centers, on 6-inch stems, in early May. The leaves are very thin and grasslike.

T. patena. (*T. persica*) A very beautiful little dwarf, producing several flowers, on an 8-inch branching stem, in May. The interior of the fragrant flowers is a brilliant yellow, the exterior golden-bronze.

T. praestans. Ten-inch stems, with light-red flowers in April. The named form 'Fusilier' has 3 to 5 flaming scarlet flowers to a stem.

T. pulchella. A rare species of breath-taking beauty. Rich imperial-purple cup-shaped flowers on decumbent stems, in early March.

T. saxatilis. Difficult but well worth a try. Very large goblet-shaped flowers, with the upper half of the petals a delicate mauve and the lower portion pale yellow.

T. suaveolens. Four inches high, with bright-yellow, very fragrant flowers in late March and April. This is the 'Duc Van Thol,' one of the first species cultivated.

T. sylvestris. Nodding bright-yellow fragrant flowers, on 10-inch stems, in late May. It must be well established (two or three years) before it flowers freely.

CHAPTER IX

ANNUALS IN THE ROCK GARDEN

The advanced rock gardener never uses the word annual when speaking of subjects for his garden. He considers the rock garden a place for the cultivation of hardy perennials that will be more or less permanent, obviating the necessity of constant replanting. Nevertheless, annuals should not be dogmatically banned. In new gardens, they are particularly useful for filling voids and helping to hold the soil until the newly-planted perennials have had time to take over.

All too many established gardens lack color in August due to faulty planning, and the use of summer-flowering annuals can greatly enhance their attractiveness. The skillful placing of even only one or two flowering plants will often change a drab setting to one of colorful vivacity.

The indiscriminate use of annuals, however, is to be avoided at all cost. It would be foolish to give over a well-built rock garden to the exclusive use of annual bedding plants. Many of them self-sow very freely, thus posing the problem of constant weeding to keep them in check. If the seedling annuals were left to grow, they would soon obliterate the slower-growing and more desirable perennials. Usually, one or two annuals with a profusion of bloom over a long period are as effective as closely set masses of gaudily colored flowers, and more in keeping with the theme of rock gardening.

As much care should be used in selecting annuals for temporary use in the rock garden as is used in choosing the perennials. They should be of definite rock-garden character — of low growth and with tufted, creeping, procumbent habits rather than upright and stiff. As I have pointed out before, the rock garden is a place for the rarest of plants. The annuals selected should be kinds that are not usually seen in neighborhood gardens. The

Great American Triumvirate of petunia-zinnia-marigold should be ruthlessly banned, not because these flowers lack charm but because their omnipresence on the American scene makes them undesirable in a collection of rare and dainty flowering plants.

Some of the annual plants in the following list are fairly common but are included because of their affinity to rock culture, or because they are adapted to special use. I use the common or vernacular names first in this alphabetized list because the plants are most generally known by them and are usually so listed in seed catalogues. These are not the only annuals that can be used in the rock garden, but they represent a fairly good assortment. In recommending them, I am assuming that the rock gardener will *avoid* using them as much as possible. They will all thrive in a sunny location and in ordinary garden soil unless otherwise noted.

AGERATUM (*Ageratum houstonianum nanum*). Dense cushions of dark-green leaves, topped with a continuous profusion of fluffy blue flowers all summer. The best plants are available at florists' shops and greenhouses. Set them out after danger of frost is past.

BABY BLUE-EYES (*Nemophila menziesii*). Mats of trailing stems with long finely-cut foliage, and large round flowers of a lovely sky-blue color. Sow the seeds where the plants are to grow—in early spring for midsummer bloom. Excellent for partial shade.

BABYS-BREATH (*Gypsophila elegans* and *G. muralis*). Airy sprays of tiny white, rose, or carmine flowers on slender branching stems, to 12 inches high, in late spring and summer. Sow seed directly in the garden in early spring.

BEGONIA (*Begonia semperflorens* and hybrids). This is the common bedding begonia. Small waxy-green and reddish-green leaves, and showy flowers in shades of pink and white all summer. A tender perennial from Brazil, usually grown from seeds by experts. It is best to purchase small plants from the florist and set them out after danger of frost is past. They require an acid leaf-mold soil, in shade.

CALIFORNIA-POPPY (*Eschscholzia californica* var. *maritima* and *E. tenuifolia*). Maritima has lovely lemon-yellow poppies two inches across, on prostrate stems, in summer. *E. tenuifolia* is an upright species, to 12 inches high, with small light-yellow flowers. These do not transplant well; seeds should be sown where the plants are to stand. They need full sun and a well-drained soil.

CANDYTUFT (*Iberis amara* and *I. umbellata*). *I. amara* is the rocket candytuft with large fragrant flowers in spiky racemes, to 12 inches high. *I. umbellata* has very showy umbels of violet, pink, red, or purple flowers in spring and summer, on branching stems about 15 inches high. Seeds can be sown in flats in winter and the seedlings transferred to the garden, or seeds may be sown where the plants are to grow (*illustration page 346*).

CROSSWORT (*Crucianella stylosa*). Prostrate stems with tiny green leaves, and rounded heads of deep-pink flowers. It prefers acid soil, in shade and half-shade. Sow the seeds in early spring where the plants are to grow.

CUP-FLOWER (*Nierembergia caerulea*). Usually listed as *N. hippomanica.* Dense clumps of thin stems and tiny bright-green leaves, about 8 inches high, with cup-shaped flowers in shades of lavender and blue. Sow seeds indoors in February for flowers from July to frost. In warm climates, cup-flowers are perennial. They can be held over winter in the North with heavy protection.

DIAMOND-FLOWER (*Ionopsidium acaule*). A tiny creeping plant with little leaves, on 3-inch petioles, and dainty four-pointed violet flowers, on thin stems to 4 inches high. Seeds should be sown in late spring for summer bloom, in summer for fall flowers. It likes partial shade, in a well-drained soil.

ENGLISH DAISY (*Bellis perennis*). This is a perennial but rather tender. From my experience, it is best to treat it as a biennial. It has spreading tufts of small leaves and 6-inch stems, with lovely little daisies in white and shades of pink

Annual Candytuft, *Iberis umbellata.*

in spring and early summer. Sow seeds in spring for flowers the following year, or hold over divisions in a cold frame. 'Dresden China' has double flowers of an exquisite pale-pink color.

FLOWERING FLAX (*Linum grandiflorum*). Rather tall, but useful in a large garden. It has stems to 24 inches high, clothed with very narrow leaves, and topped by bold masses of flowers in bright shades of red and purple. Sow seeds in early spring where the plants are to grow.

GROUND-PINK (*Gilia dianthoides*). Tufts of tiny threadlike leaves and 6-inch stems, with little clusters of pink flowers that somewhat resemble those of *Dianthus*. Sow the seeds in the garden in late spring.

ICE-PLANT (*Cryophytum*). Thick prostrate stems, with the first leaves very large but soon disappearing, and small white flowers. Grown mostly for the glistening crystal-like blisters on the stems. Usually available from florists. Plant when the danger of frost is gone.

LADY'S POCKETBOOK (*Calceolaria biflora*). Rosettes of spoon-shaped leaves that produce branching stems to 12 inches high, bearing masses of delightful yellow pouchlike flowers over a long season. It is a perennial but not hardy in the North. Seeds should be sown indoors in the winter for summer bloom. It likes an acid soil, in partial shade.

LANTANA (*Lantana camara*). A shrub, but tender and often used as a bedding plant in the North. It has decumbent or trailing stems and provides a continuous display of small flowers in tight clusters, of many colors and combinations of colors. It is rather big and rampant, but it can be used in large gardens where bold accent is desired. Small potted plants are usually offered by florists in spring.

LOBELIA (*Lobelia erinus*). A lovely little plant comprised of tufts of small shining-green leaves on trailing stems, about 4 inches high, and literally covered with little blue flowers in summer. The form called 'Crystal Palace' is a choice variety with flowers of the most intense blue imaginable. If I were permitted only one annual in my garden, I believe this would be it. Easy to grow in ordinary soil in sun or light shade. Sow the seeds in early spring in the garden, or indoors in winter if earlier bloom is desired.

MALCOLM STOCKS (*Malcomia maritima*). A loose-growing, spreading plant with grayish leaves, and a profusion of pink, lavender, red, and white flowers. This is the plant usually called Virginia stocks. Sow the seeds in spring where the plants are to grow.

PANSY (*Viola tricolor*). Universally known and accepted as a desirable plant. Need I say more?

PEACOCK POPPY (*Papaver pavoniunum*). Brilliant scarlet poppies with a dark eye, on 12-inch stems. Sow seeds in spring where the plants are to grow.

PHLOX (*Phlox drummondii*). Large clusters of purple, red, pink, and white flowers, on stems 6 to 12 inches high. The flowers vary greatly in color and in form; many are striped and fringed. Sow seeds indoors in winter for early flowers, or in the garden in early spring.

PIMPERNEL (*Anagallis arvensis*). A little creeping plant with tiny white or scarlet flowers. It is apt to become a weed if left unchecked. Sow the seeds where the plants are to grow.

RAINBOW PINKS (*Dianthus chinensis heddewigii*). Tufts of broad green leaves, and stems to 12 inches high, bearing gay flowers of many colors and markings, often with cut and frilled petals. Sow seeds in the garden in spring for summer color.

ROSE-MOSS (*Portulaca grandiflora*). Thick, fleshy, trailing stems with sharp-pointed terete leaves. Stems and leaves are usually colored a dark reddish-green. Large satiny single roselike flowers in bright shades of yellow, pink, and red —often striped. A fine plant for hot and sunny situations. Sow the seeds at any time where the plants are to grow. Self-sown seedlings must be removed constantly, once the plant is established in the garden.

SAND-VERBENA (*Abronia umbellata*). Prostrate stems, with clusters of very fragrant, rosy-purple flowers. It must have a sunny exposure, in very well-drained soil. For early summer bloom, sow the seeds indoors in February. Seeds can be sown directly in the garden in spring for fall blooming. This is a tender perennial from the West Coast that is usually treated as an annual.

SANVITALIA (*Sanvitalia procumbens*). A trailing plant with masses of bright-yellow tiny daisies in summer. Sow seeds in a sandy, well-drained soil, where they will get full sun.

SWEET ALYSSUM (*Lobularia maritima*). A well-known bedding plant with somewhat procumbent stems, to 6 inches high, and continuous masses of white or violet flowers. Sow seeds in the spring where the plants are to grow.

TWINSPUR (*Diascia barberae*). Spikes of attractive pink flowers, on 12-inch stems. Each flower has two spurs on the underside. A lovely and desirable plant for profuse summer bloom. Sow seeds where the plants are to grow.

VERBENA (*Verbena hortensis*). A very fast-growing plant that is useful only for large gardens. Showy clusters of red, yellow, and white flowers all summer. Seeds should be sown indoors in winter. Move plants to the garden after danger of frost is past. Divisions can be carried over winter in a tight cold frame.

WALLFLOWER (*Erysimum asperum*). Usually listed as *Cheiranthus allionii.* Tufts of small leaves that produce upright stems, to 12 inches high, bearing elongating racemes of bright-yellow-orange fragrant flowers in late spring. This is a biennial or short-lived perennial. Seeds should be sown in spring for bloom the following year. Seedlings grown indoors in winter, and transferred to the garden, will produce flowers in late summer.

WANDERING JEW (*Tradescantia fulminensis* and *Zebrina pendula*). These are tender perennials that are common house plants, prized for their quick luxuriant growth of long trailing stems and attractively striped and colored leaves. The small, not too showy, oddly-shaped flowers come in white, pink, and purple-red. They are useful as quick-growing ground covers in newly planted shady rock gardens. Propagate by clipping off and planting shoots from plants kept indoors all winter. The shoots can be planted, even without roots, after the danger of frost is past.

WOODRUFF (*Asperula orientalis*). Another good annual for the shady garden. Procumbent stems with small leaves in whorls of eight, and small blue flowers in terminal clusters. Sow the seeds in spring where the plants are to grow. Blooms in early summer.

CHAPTER X

CONIFERS OF DWARF HABIT AND ODD FORM

All the plants referred to here as conifers (meaning cone-bearing) are members of the pine family (*Pinaceae*). They include the firs, spruces, false cypresses, pines, junipers, hemlocks, cedars, cryptomerias, and arborvitaes. The yews are also included because they are closely related, narrow-leaved evergreens belonging to *Taxaceae*. They are listed here separately because of their special worth, both as rock-garden plants and for general landscaping. Modern home architecture, stressing long low lines, has created a demand for more trees and shrubs of dwarf habit and slow growth for foundation planting.

Collecting dwarf and odd forms is a fascinating pursuit in itself, and many people devote most of their gardening time to searching for them and growing every possible kind. They are always on the lookout for new sports or clones not yet discovered. There are now many hundreds of different kinds, and new ones are always appearing. The world-wide search for these treasures is a rewarding hobby but one that can become extremely expensive. Often collectors devote their entire gardens to these dwarfs. Sometimes a section of the garden is set aside for them. These arboretums in miniature are extremely interesting, but I feel that the best place to display dwarfs is in a naturalistic rock garden. Here the diminutive trees are in scale with the tiny alpines and saxicoles. They are essential as focal points, pyramids of strength for the delicate flowering plants to lean on.

Of all rock plants, dwarf conifers alone have an aspect of permanence, stability, and old age that matches the timeless rigidity of the rocks. It is true that they lack the brilliance of the alpine flowers and the grace of filigree foliage, but they do have the sturdiness of their forebears, the majestic forest trees. They do not fade away after a brief burst of splendor, and they seldom need replacing. Once established, they will last for years, endearing themselves more and more with the passing of time. How often has an eager gardener remarked to a visitor, "You should have seen it two weeks ago. It was lovely then." Not so with the little conifers, for they are always at their best. Every time I tour a garden with a group, there are enthusiastic comments on the brilliance of the gentians, the magnificence of the saxifragas, the heavenly beauty of the campanulas, and the splendor of the pinks, but the most lasting impressions are made by the diminutive evergreen trees.

One basic reason for the awesome respect inspired by well-developed dwarf conifers is their relative scarcity. They are scarce because they are difficult to propagate in quantity, and because they are extremely slow growers. In a goodly number of years, they reach a height or breadth of only a few inches. There are some semidwarfs of fairly rapid growth that are quite commonplace. These are grown in moderate quantities by large nurseries. But the real dwarfs require a great deal of loving care and hand labor that cannot be supplied by the tractor-driven equipment and the unskilled itinerant labor of a big nursery operation. Thus, the growing of these little gems is left to the small neighborhood grower who has the time and inclination to hover over them like a mother hen over her chicks. Understandably, he is limited to a few varieties in modest numbers so that the rock gardener's quest for additional kinds is arduous, though highly rewarding when he makes a find.

In the search for dwarf conifers, be wary of the names given them in listings. For some unfathomable reason, nurserymen who are otherwise responsible do not put much store in correct names and do not strive to label their plants accurately. Several times I have obtained identical plants from three or four sources under as many names. In making this list, I have tried to find the correct names, but I am by no means infallible. If there are errors, they are honest ones, not meant to mislead my readers. My knowledge of conifers is scanty, but I am so much in love with them that I feel I should advocate their use to the best of my ability. I limit this list to plants with which I have had personal experience, though tempted to add varieties I have read about and one day hope to grow. However, if I were to rely on another person's descriptions, I would be confusing myself as well as my readers. Even so, I know some of these varieties only as young plants of small size and may be wrong in giving their ultimate height and spread. The only reference used for the verification of names has been Alfred Rehder's *Manual of Cultivated Trees and Shrubs.*

The cultivation of dwarf conifers is generally quite simple. They all do well in an ordinary neutral to acid garden soil (pH 5–7). Heavy loam is preferable to a sandy or peaty soil. Drainage should be good and moisture adequate. A few varieties like shade, at least for part of the day, but the majority need full sun. Special note is made of the shade lovers in the descriptive list. In most cases pruning is not necessary because of the slow rate of growth. Moderately rapid growers should be trimmed annually, preferably in winter. Even the tiniest trees will grow to considerable size with advanced age. To prolong their usefulness in a small rock garden, periodic pruning is recommended to maintain scale. Most of these small conifers are about the hardiest plants available for the rock garden. Even the dwarf varieties of borderline or tender species, such as the cryptomerias and false cypresses, are quite hardy, although they need some protection from drying winds and winter sun.

Long strings of latinized names are frowned upon by botanists, but I use them here for convenience and because that is the way the plants are usually listed in catalogues.

Abies balsamea hudsonia. A form of the balsam fir that grows in the shape of a tight dark-green ball. It has short linear flat leaves, set very close together on short stiff branches. Annual growth is only about half an inch, producing trees about 6 inches high in 8 to 10 years.

Abies grandis nana. It is difficult to believe that the giant fir which attains a height of about 300 feet on Vancouver Island has a rock-garden-sized offspring. The dwarf version has a dense broad pyramidal form, with wide flat leaves colored a rich dark green above and glaucous beneath. Annual growth on my plants is 2 to 3 inches.

Cedrus brevifolia. I do not know whether this is a dwarf or not, but the trees I have seen are small enough and grow slowly enough to be used in the average rock garden. A graceful open tree or bush, with needles only half an inch long in small tufts. Annual growth 3 to 5 inches.

Cedrus deodara prostrata. A completely prostrate tree, with long slender branches that follow the contour of the ground. It has long glaucous-green leaves in tufts like little bottle brushes. Annual growth is 3 or 4 inches, often much less.

Chamaecyparis lawsoniana ellwoodii. A compact upright bush, maturing about 3 feet high. It has many straight branches coming from the ground, with soft feathery lovely blue foliage. Useful in large rock gardens. Annual growth 4 to 6 inches.

Chamaecyparis lawsoniana forsteckiana. An intriguing rock-garden tree that forms a low compact mound only a few inches high, with tiny scalelike bright-green leaves on twisted and gnarled cockscomb branches. Annual growth about 1 inch.

Chamaecyparis lawsoniana nana. A very slow-growing tree of broad pyramidal shape, with stout stiff branches and deep-green scalelike leaves on branches arranged like a flat fan. Annual growth 1 to 2 inches.

Chamaecyparis lawsoniana nidiformis. A semidwarf that can be used in the rock garden as small-sized young plants or in the approach planting. It forms a broad low bush about 3 feet high and 4 to 6 feet across, with an open center. Rather plumy light-green foliage on drooping branchlets. Annual growth 6 to 8 inches.

Chamaecyparis nootkatensis compacta. A compact columnar tree, with drooping branchlets and light-blue-green clasping leaves, with sharp prickly points. I don't know how big it finally becomes, but my plants grow about 3 inches a year. A hardy Alaskan that should be sheltered from drying winds in winter when the ground is frozen.

Chamaecyparis obtusa caespitosa. A tiny ball of deep-green drooping branchlets, very close together, that reaches the majestic height of about 4 or 5 inches in 10 or 12 years. An extremely rare, very dwarf tree that is greatly coveted by the connoisseur. Annual growth about a half-inch. Prefers shade at midday, and should be protected from the winter and the wind.

Chamaecyparis obtusa caespitosa nana. A small tight bun of mosslike deep-green nodding branches, about half the size of the preceding. The name is probably incorrect. The plant is so tiny and the growth so slow that it will always be a very scarce item. Annual growth a quarter of an inch. Provide shade and wind protection as described for preceding.

Chamaecyparis obtusa nana. A dwarf tree in a broad pyramidal form that attains a height of about 2 feet in 15 to 20 years. Deep-green scalelike leaves on close growing branchlets, in a lovely fan shape but with a wavy, crinkly effect. Annual growth 1 to 3 inches. Perfectly hardy, and will stand both full sun and fairly dense shade. It is often listed as *C. obtusa gracilis nana compacta* (*illustration page 356*).

Chamaecyparis pisifera filifera aurea nana. Same as the preceding, except that the branchlets are a rusty-golden color all year.

Chamaecyparis pisifera filifera nana. A lovely low symmetrical mound of long sweeping threadlike branches that reaches a height of about 3 feet after many years. Its annual growth is 6 to 8 inches, but its actual height does not increase very rapidly because of its weeping habit.

Chamaecyparis pisifera plumosa aurea compacta. A dense globe of small awl-shaped leaves on soft feathery branchlets, colored light green with golden tips. A fairly rapid grower, with annual growth of about 6 inches, but it can be sheared severely to maintain a dwarf dense ball.

Chamaecyparis pisifera squarrosa minima. A dense mound from 4 to 6 inches high, with tiny mossy foliage of a lovely silvery-blue, winter and summer. In old age it forms a spreading, almost prostrate, mat. The annual growth is about 2 inches, with an occasional shoot coming 4 to 6 inches long, which should be promptly cut off. It will stand full sun in summer but should be shaded in winter to prevent sun scald.

Chamaecyparis pisifera squarrosa nana. A soft fluffy mound of light-blue-green foliage that will reach a height of about 3 feet, but it can be sheared severely to keep it in bounds. An-

Chamaecyparis obtusa nana—over forty years old.

nual growth about 4 inches. It may turn rusty-colored if it is exposed to sun and wind during open winters.

Chamaecyparis plumosa minima. A very tight ball of curly feathery branchlets of deep-green color. Annual growth 2 or 3 inches. In full sun it may turn a dull russet color. To avoid this, give it light shade in summer, and protect it from drying winds in winter.

Chamaecyparis plumosa platinus nana. Soft feathery light-green ball, with the new growth in spring a striking platinum white. Annual growth about 6 inches, but it can be sheared severely. Give it part shade and protection from winter winds.

Chamaecyparis squarrosa cyano-viridis. A rounded mound of soft fluffy mossy foliage of a shimmering silvery blue-green color. Its ultimate height is about 3 feet, but it takes a number of years to attain it. Annual growth 3 or 4 inches. One of the handsomest for the rock garden; also, for foundation planting.

Chamaecyparis squarrosa pygmaea. A tiny tight ball of soft light-blue-green mossy foliage, only 5 or 6 inches high after many years. Annual growth an inch or less. It prefers part shade and wind protection.

Chamaecyparis squarrosa pygmaea aurea. The same attractive tight ball as the preceding form, with golden-yellow foliage.

Cryptomeria japonica bandai-tsuga. An elegant shrub of compact habit, with deep-green foliage. The sharp-pointed keeled leaves are on nodding branchlets that are thickened and crested in cockscomb fashion. A rather vigorous plant, with annual growth about 4 inches. This and the other cryptomerias prefer part shade in summer, and adequate winter protection north and inland from the New York City area.

Cryptomeria japonica moriniana. An extremely compact upright oval-shaped little bush resembling var. *nana,* but much more compact and grows more slowly. Annual growth about 1 inch.

Cryptomeria japonica nana. A dense globe-shaped plant, with short stiff keeled leaves on attractively drooping branchlets. A slow grower that forms a compact mound about 18 inches high and just as broad in about 15 years. Annual growth about 2 inches.

Juniperus chinensis alba. A fast-growing broadly-spreading mat-forming plant, with light-gray-green foliage tipped and feathered with white. A good ground-cover plant that can also be used in the rock garden, if it is trimmed severely each year. Annual growth 6 to 12 inches.

Juniperus chinensis aureo-globosa. A very slow-growing ball-shaped plant, with blue-green foliage and the young growth golden yellow. An excellent rock-garden subject. Annual growth 3 to 4 inches.

Juniperus chinensis blaauii. Probably too big for the average rock garden as a mature tree, but it is so strikingly handsome that a place should be found for it. It is a rather tall, more or less upright, vase-shaped bush, with stiff sturdy branches and the foliage a very deep blue. Annual growth 6 to 8 inches, or more.

Juniperus chinensis globosa. The green counterpart of var. *aureo-globosa.*

Juniperus chinensis pfitzeriana nana. A dwarf compact form of the well-known pfitzer juniper that is not too large for the average rock garden. It forms a low, almost prostrate, vase-shaped shrub, with plumy light-gray-green foliage. Annual growth 4 to 6 inches.

Juniperus communis compressa. An Irish juniper in miniature. A very slender columnar plant with feathery blue-green foliage that will reach a height of about 2 feet, with a diameter of only 3 or 4 inches. Annual growth about 3 inches.

Juniperus communis saxatilis. A natural rock plant from high mountain and arctic regions. It forms a low slowly-spreading bush, only about 6 inches high, with lovely blue foliage. The annual growth is 2 to 6 inches; but if the longest shoots are cut back, it forms a very dense little plant.

Juniperus conferta. A rather fast-growing wide-spreading billowy mat of lovely blue-green foliage, about 6 inches high. Annual growth 6 to 8 inches, or more. It can be used as a ground cover or in the rock garden, if it is sheared normally.

Juniperus horizontalis 'Bar Harbor.' The best and most coveted of the prostrate junipers for the large rock garden or as a ground cover. It is excellently used to soften huge rocks that cannot otherwise be planted. The long trailing branches have a tendency to drape downward in an attractive way, and even shallow soil in a rock crevice will satisfy its meager requirements. It has long slender growth of the finest blue-green imaginable. The annual growth can be 18 inches or more, but the plant can be cut back severely to keep it in bounds.

Juniperus horizontalis 'Blue Horizon.' A form with very slender tapering growth, colored a misty blue-purple in summer and a bronzy blue-purple in winter. Grows more slowly than Bar Harbor. Annual growth 6 to 12 inches.

Juniperus horizontalis glomerata. A deep-green plant, with short gnarled branches and very short bunchy growth, forming a compact little bush, about 6 inches high and as much as 18 inches broad after about 10 years. The normal annual growth is about 2 inches, but occasionally it will send out a long shoot that has reverted to the type. If this shoot is cut off, the remainder of the plant will retain its dwarf characteristics.

Juniperus horizontalis marcellus. A broad, rapidly-growing prostrate mat of fine gray-green color, with broad plumy growth. It spreads too fast for the average rock garden but makes an excellent ground cover and bank plant. Annual growth 10 to 18 inches, occasionally as much as 2 feet.

Juniperus horizontalis wilsonii. Very much like the Bar Harbor juniper in color and habit, except that the annual growth is much shorter without the characteristic long slender roots.

Juniperus procumbens nana. An attractive and very slow-growing hummock, about 12 inches high at maturity, with nice silvery blue-green sharp-pointed leaves that are very prickly to the touch. The short sturdy branches are procumbent, slowly forming spreading mounds. Annual growth about 2 inches, with occasional vigorous shoots reaching 6 inches (*illustration page 360*).

Juniperus squamata meyeri. A large upright shrub of unsymmetrical shape that goes several feet high. It is recommended here because it is quite a slow grower, and young plants can be used in large rock gardens. Its dense foliage is a glistening bluish-white. In fall and winter the tips of the branches are attractively tinted with pink and purple. Annual growth about 12 inches.

Juniperus squamata prostrata. A slow-growing prostrate mat of sharp-pointed blue-gray foliage in a billowy effect, about 10 inches high. It is very slow growing when young, with the

Juniperus procumbens nana.

annual growth usually less than 3 inches. After about five years, its tempo of growth increases; the trailing branches become elongated, and the annual growth is 12 inches or more. This is undoubtedly one of the best mat-formers for the rock garden.

Picea abies clanbrasiliana. A very slow-growing rounded bush, with bright-green sharp needle-pointed leaves. It eventually develops into a broad flat-topped bush, about 4 feet high and 8 feet broad, but it takes a lifetime to do it. Excellent as a rock-garden plant for its first 25 years. Annual growth 2 to 4 inches.

Picea abies maxwellii. Very similar to the preceding but slower growing, and the stiff leaves have a bluish cast. I once had some 35-year-old plants that were about 20 inches high and 3 feet across. Annual growth 2 or 3 inches.

Picea abies minima. The smallest spruce that I know. It forms a very dense ball, with thin branchlets and very fine deep-green needles, that will reach a height of 12 inches in 12 to 20 years. Extremely slow-growing, the annual growth being usually less than 1 inch.

Picea abies mucronata. A moderately rapid grower, but very dense and compact in a broad pyramidal shape. Sharp-pointed bright-shiny-green needles on stout branches. Annual growth about 4 inches.

Picea abies nidiformis. The well-known and much-loved Bird's Nest Spruce. A very dense open-topped shrub, with fine deep-green needles. It will eventually become about 3 feet high and just as broad, but it takes a great many years to do it. Annual growth to 3 inches.

Picea abies procumbens. A very noteworthy variety with deep-green foliage and yellow branches. It forms a broad low mound, with weeping or drooping branches, about 12 inches or more high and quite wide in old age. Annual growth 2 to 4 inches.

Picea abies pumila. A dense depressed globe, with fine very dark-green needles on stout red-brown branchlets. Annual growth 2 or 3 inches.

Picea abies sherwoodii. A grotesque plant, with widespread crooked and looping branches that form a broad unsymmetrical bush suggestive of a Japanese garden. With little pruning, it can be trained into an intriguing oriental shape that will make it the envy of the town. Annual growth 6 to 8 inches.

Picea glauca conica. A very dwarf slow-growing form of the dwarf Alberta Spruce, of dense slender pyramidal growth, with very fine soft blue-green leaves. Fifty-year-old trees have a height of 6 or 8 feet. Annual growth 2 to 4 inches, but more often less.

Picea pungens Col. Montgomery. A dwarf compact bush form of the Colorado blue spruce. After many years, it reaches a height of 4 or 5 feet. As a young plant it takes the form of a dense rounded cushion, with attractive silvery-blue stiff needles. Annual growth of young plants is 2 to 4 inches, of older plants 6 inches or more.

Picea pungens prostrata. The Colorado blue spruce in prostrate form. This variety grows less than a foot high, with long trailing branches forming dense mats many feet in diameter after a number of years. Annual growth 4 to 6 inches.

Picea pungens tabuliformis. A fantastic dwarf blue spruce, with wide horizontally spreading branches, one flat layer on top of another to form a low table-top bush. It has a fine blue color. Annual growth 4 to 6 inches.

Pinus aristata. Aged specimens in Arizona are said to be the oldest living things in the world, estimated to have lived more than 4000 years. This is an ideal pine for the rock garden. It remains dwarf, with procumbent or ascending branches thickly covered with short needles that are dotted with white exudations of resin. Annual growth less than 2 inches.

Pinus cembra. This is not a dwarf, but it is of such slow growth that it can be used in the rock garden for many years before it outgrows its allotted space. It forms a dense short-twigged bush, with very long needles in clusters of five. Annual growth about 3 inches under normal garden conditions.

Pinus mugo. The dwarf Swiss alpine pine that has many uses in the home landscape plan as well as the rock garden. Because all of the plants available are grown from seed, there is a great variation in habit of growth and eventual height. If careful selections are made, some real dwarf and slow growers can be found. There are several named kinds on the market that are purported to be true dwarfs, but these are also grown from seed, and even if the parent plant was a dwarf, the seedlings will vary considerably. Presently, I am working on several forms and propagating them by cuttings to insure uniform progeny. The typical seedlings have an annual growth of 2 to 4 inches, in some cases a little more.

Pinus mugo elongata. My own name for an odd plant. It forms a low spreading bush, with procumbent branches. The annual growth in a horizontal plane is greatly elongated to as much as 6 inches.

Pinus mugo glaucus. A recent selection of dense compact habit, with 2-inch needles colored a light blue-green. Annual growth less than 2 inches.

Pinus mugo pumilio. An extremely dwarf pine, with thin prostrate branches that form a little mound about 6 inches high, with very short deep-green needles. Annual growth seldom more than 1 inch. Occasional vigorous shoots will go to 3 inches.

Pinus strobus contorta. A low bush form of our eastern white pine, with short twisted twigs and fine-textured needles, curled in a most attractive fashion. Annual growth about 3 inches.

Pinus strobus nana. A dense ball-shaped plant that reaches an eventual height of about 4 feet after several years. Soft needles of a deep-green color, very close together on short twigs. Annual growth 3 to 4 inches.

Pinus sylvestris watereri. A dwarf Scots pine of dense pyramidal habit, with leaves a shimmering steel-blue. Annual growth of about 2 inches.

Pinus thunbergii prostrata. This may possibly be *P. nigra prostrata.* A very slow-growing cushion of stout prostrate stems and very dark-green long rigid needles. Annual growth about 3 inches.

Pseudotsuga taxifolia fletcheri. An ideal rock garden Douglas fir that forms a low dense cushion of prostrate branches, covered with very dark-green wide and flat leaves. I saw a plant of considerable age in the garden of Mr. Harold Epstein, that was about 6 inches high and perhaps 18 inches across. Annual growth about 2 inches.

Taxus cuspidata minima. A very tiny form of the Japanese yew, of very dense and dwarf habit, with tiny dark-green leaves on very stout short twigs. Annual normal growth is about 1 inch, with an occasional shoot to 3 inches long. I know two 15-year-old plants that are about 8 inches high and 10 inches across.

Thuja occidentalis ellwangeriana. A low squat pyramid in old age but a round fluffy ball when young. It has both juvenile and adult leaves, but is very unlike an arbor-vitae, with a predominance of soft, deep-green linear leaves. Annual growth 3 or 4 inches, but spreading rather than upright. It can be sheared severely to keep it in a tight ball shape.

Thuja occidentalis ellwangeriana aurea. Identical to the preceding, except that the foliage is a rich golden-yellow, with a deep bronzy tint in fall and winter.

Thuja occidentalis minima. A typical arbor-vitae but extremely small. It forms a very compact oval shape, with tight fan-shaped branchlets with dark-green foliage. Annual growth 1 inch or less. I have a 15-year-old tree that is barely 8 inches high.

Thuja occidentalis nana. A dense low pyramidal form of fairly rapid growth that can be used in large gardens. Typical dark-green arbor-vitae foliage. Annual growth about 4 inches.

Thuja occidentalis pumila sudworthii. A dense, very compact, ball-shaped plant, with dark-green foliage tipped with rich and vivid golden-yellow. A most attractive plant. Annual growth 2 to 4 inches.

Tsuga canadensis. There are many dwarf and odd forms of our beloved Canadian hemlock. The named kinds now number in the hundreds and new ones are always being found, either in the wild or in nurseries specializing in growing seedlings by hundreds of thousands. Recently, I visited one of these nurseries and saw 50 or 60 different kinds of dwarf and odd forms that have been selected from great batches of seedlings over the past 30 years or so. Most of these have not been named and perhaps never will be. There are so many now, with such close similarity, that it is difficult to tell many of them apart. I do not condemn any of them because they are all desirable and have a place in the rock garden. Those listed here I recommend very highly, but I cannot consider them the best of all the varieties known. I have selected these few only because they are the best of the ones I have been able to add to my collection to date. I am quite sure that if I were to rewrite this list ten years from now, many additional kinds would be included.

Tsuga canadensis bennett. A low spreading bush about 3 feet high with age. Horizontally spreading branches with the small green leaves densely covering the short twigs in graceful fans. Annual growth 2 to 4 inches.

Tsuga canadensis bradleyi. A very dense and dwarf slow-growing tree of broad pyramidal form, with short stiff very dark-green leaves. Annual growth about 3 inches, usually much less.

Tsuga canadensis 'Cole's Prostrate.' A magnificent rock-garden subject, with slender, completely prostrate branches forming a broad evergreen mat, only 2 or 3 inches high but 2 to 3 feet wide. Annual growth 4 to 8 inches.

Tsuga canadensis compacta. A semidwarf plant, forming a broad dense globular bush with attractively nodding branchlets. The largest I have seen was about 3 feet high but only 10 years old. Useful in large rock gardens, especially if it is trimmed regularly. Annual growth about 6 inches.

Tsuga canadensis 'Esta M.' A charming dense ball, 6 or 8 inches high, with very thin twigs and small light-green leaves. Annual growth about 1 inch or slightly more.

Tsuga canadensis 'Horsford Dwarf.' A very slow-growing dwarf, with tiny dark-green blunt leaves on short stubby twigs. Annual growth 1 inch, or less.

Tsuga canadensis hussii. An extremely slow-growing dwarf, forming an open-topped irregular shrub, 2 to 3 feet high. The small leaves are dense on short stout branches that are thickened at the tips. Annual growth about 2 inches when young, to 4 inches in old well-established plants.

Tsuga canadensis jervis. An intriguing plant of dense but irregular habit, with short gnarled branches covered with tiny light-green leaves. Extremely slow-growing, with the normal annual growth of an inch or less. Occasionally a shoot will come as much as 3 inches long, but subsequent growth is again very short.

Tsuga canadensis minuta. The tiniest hemlock that I know. Thirty-year-old plants are only about 6 inches high, with branches clothed in tiny bright-green leaves compressed into a perfect little ball. Annual growth about half an inch, usually less.

Tsuga canadensis ruggii. A tiny ball-shaped plant, with thin nodding branchlets and tiny light-green leaves. The tips of the branchlets are elongated, leafless, and colored in light brown. Annual growth about 1 inch. I have a 15-year-old tree that is 10 inches high and 12 inches across.

Tsuga canadensis taxifolia. A compact bushy semidwarf that grows about 5 feet high, with short, wide yewlike dark-green leaves. Annual growth about 4 inches.

Tsuga canadensis 'Von Helm.' A dwarf dense very compact narrow pyramid, with annual growth 2 to 3 inches.

Tsuga diversifolia. A Japanese tree that remains quite dwarf in our rigorous climate. It forms a rather lacy-topped bush, with very dark-green short and wide leaves. Annual growth usually less than 3 inches.

APPENDIX

VARIOUS PLANTS FOR VARIOUS SEASONS, LOCATIONS, CONDITIONS, AND EFFECTS

FLOWERS IN SEASON

Early Spring

Adonis
Aethionema
Ajuga
Alyssum
Andromeda
Androsace
Anemone
Aphyllanthes
Arabis
Arenaria
Asperula
Aster
Aubrieta
Bergenia
Brunnera
Bulbocodium
Caltha
Chionodoxa
Cerastium
Claytonia
Coptis
Cornus
Corydalis
Crocus
Cyclamen
Daphne
Dicentra
Douglasia
Draba
Epigaea
Epimedium
Eranthis
Erica
Eritrichium
Erysimum
Euphorbia
Forsythia
Galanthus
Gentiana
Helleborus
Hepatica
Hutchinsia
Iberis
Iris
Jeffersonia
Loiseleuria
Omphalodes
Phlox
Pieris
Polemonium
Polygala
Potentilla
Primula
Pulmonaria
Pyxidanthera
Ranunculus
Rhododendron
Sanguinaria
Sarcococca
Saxifraga
Schivereckia
Scilla
Shortia
Soldanella
Thlaspi
Tiarella
Tulipa
Uvularia
Vaccinium
Veronica
Viola

Late Spring

Achillea
Actinea
Aethionema
Ajuga
Allium
Alyssum
Anacyclus
Andromeda
Androsace
Anemone
Anemonella
Antennaria
Anthemis
Anthyllis
Antirrhinum
Aquilegia

(*Late Spring continued*)

Arabis
Arenaria
Armeria
Arnebia
Arnica
Aster
Astilbe
Aubrieta
Bellis
Bellium
Brodiaea
Calochortus
Caltha
Camassia
Campanula
Carlina
Cassiope
Cerastium
Chrysanthemum
Chrysogonum
Coreopsis
Corydalis
Cuthbertia
Cymbalaria
Cypripedium
Cytisus
Delphinium
Dianthus
Dicentra
Dimorphotheca
Dionaea
Dodecatheon
Doronicum
Douglasia
Dryas
Edraianthus
Epigaea
Epimedium
Erigeron
Erinus
Eriogonum
Eriophyllum
Erodium
Erysimum
Erythronium
Euphorbia
Filipendula
Fritillaria
Genista
Gentiana
Geranium
Geum
Globularia
Gypsophila
Haberlea
Hebe
Helianthemum
Helonias
Heuchera
Hieracium
Houstonia
Hudsonia
Hyacinthus
Hypericum
Hypoxis
Iberis
Incarvillea
Iris
Jasione
Jasminum
Kalmia
Lamium
Leiophyllum
Leucojum
Lewisia
Linaria
Linum
Lithospermum
Lotus
Lychnis
Mahonia
Mazus
Mentha
Mertensia
Maianthemum
Mitchella
Moneses
Montia
Muscari
Myosotis
Narcissus
Narthecium
Nemophila
Nepeta
Nierembergia
Oenothera
Opuntia
Orchis
Parnassia
Pedicularis
Penstemon
Petalostemum
Petrophytum
Phlox
Phyllodoce
Phyteuma
Polygala
Potentilla
Primula
Puschkinia
Pterocephalus
Pyxidanthera
Ramonda
Rhododendron
Rosa
Saponaria
Sarracenia
Satureja
Saxifraga
Scabiosa
Scilla
Scutellaria
Sedum
Sempervivum
Silene
Sisyrinchium
Spiraea
Stachys
Stylophorum
Symphyandra
Synthyris
Talinum
Thalictrum
Thymus
Townsendia
Trillium
Tulipa
Tunica
Vancouveria
Waldsteinia
Verbena
Veronica
Viola

Summer

Abronia	Convallaria	Houstonia	Petalostemum
Achillea	Coreopsis	Hypericum	Physostegia
Ageratum	Corydalis	Iberis	Polygonum
Ajuga	Cuthbertia	Inula	Potentilla
Allium	Cyclamen	Jasione	Prunella
Alyssum	Cymbalaria	Lamium	Pterocephalus
Androsace	Daboecia	Lantana	Pyrola
Anemone	Dalibarda	Lavandula	Rhexia
Anthemis	Delphinium	Liatris	Rosa
Anthyllis	Dianthus	Lilium	Santolina
Antirrhinum	Dicentra	Linaria	Saponaria
Armeria	Drosera	Linum	Satureja
Aster	Dryas	Liriope	Scilla
Astilbe	Echinocereus	Lithospermum	Scutellaria
Begonia	Edraianthus	Lobelia	Sedum
Bellis	Erica	Lotus	Silene
Bellium	Erinus	Leucojum	Sisyrinchium
Bletilla	Eriogonum	Lychnis	Solidago
Bruckenthalia	Erodium	Lycoris	Spiraea
Calceolaria	Eschscholzia	Malvastrum	Talinum
Callirhoe	Filipendula	Micromeria	Teucrium
Calluna	Fragaria	Myosotis	Thymus
Calochortus	Genista	Nemophila	Tunica
Calopogon	Gentiana	Nierembergia	Valeriana
Ceratostigma	Geranium	Oenothera	Verbena
Chimaphila	Geum	Opuntia	Veronica
Chrysanthemum	Gypsophila	Oxalis	Viola
Chrysogonum	Heuchera	Papaver	Xyris
Chrysopsis	Hieracium	Penstemon	

Autumn

Allium	Campanula	Colchicum	Daphne
Anemone	Ceratostigma	Coreopsis	Dianthus
Aster	Chrysanthemum	Corydalis	Dicentra
Callirhoe	Chrysogonum	Cyclamen	Draba
Calluna	Chrysopsis	Daboecia	Erica

(*Autumn continued*)

Gentiana
Geum
Iberis
Liatris
Lithospermum
Micromeria
Potentilla
Rosa
Sedum
Serratula
Silene
Solidago
Talinum
Thymus
Tunica
Verbena
Viola

PLANTS FOR BETWEEN FLAGSTONE

Acaena
Achillea
Antennaria
Arabis
Arenaria
Artemisia
Bellium
Cerastium
Dianthus
Draba
Galium
Herniaria
Lotus
Mazus
Micromeria
Paronychia
Thymus
Veronica

PLANTS FOR HOT, DRY, SUNNY LOCATION

Acaena
Achillea
Actinea
Aethionema
Alyssum
Anacyclus
Antennaria
Arabis
Armeria
Arnebia
Artemisia
Aubrieta
Callirhoe
Carlina
Cerastium
Coryphantha
Cytisus
Dianthus
Dimorphotheca
Douglasia
Draba
Echinocereus
Erigeron
Eriogonum
Eriophyllum
Euphorbia
Genista
Hebe
Helianthemum
Hieracium
Lavandula
Lewisia
Lotus
Malvastrum
Micromeria
Neobesseya
Oenothera
Opuntia
Papaver
Paronychia
Penstemon
Petalostemum
Physaria
Raoulia
Santolina
Sedum
Sempervivum
Stachys
Talinum
Thlaspi
Thymus
Townsendia
Tunica
Valeriana
Veronica
Zinnia

PLANTS FOR MORAINE

Androsace
Arnica
Betula
Cassiope
Dianthus
Diapensia
Dicentra pusilla
Douglasia
Eritrichium
Gentiana verna
Primula
Pyxidanthera
Saxifraga
Shortia
Silene
Soldanella

TRUE ALPINE AND ARCTIC PLANTS

Androsace
Anemone
Aquilegia
  A. alpina
  A. jonesii
  A. saximontana
  A. scopulorum
Arabis
Arenaria
Arnica
Artemisia
Aster
Betula
Caltha leptosepala
Campanula
  C. cochlearifolia
  C. parryi
  C. pilosa
  C. piperi
Cassiope
Cerastium
Chiogenes
Chrysanthemum
  C. alpinum
  C. arcticum
Coptis
Daphne
Dianthus
Diapensia
Dicentra
Dodecatheon
  D. cusickii
Douglasia
Draba
  D. sibirica
Dryas
Epimedium
Erigeron
Erinus
Eritrichium
Gentiana
Geranium
Haberlea
Hutchinsia
Kalmia microphylla
Jasione
Leontopodium
Lewisia
Linaria
Linnaea
Loiseleuria
Lychnis
Papaver
Penstemon
Phyllodoce
Polemonium
Polygala
Potentilla
Primula
Ranunculus
Rhododendron
Salix
Saponaria
Saxifraga
Sempervivum
Shortia
Silene
Sisyrinchium
Soldanella
Synthyris
Tanakaea
Thalictrum
Townsendia
Vaccinium vitis idaea
  V. vitis idaea minus
Veronica
Viola

PLANTS FOR DENSE SHADE

Actaea
Anemone
Anemonella
Arum
Asarum
Asperula
Asplenium
Athyrium
Begonia
Bergenia
Blechnum
Brunnera
Camptosorus
Chimaphila
Chiogenes
Chrysogonum
Claytonia
Convallaria
Coptis
Cryptogramma
Cyclamen
Cymbalaria
Cypripedium
Dalibarda
Dicentra
Dodecatheon
Dryopteris
Epimedium

(*Plants for Dense Shade continued*)

Galax
Gaultheria
Gaylussacia
Goodyera
Haberlea
Helleborus
Hepatica
Heuchera americana
Hypoxis
Iris
Jeffersonia
Linnaea
Liriope
Lygodium
Mahonia
Mitchella
Mitella
Moneses
Omphalodes
Orchis
Pachysandra
Phlox
Polypodium
Pulmonaria
Pyrola
Ramonda
Sarcococca
Saxifraga
Shortia
Synthyris
Tanakaea
Tiarella
Trillium
Uvularia
Vancouveria
Viola
Woodsia

PLANTS FOR CREVICES

Aethionema
Androsace
Arabis
Arenaria
Armeria
Asplenium
Aubretia
Campanula
Camptosorus
Cerastium
Cheilanthes
Corydalis
Cryptogramma
Cystopteris
Dianthus
Douglasia
Draba
Erigeron
Erinus
Erysimum
Haberlea
Heuchera
Jasione
Leontopodium
Linaria
Lychnis
Montia
Papaver
Paronychia
Pellaea
Penstemon
Physaria
Phyteuma
Potentilla
Ramonda
Saponaria
Saxifraga
Sedum
Sempervivum
Silene
Townsendia

LIST OF FERNS

Adiantum
Asplenium
Athyrium
Blechnum
Camptosorus
Cheilanthes
Cryptogramma
Cystopteris
Dryopteris
Lygodium
Pellaea
Polypodium
Polystichum
Woodsia

BOG PLANTS

Andromeda
Calopogon
Caltha
Chiogenes
Daboecia
Dionaea
Drosera
Geum
Helonias
Kalmia
Narthecium
Parnassia
Rhexia
Sarracenia
Xyris

PLANTS FOR ORNAMENTAL BERRIES

Actaea
Berberis
Arctostaphylos
Chiogenes
Cornus
Cotoneaster
Daphne
Empetrum
Gaultheria
Ilex
Mitchella
Pernettya
Vaccinium

PLANTS PREDOMINANTLY FOR FOLIAGE

Green

Adiantum
Arctostaphylos
Asarum
Asplenium
Berberis
Betula
Blechnum
Buxus
Cheilanthes
Chimaphila
Corema
Corydalis
Cotoneaster
Cryptogramma
Cystopteris
Dryopteris
Epimedium
Galax
Hedera
Ilex
Lygodium
Mahonia
Muehlenbeckia
Pachistima
Pachysandra
Polystichum
Santolina
Sarcococca
Sedum
Sempervivum
Shortia
Tanakaea
Teucrium
Thymus

Blue

Aethionema
Andromeda
Aquilegia
Corydalis
Dianthus
Euphorbia
Festuca
Gypsophila
Hebe
Linaria
Pellaea
Penstemon
Sedum
Sempervivum
Thalictrum

Silver

Acaena
Achillea
Alyssum
Androsace
Antennaria
Anthemis
Antirrhinum
Arabis
Artemisia
Athyrium
Aubrieta
Cerastium
Cymbalaria
Eriogonum
Eriophyllum
Helianthemum
Hypericum
Lavandula
Leontopodium
Malvastrum
Micromeria
Nepeta
Papaver
Paronychia
Petalostemum
Physaria
Potentilla
Pterocephalus
Raoulia
Santolina
Saxifraga
Schivereckia
Sedum
Sempervivum
Stachys
Teucrium
Thymus
Veronica

(*Plants for Foliage continued*)

Variegated

Aegopodium
Arrhenatherum
Chimaphila
Cyclamen
Daphne
Goodyera
Lamium
Liriope
Ophiopogon
Pachysandra
Phlox
Pieris
Pulmonaria
Saxifraga
Sedum
Thymus

CUSHION TYPE PLANTS

Androsace
Arabis
Arenaria
Armeria
Coprosma
Dianthus
Diapensia
Douglasia
Draba
Erigeron
Erinus
Erysimum
Globularia
Houstonia
Hutchinsia
Iberis
Lewisia
Limonium
Lychnis
Pyxidanthera
Saponaria
Saxifraga
Schivereckia
Sedum
Sempervivum
Silene
Thlaspi
Townsendia
Valeriana

GROUND COVERS

Acaena
Achillea
Aegopodium
Ajuga
Antennaria
Anthyllis
Asarum
Arctostaphylos
Asperula
Calluna
Chiogenes
Coptis
Corema
Cymbalaria
Dalibarda
Dryas
Erica
Euonymus
Galax
Galium
Gaultheria
Gaylussacia
Gypsophila
Herniaria
Houstonia
Hydrocotyle
Lamium
Linnaea
Liriope
Lotus
Mazus
Micromeria
Mitchella
Muehlenbeckia
Nepeta
Nierembergia
Omphalodes
Pachistima
Pachysandra
Penstemon
Phlox
Polygonum
Potentilla
Satureja
Sedum
Stachys
Thymus
Tiarella
Vaccinium
Vancouveria
Verbena
Veronica
Waldsteinia

PLANTS IN COLOR

Blue

Ajuga
Allium
Anemone
Aphyllanthes
Aquilegia
Asperula
Aster
Aubrieta
Brodiaea
Brunnera
Calochortus
Camassia

(*Blue continued*)

Campanula
Ceratostigma
Chionodoxa
Delphinium
Edraianthus
Erigeron
Eritrichium
Gentiana
Globularia
Hepatica
Houstonia
Hyacinthus
Iris
Jasione
Jeffersonia
Linaria
Linum
Lithospermum
Mertensia
Myosotis
Muscari
Nepeta
Nierembergia
Omphalodes
Penstemon
Phlox
Phyteuma
Polemonium
Polygala
Primula
Pulmonaria
Puschkinia
Ramonda
Rhododendron
Scabiosa
Shortia
Sisyrinchium
Symphysandra
Veronica

Pink

Aethionema
Allium
Andromeda
Androsace
Anemone
Antennaria
Anthyllis
Arabis
Armeria
Asperula
Aster
Astilbe
Aubrieta
Bellis
Bergenia
Brodiaea
Bruckenthalia
Calluna
Calochortus
Calopogon
Chionodoxa
Claytonia
Colchicum
Cornus
Cuthbertia
Cyclamen
Cypripedium
Daphne
Dianthus
Dicentra
Dodecatheon
Enkianthus
Epigaea
Erica
Erodium
Erythronium
Filipendula
Geranium
Gypsophila
Heuchera
Helianthemum
Helonias
Hepatica
Kalmia
Lewisia
Linnaea
Loiseleuria
Lycoris
Magnolia
Moneses
Montia
Myosotis
Oenothera
Oxalis
Papaver
Penstemon
Phlox
Phyllodoce
Polemonium
Polygala
Polygonum
Potentilla
Primula
Prunella
Pterocephalus
Pulmonaria
Rhexia
Rhododendron
Rosa
Saponaria
Saxifraga
Scilla
Sedum
Sempervivum
Shortia
Silene
Spiraea
Thymus
Tradescantia
Trillium
Tulipa
Tunica
Vaccinium
Valeriana
Viola

Purple

Abronia
Allium
Anemone
Aquilegia
Arabis
Arenaria
Aster
Astilbe

(*Purple continued*)

Aubrieta
Bletilla
Brodiaea
Callirhoe
Calluna
Calochortus
Campanula
Cercis
Colchicum
Corydalis
Coryphanta
Cotinus
Crocus
Cymbalaria
Cypripedium
Cytisus
Daboecia
Delphinium
Dicentra
Dimorphotheca
Dodecatheon
Douglasia
Epimedium
Erica
Erigeron
Erinus
Erodium
Erysimum
Erythronium
Fritillaria
Gentiana
Geranium
Haberlea
Houstonia
Incarvillea
Iris
Kalmia
Lamium
Lavandula
Limonium
Liriope
Lobularia
Lychnis
Mazus
Mentha
Micromeria
Muscari
Nepeta
Ophiopogon
Oxalis
Petalostemum
Phlox
Phyllodoce
Phyteuma
Polygala
Primula
Prunella
Pulmonaria
Pyrola
Ramonda
Rhododendron
Satureja
Saxifraga
Scabiosa
Scutellaria
Serratula
Sisyrinchium
Soldanella
Stachys
Snythyris
Teucrium
Thalictrum
Thlaspi
Thymus
Tulipa
Verbena
Viola

Red

Aquilegia
Astilbe
Bulbocodium
Calluna
Cyclamen
Dianthus
Douglasia
Epimedium
Erica
Erodium
Erythronium
Helianthemum
Heuchera
Iris
Lilium
Lychnis
Lycoris
Malvastrum
Opuntia
Papaver
Penstemon
Physostegia
Potentilla
Primula
Rhododendron
Rosa
Saxifraga
Scilla
Sedum
Sempervivum
Silene
Talunum
Trillium
Tulipa

White

Achillea
Actaea
Aethionema
Ajuga
Amelanchier
Anacyclus
Anemone
Anemonella
Antennaria
Anthemis
Antirrhinum
Aquilegia
Arabis
Arctostaphylos
Arenaria
Armeria
Asperula
Aster
Astilbe
Bellium

(*White continued*)

Brodiaea
Calluna
Calochortus
Caltha
Cassiope
Cerastium
Chionodoxa
Chrysanthemum
Clethra
Colchicum
Convallaria
Cornus
Cotoneaster
Crocus
Delphinium
Dianthus
Dicentra
Dodecatheon
Dryas
Erica
Erigeron
Erodium
Erythronium
Filipendula
Fritillaria
Galanthus
Galax
Gypsophila
Helianthemum
Helleborus
Hepatica
Heuchera
Houstonia
Hutchinsia
Iberis
Jeffersonia
Lamium
Leiophyllum
Leontopodium
Leucojum
Lycoris
Magnolia
Maianthemum
Muscari
Narcissus
Nierembergia
Oenothera
Oxydendrum
Papaver
Physostegia
Pieris
Petrophytum
Potentilla
Primula
Prunella
Pyrola
Pyxidanthera
Ranunculus
Rhododendron
Sanguinaria
Satureja
Saxifraga
Scilla
Schivereckia
Scutellaria
Sedum
Shortia
Silene
Tiarella
Trillium
Tunica
Vaccinium
Vancouveria
Veronica
Viola

Yellow

Achillea
Actinea
Adonis
Allium
Alyssum
Anemone
Anthemis
Antirrhinum
Arnebia
Arnica
Berberis
Calochortus
Caltha
Chrysogonum
Chrysopsis
Coreopsis
Corydalis
Crocus
Cypripedium
Cytisus
Doronicum
Douglasia
Draba
Dryas
Epimedium
Eranthis
Eriogonum
Eriophyllum
Erythronium
Erysimum
Euphorbia
Forsythia
Fritillaria
Genista
Geum
Helianthemum
Hieracium
Hudsonia
Hypericum
Hypoxis
Inula
Iris
Jasminum
Linum
Lithospermum
Lotus
Lycoris
Mahonia
Narcissus
Narthecium
Oenothera
Ophiopogon
Opuntia
Papaver
Pedicularis
Physaria
Polygala
Potentilla
Primula
Ramonda
Ranunculus
Rhododendron
Rosa
Santolina
Saxifraga
Sedum
Sempervivum
Sisyrinchium

(*Yellow continued*)

Solidago
Teucrium
Thalictrum
Thlaspi
Thymus
Tiarella
Tulipa
Uvularia
Vancouveria
Viola
Waldsteinia
Xyris
Zinnia

PLANTS FOR WALL GARDEN

Achillea
Aethionema
Alyssum
Androsace
Antennaria
Anthemis
Aquilegia
Arabis
Arenaria
Artemisia
Aubrieta
Campanula
Cerastium
Cymbalaria
Cytisus
Dianthus
Dicentra eximia
Douglasia
Draba
Edraianthus
Epimedium
Erinus
Eriogonum
Eriophyllum
Erysimum
Euphorbia myrsinites
Genista
Geranium sanguineum
Gypsophila
Helianthemum
Heuchera sanguinea
Hutchinsia
Hypericum
Iberis
Jasione
Lavandula
Leontopodium
Linaria
Linum
Lotus
Micromeria
Papaver
Pellaea
Penstemon
Phlox
Phyteuma
Potentilla
Santolina
Saponaria ocymoides
Schivereckia
Sedum
Sempervivum
Silene
Thymus
Tiarella
Tunica
Verbena
Veronica

PLANTS FOR SCREE

Achillea ageratifolia
Achillea argentea
Actinea
Aethionema
Alyssum
Anacyclus
Androsace villosa
Arabis androsacea
Arabis kellereri
Callirhoe
Cerastium alpinum
Chrysanthemum alpinum
Chrysanthemum mawii
Chrysopsis falcata
Douglasia
Draba
Echinocereus
Erigeron
Eriogonum
Malvastrum
Oenothera
Penstemon
Petalostemum
Physaria
Potentilla nevadensis
Potentilla nitida
Pterocephalus
Saponaria cespitosa
Valeriana
Zinnia

INDEX